The Chief Eunuch of the Ottoman Harem

Eunuchs were a common feature of pre- and early modern societies but are now poorly understood. Here, Jane Hathaway offers an in-depth study of the chief of the African eunuchs who guarded the harem of the Ottoman Empire. A wide range of primary sources are used to analyze the Chief Eunuch's origins in East Africa and his political, economic, and religious role from the inception of his office in the late sixteenth century through the dismantling of the palace harem in the early twentieth century. Hathaway highlights the origins of the institution and how the role of eunuchs developed in East Africa, as well as exploring the Chief Eunuch's connections to Egypt and Medina. By tracing the evolution of the office, we see how the Chief Eunuch's functions changed in response to transformations in Ottoman society, from the generalized crisis of the seventeenth century to the westernizing reforms of the nineteenth century.

JANE HATHAWAY is professor of history at Ohio State University and one of the world's leading authorities on the Ottoman Empire and on eunuchs in Islamic societies. She is the author of five books, including *The Arab Lands under Ottoman Rule* (2008), which won the Turkish Studies Association's M. Fuat Köprülü Book Prize. She also authored the article "Eunuchs" for the third edition of the *Encyclopaedia of Islam*, a seminal reference work. Her research has been funded by prestigious grants from the National Endowment for the Humanities, the American Council of Learned Societies, and the Institute for Advanced Study.

The Chief Eunuch of the Ottoman Harem

From African Slave to Power-Broker

Jane Hathaway

The Ohio State University

CAMBRIDGE
UNIVERSITY PRESS

University Printing House, Cambridge CB2 8BS, United Kingdom

One Liberty Plaza, 20th Floor, New York, NY 10006, USA

477 Williamstown Road, Port Melbourne, VIC 3207, Australia

314-321, 3rd Floor, Plot 3, Splendor Forum, Jasola District Centre, New Delhi - 110025, India

79 Anson Road, #06-04/06, Singapore 079906

Cambridge University Press is part of the University of Cambridge.

It furthers the University's mission by disseminating knowledge in the pursuit of education, learning and research at the highest international levels of excellence.

www.cambridge.org
Information on this title: www.cambridge.org/9781107519206
DOI: 10.1017/9781316257876

© Jane Hathaway 2018

First published 2018
First paperback edition 2020

A catalogue record for this publication is available from the British Library

ISBN 978-1-107-10829-5 Hardback
ISBN 978-1-107-51920-6 Paperback

In memory of Meg Hathaway (1927–2014)

Contents

Figures

Maps

Tables

Acknowledgments

This book has been a long time coming, and I have many people and institutions to thank. I have used the notes for this purpose where appropriate, but they cover only part of the debt.

Early research for this project was funded by generous grants from the National Endowment for the Humanities and the American Council of Learned Societies. I began writing the book while holding the Douglas Southall Freeman Professorship in History at the University of Richmond, Virginia, and finished drafts of most of the chapters while holding the Gladys Kreible Delmas Membership at the Institute for Advanced Study in Princeton, NJ. I am grateful to Ohio State's College of Arts and Sciences for allowing me to accept these positions and for funding a Special Assignment in spring 2017 that allowed me to complete a full draft of the book.

I am grateful to the staff and directors of the Başbakanlık Ottoman Archives, the Süleymaniye Library, the Köprülü Library, and the Topkapı Palace Museum Library and Archive in Istanbul for access to their collections, and to Dr. Anthony Greenwood and the staff of the American Research Institute in Turkey's Istanbul branch for providing a haven on numerous occasions. Over the years, a number of colleagues and students have provided access to research materials. Here, I must single out Muhammad Husam al-Din Ismail Abd al-Fattah, Günhan Börekçi, Emine Fetvacı, Betül İpşirli Argıt, George Junne, Svetlana Kirillina, Mikhail Meyer, Özgül Özdemir, Doğa Öztürk, and Ata Potok. For helping me track down eunuch monuments and tombs, I thank Caroline Finkel (who also gave the book manuscript a close read), Catalina Hunt, Davidson McLaren, Darin Stephanov, and Professor Abd al-Fattah's graduate students at Ayn Shams University.

I thank Nicolas Vatin for inviting me to deliver a series of lectures, sponsored by the École des Hautes Études en Sciences Sociales, at the Sorbonne in spring 2008 that were instrumental in my conceptualization of this project. I likewise thank the late Patricia Crone for commissioning my short biography of el-Hajj Beshir Agha (2006), which served as a forerunner for this project.

I am grateful to two anonymous readers for Cambridge University Press and, above all, to my retired colleague Stephen Dale, who during summer 2017 read the entire book manuscript and offered chapter-by-chapter comments. Needless to say, responsibility for any errors or omissions is entirely mine. Laura Seeger of Ohio State's Goldberg Center for Excellence in Teaching proved vital to the preparation of the maps and images.

I could not have completed this book without the support of my husband, Robert ("Mimar Bob") Simkins, and Pelin and Tasha, the worthy successors to the legendary Beshir and Stella. I dedicate this book to the memory of my mother, Meg Hathaway, the only member of my family to have read all my books. The last time I saw her, in May 2014, she asked me if I had another book for her to read. Here it is, Mom, only a few years late.

Note on Transliteration and Diacritics

Since I use both Ottoman Turkish and Arabic primary sources in my research, I constantly confront the question of which transliteration system to employ in my publications. Since this is a book about an Ottoman official who served mainly in the imperial capital (even though he might be exiled to Cairo), I have chosen to give pride of place to Turkish transliterations. Thus, I use Turkish transliteration for the names and offices of Ottoman officials, most Ottoman institutions, titles of books composed in Ottoman Turkish, and the Islamic (*hijri*) months. I use Arabic transliteration for Arabic book titles and the names of most Arabophone authors. I follow the transliteration system of the *International Journal of Middle East Studies*, although, in consultation with my editor, I have elected to omit diacritics apart from *'ayn*, which is indicated by a backward apostrophe, and *hamza*, which is indicated by a forward apostrophe.

Names of Islamic institutions and offices that can be found in a present-day English dictionary (e.g., *hadith*, *madrasa*, *qadi*, Sufi) retain the spellings found there.

Otherwise, the sounds indicated by the distinctive letters of the modern Turkish alphabet are as follows:

Letter	Sound
c	j
ç	ch
ğ	elongated vowel, as in "espagnol"
ı	short *u*, as in "put"
ö	*er*, as in "pert," or French *oe*
ş	sh
ü	long *u*, as in "cute," or French *u*

Abbreviations

BOA	Başbakanlık Osmanlı Arşivi (Prime Ministry Ottoman Archives, Istanbul)
EI^2	*Encyclopaedia of Islam*, 2nd edition (Leiden, 1960–2004)
EI^3	*Encyclopaedia of Islam Three* (Leiden, 2007–present)
MD	Mühimme Defteri (Register of Important Affairs)
TDVİA	*Türkiye Diyanet Vakfı İslam Ansiklopedisi*

Because I find the classification abbreviations currently employed by the Başbakanlık Osmanlı Arşivi to be a source of considerable confusion, I do not use them in my notes. They are, however, provided in the Works Cited, in parentheses after the title of each major classification.

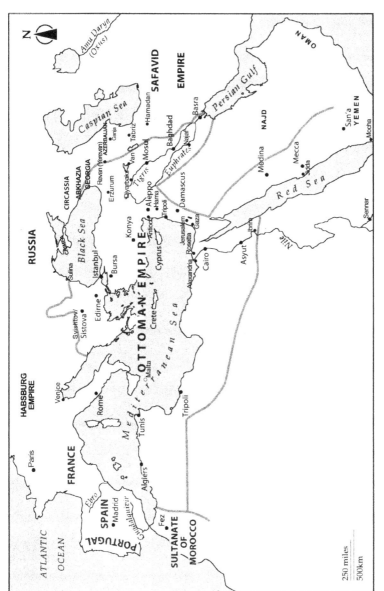

Map 0.1 The Ottoman Empire in the mid-sixteenth century.

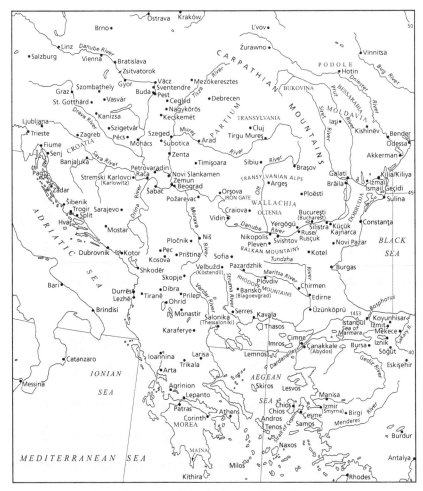

Map 0.2 The Ottoman Balkans in the late sixteenth century.

1 Introducing the Chief Harem Eunuch

Let's start with the cover illustration. It shows the most powerful Chief Harem Eunuch in Ottoman history, el-Hajj Beshir Agha, leading three sons of Sultan Ahmed III through the Third Court of Topkapı Palace. The year is 1720. The princes are about to be circumcised in the Circumcision Room in the palace's Fourth Court. Each of them is held on either side by a vizier, or government minister. Beshir Agha is right at the front of the painting, flush with the picture frame. Even the grand vizier, supposedly the most powerful figure in the Ottoman Empire at the time, walks behind him, holding the right arm of the oldest prince. What is the message of this painting? El-Hajj Beshir Agha is the most powerful person in the palace, more powerful than the grand vizier or any of the princes. He holds the princes' fates and, by implication, the fate of the empire in his hands. But he also guards the barrier separating the princes and the viziers from the viewer. In this sense, he is both a central figure and a marginal figure, both the master of the princes and viziers and their servant. He is also the only dark-skinned figure in the painting, yet he is leading all the pale-skinned figures.

Does this image seem contradictory? It should. The Chief Eunuch of the Ottoman Empire's imperial harem embodied all these contradictions. He was a castrated African slave, permanently separated from his family of origin and incapable of founding a family of his own, yet someone who was on intimate terms with the Ottoman royal family, to the extent of announcing the birth of a prince or princess to the sultan, overseeing the princes' education, representing the bridegroom at the wedding of a princess, or informing the sultan of his mother's death. The very existence of such a person might seem outlandish and incomprehensible to us, and yet the office of Chief Harem Eunuch existed for more than three hundred years, building on precedents that may have gone back to the earliest human civilizations. This book's task is to explore this office and the characteristics of the people who held it over these three centuries, examining how the office changed in response to the transformations in Ottoman society and Ottoman court life that occurred during this lengthy period.

Introducing This Book

Astonishingly enough, no book-length study has yet been devoted to this pivotal yet enigmatic figure. The Turkish historian İ. H. Uzunçarşılı provided the best description of the office's duties in a seminal study of Ottoman palace institutions published in 1945.[1] Since then, various works on Topkapı Palace and on the Topkapı harem, both scholarly and popular, have discussed the role of both African and white palace eunuchs, including the Chief Eunuch.[2] A popular Turkish overview of the harem eunuchs appeared in 1997, while an English-language book based on secondary sources appeared in 2016.[3] What I attempt here is a study of the office's development based on primary sources. But this is, I hope, more than simply a research monograph. It is also a wide-ranging consideration of how the development of the office of Chief Harem Eunuch paralleled the empire's development during this era.

We start by framing the subject: Which societies used eunuchs? Where did they come from? What functions did they perform? Then we narrow the focus: Where did the practice of employing African eunuchs, as harem guardians and in other capacities, originate, and how did the Ottoman Empire come to adopt it? Finally, what was the Ottoman harem like, and what place did it occupy in the imperial palace? These institutional concerns occupy Chapters 1–3.

We then turn to the career of the Ottoman Chief Harem Eunuch specifically. Rather than simply tracing the accomplishments and failures of all seventy-six Chief Eunuchs, one after another, I attempt to show how the careers of key Chief Eunuchs reflected and were affected by transformations in Ottoman political, social, and institutional history. The office of Agha of the Abode of Felicity (Ağa-yı Darü's-sa'ade, or Darüssaade Ağası) was founded just after Sultan Murad III (r. 1574–95) moved into the harem and began to spend most of his "free" time there, more or less abandoning his privy chamber in the palace's Third Court. This move made the head of the harem eunuchs, Habeshi Mehmed Agha, one of the people he saw most frequently. Around the same

---

[1] İ. H. Uzunçarşılı, *Osmanlı Devletinin Saray Teşkilatı* (Ankara, 1945; reprinted 1984, 1988), 72–83.

[2] Gülru Necipoğlu, *Architecture, Ceremonial, and Power: The Topkapı Palace in the Fifteenth and Sixteenth Centuries* (New York and Cambridge, MA, 1991), 43, 49, 73, 74, 79, 89–90, 102, 111, 115, 117, 121, 133–35, 160–64, 174, 177–83, 225, 230; Leslie Peirce, *The Imperial Harem: Women and Sovereignty in the Ottoman Empire* (New York, NY, 1993), 11–12, 46, 49, 125, 135–37, 195–96, 206, 235, 241–42; M. Çağatay Uluçay, *Harem II* (Ankara, 1971), 117–26; N. M. Penzer, *The Harem: An Account of the Institution as It Existed in the Palace of the Turkish Sultans, with a History of the Grand Seraglio from Its Foundation* (Philadelphia, 1936; 2nd ed. London, 1965; reprint New York, NY, 1993), especially 117–92.

[3] Sema Ok, *Harem Dünyası: Harem Ağaları* (Istanbul, 1997); George H. Junne, *The Black Eunuchs of the Ottoman Empire: Networks of Power in the Court of the Sultan* (London, 2016).

time, not coincidentally, he made Habeshi Mehmed superintendent of the imperial pious foundations for the Muslim holy cities of Mecca and Medina, known in Ottoman Turkish as Evkafü'l-Haremeyn; this post had previously been held by the head of the white eunuchs of the Third Court.

Chapter 4 dissects the career of Habeshi Mehmed Agha, who set a number of lasting precedents in the course of his seventeen years in office. He died shortly before the onset of the prolonged crisis of the seventeenth century, which coincided with the reigns of a series of youthful sultans who either died heirless or left behind only young children. The sultan's mother and favorite concubines competed to fill the resulting power vacuum, and the Chief Harem Eunuchs became their allies in this effort. Chapter 5 explains how the chaotically competitive atmosphere of the crisis years gave rise to factionalism within the harem and how the Chief Eunuch participated in, and manipulated, this brand of factionalism.

The reforms of the Köprülü family of grand viziers mark the end of the crisis, and Chapter 6 demonstrates how they channeled their own clients into the office of Chief Harem Eunuch or, at the least, promoted Chief Eunuchs whose priorities matched their own. With the Köprülüs, the office of Chief Harem Eunuch begins to intersect directly with the corps of eunuchs who guarded the Prophet Muhammad's tomb in Medina, for the Köprülüs introduced the practice of naming a former Chief Eunuch to head the tomb eunuchs. In general, the Köprülüs tried to ensure the grand vizier's control over all appointments and decisions made in the imperial capital. As Chapter 7 demonstrates, though, only after the middle of the eighteenth century was the grand vizier truly able to transcend the Chief Eunuch's influence, and even then, the Chief Eunuch was far from powerless. One of his unfailingly reliable channels of influence, at least before the westernizing reforms of the nineteenth century, was Egypt, which supplied grain to the Evkafü'l-Haremeyn and provided deposed Chief Harem Eunuchs with a comfortable place to spend their retirement. Accordingly, Chapter 8 addresses the Chief Eunuch's connections to this critical Ottoman province.

Despite the largely chronological flow of the discussion in Chapters 4–8, several key themes keep surfacing: the Chief Eunuch's relationship to the sultan and his mother, his concern with the Evkafü'l-Haremeyn, the interplay of several different kinds of palace factionalism, the Chief Eunuch's competition with the grand vizier, and his connections to Egypt. I have chosen to emphasize these themes in my treatment of the office of Chief Harem Eunuch, rather than trying to impose an externally derived theoretical framework on the subject. Above all, I seek to show how the office of Chief Harem Eunuch mirrored the Ottoman Empire's experience of a wrenching, multifaceted crisis during the seventeenth century, followed by gradual adaptation in the late seventeenth and early eighteenth centuries, and economic prosperity, an expansion of international trade, and a growing regularization of imperial institutions in the later eighteenth, before the nineteenth-century reforms transformed the imperial administration.

Three of the book's last four chapters treat themes that run through most of the three hundred years during which the office of Chief Harem Eunuch was active while also considering how the story of the Chief Harem Eunuch came to an end. Chapter 9 examines the Chief Eunuch's considerable impact on Ottoman religious and intellectual life through the establishment of educational institutions, religious complexes, and libraries, many of which are still functioning today. In Chapter 10, we see how the westernizing reforms of the nineteenth century drastically curtailed this kind of society-wide influence. For the last seventy-five years of its existence, roughly 1834–1909, the office of Chief Harem Eunuch was purely a palace position, largely irrelevant to the broader concerns of empire.

In view of these dramatic shifts in the Chief Eunuch's status and fortunes over three centuries, Chapter 11 asks how the Chief Harem Eunuch is remembered, and how he fashioned his own memorials through miniature paintings, on the one hand, and tombs and gravestones, on the other. These considerations provide an appropriate segue to the Conclusion, which considers the Chief Eunuch's place in the *longue durée* of Ottoman history and, even more broadly, in world history.

Why Eunuchs?

Nowadays, many students, to say nothing of the reading public, find it impossible to understand why eunuchs were ever an institution. Castration, they believe, was a dastardly punishment that the victim must have resented for the rest of his life, dreaming ceaselessly of revenge. But how could this have been the case when much of the world, excluding western Europe and possibly the precolonial Americas, employed eunuchs in positions of trust close to the ruler? Eunuchs were a deeply rooted institution in most, if not all, of the great Mediterranean and Asian empires: the ancient Mesopotamian empires, beginning at least with the Neo-Assyrians (911–612 BCE), all the Persian empires (Achaemenid, 550–331 BCE; Parthian, 240 BCE–220 CE; and Sasanian, 220–651 CE), the Roman and Byzantine Empires (27 BCE –1453 CE), all Chinese empires beginning with the Zhou (1045–771 BCE) and ending only with the overthrow of the Qing in 1911, and even many sub-Saharan African kingdoms, which will be discussed in Chapter 2. The only ancient Old World civilization about which we are unsure is Pharaonic Egypt.[4] The tradition

---

[4] See Chapter 2 on Egypt and the "Eunuchs in Africa and Related Topics" and "Eunuchs in Other Societies" sections of the Works Cited.

continued under the major medieval and early modern empires of Asia and Africa, including all Islamic empires from at least the Abbasids (750–1258 CE) onward. Even in the kingdoms of western Europe, where such "guardian" eunuchs were unknown, the eunuch singers known as *castrati*, a possible evolution of castrated church singers in the Byzantine Empire, were performing in the church choirs of the Vatican by the mid-sixteenth century and were wildly popular on opera stages until the 1820s.[5] In fact, the eunuch institution was so widespread that the appropriate question may be not why so many societies employed eunuchs but why certain others did not.

So why did these polities use eunuchs, and court eunuchs in particular? Apart from the western European kingdoms, all of them shared three features that required the use of eunuchs. First, they all featured more or less absolute rulers who lived in isolation from their subjects and were sometimes quasi-deified. Orlando Patterson has noted that "rulers who claim absolute power, often with divine authority, seem to prefer – even to need – slaves who have been castrated."[6] Because of the risk of assassination or rebellion, access to the ruler had to be strictly controlled, fueling a need for servants and confidants with no family or locational ties that would dilute their utter loyalty to the sovereign. Eunuchs, and particularly eunuchs who came from outside the empire or from its peripheries, supplied this need.

But the absolute ruler's need for eunuchs went beyond the practicalities of protection. Absolute rulers inhabited a quasi-sacred, inviolate space, comparable to the inner sanctum of a temple. Eunuchs provided a sort of *cordon sanitaire* around this taboo precinct, so that it could not be "polluted" by contact with commoners. In their mediating role, they arguably resembled demigods or angels.[7] Yet they differed from angels and demigods in occupying a dangerously ambivalent zone, for they could not become so intimate with the "sacred" ruler that they would diminish his status while, at the same time, losing their connection with the common population. Figuratively, then, they walked a fine line between the ruler's sacred purity and the mundane impurity of the mass of his subjects.

---

[5] Helen Berry, *The Castrato and His Wife* (Oxford, 2011), especially 13, 15–16, 18, 68, 76–77, 183; Neil Moran, "The Choir of the Hagia Sophia," *Oriens Christianus* 89 (2005): 1–7; Georges Sidéris, "Une Société de ville capitale: les eunuques dans la Constantinople byzantine (IVe–XIIe siècle)," in *Les Villes capitales au Moyen Âge – XXXVIe Congrès de la SHMES (Istanbul, 1er-6 juin 2005)* (Paris, 2006), 262. I thank Professor Sidéris for providing me with a copy of his article.

[6] Orlando Patterson, *Slavery and Social Death: A Comparative Study* (Cambridge, MA, 1982), 323.

[7] Kathryn Ringrose, *The Perfect Servant: Eunuchs and the Social Construction of Gender in Byzantium* (Chicago, IL, 2003), chapters 4, 7; Shaun Tougher, *The Eunuch in Byzantine History and Society* (London, 2008), 86, 89, 106–7, 113–15.

As to the second shared feature, all these empires practiced seclusion of royal women as a means of controlling dynastic reproduction. A designated, circumscribed place for all the ruler's potential sexual partners (and their numerous servants and assistants) made it possible to limit the number of children, particularly sons, that each wife or concubine bore and to ensure that these women never had sexual partners apart from the ruler. This was the famous harem or "inner sanctum" institution, practiced not only in Islamic empires and kingdoms but also in imperial China and in the Roman, Byzantine, and ancient Persian empires. Even if some of these empires cultivated marriage alliances with neighboring polities, the foreign princesses entered the harem after their weddings, often sharing quarters with concubines. In this scheme of things, eunuchs policed the boundary between the women's space and that of the ruler and his (castrated or uncastrated) male pages.[8]

The third shared feature is somewhat less obvious: many, if not all, of these regimes employed elite military-administrative slaves, who in Islamic empires were usually called *mamluks* or *ghulams*. The late David Ayalon has argued that the use of eunuchs invariably accompanied the use of these uncastrated elite male slaves, if not for military purposes, then as pages to the ruler. His reasoning is logical: a large corps of young male recruits, usually from far-flung lands, usually ignorant of the language and customs of their new masters, inhabited a barracks or similar quarters for training with older recruits who could easily abuse them, sexually and otherwise. The ruler therefore stationed eunuchs in the barracks to prevent this eventuality.[9] Their function in the barracks mirrored their role in the women's quarters: they policed the sexuality of the inhabitants. Ayalon's analysis points up the fact, also noted by scholars of the Ottoman Empire, that the space occupied by the ruler and his pages resembled a "male harem."[10] In the Ottoman palace, this male harem – the Third Court, including the sultan's privy chamber – had its own corps of eunuchs who might compete with the harem eunuchs.

These three features describe the distinctive practices of the ruling elite in polities that employed eunuchs. Broader socioeconomic considerations, however, may help to explain why castration was accepted by the societies that these elites ruled. Consider the life of the average subject of a premodern polity in Asia, eastern Europe, or Africa. Such a person would have lived in a rural region and had a short life expectancy – hardly beyond thirty or forty in most

---

[8] Peirce, *Imperial Harem*, 136.

[9] David Ayalon, *Eunuchs, Caliphs, and Sultans: A Study in Power Relationships* (Jerusalem, 1999), 33–34, 45–58.

[10] Peirce, *Imperial Harem*, 11; Koçi Bey, *Koçi Bey Risaleleri*, ed. Zuhuri Danışman, prepared by Seda Çakmakoğlu (Istanbul, 2008), 103.

cases – subject to disease, food shortages, natural disasters, and the myriad accidents that could occur in a premechanized rural environment.

The life of an elite slave was very different. An elite slave lived in the ruler's palace, had decent, even elegant, clothing, never went hungry, received the best medical care available, and in many (though not all) cases, acquired an education. And if he were castrated, that slave would be able to function in very close proximity to the ruler. Despite the physical hardships that eunuchs suffered, castration might have seemed an acceptable price to pay for this kind of security and privilege – at least to the ruling elite and society at large; the eunuchs themselves, virtually all of whom were slaves, almost never got to choose whether or not to be castrated. In the context of a premodern or early modern society, castration resembled a security clearance. There were serious costs involved, but there were also tremendous benefits.

The Harem, Gender, and Sexuality

The harem women's sexuality was, obviously, essential to dynastic reproduction. Still, it was a tightly controlled sexuality. The Ottoman imperial household sought to ensure that imperial wives and concubines produced only a limited number of potential male heirs to the throne. This guaranteed the succession while avoiding the chaos of large numbers of sons, with their mothers' active support, competing for the throne. As Leslie Peirce has pointed out, the Ottoman harem by the late sixteenth century – just when the Chief Eunuch became an influential figure – featured a rigid age and status hierarchy among its inhabitants. Imperial wives and concubines who had borne male children held pride of place, with a pecking order descending from the mother of the eldest son to that of the youngest. The sultan's mother dominated all, particularly during the crisis years of the seventeenth century, when these formidable women often ruled de facto on behalf of their young sons. This period came to be called "the sultanate of women" as a result.[11]

As in other absolutist empires, the harem eunuchs occupied an asexual liminal space between the male harem – that is, the Third Court, inhabited by the ruler and his male pages – and the female harem. As Peirce explains, "With the exception of the sultan, only those who were not considered to be fully adult males were routinely permitted in the inner worlds of the palace: in the male harem household, boys and young men, eunuchs, dwarves, and mutes; and in the family harem household women and children."[12] As her description implies, the harem eunuchs almost never entered the living quarters of the palace women but remained in the corridors just inside the harem entrance, where they had their

[11] The term was coined in 1916 by the historian Ahmet Refik (Altınay) (1881–1937).
[12] Peirce, *Imperial Harem*, 11.

lodgings.[13] The Chief Eunuch acted as a sort of liaison between the top woman in the harem – either the sultan's favorite concubine or, by the seventeenth century, his mother – and the sultan and his male pages, at least some of whom were white eunuchs from the Balkans and the Caucasus.

Both the African and the white eunuchs could function in this space because their sexuality had never fully developed. They arguably comprised not so much a third gender as an arrested male gender, much as if they were young boys, with all the androgyny that young boys can exhibit. Shaun Marmon has eloquently compared harem eunuchs to the three boys in Mozart's opera *The Magic Flute*, who "act as neutral messengers between the dangerous and disorderly female world of the Queen of the Night and the sunlit, rational world of Sarastro." "The eunuch/child," she adds, "is an intermediate being, safe in both worlds and belonging to neither."[14] Just so the harem eunuchs, like perpetual children, were able to mediate between the taboo space of the female or male harem and the public spaces of Topkapı Palace. In this sense, too, they resembled guardian demigods or angels, as noted above.

This liminality has been one of the main reasons that eunuch gender has proven so challenging, not only for the societies in which eunuchs have historically existed but also in scholarship on the subject. There is still disagreement on whether court eunuchs, who generally dressed in clothing designed for men, were male-gendered or belonged to some other gender entirely; this is the case above all in scholarship on the Roman and Byzantine Empires, where eunuchs have been most thoroughly examined from the perspective of gender.[15] If court eunuchs were male-gendered, then theirs was not a normative adult male gender but a nonnormative or alternative male gender. As such, it quite obviously subverted societal norms of masculinity, which, in most Islamic societies, included the ability to father children and to grow facial hair. This subversive gender, moreover, resulted from surgical intervention. Premodern and early modern societies worldwide perceived a need to intervene to complicate normative gender categories. But in so doing, they were also emphasizing these normative categories, for eunuchs, in a sense, enforced them. As Marmon stresses, the figure guarding the boundary between two realms must be comfortable in both while belonging to neither. It was as if the eunuch, by being neither/nor, sharpened the boundary between either/or.

---

[13] Ibid., 136.

[14] Shaun Marmon, *Eunuchs and Sacred Boundaries in Islamic Society* (New York, NY, 1995), 90.

[15] Sidéris, "Les Eunuques dans la Constantinople byzantine," 245; Pascal Boulhol and Isabelle Cochelin, "La Réhabilitation de l'eunuque dans l'hagiographie antique (IVe–VIe siècles)," *Studi di antichita cristiana* 48 (1992): 48, 49–76; Ringrose, *Perfect Servant*, chapters 1–3, 6; Tougher, *The Eunuch in Byzantine History and Society*, 3, 5, 34–35, 50–51, 52, 96–118, 129; Mathew Kuefler, *The Manly Eunuch: Masculinity, Gender Ambiguity, and Christian Ideology in Late Antiquity* (Chicago, IL, 2001), 96–102, 218–44.

Distinctive Features of Ottoman Eunuchs

The Ottoman eunuch system was heavily influenced by those of earlier Islamic polities, including the Abbasids (750–1258 CE), the Great Seljuks (ca. 1037–1153), and their various subordinate dynasties in Iraq, Iran, and Central Asia; the Seljuks of Rum (ca. 1077–1308) in Anatolia; and the Mamluk Sultanate (1250–1517) in Egypt, Syria, and southeastern Anatolia. But it also bore the influence of non-Muslim dynasties, most notably the Byzantines, who, as Chapter 3 will point out, were direct models for Ottoman court institutions, although certainly not the only models. There were key differences in the Byzantine eunuch institution, particularly the fact that Byzantine eunuchs were not radically castrated, as their counterparts in Islamic empires were, and that Byzantine eunuchs could join the church hierarchy and even become patriarchs of the Orthodox Church, at least before the thirteenth century CE or thereabouts.[16] In Islamic empires, by contrast, eunuchs could not hold official religious appointments, such as judge (*qadi*) of a Muslim law court or Chief Mufti, the official who dispensed legal decisions (*fetva*s) in accordance with Islamic law. On the other hand, they could be, and often were, extremely well read in Islamic law and theology, and might amass impressive libraries of texts in these and other fields. They could even found mosques, Qur'an schools, and madrasas, or Islamic theological seminaries. Their engagement in intellectual life stands in marked contrast to the experience of their counterparts in Ming dynasty China (1368–1644 CE), where eunuchs were sometimes totally uneducated and even illiterate, despite the wide variety of political and economic roles they performed.[17] Eunuchs also served in military roles in a number of these polities, including the Byzantine Empire, imperial China, and most medieval Muslim empires. In some of the medieval Muslim empires, military eunuchs could serve in the harem and vice versa.[18] The Ottomans, however, introduced a rigid barrier between the two categories.

The Evkafü'l-Haremeyn. Although the Chief Harem Eunuch's duties by definition revolved around the palace harem, the office of Chief Harem Eunuch owed its existence to the Muslim holy cities of Mecca and Medina. It was created in 1588, when Sultan Murad III transferred supervision of the imperial pious foundations for the holy cities from the head of the white Third Court

---

[16] Ringrose, *Perfect Servant*, chapter 5; Tougher, *The Eunuch in Byzantine History and Society*, chapter 5 and 120, 123; Sidéris, "Les Eunuques dans la Constantinople byzantine," 253, 256.

[17] Shih-shan Henry Tsai, "Eunuch Power in Imperial China," in *Eunuchs in Antiquity and Beyond*, ed. Shaun Tougher (Swansea, 2002), 227–29; Shih-shan Henry Tsai, *The Eunuchs in the Ming Dynasty* (Albany, NY, 1996), 42–43 and chapters 4–9.

[18] Ringrose, *Perfect Servant*, 130–41; Tougher, *The Eunuch in Byzantine History and Society*, 5, 35, 40, 97, 116, 120, 121, 122, 126, appendix 2 passim; Tsai, *Eunuchs in the Ming Dynasty*, chapter 4. On the medieval Islamic empires, see Chapter 2 of the present work.

eunuchs to the head of the mostly African harem eunuchs. As noted above, these endowments were known as Evkafü'l-Haremeyn, or Awqaf al-Haramayn in Arabic, literally, "endowments of the two *harams*," since the Great Mosque in Mecca and the Prophet's Mosque in Medina were both considered *harams*, or spaces that were sacred, on the one hand, and forbidden to outsiders and the ritually impure, on the other hand. The Arabic word comes from the same root as harem (*harim* in Arabic), which is similarly a taboo space that is off-limits to outsiders – in this case, adult males, particularly those not related to the ruler by blood.

Supervision of the Evkafü'l-Haremeyn was a key part of the Chief Eunuch's duties almost as long as the office existed; the office lost much of its influence toward the middle of the nineteenth century, just as a Ministry of Pious Endowments was taking shape as part of the wave of top-down reforms. Reminders of the palace harem's link to the holy cities were ubiquitous in Topkapı Palace: the foundation documents were stored in cupboards lining the walls just inside the harem entrance,[19] and the tiles adorning the harem's entry corridor were painted with scenes of the Ka'ba in Mecca. The Chief Harem Eunuch spent much of his time in office worrying about collecting revenues earmarked for the endowments from the far-flung provinces of the empire. Even if he were deposed and exiled to Egypt, he could hardly forget the Evkaf since the villages that produced grain for Mecca and Medina were located in that province.

Beginning in the late seventeenth century, as Chapter 6 will make clear, deposed Chief Harem Eunuchs were often reassigned to Medina to head the corps of eunuchs who guarded the tomb of the Prophet Muhammad, a venerable institution dating to the late twelfth century. This practice underlined the importance of the Evkafü'l-Haremeyn to the Chief Eunuch, even well after deposition. "Making the *hijra* to the Prophet" – referring to Muhammad's emigration (*hijra*) from Mecca to Medina in 622 CE – symbolically transformed a harem eunuch's identity; eunuchs were usually manumitted when they left the palace, and in Medina, they took enslaved African women as wives. They thus claimed, for the first time in their lives, the status of free, mature Muslim males. This was a mark of spiritual fulfillment that had obvious implications for the eunuchs' sexuality as well, although it is impossible to tell if married tomb eunuchs were sexually active in any fashion.[20] The paradox is striking: in the presence of the dead, the eunuchs enjoyed the perquisites of family life, at least in appearance, whereas at the site of dynastic reproduction,

---

[19] Necipoğlu, *Architecture, Ceremony, and Power*, 180.
[20] John Lewis Burckhardt, *Travels in Arabia* (Beirut, 1972), 342, 344; Richard Francis Burton, *Personal Narrative of a Pilgrimage to al-Madinah and Meccah*, memorial ed. (London, 1893; reprint, New York, NY, 1964), I: 372.

they maintained a monklike bachelorhood. Yet it makes sense at the same time: the eunuchs' sexuality, real or fictive, was no threat to the Prophet, who was dead and whose succession had long since been determined, at least so far as Sunnis were concerned. As free Muslim men, moreover, they were fitting companions to the Prophet.

We are justified, in any case, in saying that the Chief Harem Eunuch's mind was to some degree always on "the other harem," that is, the sacred precinct encompassing the Prophet's mosque and tomb in Medina, even if the Muslim holy city seemed to recede amid the daily exigencies of palace life. But by invoking the link to Medina, and to the pious endowments for the holy cities more specifically, I hope to stress the point that the office of Chief Harem Eunuch was an administrative position inextricably tied to these foundations. After the conquest of the Mamluk Sultanate in 1517, the Ottoman sultan drew a great deal of prestige from his role as Khadim al-Haramayn, or "servant of the two *haram*s," referring to Mecca and Medina. Coincidentally or not, the Arabic word for "servant," *khadim*, came to designate a eunuch as early as the Abbasid era; by the Ottoman era, it was a virtual synonym.[21] The Chief Eunuch was likewise the "servant of the two *haram*s," only in his case, the two in question were the palace harem and the Prophet's tomb in Medina. In some respects, we can see the Chief Harem Eunuch's career unfolding between these two harems, although the balance between the two shifted over the years.

Because he guaranteed dynastic reproduction while, at the same time, controlling the pious foundations for the holy cities – two pillars of Ottoman legitimacy – the Chief Eunuch was indispensable to Ottoman authority, at least until the westernizing reforms of the nineteenth century. This fact helps to explain why the office of Chief Harem Eunuch persisted for more than three hundred years, despite the excesses of individual holders of the office, the machinations of political enemies within and outside the palace, and the attempts of certain grand viziers, particularly in the eighteenth century, to bar the importation of African eunuchs into imperial territory.

The evolution of the Ottoman harem institution, which made the Chief Harem Eunuch's role possible (and necessary), is the subject of Chapter 3. Before we get to the harem, however, we need to ask a fundamental question, namely, why were almost all Chief Harem Eunuchs, and all Ottoman harem eunuchs more generally, African? This is the subject of Chapter 2.

---

[21] Ayalon, *Eunuchs, Caliphs, and Sultans*, appendix A.

2   The African Connection

Most of the eunuchs who guarded the Ottoman imperial harem – as well as the harems of high government officials and provincial governors and notables – were African. Why was this? Four key considerations probably came to bear on this choice. First, and perhaps most important, was convenience and availability. Africa, more specifically eastern Africa, was adjacent to Ottoman territory after the Ottomans' 1517 conquest of Egypt; at different periods, large swaths of it were even part of Ottoman territory. This meant that the pool of potential eunuchs was ready to hand.

A second consideration was the widespread (although by no means absolute) taboo against enslaving and castrating the core population of an empire. Most empires that employed eunuchs acquired them from outside imperial territory or from the empire's peripheral regions.[1] East Africa was unquestionably such a region in relation to the Ottoman Empire. Muslim empires, in addition, had to contend with the fact that enslaving Muslims violates Islamic law, as does castration. Thus, the procedure had to be performed on non-Muslim captives by non-Muslims, preferably outside or on the fringes of Muslim territory. While the Christian and animist populations of East Africa fulfilled the first requirement – which was sometimes violated – the overwhelmingly Coptic areas of Upper Egypt fulfilled the second, as we will soon see.

A third factor was a preexisting slave trade in the region. In the case of eastern Africa, a well-developed slave trade existed long before the Ottoman conquest of Egypt and North Africa in the sixteenth century, so it was relatively easy for the Ottomans to tap into it. This brings up a fourth, and related, consideration: eunuchs were almost always a subset of a larger population of slaves, elite and nonelite, male and female, from their land of origin. Thus, we would expect eunuchs to come from regions that already supplied the Ottoman Empire with slaves. East Africa certainly fulfilled that function. At the same time, African eunuchs were more often than not a subset of a

---

[1] Tougher, *The Eunuch in Byzantine History and Society*, 60–65, 103, appendix 2, passim; Tsai, *Eunuchs in the Ming Dynasty*, 14–15, 115, 127, 135, 138–39, 144, 202, 205.

larger population of eunuchs from a variety of provenances. A court that employed African eunuchs might therefore choose to assign them duties that non-African eunuchs did not perform. Harem service was chief among such duties.

But there was also a fifth, more nebulous factor: the color and racial prejudices, combined with a perception of "otherness," that made East African eunuchs ubiquitous as harem guardians in the Islamic world for more than a thousand years. So far as the Ottomans specifically were concerned, their initial exposure to a critical mass of East Africans came at a time when the empire was undergoing rapid demographic change on a number of fronts. Broader ethnoregional antagonisms helped to shape the kinds of racism that emerged in Ottoman society.

This chapter will address these considerations as they pertain not only to the Ottoman Empire but also to earlier Muslim empires and to the polities of East Africa. We will observe how the use of enslaved Africans, including eunuchs, among the Muslim polities that preceded the Ottomans in the eastern Mediterranean and the Fertile Crescent established patterns that the Ottomans followed. At the same time, we will not lose sight of the fact that employment of eunuchs was part of a broader pattern of elite slavery in these societies. Practices in Africa itself likewise affected Ottoman access to African slaves, eunuchs and otherwise, and accordingly the second section will address the circulation of East African eunuchs and non-eunuch slaves in the various kingdoms of that region, as well as the rather anomalous part taken by the Christian kingdom of Ethiopia. New sixteenth-century geopolitical realities that facilitated Ottoman acquisition of East African slaves form the subject of the third section. Turning to the logistics of the trade in African eunuchs, the fourth section describes the major routes of the East African slave trade and the methods by which East African slaves were castrated. A final section broaches the vexed question of racism and sexual stereotypes.

African Eunuch and Non-Eunuch Slaves in Pre-Ottoman Muslim Empires

In using African slaves, and more particularly African eunuchs, the Ottomans were influenced by a long line of earlier Muslim empires. While evidence of African eunuchs in the Middle Eastern heartland is spotty before the rise of the Abbasid caliphate in the eighth century CE, trade in non-eunuch East African slaves was firmly rooted in the region well before the rise of Islam, and the early Muslim state participated in it to some degree. After failing to conquer the Nubian Christian kingdom of Muqurra in 652, the Muslim governor of Egypt famously concluded an agreement (*baqt*) with the Nubians that guaranteed their independence if they would undertake a number of obligations, including sending a specified number of slaves to Egypt each year.[2] Whether these slaves included eunuchs cannot be determined. Certainly, the early Muslims would have been familiar with eunuchs from contact with the Byzantines and Sasanians. In fact, the biographical traditions of the Prophet Muhammad assert that when he received the Coptic concubine Marya as a gift from the Byzantine Patriarch of Alexandria, she was accompanied by her eunuch Jurayj.[3]

In any event, there is reason to believe that court eunuchs were a feature of the Umayyad empire (680–750 CE), although the meager sources available for Umayyad institutions and court practices make it impossible to be completely certain. Lore of the Umayyads transmitted by later authors, however, attributes the introduction of the eunuch institution to the founder of the Umayyad dynasty, Mu'awiya ibn Abi Sufyan (r. 661–80).[4]

This lack of certainty ends with the Abbasids, who overthrew the Umayyads in 750 CE and established a new capital at Baghdad. They unquestionably employed African eunuchs, who, in turn, were a subset of an enormous number of slaves, eunuchs and otherwise, from a wide variety of locales. In a description of Baghdad in the late ninth century, the traveler al-Ya'qubi notes the quarters of "the black slaves attached to [the caliph's] personal service" – almost certainly eunuchs – surrounding the caliphal palace at the exact center of the city.[5] African eunuchs likewise appear in virtually all Abbasid-era sources, from official chronicles to the *Thousand and One Nights*. In the latter source, they are almost always harem guardians and not infrequently lascivious foils for the women who inhabit the harem.[6]

In fact, the Abbasids are the first Muslim empire known to have adopted the custom of grooming East African eunuchs as harem guardians. This did not mean, however, that East Africa was the dynasty's sole source of eunuchs. The bureaucrat Hilal al-Sabi (969–ca. 1056), who composed a description of the Abbasid court and its etiquette, reports 11,000 eunuchs in the imperial palace, of whom 7,000 were "blacks" while 4,000 belonged to the Slavic population known as *Saqaliba*, who were also a prime source of eunuchs in Muslim

---

[2] Stanley Burstein, ed. and trans., *Ancient African Civilizations: Kush and Axum* (Princeton, NJ, 1998), 118–20, 127–31.

[3] Ayalon, *Eunuchs, Caliphs, and Sultans*, 277; *EI²*, s.v. "Khasi," by Charles Pellat.

[4] *Encyclopaedia Iranica*, s.v. "Eunuchs, III. The Early Islamic Period," by C. Edmund Bosworth; Ayalon, *Eunuchs, Caliphs, and Sultans*, 66–68.

[5] Al-Ya'qubi, *Buldan*, in Bernard Lewis, ed. and trans., *Islam from the Prophet Muhammad to the Capture of Constantinople*, vol. 2: *Religion and Society* (Oxford, 1974, 1987), 75.

[6] N.J. Dawood, trans., *Tales from the Thousand and One Nights* (Hammondsworth, Middlesex, 1954; reprint, 1985), 15–17. As is well known, many of the *Nights* tales were retransmitted under the Mamluk Sultanate; some even reflect Ottoman-era influences.

Spain.[7] Intriguingly, the caliph al-Amin (r. 809–13), eldest son of the legendary Harun al-Rashid, is reported by the chronicler al-Tabari (838–923) to have divided the palace eunuchs into a black corps and a white corps. In so doing, he anticipated the Ottoman division by some seven centuries, although the duties of the two corps do not seem to have differed significantly, and there is no evidence that the division, which lapsed with the end of al-Amin's brief reign, influenced the Ottomans.[8]

The Abbasids fulfill Ayalon's dictum that societies that employed eunuchs also employed elite military slaves, known as mamluks or *ghulam*s: the Central Asian Turks who, beginning in the mid-ninth century, served the Abbasids in this capacity are well known.[9] A eunuch of unspecified origin supervised the young non-eunuch *ghulam*s who guarded the halls of the Abbasid caliph's palace; this was a role that eunuchs typically played, in Ayalon's schema, in order to prevent sexual abuse.[10] Eunuchs likewise served as companions to the caliph, oversaw the education of his sons, and delivered confidential messages between imperial family members.[11] Iranian eunuchs and eunuchs of Central Asian Turkic origin also appear in the seminal history of al-Tabari, who was well familiar with the Abbasid court.[12] These eunuchs, however, were not restricted to the palace but could serve as military commanders.

Virtually all the regional powers that administered the Abbasid provinces beginning in the mid-tenth century employed a combination of African and non-African eunuchs, as well as Turkish mamluks.[13] The only one of these

---

[7] Hilal al-Sabi, *Rusum dar al-khilafa: The Rules and Regulations of the 'Abbasid Court*, trans. Elie A. Salem (Beirut, 1977), 14; David Ayalon, "On the Eunuchs in Islam," *Jerusalem Studies in Arabic and Islam* 1 (1979): 110–14, 123; Ayalon, *Eunuchs, Caliphs, and Sultans*, 349–52; Eliyahu Ashtor, *The Jews of Moslem Spain* (Philadelphia, 1973, reissued 1992), I: 290, II: 69 ff., 105; Jane Hathaway, "Eunuchs," *EI³*, http://referenceworks.brillonline.com./entries/encyclo paedia-of-islam-3/eunuchs-COM_27821?s.num=19.

[8] Ayalon, *Eunuchs, Caliphs, and Sultans*, 128–31.

[9] Matthew S. Gordon, *The Breaking of a Thousand Swords: A History of the Turkish Military of Samarra, A.H. 200–275/815–889 C.E.* (Albany, NY, 2001); David Ayalon, "The Muslim City and the Mamluk Military Aristocracy," *Proceedings of the Israel Academy of Sciences and Humanities* 2 (1968): 311–29.

[10] Al-Sabi, *Rusum dar al-khilafa*, 14 n. 1; Ayalon, *Eunuchs, Caliphs, and Sultans*, 45–46.

[11] Ayalon, *Eunuchs, Caliphs, and Sultans*, 39–42, 71–103.

[12] E.g., Muhammad b. Jarir al-Tabari, *The History of al-Tabari*, vol. 31: *The War between Brothers: The Caliphate of Muhammad al-Amin, A.D. 809–813/A.H. 193–198*, trans. Michael Fishbein (Albany, NY, 1992), 14, 57, 178, 188, 242.

[13] E.g., Milton Gold, trans., *Tarikh-e Sistan* (Rome, 1976), 206, 208, 224, 270–72; C. Edmund Bosworth, "The Army of the Ghaznavids," in *Warfare and Weaponry in South Asia, 1000–1800*, eds. Jos J.L. Gommans and Dirk H.A. Kolff (New Delhi, 2001), 153–84; *Encyclopaedia Iranica*, s.v. "Eunuchs, III. The Early Islamic Period," by C. Edmund Bosworth; Donald S. Richards, ed. and trans., *The Annals of the Saljuq Turks: Selections from* al-Kamil fi'l-Ta'rikh *of 'Izz al-Din Ibn al-Athir* (London, 2002), 44, 48, 206; Kenneth Allin Luther, trans., *The History of the Seljuq Turks from the* Jami' al-Tawarikh, *an Ilkhanid Adaption [sic] of the* Saljuq-nama *of Zahir al-Din Nishapuri*, ed. C. Edmund Bosworth (Richmond, Surrey,

regimes that apparently did not have recourse to African eunuchs was the Seljuks of Rum, so called because they ruled former Roman – i.e., Byzantine – territory in central and eastern Anatolia. Although they employed Greek and Armenian eunuchs, in addition to Turkish and other mamluks (or *ghulam*s in Seljuk usage),[14] there is no record of African slaves of any kind in their domains, probably because their territory lay relatively far to the north of Africa, across hostile territory.

Perhaps the most famous eunuch ever to serve the Abbasid caliph – even if only indirectly – was Kafur al-Ikhshidi, an Ethiopian eunuch who acted as regent for the last two rulers of the provincial dynasty that administered Egypt on the Abbasids' behalf; rulers of this dynasty, which was founded by a Turkish mamluk, held the ancient Soghdian title Ikhshid, meaning "prince." As the late fourteenth-century historian al-Maqrizi says of Kafur, "He appointed and dismissed, bestowed and withheld; he was named in the Friday bidding-prayer in all the pulpits."[15] Kafur was likewise a military commander and, in that capacity, inflicted a defeat on the Fatimids, proponents of an Ismaili counter-caliphate who were attempting to conquer Egypt from the west. His death shortly afterward arguably enabled the Fatimid takeover.[16]

During the two hundred years (969–1171) of their rule over Egypt, the Fatimids imported large numbers of slaves from Sudan. The long-reigning caliph al-Mustansir billah (r. 1036–94) was the son of a Sudanese slave girl; supposedly under her influence, he acquired a regiment of Sudanese military slaves, who clashed violently with his existing corps of Central Asian Turkish mamluks.[17] Like the Ikhshidids and several other regional dynasties, then, the Fatimids pressed African slaves into military service, although none of the Fatimids' Sudanese fighters was a eunuch, to the best of our knowledge. In contrast, Ethiopian and Nubian eunuchs did hold military commands under smaller pro-Abbasid regional dynasties.[18]

Nonetheless, the Fatimids did employ enormous numbers of eunuchs, both African and otherwise. By the time the Fatimid regime came to an end, in 1171, the palace in Cairo housed several thousand eunuchs; the only non-eunuch

2001), 77–78, 110, 116; Ayalon, *Eunuchs, Caliphs, and Sultans*, 39–41, 47–48, 153–73, 163–64, 169–73, 176–90, 274, 286–87, 323, 326–29, 343–44.

[14] Speros Vryonis, Jr., "Seljuk Gulams and Ottoman Devishirmes," *Der Islam* 41 (1965): 224–52.

[15] Al-Maqrizi, quoted in Lewis, ed. and trans., *Islam...*, vol. 1: *Politics and War* (Oxford, 1974, 1987), 44–45.

[16] Lewis, ed. and trans., *Islam...*, I: 43–46; Bernard Lewis, *Race and Slavery in the Middle East: An Historical Enquiry* (New York, 1990), 59–60; Ayalon, *Eunuchs, Caliphs, and Sultans*, 340.

[17] Yaacov Lev, "Army, Regime, and Society in Fatimid Egypt, 358–487/968–1094," *International Journal of Middle East Studies* 19 (1987): 340–42, 347–51, 357.

[18] Ayalon, *Eunuchs, Caliphs, and Sultans*, 160–61, 184, 188–90, 343; Luther, trans., *History of the Seljuq Turks*, 121; *Encyclopaedia Iranica*, s.v. "Eunuchs, III. The Early Islamic Period," by Bosworth.

residents, in fact, were members of the imperial family. Like the Abbasid palace eunuchs, these consisted of both East Africans and *Saqaliba*.[19] Among the palace eunuchs' duties was supervising the young boys from among the Fatimids' prisoners of war, on the one hand, and the sons of deceased military commanders and high administrators, on the other, who were trained as soldiers; here again, they policed the sexuality of young military recruits.[20] Prominent Fatimid eunuchs served as confidants to the caliphs, keepers of the imperial treasury, provincial governors, and military commanders.[21] Although very little is known about the Fatimid harem, it was certainly guarded by eunuchs, some, if not most, of whom probably originated in eastern Africa. In contrast, most of the eunuchs who served the Fatimids as military and naval commanders were *Saqaliba* – including the general who conquered Egypt and founded Cairo, Jawhar al-Siqilli.[22]

In general, all these medieval Muslim dynasties preferred African eunuchs for harem duty over eunuchs of other ethnoregional origins. Only if Africans were not available did these various regimes resort to non-African eunuchs, particularly Saqaliba and occasionally Indians, en masse.[23] The same was true of the Sunni Mughals and the Twelver Shi'ite Safavids, who dominated India and Iran, respectively, during much of the Ottoman period. Both employed East African eunuchs as harem guardians, supplementing them with Georgians, in the Safavid case, and Bengalis, in the case of the Mughals.[24] In any number of Muslim polities, it is true, small numbers of non-African eunuchs served in the harem alongside Africans; if Africans were regularly available in sufficient numbers, however, these regimes did not exploit alternative sources of harem eunuchs to any significant degree. We might make the analogy to the manner in which, from roughly the ninth through the thirteenth centuries CE, Central Asian Turks were the preferred source of mamluks among many of these same polities. Only kingdoms, such as those of Muslim Spain, that were too distant from the Central Asian steppe to import a critical mass of Turkish mamluks made do with mamluks from other populations, notably the *Saqaliba*.[25] It was not the case that no other people

---

[19] Ayalon, *Eunuchs, Caliphs, and Sultans*, 139.   [20] Ibid., 21, 49–54.

[21] Ibid., 141–43, 340–42.

[22] Delia Cortese and Simonetta Calderini, *Women and the Fatimids in the World of Islam* (Edinburgh, 2006), 37, 74, 78, 80, 81, 82, 84–85, 88, 162; *EI²*, s.v. "Djawhar al-Sikilli," by Hussein Monés.

[23] *Encyclopaedia Iranica*, s.v. "Eunuchs, III. The Early Islamic Period," by Bosworth; Gold, trans., *Tarikh-e Sistan*, 282; Richards, trans., *Annals of the Saljuq Turks*, 284.

[24] Gavin Hambly, "A Note on the Trade in Eunuchs in Mughal Bengal," *Journal of the American Oriental Society* 94, 1 (1974): 125–30; Jessica Hinchy, "Eunuchs and the East India Company in North India," in *Celibate and Childless Men in Power: Ruling Eunuchs and Bishops in the Pre-Modern World*, eds. Almut Höfert et al. (London, 2018), 149–74; *Encyclopaedia Iranica*, s.v. "Eunuchs, IV. The Safavid Period," by Kathryn Babayan.

[25] Ayalon, *Eunuchs, Caliphs, and Sultans*, 349–52.

were fit to be mamluks, although the Turks' extraordinary military prowess had been noted by many observers. Rather, mamluks were, from the ninth to the thirteenth century, automatically identified with Turks because of the sheer mass of Turkic populations moving through the Central Asian steppe at the time, many of whom the Abbasids and their vassals encountered as they expanded eastward, and by the example that the Abbasids and their vassals set by employing them. By the same token, harem eunuchs had by the fifteenth century come to be automatically identified with East Africans, and for the same basic reasons of availability and example, although prejudices and stereotypes of the sort described at the end of this chapter must also have played a role.

The Model of the Mamluk Sultanate. All of these medieval Islamic polities – and above all the neighboring Seljuks of Rum – influenced the early Ottomans in their use of eunuch and non-eunuch slaves, whether African or otherwise. By the late fifteenth century, though, the Mamluk Sultanate had arguably become the most immediate and far-reaching model of any Muslim empire. The Mamluk Sultanate derived its name from the fact that its founders were Turkish mamluks of the Ayyubids, the dynasty founded in 1171 by the famous Crusader-fighter Salah al-Din (Saladin). Most of the sultanate's rulers were likewise manumitted mamluks, and mamluks dominated the officer ranks and the elite regiments of its armies.[26] (Neither the Mamluks nor the Ayyubids, who preceded them as overlords of Egypt and Syria, continued the Fatimids' practice of employing East African slave soldiers.)

By the time of the Ottoman conquest of Constantinople in 1453, the Mamluk Sultanate's supply of military slaves came overwhelmingly from the Caucasus, above all Circassia in what is now southern Russia. They were transported along the southern Black Sea coast, then through Constantinople or overland through central Anatolia; the early Ottomans not only would have been familiar with this slave traffic but would have sought to control it.[27] When the Ottomans engaged the Mamluks in warfare in southeastern Anatolia in the late fifteenth century,[28] and above all when they absorbed the Mamluk empire into their own in 1516–17, they became intimately acquainted with this slave procurement system, to say nothing of the sultanate's administrative institutions, which had a profound influence on the Ottomans' own developing state. By the seventeenth century, the Ottomans themselves were importing

[26] Robert Irwin, *The Middle East in the Middle Ages: The Early Mamluk Sultanate, 1250–1382* (London, 1986), especially 1–61.
[27] *EI²*, s.v. "Mamluk," by David Ayalon; Halil Inalcik, "The Question of the Closing of the Black Sea under the Ottomans," in Inalcik, *Essays in Ottoman History* (Istanbul, 1998), 416–45, especially 424, 426, 431–32, 434–35, 441, 443–44.
[28] Shai Har-El, *The Struggle for Domination in the Middle East: The Ottoman-Mamluk War, 1485–91* (Leiden, 1995).

Circassian and Georgian mamluks as an alternative to the rebellious palace slaves (Turkish plural, *kullar*) who came into Ottoman service through the *devshirme*, the peculiarly Ottoman practice of "collecting" boys from among the empire's Balkan and Anatolian Christian subjects, converting them to Islam, and training them to be either Janissaries or palace pages.[29]

Similarly, the manner in which the Mamluk Sultanate employed eunuchs served as a key model for the Ottoman Empire, although this is not to say that the Ottomans were not influenced by other polities, both Muslim and non-Muslim. Under the Mamluks, eunuchs of East African, Greek, other Balkan, and Indian origin served as guardians not only of the women's quarters but also of the barracks where mamluk recruits received their training; their presence there helped to prevent sexual abuse of young new recruits by older mamluks.[30] This was, to a large extent, a continuation of the practice, observed under the Abbasids, the Fatimids, and the various regional potentates, whereby eunuchs served as educators to crown princes, and supervised soldiers and pages in training. While the Ottomans did not install eunuchs in their own military barracks, white eunuchs did supervise the Ottoman corps of palace pages, while African eunuchs were in charge of the princes' early education (see Chapter 3). In all these cases, the use of eunuchs to police the sexuality of uncastrated young men in training followed the pattern observed by Ayalon.

Under the Mamluks, a permanent eunuch guard patrolled the entrance to the sultan's audience chamber in Cairo's citadel.[31] A similar phalanx of white eunuchs came to guard the threshold in front of the Ottoman sultan's audience hall in Topkapı Palace. In an even more far-reaching precedent, eunuchs guarded the tombs of Mamluk sultans in Cairo and the tomb of the Prophet Muhammad in Medina. This latter custom seemingly originated with either the Ayyubids or their Zengid predecessors, although its roots are shrouded in mystery. Already in 1184, thirteen years into Ayyubid control of Medina, the Andalusian traveler Ibn Jubayr could report, "The guardians [of the tomb] are Ethiopian and Slavic eunuchs. They present an elegant appearance and are meticulous in their clothing and bearing."[32] Under the Mamluks, as under their Ayyubid predecessors, the corps of "tomb eunuchs" in Medina was not

---

[29] Jane Hathaway, "The 'Mamluk Breaker' Who Was Really a *Kul* Breaker: A Fresh Look at Kul Kıran Mehmed Pasha, Governor of Egypt 1607–1611," in *The Arab Lands in the Ottoman Era: Essays in Honor of Professor Caesar Farah*, ed. Jane Hathaway (Minneapolis, MN, 2009), 93–109; Jane Hathaway, "The *Evlad-i 'Arab* ('Sons of the Arabs') in Ottoman Egypt: A Rereading," in *Frontiers of Ottoman Studies: State, Province, and the West*, vol. 1, eds. Colin Imber and Keiko Kiyotaki (London, 2005), 203–16.

[30] Ayalon, *Eunuchs, Caliphs, and Sultans*, 41–42, 54–57, 309; Marmon, *Eunuchs and Sacred Boundaries*, 11–12.

[31] Marmon, *Eunuchs and Sacred Boundaries*, 10–13.

[32] Ibn Jubayr, *Rihla*, quoted in Marmon, *Eunuchs and Sacred Boundaries*, 131.

exclusively African but included Indian, Greek, and other Balkan eunuchs, as well.[33] Under the Ottomans, an exclusively African eunuch corps would guard the Prophet's tomb into the twentieth century.

African Eunuchs in Africa

Of course, the fact that Muslim empires sought to acquire eunuchs, to say nothing of female slaves and uncastrated male slaves, from East Africa does not mean that East Africa was simply a passive source of man- and woman-power. The infrastructure for the creation and dissemination of eunuchs existed internally in eastern Africa well before the Ottomans extended their conquests to the African continent. In contrast to the Fertile Crescent, though, use of court eunuchs apparently does not go back to the earliest civilizations in Africa. There is no convincing evidence for the presence of eunuchs in Pharaonic Egypt. They were apparently introduced to Egypt in the wake of Alexander the Great's conquest in 331 BCE and became staples of court culture under the dynasty founded by Alexander's general Ptolemy, which ruled Egypt until the Roman takeover in 30 BCE, and under Roman and Byzantine rule. These eunuchs, however, tended to come from European and Asiatic populations.[34]

The earliest mention of an African eunuch at an African court appears in the well-known story from the New Testament Book of Acts of "a man of Ethiopia, an eunuch of great authority under Candace queen of the Ethiopians, who had the charge of all her treasure" (Acts 8:27). Apparently a Jew, the eunuch was converted to Christianity by Philip the Evangelist while returning from a pilgrimage to Jerusalem. Although the story describes the queen as Ethiopian, she would more realistically have been the ruler of the kingdom of Kush in what is now Sudan, with its capital at Meroë on the Nile (see Map 2.1). Candace, or Kandake, was an ancient Nubian title for a queen, and Kush had a total of eleven Kandakes between the fourth century BCE and the fourth century CE.[35] The very existence of this story, naturally, suggests that eunuchs from the surrounding region were employed at the Kushite court before the three Nubian successor kingdoms to Kush accepted

---

[33] Marmon, *Eunuchs and Sacred Boundaries*, 15–77.

[34] Frans Jonckheere, "L'Eunuque dans l'Égypte pharaonique," *Revue d'Histoire des Sciences* 7, 2 (1954): 139–55; Gerald E. Kadish, "Eunuchs in Ancient Egypt?," in *Studies in Honor of John A. Wilson* (Chicago, 1969), 55–62; John Cameron, "The Anatomy of the Mummies," in *The Tomb of Two Brothers*, ed. Margaret Alice Murray (Manchester and London, 1910), 33–47, especially 33.

[35] James Bruce, *Travels to Discover the Source of the Nile in the Years 1768, 1769, 1770, 1771, 1772, and 1773* (Dublin, 1790–91), II: 115; J. Spencer Trimingham, *Islam in Ethiopia* (London, 1965), 38 n. 1; László Török, *The Kingdom of Kush: Handbook of the Napatan-Meroitic Civilization* (Leiden, 1997), 443, 452, 455, 456, 459, 484; David M. Goldenberg, *The Curse of Ham: Race and Slavery in Early Judaism, Christianity, and Islam* (Princeton, NJ, 2003), 17–25.

Map 2.1 Ethiopia and adjacent regions, showing major ethno-regional groups.

Christianity sometime in the sixth century.[36] So when the early Muslims made their treaty with Christian Nubia in 652, eunuchs would have been well established there.

During the medieval and early modern eras, certain of the Muslim kingdoms of East Africa oversaw the production and marketing of eunuchs while also

---

[36] Laurence Kirwan, *Studies on the History of Late Antique and Christian Nubia*, eds. Tomas Hägg et al. (Aldershot, Hampshire, UK, 2002).

employing eunuchs at their own courts. Before its conquest by Ethiopia in 1332, the city of Hadiya, capital of a kingdom of the same name that had controlled the region southwest of the present Ethiopian capital, Addis Ababa, for some decades, was a key center for the export of eunuchs and other slaves to Muslim lands, including Egypt.[37] Castration took place inside the kingdom's territory, at a town called Washilu south of the city of Hadiya.[38] To the east, the kingdom of Adal employed eunuchs at its court in the Somali port of Zayla', as attested by a story purporting to explain Ethiopia's decision to attack the Muslim kingdom: the emperor accused the ruler of Adal of "upbraiding him as a eunuch, fit only to take care of the women of their seraglio."[39] Over five centuries later, Richard Francis Burton, ensconced in Harar, which became Adal's capital in the sixteenth century, described one "Sultan, a sick and decrepid [sic] Eunuch who, having served five Amirs, was allowed to remain in the palace."[40] In eastern Sudan, the Funj sultans, who ruled a regional trading power from their capital at Sennar from 1505 to 1821, employed what the Scottish explorer James Bruce, who traveled extensively in the region between 1768 and 1773, calls "black slaves" in the harems where their wives lived.[41]

In western Sudan, the kingdom of Darfur apparently drew on the traditions of the Muslim kingdoms to the west, around Lake Chad and in northern Nigeria, notably Kanem-Bornu, Baguirmi, and Wadai. Under all these regimes, a highly specialized hierarchy of palace eunuchs developed, with the top two or three in charge of, variously, military expeditions, diplomatic missions, tax collection, the administration of peripheral territories, the harem, the education of princes and princesses, the palace treasury, and palace provisioning.[42] These traditions extended as far west as the kingdom of Songhay, which controlled a swath of western Africa stretching from present-day Nigeria to the Atlantic from the early fourteenth century through the late sixteenth century.[43] Eunuchs employed in these kingdoms were drawn from prisoners of war and from miscreants who were castrated as a form of judicial punishment, as well as from animist populations to the south.[44] Both Baguirmi and Bornu supplied eunuchs to the Great Mosque of Mecca, and the

---

[37] Richard Francis Burton, *First Footsteps in East Africa, or, An Exploration of Harar*, ed. Isabel Burton (London, 1894), II: 2–3. See also Trimingham, *Islam in Ethiopia*, 182; Taddesse Tamrat, *Church and State in Ethiopia, 1270–1527* (Oxford, 1972), 135–37, 155, 173.

[38] Tamrat, *Church and State in Ethiopia*, 86, 87 and 86–87 n. 6, 136–37; Trimingham, *Islam in Ethiopia*, 66–67; Ayalon, *Eunuchs, Caliphs, and Sultans*, 305–6; Humphrey Fisher, *Slavery in the History of Muslim Black Africa* (New York, 2001), 280.

[39] Bruce, *Travels*, II: 228; Burton, *First Footsteps*, II: 3 (conflating Adal and Hadiya).

[40] Burton, *First Footsteps*, II: 34–35.   [41] Bruce, *Travels*, V: 110.

[42] Fisher, *Slavery in the History of Black Africa*, 281, 285–90, 292–93.   [43] Ibid., 282.

[44] Ibid., 281–84, 98.

rulers and notables of these two kingdoms and Wadai occasionally presented eunuchs to the Ottoman palace.[45]

Nor was the employment of eunuchs in central and western Africa exclusive to Muslim kingdoms. The ruler of the Oyo empire, which emerged from among the animist Yoruba people in the fourteenth century and ruled northern and western Nigeria until the late 1800s, employed a large staff of eunuchs and delegated judicial, religious, and executive functions to the three highest-ranking.[46] Eunuchs performed similar functions in the kingdom of the nearby Igala people, which lasted from the sixteenth century through the early twentieth century; the Igala's chief source of eunuchs was subjects who rebelled or otherwise committed crimes against the king.[47]

Ethiopia. Ethiopia was unique among all these African polities in being officially Christian; the religion took root there in the fourth century CE. By the medieval era, a Christian elite belonging largely to the Amharic population at the kingdom's geographical center ruled an assortment of ethnoregional groups, some animist, an increasing number Muslim. Despite the Ethiopian Church's official opposition to the slave trade, Ethiopia had a lengthy tradition of elite slavery, although most such slaves came from the kingdom's peripheral non-Christian populations.

On the other hand, the emperor seems to have enforced the Church's prohibition of castration more or less rigorously.[48] As a result, the Ethiopian court made only very occasional use of eunuchs. Notwithstanding, the court had a hierarchy of offices close to the monarch that directly paralleled those routinely filled by eunuchs in other societies. By James Bruce's account, these were, from lowest to highest, gentleman of the king's bedchamber; groom of the king's stole, referring to a ceremonial garment; and master of the king's household.[49] The last office supervised all of Ethiopia's provincial governors and collected revenues from them.[50]

These are exactly the sorts of positions of trust, involving regular close, even intimate, contact with the ruler, that were held by eunuchs in the Byzantine, Chinese, and various Islamic empires, not to mention the West African kingdoms. Under the Ottomans, such posts were ordinarily held by the white eunuchs of the Third Court, although once Sultan Murad III (r. 1574–95) moved his residential quarters into the harem, his bedchamber was guarded by

---

[45] Ibid., 292; Bruce, *Travels*, V: 248.

[46] Fisher, *Slavery in the History of Black Africa*, 293; J.S. Eades, *The Yoruba Today* (Cambridge, 1980), 20–21.

[47] J.S. Boston, *The Igala Kingdom* (Ibadan, 1968), 21, 54, 93, 105, 163–75, 197–99, 209–13.

[48] Burton, *First Footsteps*, II: 25 n. 1; Trimingham, *Islam in Ethiopia*, 67 n. 1; Harold G. Marcus, *A History of Ethiopia* (Berkeley, CA 1994), 55.

[49] Bruce, *Travels*, III: 273, 596; Tamrat, *Church and State in Ethiopia*, 104–5, 269–75.

[50] Bruce, *Travels*, III: 273; Samuel Johnson, *A Voyage to Abyssinia*, ed. Joel L. Gold, trans. from the French (New Haven, CT, 1985), 44.

elderly women (see Chapter 3). In Ethiopia, though, these positions, while often filled by slaves, were only occasionally held by eunuchs. Bruce describes six masters of the king's household; of these, only one, Kefla Wahad, active in the early seventeenth century, can be identified with certainty as a eunuch.[51] In contrast, other holders of this post included a relative of the ruler and even a future king.[52]

Ethiopia is, in fact, something of a curiosity: a society that possessed all the offices, duties, and career paths that ordinarily accompanied widespread use of eunuchs, yet one that only very rarely had recourse to them. Bruce observed "black servants" – again, not specified as eunuchs – who guarded the door of the king's "presence chamber," not unlike the white eunuchs who guarded the threshold in front of the Ottoman sultan's audience chamber. He refers repeatedly to young boys and girls taken in slavery by the Ethiopian court;[53] in other polities, including those bordering Ethiopia, young boys would have been the most likely candidates for castration, which, according to the logic of many early modern empires, would have cemented their loyalty to the dynasty. Bruce likewise describes a system whereby both male and female slaves under the age of seventeen or eighteen were converted to Christianity and educated by the king; they were then sent to serve in the "great houses of Abyssinia." The cream of these slaves became the king's personal attendants.[54] This custom appears analogous to the process by which, in the Ottoman Empire, an African eunuch might serve in the household of the governor of Egypt or one of Egypt's grandees before being presented to the imperial palace.[55] Yet Bruce gives no indication that the young male slaves were castrated, and given the ecclesiastical injunction, we may assume that they were not.[56]

Since castration was not practiced in Ethiopia, we have to conclude that any eunuchs who entered the service of the Ethiopian court had been castrated somewhere else. Eunuchs such as Kefla Wahad may have been previously castrated prisoners of war from the Funj Sultanate or from the Ottoman province of Habesh. Certainly, Ethiopia had a history of attacking its Muslim neighbors and enslaving large numbers of captives, despite the Ethiopian Church's official prohibition of slavery.[57]

---

[51] Bruce, *Travels*, III: 518.   [52] Ibid., III: 142, 144, 273–74, 291–92, 418–19; IV: 696.

[53] Ibid., II: 480–81, 489; III: 52, 56, 156, 172, 213.   [54] Ibid., III: 156.

[55] Jane Hathaway, *The Politics of Households in Ottoman Egypt: The Rise of the Qazdağlıs* (Cambridge, 1997), 158, 160–64; Jane Hathaway, *Beshir Agha, Chief Eunuch of the Ottoman Imperial Harem* (Oxford, 2006), 25–26.

[56] My thanks to Professors Ralph Lee and Glen Bowersock for their insights on this issue.

[57] Alice Moore-Harell, "Economic and Political Aspects of the Slave Trade in Ethiopia and the Sudan in the Second Half of the Nineteenth Century," *International Journal of African Historical Studies* 32, 2 (1999): 407, 409, 412; Bruce, *Travels*, II: 489, III: 242, 263; J.H. Arrowsmith-Brown, ed. and trans., *Prutky's Travels in Ethiopia and Other Countries* (London, 1991), 152.

On the other hand, Ethiopia, true to the pattern observed in many other polities, routinely raided the populations of its own peripheral territories for non-eunuch slaves. These populations were almost uniformly non-Christian, and in most cases animists of one kind or another. In numerous cases, rebellions on the parts of these peoples against the Ethiopian monarch served as justifications for punitive expeditions that resulted in the capture of large numbers of slaves. In the space of two pages, Bruce describes an early seventeenth-century monarch attacking the ancient Jewish population popularly known by the derogatory term "Falasha" and two different groups of the Oromo, popularly known by the derogatory term "Galla." In each case, the king and his forces forced the survivors to convert to Christianity and sold the captured women and children into slavery.[58] Before the same king conquered and converted the animist principality of Narea, in the far south of Ethiopia, Oromo warriors routinely raided the region for prisoners, whom they sold to Muslim slave traders, who, in turn, sold them in what was then the Ethiopian capital of Gondar.[59]

Other seventeenth-century Ethiopian emperors acquired slaves from among the Shangalla, whom Bruce describes as "black pagans" who dwelt in caves in Ethiopia's northeastern mountains and worshipped "the Nile and a certain tree."[60] The governors of the districts bordering Shangalla territory were each required to deliver a specified number of slaves to the king each year; many of the palace slaves apparently came from this source.[61] On the other hand, Bruce has the Shangalla raiding the Agew, a large animist confederation near the Nile headwaters, for slaves.[62] Agew men also served in the royal army during Bruce's stay in the late 1760s and early 1770s.[63] Slaves from among the Oromo, meanwhile, supplied the royal household cavalry, while the so-called Falasha contributed to the imperial guard.[64]

While these slaves were not castrated in preparation for their service at the Ethiopian court, that fate might well await them if they fell into the hands of the eunuch-employing polities bordering Ethiopia, whether through warfare or, more commonly, through trade conducted by enterprising merchants from Ethiopia and neighboring polities. During the medieval period, Ethiopian

---

[58] Bruce, *Travels*, II: 401ff., 480–81, 550–51.
[59] Bruce, *Travels*, II: 501–4; Cengiz Orhonlu, *Osmanlı İmparatorluğu'nun Güney Siyaseti: Habeş Eyaleti* (Ankara, 1974; 2nd printing 1996), 72–73.
[60] Bruce, *Travels*, II: 22; III: 39, 56, 149, 158–67.
[61] Ibid., II: 479; III: 155–56, 506–7, 590; IV: 336; Henry Salt, *A Voyage to Abyssinia, and Travels into the Interior of That Country* (Philadelphia, PA, 1816), 293–95; Tamrat, *Church and State in Ethiopia*, 91–92, 136, 173.
[62] Bruce, *Travels*, II: 248; III: 40; IV: 320, 437, 675; Tamrat, *Church and State in Ethiopia*, 8, 25–29, 37, 196, 201–2; Marcus, *History of Ethiopia*, 5–6, 10–11, 32.
[63] Bruce, *Travels*, III: 320, 323.   [64] Ibid., III: 206, 219, 272; Marcus, *History of Ethiopia*, 43.

merchants routinely supplied slaves to the Muslim principality of Adal to the east in return for rock salt, even though Adal was supposedly subordinate to the Ethiopian emperor.[65] By the early seventeenth century, male and female prisoners from animist Narea, mentioned above, were sold by Muslim merchants not only at Gondar but also at "Constantinople, India, and Cairo."[66] Muslim merchants likewise bought up Agew slaves captured by the Shangalla.[67] During Bruce's sojourn in Ethiopia, the powerful governor of the northern province of Tigray traded slaves to "Arabia" – presumably meaning the Ottoman-ruled Hijaz – in exchange for firearms. This human cargo included not only "pagans" from the market at Gondar but hundreds of kidnapped Christian children, as well. The governor himself had first pick of all slaves passing through.[68]

In addition, Ethiopian Christians, including members of the core Amharic population, were often enough captured by enemy raiders and sold to Muslim slave traders, who occasionally transported them across the Red Sea to the Hijaz and Yemen, or overland to Egypt, from where they might be trans-shipped to Anatolia and Syria. A powerful fourteenth-century king complained that the rulers of Adal and the neighboring Muslim state of Mora made war on him for the express purpose of "carry[ing] Ethiopian children into slavery."[69] The governor of Harar, which later became Adal's capital, was accused of selling whole Ethiopian villages to Arabia, India, and "all parts of Asia."[70] In the years following the Ottoman conquest of Egypt in 1517, the caravan carrying Ethiopian Christians on pilgrimage to Jerusalem was repeatedly attacked by Ottoman troops; on at least one occasion, the elderly pilgrims were killed while the young were sold as slaves.[71] In the later part of the sixteenth century, the Ottoman governor of Habesh routinely raided Ethiopian territory and drove his captives to the slave markets of Massawa.[72] The Franciscan Remedius Prutky, a native of Bohemia who was invited by the emperor to lead a mission to Ethiopia in 1751, describes Arab raiders in the border regions kidnapping Ethiopian boys and girls, then selling them to slave traders who transported them to Egypt, the Hijaz, Yemen, "and other parts of the world."[73]

During Bruce's stay, some twenty years later, civil war between the king and the governor of Tigray created horrific conditions under which Ethiopian Christians even sold children stolen from their coreligionists to Muslim

[65] Burton, *First Footsteps*, II: 3; Tamrat, *Church and State in Ethiopia*, 87.
[66] Bruce, *Travels*, II: 503.   [67] Ibid., III: 40.   [68] Ibid., III: 582.
[69] Ibid., II: 200–201; III: 419–20; Burton, *First Footsteps*, I: 50, quoting the Italian traveler Ludovico di Varthema (Bartema) (1503).
[70] Bruce, *Travels*, II: 294–95, 306, 308; Burton, *First Footsteps*, II: 3–4.
[71] Bruce, *Travels*, II: 340.   [72] Ibid., II: 416.
[73] Arrowsmith-Brown, ed. and trans., *Prutky's Travels in Ethiopia*, 178–79.

traders, who transported them to Massawa to sell to merchants from Arabia and India. This was the case in the mixed Christian-Muslim town of Dixan (Dessie) on the border between Tigray and Begmender provinces, where the governor of Tigray allowed the priests of that province to engage in this trade in exchange for supplying him with firearms from Habesh.[74] "Straggling soldiers" from both sides snatched Christian women and children "to sell them to the Turks for a very small price."[75]

As the examples cited above demonstrate, many of the Ethiopians swept up in the East African slave trade were children aged fifteen or younger. This was precisely the pool from which eunuchs were taken, and we can assume that a significant percentage of the captured boys ended up as eunuchs at one court or another, or in one great household or another. As if to underline this point, the French pharmacist Charles Jacques Poncet, who traveled to Gondar from Cairo to treat the emperor and his son for a skin disease, reports that an Ethiopian boy purchased by the Armenian merchant who accompanied him on his return was seized by Egypt's Janissaries as Poncet and the merchant were boarding a ship at the Nile port of Bulaq and taken to the *kethüda* of their regiment, Mustafa al-Kazdağlı, founder of the household that came to dominate Egypt by the late eighteenth century.[76] If this boy were not already a eunuch, he was certainly destined to become one in short order, for this, as Chapter 8 will make clear, was the capacity in which the Kazdağlı household habitually employed Ethiopian slaves.

In short, Ethiopia was an unwilling, or at least unwitting, source of eunuchs to neighboring polities and to the Ottoman Empire. To judge from the numerous references to the shipment of Ethiopian slaves to India, the Mughals were likewise recipients, as perhaps were the Safavids.[77] And while these "Ethiopian" eunuchs could well include members of the kingdom's core Amharic population, most of them came from Ethiopia's peripheral populations. Although we can only speculate as to the proportions of these various peoples represented in the total, we can assume that Oromos made up a large share, particularly given their predominance in the nineteenth and early twentieth centuries.

The Funj Sultanate and the Ottoman Province of Habesh

Before the Ottoman conquest of the Mamluk Sultanate, Ethiopia's relations with the various Muslim rulers of Egypt and the eastern Mediterranean were,

---

[74] Bruce, *Travels*, III: 416–18.   [75] Ibid., IV: 92–93.

[76] Sir William Foster, ed., *The Red Sea and Adjacent Countries at the Close of the Seventeenth Century, as Described by Joseph Pitts, William Daniel, and Charles Jacques Poncet* (London, 1949), xxix; Bruce, *Travels*, III: 92.

[77] The sultanates of the central Indian region known as the Deccan employed non-eunuch Ethiopian military commanders. See Omar H. Ali, *Malik Ambar: Power and Slavery across the Indian Ocean* (Oxford, 2016).

for the most part, indirect. Slave traders from these regions acquired Ethiopian slaves, in the vast majority of cases, not from Ethiopia itself but from intermediaries, usually merchants who were subjects of the Muslim coastal kingdoms located in present-day Somalia, Eritrea, and Djibouti, or of the various kingdoms occupying what is now Sudan.

This circumstance began to change early in the sixteenth century, not only with the Ottomans' expansion into Egypt and the Red Sea region but also with the rise of the Funj Sultanate in Sudan. A population of rather mysterious origin, apparently from the extreme south of present-day Sudan, the Funj moved northward and established their capital at the southeastern Sudanese city of Sennar, strategically located on the Blue Nile, in 1504–5. In succeeding decades, they extended their sway over a wide swath of southeastern and central Sudan, including the territory of the ancient Christian kingdom of Upper Nubia, which had been conquered by an Arab tribal confederation around 1500. They also forged alliances with neighboring kingdoms, including Darfur in western Sudan.[78] Originally animist, the Funj converted to Islam in the 1520s under the tutelage of a Sudanese Sufi scholar.[79]

For the four centuries during which the Funj sultans and, beginning in 1761, the influential members of the Hamaj tribe who served as their regents[80] ruled this territory, the starting points of the major slave caravans lay within their domains. Since the Funj Sultanate effectively united much of central and southern Sudan, its presence made the passage of Ethiopian slaves, as well as slaves from Nubia and other parts of East Africa, into Ottoman territory logistically easier. Certainly, the transport of thousands of African slaves through Sudan to Ottoman Egypt every year would not have been possible without the Funj Sultanate's active cooperation – and this despite friction with the Ottomans in the later part of the sixteenth century.

The kingdom of Ethiopia itself was hostile toward the Funj and launched a number of invasions of its territory across the border region of southeastern Sudan, home to an Ethiopian population that the Funj routinely raided for slaves.[81] Although the *Funj Chronicles*, the only known internally produced histories of the sultanate, are silent on relations between the Funj and Ethiopia before the eighteenth century, they note an Ethiopian invasion in the 1740s and

[78] P.M. Holt, ed. and trans., *The Sudan of the Three Niles: The Funj Chronicles, 910–1288/ 1504–1871* (Leiden, 1999), 4, 34, 155, 163 n. 13; P.M. Holt and M.W. Daly, *A History of the Sudan from the Coming of Islam to the Present Day*, 5th ed. (Harlow, Essex, UK, 2000), 24–27, 31–32; P.M. Holt, *Egypt and the Fertile Crescent: A Political History, 1516–1922* (Ithaca, NY, 1966), 53–54; Bruce, *Travels*, II: 487–89; Orhonlu, *Habeş Eyaleti*, 73–75.

[79] Holt, ed. and trans., *Sudan of the Three Niles*, 4; Holt and Daly, *History of the Sudan*, 28–29.

[80] Holt, ed. and trans., *Sudan of the Three Niles*, 19, 72–73, 76, 184–85; Holt and Daly, *History of the Sudan*, 33–35.

[81] Holt, ed. and trans., *Sudan of the Three Niles*, 14; Evliya Çelebi, *Seyahatname*, vol. 10, eds. Seyit Ali Kahraman et al. (Istanbul, 2007), 438–39, 462, 519.

border raids in the 1830s and 1840s, by which time the Funj territories had been conquered by the regime of Mehmed Ali Pasha, the autonomous Ottoman governor of Egypt. In all the reported cases, the Ethiopians were repulsed, and all captives from their armies were enslaved.[82]

If the emergence of the Funj Sultanate facilitated the transport of Ethiopian slaves into Ottoman territory, the foundation of the Ottoman province of Habesh, comprising essentially what is now Eritrea, in 1560, following the spectacular conquests of the former Mamluk emir Özdemir Pasha,[83] virtually guaranteed a steady supply. It cannot be a complete coincidence that the number of Ethiopian eunuchs employed in the harem of Topkapı Palace in Istanbul peaked, at perhaps four hundred, only a few decades after Özdemir Pasha's exploits – a time, moreover, when the Ottomans were actively pursuing their imperial ambitions in the Red Sea. Yet even when the kingdom of Ethiopia appeared to hold the upper hand militarily against both the Funj Sultanate and Habesh, the slave trade continued apace. This suggests that Ethiopia itself had a certain interest in this trade and that slave traders within Ethiopia may have channeled some of their supply – drawn, as it was, chiefly from the kingdom's peripheral, largely non-Christian populations – into the Sudanese caravan and Red Sea slave trade. Slaves routed into this international market would undoubtedly have included future eunuchs.

Enslavement and Castration

Slave Trade Routes. As noted above, East African eunuchs were part of a much larger population of slaves entering Ottoman territory from Africa. Each year, from the sixteenth century through the late nineteenth century, thousands of slaves from Ethiopia, Nubia, and southern Sudan arrived in the slave market of Cairo,[84] whence hundreds of them made their way to Istanbul and to other Ottoman provincial capitals. The majority arrived with the slave caravans that set out each year from Sudan. The larger of these, from the western district of Darfur, site of unspeakable carnage during the early 2000s, carried several thousand slaves to Egypt. Meanwhile, the Funj capital of Sennar in southeastern Sudan, along with several other Sudanese trading hubs, sent out smaller caravans that converged at the Egyptian border. These were known in Egypt as Sennar caravans; collectively, they carried several hundred

---

[82] Holt, ed. and trans., *Sudan of the Three Niles,* 15–16, 100, 106, 108–9, 116; Bruce, *Travels,* III: 242–45, 263.

[83] Giancarlo Casale, *The Ottoman Age of Exploration* (Oxford, 2010), 107–8; Holt and Daly, *History of the Sudan,* 26–27; Holt, *Egypt and the Fertile Crescent,* 52–54; Orhonlu, *Habeş Eyaleti,* 31–42, 93–128.

[84] Jean Carlier de Pinon, *Relation du voyage en Orient de Carlier de Pinon (1579),* ed. Edgar Blochet, *Revue de l'Orient latin* 12 (1911), 412–13, and 413 n. 2.

slaves.[85] Conditions along these routes could be dire as avaricious slave traders commonly deprived their charges of food, water, and adequate shelter so as to minimize travel expenses.[86]

Yet by the early nineteenth century, the Swiss archaeologist John Lewis (Johann Ludwig) Burckhardt tells us, few of the slaves traded northward from Sudan were Ethiopian since "in Arabia and Egypt Abyssinian slaves may be had cheaper by the Djebert traders from Massouah, who sell them at Djidda."[87] While slaves from Nubia, Darfur, and other westerly regions of Sudan entered Egypt overland, in other words, most Ethiopian slaves followed an alternative route that took them by boat from Massawa and other port cities in the Ottoman province of Habesh through the Red Sea to Jidda, the Arabian peninsula port serving Mecca.[88] The seaborne slave traders in this case were the Ethiopian Muslims known as Jabart. This mode of transport had the virtue of being generally swifter than the overland caravans, so that the slaves might have suffered somewhat less. If, on the other hand, some of these slaves were sold at Jidda to Egyptian buyers, they would have been transported back across the Red Sea to Suez, then taken overland to Cairo or another town. This would have entailed lengthy waits in the ports of Massawa and Jidda, to say nothing of the slave markets of those cities. Such delays might have added up to several months, easily the equivalent of the time necessary for the various southeastern Sudanese overland caravans to converge at Egypt's southern border.

Regardless of which route they took, these East African slaves, future eunuchs included, would have experienced the common lot of slaves imported into Egypt: numerous changes of location and master, long months or even several years of bondage before being settled in a household.[89] What is worth noting is that the routes themselves were specifically designed to bring East African slaves into the eastern Mediterranean for purchase by the Muslim powers that predominated there. Although a caravan occasionally arrived in Cairo from what is now Libya, bringing slaves from the Lake Chad region,[90] West Africa was never a significant supplier of slaves to the Ottoman Empire and earlier Islamic empires, except in the westernmost reaches of North Africa.[91]

---

[85] Burckhardt, *Travels in Nubia*, 38, 58–59, 217; P.S. Girard, *Mémoire sur l'agriculture, l'industrie et le commerce de l'Égypte*, vol. 17 of the *Description de l'Égypte*, 2nd ed. (Paris, 1824), 278–96; Orhonlu, *Habeş Eyaleti*, 100–102, 130.

[86] Louis Frank, "Memoir on the Traffic in Negroes in Cairo and on the Illnesses to Which They Are Subject upon Arrival There," trans. Michel LeGall, in *Slavery in the Islamic Middle East*, ed. Shaun E. Marmon (Princeton, NJ, 1999), 73–74.

[87] Burckhardt, *Travels in Nubia*, 276–79, 288, 290.

[88] Frank, "Memoir on the Traffic in Negroes in Cairo," 77; Orhonlu, *Habeş Eyaleti*, 102.

[89] Burckhardt, *Travels in Nubia*, 291, 293.

[90] Frank, "Memoir on the Traffic in Negroes in Cairo," 75.

[91] Lewis, *Race and Slavery*, 51; R.W. Beachey, *The Slave Trade of Eastern Africa* (New York, NY, 1976), 172.

Castration Practices in East Africa and Egypt. Available evidence strongly suggests that most eunuchs in the service of Muslim kingdoms and empires, going back at least to the Abbasid era, were radically castrated. That is to say, their genitalia, including the penis and testicles, were removed in their entirety. This was true regardless of whether the eunuchs in question came from Africa, Anatolia, the Balkans, or the Caucasus, and regardless of where the operation was performed.[92] Radical castration was, moreover, the norm not only for harem eunuchs but for eunuchs employed as companions to the ruler, supervisors of young military recruits, and military commanders, as well. The practice was similar to the traditions of imperial China, and it is conceivable that the Abbasids and regional potentates in the eastern reaches of their empire were influenced by Chinese custom, although there is no clear evidence to that effect.

On the other hand, radical castration ran counter to the usages of the Byzantine Empire, which was otherwise a key model for many Islamic institutions, including the employment of eunuchs. Byzantine eunuchs in most cases suffered the removal of their testicles but kept their penises. The ninth-century belle-lettrist al-Jahiz disparages the Byzantines' laxity in this regard: "It is as if they only hate that their children [whom they castrate and dedicate to the church] would impregnate their women and their nuns and nothing else!"[93] The more prudent course, in al-Jahiz's opinion and in that of many other premodern Muslim commentators, was to eliminate, or at least minimize, any chance of sexual contact between eunuchs and other members of the ruler's court, whether harem women, the ruler and his sons, or young soldiers-in-training. In this way, those in authority not only prevented illegitimate children but preserved the innocence of young girls and boys affiliated with the court while ensuring that the eunuchs' respect for and loyalty to the ruler continued undiminished.[94]

Most accounts of radical castration within East Africa itself focus on the production of eunuchs for export. The role played in that process before the fourteenth century by the kingdom of Hadiya and the town of Washilu, south of the city of Hadiya, has already been mentioned. In the late sixteenth century, a Portuguese priest encountered a tribe near the Somali port of Mogadishu who allegedly castrated their own boys, perhaps for export across the Red Sea.[95] For the most part, though, Ethiopian, Nubian, and Sudanese slaves bound for Egypt and points north and east were castrated in Upper Egypt after they had

---

[92] Ayalon, *Eunuchs, Caliphs, and Sultans*, 304–14; Carlier de Pinon, *Relation du voyage en Orient*, 414 (on the Bulgarian eunuch Mesih Pasha).
[93] Quoted in Ayalon, *Eunuchs, Caliphs, and Sultans*, 305.
[94] Ayalon, *Eunuchs, Caliphs, and Sultans*, 309.
[95] Beachey, *Slave Trade of Eastern Africa*, 170.

completed their journeys with the slave caravans or the Red Sea boats because of the danger of moving them before their wounds had healed completely.[96] Thus, Burckhardt observes that few eunuchs were produced in Sudan for export. Only in Borgho, west of Darfur, was castration carried out for this purpose on a small number of slaves who were then either transported to Egypt or "sent as presents by the Negro sovereigns to the great mosques at Mekka and Medina, by the way of Souakin."[97]

Throughout much of the Islamic era, it seems, eunuchs were produced near the city of Asyut on the Middle Nile. Before the French occupation of Egypt in 1798–1801, according to the French physician Louis Frank (1761–1825), who traveled throughout Egypt just before the invasion, the hub of castration was the town of Abu Tig.[98] Yet what Burckhardt, writing some twenty years later, calls "the great manufactory" of African eunuchs for the Ottoman Empire was the nearby Coptic Christian village of Zawiyat al-Dayr. At the time of Burckhardt's sojourn in the region, in 1813–14, the practitioners were "two Coptic monks, who were said to excel all their predecessors in dexterity, and who had a house in which the victims were received."[99] Once a contingent of slaves arrived in Asyut, a selection of boys was taken immediately to the monks' house for the procedure. We do not know how slaves were selected for castration. The slave traders probably had a rough idea of how many eunuchs were required by the imperial palace and by the various viziers and provincial governors in a given year. Burckhardt asserts that roughly 150 eunuchs were produced each year. Numbers must have been higher before the nineteenth century, for he also claims that "the custom of keeping eunuchs has greatly diminished in Egypt, as well as in Syria."[100] Beyond this, prepubescent boys, usually between the ages of eight and twelve, were preferred for castration since they had not yet undergone the hormonal changes that lead to facial hair, deepened voices, and sexual desire.[101]

Imagine, then, the bewilderment and terror of a young Ethiopian, Nubian, or Sudanese boy who had just suffered through months in a slave caravan, or weeks in a boat on the Red Sea, only to find himself, with other boys of similar age, not transported directly to the slave market in Cairo but shunted off to a village in Upper Egypt for a painful and life-changing operation. He would have undergone one of two basic procedures, both described as early as the tenth century by the traveling geographer al-Muqaddasi (ca. 945–1000). In one, the penis and scrotum were sliced off with a single stroke of a razor. In the other, "the scrotum is cut open and the testicles are taken out of it. Then a piece

[96] Ayalon, *Eunuchs, Caliphs, and Sultans*, 306.   [97] Burckhardt, *Travels in Nubia*, 294.
[98] Frank, "Memoir on the Traffic in Negroes in Cairo," 74.
[99] Burckhardt, *Travels in Nubia*, 294.   [100] Ibid., 294–95.   [101] Ibid., 295.

of wood is put under the male organ, which is cut to its very root."[102] In both cases, a lead rod was inserted into the urethra afterward to prevent its scarring over as the area healed (a step apparently not followed in Washilu, where urethral obstruction and infection were distressingly common). Some 700 years later, the Ottoman traveler Evliya Çelebi, in his description of Egypt's "slave surgeons'" guild, depicts a similar process, although he portrays the scale as industrial, with the "surgeons" – presumably numbering more than the two described by Burckhardt – castrating 100–200 African boys at once, after drugging them.[103] Nineteenth-century European observers describe virtually the same procedure – which, it must be added, few of them actually witnessed – while adding a few piquant details on techniques to prevent infection and consequent obstruction of the urethra, which was clearly the chief danger.[104]

Given the absence of antibiotics, one would expect the death rate from this sort of infection to have been quite high. Observers differ on this point. In medieval Washilu, where unsanitary conditions prevailed and no attempt was made to protect the urethra, al-'Umari (1300–49) claims that more boys died as a result of castration than survived.[105] Similarly, Evliya Çelebi's description of Egypt's "surgeons," written in the 1670s, when Egypt apparently produced several hundred eunuchs a year, implies that about half the castrated boys died, often in quite agonizing fashion.[106] Some 250 years later, the German physician Gustav Nachtigal (1834–85) relates that of 100 boys castrated in the kingdom of Baguirmi, southeast of Lake Chad, fewer than one-third survived.[107] Meanwhile, the French physician Antoine Clot, known as Clot Bey, writing in the 1840s, reports a death rate of 25 percent even at the hands of the practiced monks at Zawiyat al-Dayr.[108] In contrast, Burckhardt asserts that of sixty boys castrated in the same location in the fall of 1813, only two died – a mortality rate similar to that reported by Frank at the end of the eighteenth century.[109] Castration was generally performed in the autumn at Zawiyat al-Dayr, a practice that seems to have reduced mortality relative to other times of year,[110] probably because the weather was cool enough to curb the rapacity of infectious bacteria while not cold enough to pose a danger from

[102] Al-Muqaddisi, quoted in Ayalon, *Eunuchs, Caliphs, and Sultans*, 304–5, also 219–20.
[103] Evliya Çelebi, *Seyahatname*, X: 205.
[104] Burckhardt, *Travels in Nubia*, 295; John Lewis Burckhardt, *Notes on the Bedouins and the Wahabys, Collected during His Travels in the East* (London, 1831), II: 329; Ayalon, *Eunuchs, Caliphs, and Sultans*, 306–7; Frank, "Memoir on the Traffic in Negroes in Cairo," 74.
[105] Quoted in Ayalon, *Eunuchs, Caliphs, and Sultans*, 306.
[106] Evliya Çelebi, *Seyahatname*, X: 205.
[107] Quoted in Fisher, *Slavery in the History of Muslim Black Africa*, 282–83; see also 284.
[108] Ayalon, *Eunuchs, Caliphs, and Sultans*, 307, 315.
[109] Burckhardt, *Travels in Nubia*, 294–95; Frank, "Memoir on the Traffic in Negroes in Cairo," 74–75; Ayalon, *Eunuchs, Caliphs, and Sultans*, 314.
[110] Ayalon, *Eunuchs, Caliphs, and Sultans*, 315.

exposure. We can probably hazard the conclusion that mortality varied according to the conditions prevailing at individual eunuch "manufactures"; it tended to be lowest in long-established centers where castration had been standardized and conditions were relatively sanitary.

Even if he survived, the new eunuch could expect to suffer from various physical abnormalities, most caused by hormonal deficiencies or imbalances. He would grow unusually tall, with a small head in proportion to his torso but an unusually large face, and unusually long arms and legs. He would probably incline either to obesity or to extreme thinness. Burckhardt claims that the eunuchs whom he encountered in the Hijaz – no doubt those who guarded the Prophet Muhammad's tomb in Medina and the Ka'ba in Mecca – were preternaturally thin.[111] He may simply have visited Mecca and Medina at a time when thin eunuchs happened to predominate. Eunuchs castrated before puberty never acquired facial hair, and their faces often grew excessively wrinkled.[112] Likewise, their voices never broke but grew increasingly shrill with age, so that if they lived past sixty or so, as many of them did, they might sound like shrieking women.[113]

Chronic medical complaints were also a common byproduct of early castration. Many eunuchs suffered from osteoporosis since their bones had not been strengthened by the surge of testosterone that occurs at puberty.[114] For radically castrated eunuchs, urinary tract infections were common as a result of the foreshortening of the urethra. The Chinese folk saying "as stinky as a eunuch" alludes to the pervasive odor of urine that clung to many eunuchs in imperial China, where, as in most Muslim empires, radical castration was the norm.[115]

Race and Sexuality Stereotypes

Quite apart from their proximity to Ottoman territory, well-trodden slave caravan routes, and long-established castration facilities, though, Ethiopian slaves were in demand in the Ottoman Empire because of their perceived positive qualities. These are enumerated by John Lewis Burckhardt, who traveled through Egypt and Nubia in 1813–14, before Mehmed Ali's 1821 invasion of Sudan radically changed the conditions of the slave trade. Ethiopian males, Burckhardt tells us, "are esteemed for their fidelity, and make excellent house servants, and often clerks, their intellects being certainly much superior to those of the Blacks"[116] – by whom he presumably means the population popularly known as Zanj, comprising the indigenous peoples of East Africa apart from Nubians and the inhabitants of the Horn of Africa.

---

[111] Burckhardt, *Travels in Nubia*, 295.   [112] Patterson, *Slavery and Social Death*, 320.
[113] Ibid.   [114] Ringrose, *Perfect Servant*, 1.   [115] Mitamura, *Chinese Eunuchs*, 42.
[116] Burckhardt, *Travels in Nubia*, 278–79.

Nubians, by contrast, were preferred as laborers since they were considered to be of good character but constitutionally sturdier than the Ethiopians.[117] Of the various other East African populations, Burckhardt relates that the Amharas, the ethnic group from which the Ethiopian royal family usually came, "are noted for their amiable tempers."[118] All of this is, naturally, the language of the slave market, informed by subjective experience and oral lore rather than by any objective reality. Nonetheless, the stereotypes relayed by Burckhardt are consistent with those recorded in the Middle Ages.[119] If Ethiopian males were widely regarded as intelligent and trustworthy, suitable for household tasks and record-keeping, then it is little wonder that they became the preferred pool for palace eunuchs. These perceived positive qualities, together with the complexities of castration and transport, help to explain why, in Cairo's slave market, East African eunuchs commanded prices two or three times higher than uncastrated African slaves.[120]

These attitudes reflect deep-rooted assumptions on the part of the core population of the Ottoman Empire about the qualities of various populations of the world, and of Africa more specifically. While these assumptions were definitely not identical to the kinds of race and color prejudice present in modern-day North America and western Europe, they did constitute a kind of "indigenous racism" that shaped the experiences of enslaved Africans in Ottoman society. Where African populations were concerned, Ottoman categorizations inevitably drew on medieval literary precedents. Yet Ottoman attitudes toward different peoples and toward skin color were heavily influenced by the fact that before the mid-seventeenth century, the empire was administered by a Rumi elite – that is, an elite with roots in the empire's central lands: Istanbul and vicinity, the Balkans, and western Anatolia, collectively known as Rum ("Rome") because they had once been ruled by the Byzantine, or Roman, Empire. As Hüseyin Yılmaz has pointed out, echoing the work of Metin Kunt, Rumi ethnoregional identity was the ideal among the Ottoman administrative and intellectual elite.[121] Members of this elite tended to judge other populations against this ideal.

In describing the peoples of Africa, Ottoman intellectuals, like their medieval predecessors, tended not to use the omnibus category "African," indicating that they did not regard these peoples as belonging to a pan-African population. They did deploy the collective noun "Zanj" (*zenc* in Turkish),

---

[117] Ibid.   [118] Ibid., 293, also 277.
[119] For example, Ibn Butlan (1001–38), in Lewis, trans., *Islam...*, II: 245–51.
[120] Girard, *Mémoire sur l'agriculture, l'industrie et le commerce*, 293.
[121] Hüseyin Yılmaz, *Caliphate Redefined: The Mystical Turn in Ottoman Political Thought* (Princeton, NJ, 2018), 10–14; Metin Kunt, "Ethno-Regional (*Cins*) Solidarity in the Seventeenth-Century Ottoman Establishment," *International Journal of Middle East Studies* 5 (1974): 233–39.

today considered somewhat pejorative, to indicate a range of populations south of the Sahara but not ordinarily including the populations of the Horn of Africa, who were usually termed Habeshi ("Abyssinian"); this label in turn encompassed a fairly large range of peoples, including Amharic peoples, the Oromo, Shangalla, and others. Yet Ottoman writers did not use Zanj in all cases but occasionally differentiated among smaller subdivisions of this category, such as Nubians (Nubi) and Sudanese (Sudani). West Africans, with whom the Ottoman core regions had relatively little contact, were often labeled Takruri, an adjective derived from an ancient Ghanaian empire.

Where skin color was concerned, Rumi intellectuals had a perception of East Africans slaves as "black" (*siyah* or, more rarely, *kara* in Turkish, *aswad* in Arabic), although, again, this term did not have the same connotations that it does in today's North America or western Europe. It seems rather to have been used to describe dark-skinned individuals, more specifically individuals whose skin was darker than the Rumis of the Ottoman central lands. Not only East Africans but the populations of the empire's "peripheral" territories, especially the Arab provinces, were appraised in relation to this Rumi "standard," and usually came up short. Hence the late sixteenth-century intellectual Mustafa Ali, very much a Rumi, in his 1599 *Description of Cairo*, is quick to disparage the locals, whom he calls *evlad-i 'Arab* ("sons of the Arabs"), in contradistinc- tion to *Rum oğlanı* ("sons of the Rumis"), whom he obviously considers superior.[122] (In the Arab provinces themselves, where a somewhat different array of peoples lived, the norm adopted by the provincial intelligentsia could be somewhat different.)[123] We must, I think, view Ottoman attitudes toward "black" East Africans in the context of this overarching ethno-regional chauvinism. Africans of various "races" (singular, *cins*, which derives from the Latin *genus*) – Habeshi, Nubi, Sudani, Takruri – along with the *evlad-i 'Arab*, occupied a spectrum that also included eastern Anatolians, Kurds, and populations from the Caucasus.

Al-Jahiz, the Abbasid-era belle-lettrist who, some eight centuries earlier, composed a treatise on the merits of dark-skinned peoples, might have recog- nized some of the attitudes at play among the Rumi elite: the notion that lighter skin is inherently superior to darker skin and that, correspondingly, people from (relatively) northerly regions are superior to those from the southerly climes. Ottoman intellectuals' appeal to the biblical "Curse of Ham," as adapted by early Muslim theologians, to explain the "backwardness" and

---

[122] Mustafa Ali, *Halatü'l-Kahire mine'l-'adati'z-zahire*, Süleymaniye Library, MS Fatih 5427/14, fols. 46b, 53b; MS Esad Efendi 2407, fol. 13b; Mustafa Ali, *Mustafa Ali's Description of Cairo of 1599*, ed. Andreas Tietze (Vienna, 1975), 40 and plates 24 and 43; Evliya Çelebi, *Seyahatname*, X: 438–39 (where "Rum" is synonymous with "white").

[123] E.g., 'Abd al-Rahman al-Jabarti, *'Aja'ib al-athar fi-l-tarajim wa-l-akhbar*, ed. Shmuel Moreh (Jerusalem, 2013), I: 454.

"depravity" of African populations would have resonated with al-Jahiz, who was himself the grandson of an African slave, as well.[124] (Indeed, al-Jahiz's treatise inspired a series of similar works stretching into the seventeenth century.)[125]

This chauvinism was not ingrained in the Rumi elite but took shape amid the rapid expansion of the Ottoman Empire in the sixteenth century, and the consequent exposure to a wide array of new populations – Bedouins, Kurds, Ethiopians, Berbers, peoples of the Caucasus, and many more. It was exacerbated by the dramatic demographic changes of the early seventeenth century, including peasant flight from the land in Anatolia, tribal migrations in Syria and Iraq, and, in Egypt, an influx of rural ulema into Cairo.[126] The initial "shock" of this exposure to a diverse spectrum of peoples often results in a chauvinistic backlash of the sort we are seeing in the United States right now.

Sexual stereotypes are a dismal yet predictable part of this kind of backlash. The Rumi intelligentsia of the Ottoman central lands and the Arabophone intelligentsia of the Arab provinces imagined ethnically "different" peoples to have outsized and/or deviant sexual appetites. This was a common means of dehumanizing them. Thus, the Cairene chronicler Ahmed Çelebi, writing in the 1730s of an event that occurred in 1711, trashes "the race of Turks" – by whom he means soldiers of Anatolian "hillbilly" origin – "who didn't distinguish between *mim* and *nun*," a crude homophobic sexual insult.[127] Even today, meanwhile, Turkish slang for masturbation incorporates the word "Abaza," i.e., Abkhazian. As for Africans, stereotypes, both positive and negative, abounded regarding their sexuality. Hypersexuality seems to be a common trope. According to the fifteenth-century Egyptian man of letters al-Abshihi, "It is said that when the black slave is sated, he fornicates."[128] Three centuries later, the chronicler al-Jabarti, though lauding the Amharic

---

[124] Goldenberg, *Curse of Ham*, 1–6, 74–75; Jane Hathaway, "Out of Africa, into the Palace: The Ottoman Chief Harem Eunuch," in *Living in the Ottoman Realm*, eds. Christine Isom-Verhaaren and Kent F. Schull (Bloomington, IN, 2015), 230. The biblical story appears in Genesis 9:20–27.

[125] Al-Jahiz, *Risalat mufakharat al-sudan 'ala al-bidan*, in *Rasa'il al-Jahiz*, ed. 'Abd al-Salam Muhammad Harun (Cairo, 1385/1965), I: 173–226; Lewis, *Race and Slavery*, 31–33; Akbar Muhammad, "The Image of Africans in Arabic Literature: Some Unpublished Manuscripts," in *Slaves and Slavery in Muslim Africa*, ed. John R. Willis, vol. 1: *Islam and the Ideology of Enslavement* (London, 1985), 47–65; Baki Tezcan, "*Dispelling the Darkness*: The Politics of 'Race' in the Early Seventeenth-Century Ottoman Empire in the Light of the Life and Work of Mullah Ali," *International Journal of Turkish Studies* 13, 1–2 (2007): 85–91.

[126] Jane Hathaway, *The Arab Lands under Ottoman Rule, 1516–1800*, with contributions by Karl K. Barbir (Harlow, Essex, UK, 2008), 63–64, 66–67, 175–76, 178–80, 183–84, 185–86.

[127] Ahmed Çelebi ibn 'Abd al-Ghani, *Awdah al-isharat fi man tawalla Misr al-Qahira min al-wuzara' wa-l-bashat*, ed. A.A. 'Abd al-Rahim (Cairo, 1978), 253. This remark has been widely misinterpreted as expressing anti-Turkish sentiment in the modern sense.

[128] Shihab al-Din ibn Ahmad al-Abshihi, *Kitab al-mustatraf fi kulli fannin mustazraf* (Cairo, 1902), II: 68; Lewis, ed. and trans., *Islam...*, II: 256, quoting a later edition.

peoples, from whom he descended, quotes a verse in which an Amharic woman replies, when asked about "the softness that was hidden," "Why ask? I am of Amharic race."[129]

Even when enslaved and emasculated, popular stereotypes held, East African men still possessed sexual impulses that could not be fully controlled. An infamous early eighteenth-century diatribe against African harem eunuchs, by an officer in one of the corps of Ottoman palace soldiery, tells the story of two palace concubines who were married off to members of the author's regiment but promptly divorced their husbands, complaining that "we did not find the pleasure in you that we found in the black eunuchs."[130] Such absurd fantasies reflect, most obviously, ignorance of the realities of the harem on the part of men who never went near it and, somewhat less obviously, a deep-seated fear of the tables turned. In the same way that slave-owners in the antebellum American South lived in constant fear of a slave rebellion, so the masters of eunuchs, or even members of societies in which eunuchs featured – most premodern societies of the Old World, in other words – lived in fear of a eunuch who was somehow, magically, sexually empowered. Unlike the fears of Southerners, this was not a "realistic" fear but something more nebulous and perhaps even unconscious. The paradox of emasculated, "exotic" men living in constant proximity to and policing the sexuality of the wealthiest, most powerful, and, in many respects, most desirable women – particularly when "real" men had no such access – no doubt fed this fear and the stereotypes that resulted from it. The same paradoxes, after all, feed the stereotypes about the harem and eunuchs that still abound today.

Conclusion

Traditions of slavery and "political eunuchism" in the empires of Egypt, the Arabian peninsula, and the eastern Mediterranean combined with ancient patterns of slavery, geopolitical rivalry, and ethnoregional diversity in East Africa to create the conditions for the trade in East African eunuchs that would culminate in their widespread employment in the Ottoman Empire. While the extent to which African eunuchs were used in African polities before the advent of Islam is uncertain, it seems clear that Muslim empires did not simply impose eunuchism on East Africa. And even if the use of eunuchs were not particularly widespread in East Africa before the expansion of Muslim empires

---

[129] Al-Jabarti, *'Aja'ib al-athar*, I: 454; Thomas Philipp and Moshe Perlmann, eds., *Al-Jabarti's History of Egypt: 'Aja'ib al-athar fi-l-tarajim wa-l-akhbar*, 4 vols. in 2 (Stuttgart, 1994), I: 648, trans. Charles Wendell and Michael Fishbein.
[130] Derviş Abdullah Efendi, *Risale-i teberdariye fi ahval ağa-yı Daru's-sa'ade*, Istanbul, Köprülü Library, MS II/233, fol. 92b, also fol. 91b.

into the region, the preexisting infrastructure of the slave trade facilitated the procurement of eunuchs both for large empires at some remove and for local kingdoms. On the other hand, the slave trade undeniably expanded as a result of the demands of such empires, while the need for new eunuchs led to castration industries of greater or lesser sophistication.

Within this context, Ethiopia presents a special case. An ancient Christian kingdom, often hostile to the Muslim polities around it, it became the preferred source of a long line of Muslim empires, culminating in the Ottomans, for harem eunuchs above all. Ethiopia's own well-developed slave trade, targeting the kingdom's marginal, non-Christian populations, was adapted to the larger transregional slave trade that served the great Muslim empires. The trade within Ethiopia was, moreover, geared in part toward filling the hierarchy of positions of trust close to the king. While these posts were usually filled, at least during the premodern era, by non-eunuchs, they mirrored those filled by eunuchs in Muslim polities. To a certain degree, in other words, Ethiopia's preexisting traditions of elite slave procurement and employment facilitated the kingdom's transformation into the chief pool of eunuchs for the Ottoman Empire and earlier Muslim powers.

At the same time, Ethiopian eunuchs in Ottoman employ fit into a constellation of racial and gender stereotypes that had existed long before the Ottoman Empire took shape but that intensified as a result of the demographic stresses that the empire faced during the sixteenth and seventeenth centuries. These stresses affected palace life as a whole, which is addressed in the following chapter.

Arrangement in Black and White
Eunuchs in the Ottoman Palace

The Chief Harem Eunuch served in the Ottoman palace. Most eunuchs, not only in the Ottoman Empire but in all Muslim empires and most non-Muslim ones, as well, served either in the ruler's palace or in the palaces or mansions of high government officials or wealthy notables. People who were not wealthy simply could not afford eunuchs, who tended to be more expensive – often far more expensive – than "ordinary" domestic service slaves.

With all this in mind, this chapter examines the Ottoman palace, where the Chief Harem Eunuch's career played out. Our first priority is to determine when and to what extent the Ottomans began to use eunuchs, and harem eunuchs in particular, systematically. Turning to the physical reality of the palace, we consider how the spatial arrangement of the various Ottoman palaces framed the Chief Eunuch's duties and *modus operandi*, as well as those of other harem eunuchs and eunuchs who did not serve as harem guardians. The size and complexity of the palace inevitably affected the Chief Eunuch's ability to navigate the boundaries between the harem and the sultan's private chambers, and between these spaces and the palace's public space.

Unfortunately, little or no trace remains of the earliest Ottoman palaces, making it difficult to trace the evolution of the space that the head of the harem eunuchs inhabited in the years before the construction of Topkapı Palace in the mid-fifteenth century. Where Topkapı itself is concerned, happily, we have a firm idea of the manner in which the eunuchs' space developed. As this chapter will show, the story of the harem at Topkapı Palace is one of steadily increasing spatial complexity that mirrored the steadily increasing influence of the harem eunuchs, particularly in relation to eunuchs in other roles.

Early Ottoman Eunuchs

The Ottoman Empire began at the end of the thirteenth century as a tiny Turkish emirate in northwestern Anatolia, on the eastern frontier of what was left of the Byzantine Empire.[1] Not surprisingly, Byzantine institutions loomed large in the early Ottoman state's development. One particularly influential institution was that of palace eunuchs, who under the Byzantines fulfilled most of the functions observed in the Muslim polities covered in Chapter 2: companions to the emperor, tutors to members of the imperial family, guardians of the women's quarters, military commanders. (As noted in Chapter 1, eunuchs also played significant roles in the church as priests and singers; their ecclesiastical functions were not emulated in the Muslim world.) Byzantine eunuchs were probably the first eunuchs whom the Ottomans ever saw. In turn, the first eunuchs whom the Ottomans employed were probably captured Byzantine eunuchs, most of whom came from the empire's peripheral territories, notably what the Byzantines called Paphlagonia, the north-central Anatolian coastal region that includes the cities of Sinop and Kastamonu.[2]

At the time of the Ottoman emirate's emergence and early expansion, Byzantine slaves, including eunuchs, were pervasive in Anatolia. They were employed by virtually all of the Turkish emirates that dominated the western parts of the peninsula in the wake of the Mongol invasions of the mid-thirteenth century and the resulting collapse of the Rum Seljuk sultanate, briefly profiled in Chapter 2. The peripatetic fourteenth-century Moroccan scholar Ibn Battuta (1304–68), passing through western Anatolia in 1333, was struck by the physical beauty of the Greek eunuchs whom he encountered at the court of the emir of Aydın in his capital near Izmir:

When we reached the vestibule [of the emir's residence], we found about twenty of his servants (*khuddam*) of strikingly beautiful appearance and dressed in silk garments. Their hair was parted and hanging down, and their color was a radiant white tinged with red. "Who," I asked the jurist, "are these beautiful forms?" "These," he replied, "are Greek eunuchs (*fityan*)."[3]

These young men were almost certainly acquired through warfare against the Byzantines. Ibn Battuta calls them *fityan* (literally, "young men"), a term he consistently uses for eunuchs,[4] and the fact that they were guarding the entrance to the emir's residence, a common eunuch occupation, reinforces this identification.

To the northeast of Aydın, the expanding Ottoman emirate was apparently employing eunuchs, as well, to judge from a pious endowment deed prepared

---

[1] Caroline Finkel, *Osman's Dream: History of the Ottoman Empire* (London, 2005), chapters 1–2; Colin Imber, *The Ottoman Empire, 1300–1650: The Structure of Power* (New York, 2002, 2nd ed. 2009), 3–24. Both works cite the contentious scholarship on the origins of the Ottoman state.

[2] Tougher, *The Eunuch in Byzantine History and Society*, 60–64, 103, 135, 136, 141–44, 146, 149, 151–55, 159, 164–66, 168.

[3] Ibn Battuta, *Rihla Ibn Battuta* (Beirut, 1964), 301–2; Lewis, ed. and trans., *Islam...*, II: 103, although Lewis translates *fityan* as "pages."

[4] E.g., Ibn Battuta, *Rihla Ibn Battuta*, 344, 491, 644.

for Orhan (r. 1326–62), the second Ottoman sultan, in 1324. This document, composed in Persian, declares that Orhan has "bequeathed the entire region of Mekece, with the distinct and well-known boundaries... [to the] eunuch Sharaf al-Din Muqbil, who is my liberated slave."[5] Mekece is a town in northwestern Anatolia, near the original Ottoman heartland, and there Orhan had founded a Sufi lodge. The deed goes on to explain that while Orhan had originally assigned the trusteeship (*tawliyat*) of Mekece to the children of the lodge's servants, he had later transferred it to Muqbil so that he would maintain the lodge and its residents. On Muqbil's death, the trusteeship would revert to the servants' descendants.

Muqbil was the first of many Ottoman eunuchs to hold the trusteeship of various pious foundations, culminating in the enormous imperial foundations endowed to the Muslim holy cities of Mecca and Medina. Unfortunately, we know virtually nothing about Muqbil beyond what little is revealed in this endowment deed, although we can probably assume that he came from one of the populations from which the Byzantines habitually drew their eunuchs. He was obviously well established at Orhan's court before the sultan's 1326 conquest of the ancient Byzantine city of Prusa (Bursa). Once Orhan had transferred his capital to the newly conquered city, many more eunuchs presumably served at his court there. Regrettably, no trace remains of Orhan's palace. According to the seventeenth-century traveler Evliya Çelebi, it was located within Bursa's citadel, but beyond this nugget of information, nothing is known about it.[6]

Ibn Battuta's description of the Aydın eunuchs suggests that they served mainly as companions to the ruler while, at the same time, controlling access to him. Orhan's eunuch Muqbil may well have performed similar duties, although he seems also to have held a position of fiscal trust. There is no indication that eunuchs in the Anatolian emirates guarded harems, or even that harems in these emirates bore any resemblance to the enormous, complex, and elaborately guarded harem of Topkapı Palace some 250 years later. In fact, when Ibn Battuta visited Iznik, the former Byzantine Nicaea, in 1333, he was received by Orhan's wife Bilun Hatun, who presided over this more modest town while her husband held court in Bursa.[7]

Orhan's son, Murad I (r. 1362–89), captured Adrianople (Edirne) from the Byzantines in the early 1360s.[8] The city became an alternative imperial residence for the next several decades, gradually displacing Bursa as the center

[5] Heath W. Lowry, *The Nature of the Early Ottoman State* (Albany, NY, 2003), 75–77, translated from İsmail Hakkı Uzunçarşılı, "*Gazi* Orhan Bey Vakfiyesi," *Belleten* 5 (1941): 277–88.
[6] Evliya Çelebi, *Seyahatname*, II: 10–11; Uzunçarşılı, *Saray Teşkilatı*, 9.
[7] Ibn Battuta, *Rihla Ibn Battuta*, 309; Uzunçarşılı, *Saray Teşkilatı*, 9.
[8] Halil Inalcik, "The Conquest of Edirne, 1361," *Archivum Ottomanicum* 3 (1971): 185–210.

of government by the early fifteenth century.[9] Even after the Ottoman conquest of Constantinople in 1453, Edirne continued in its historical role of alternative sultanic seat until the early eighteenth century. Near the site where the Selimiye Mosque would rise more than two hundred years later, Murad I built a palace, virtually no trace of which remains.[10] The far more famous New Palace, known as Hünkârbahçesi, or "The Sultan's Garden," was founded by Murad II (r. 1421–44, 1446–51) not long before his death. It originally consisted of several kiosks on the bank of the Tunca River; later sultans through the early eighteenth century continued to augment it. As constituted under Murad II and his son Mehmed II ("the Conqueror," r. 1444–46, 1451–81), the palace included a harem separate from the sultan's towering privy chamber, known as the Cihannüma Kasrı ("Panorama Castle"), and the residences of his pages. Still, the elaborate compartmentalization of space of later years did not yet exist.[11] White eunuchs guarded the palace entrance, known as the Babüssaade, or Gate of Felicity, in front of the sultan's audience hall (just south of the Cihannüma Kasrı), harking back to the function of the Aydın eunuchs and looking ahead to the function of the white eunuchs at Topkapı.

Unfortunately, the New Palace was used as an ammunition depot during the Russo-Ottoman War of 1877–78, and when the Russians advanced on Edirne, Ottoman forces deliberately blew up the stores, causing most of the palace's structures to collapse. Excavation and restoration began in earnest in 2009 but encountered serious climatic and logistical obstacles.[12] This fact, together with a dearth of archival materials from the period before 1500, makes it difficult to gauge the numbers of eunuchs employed in the New Palace during the reigns of Murad II and Mehmed II. Of the eunuchs who served in the Old Palace under Murad I and his immediate successors, meanwhile, we have no clue whatsoever. We can safely assume that all these rulers continued to acquire eunuchs from familiar Byzantine sources, although as the empire expanded, the range of populations that might supply eunuchs grew correspondingly. Eunuch acquisition would have become more regular and predictable with the

---

[9] Uzunçarşılı, *Saray Teşkilatı*, 10.

[10] Ibid., 11–12; Tosyavizade Rifat Osman, *Edirne Rehnüması* (Istanbul, 1994), 86–87.

[11] Uzunçarşılı, *Saray Teşkilatı*, 10–12; Osman, *Edirne Rehnüması*, 87–88; Necipoğlu, *Architecture, Ceremonial, and Pzower*, 6, 93.

[12] Mustafa Özer, "Edirne Sarayı Kazıları'nda Son Bulgular," İstanbul Araştırmalar Enstitüsü, 26 November 2015, www.iae.org.tr/Aktivite-Detay/Edirne-Sarayi-Kazilarinda-Son-Bulgular-Mustafa-Ozer/53; Özüm İtez, "Osmanlı Arkeolojisinin Daha Sağlam Temeller Üzerinde Gelişmesine Öncüllük Etmek İstiyoruz," *Arkitera*, 24 March 2016, www.arktitera.com/soylesi/831/osmanli-arkeolojisinin-daha-saglam-temeller-uzerinde-gelismesine-onculluk-etmek-istiyoruz; Ayşegül Parlayan, "Osmanlı'nın Kayıp Sarayı: Edirne Sarayı'nda Arkeoloji, Koruma, ve Restorasyon,"*Atlas Tarih* 45 (2017): 80–91. I am grateful to Amy Singer for alerting me to these reports. Cf. "Ottoman Palace Suffers from Flooding, Neglect," *Hürriyet Daily News*, 31 January 2012.

introduction, probably in the late fourteenth or early fifteenth century, of the *devshirme*, the "collection" of Christian boys for service as Janissaries or palace pages.[13] A small number of the boys chosen to be pages were apparently castrated, although how the selection was made remains unclear.[14]

The white eunuchs who guarded the Edirne palace's Babüssaade were probably mostly captives of war, with perhaps a few of *devshirme* origin, originating in the Ottoman Balkans or among the Greek population of Anatolia. (In later centuries, the pool of threshold eunuchs would expand to include prisoners of war from Habsburg-ruled Hungary and purchased slaves from the Caucasus.) It is plausible, too, that at least by Murad II's reign, the corps of palace eunuchs included limited numbers of East Africans, who, just as in earlier Muslim empires, would have guarded the harem. The Ottoman Empire was not yet in a position to import large numbers of African eunuchs since, after all, the Mamluk Sultanate blocked direct access to the Sudan and the Horn of Africa. However, Ottoman functionaries may have purchased African eunuchs in the Hijaz during the annual pilgrimage to Mecca. A few eunuchs may also have been presented to the sultans as gifts, most likely by the Mamluks themselves during diplomatic exchanges.[15]

After the Conquest of Constantinople (1453)

Mehmed II's conquest of the Byzantine capital of Constantinople in 1453 marks a turning point in the history of Ottoman palace eunuchs. The Conqueror made the city his capital, and it remained the imperial capital until the abolition of the Ottoman Empire in the early 1920s. A fixed capital offered new opportunities for the construction of large palaces that would house the Ottoman dynasty for many years, and potentially for centuries.

The year after the conquest, construction commenced on a palace on the site of the forum of the Byzantine emperor Theodosius (r. 379–95), originally the Forum Tauri (Forum of the Bulls) of Constantinople's founder, Constantine

---

[13] J.A.B. Palmer, "The Origin of the Janissaries," *Bulletin of the John Rylands Library* 35 (1952–53): 448–81; Paul Wittek, "Devshirme and Shari'a," *Bulletin of the School of Oriental and African Studies* 17 (1955): 271–78; V.L. Ménage, "Sidelights on the Devshirme from Idris and Sa'duddin," *Bulletin of the School of Oriental and African Studies* 18 (1956): 181–83; *EI²*, s.v. "Devshirme," by Ménage; H.A.R. Gibb and Harold Bowen, *Islamic Society and the West: A Study of the Impact of Western Civilization on Moslem Culture in the Near East*, vol. 1, part 1 (London, 1950), appendix A.

[14] A number of eunuch grand viziers were *devshirme* recruits, e.g., Hadım Ali Pasha, a.k.a. Atik Ali Pasha (Bosnian, terms 1501–3, 1506–11); Hadım Mesih Pasha (Bulgarian, 1585–86); and Hadım Hasan Pasha (possibly Albanian, 1597–98). See İ.H. Uzunçarşılı, *Osmanlı Tarihi* (Ankara, 1947–62), II: 538–39; III, part 2, 346, 357–58.

[15] On Ottomans presenting mamluks to the Mamluk court, see Cihan Yüksel Muslu, *The Ottomans and the Mamluks: Imperial Diplomacy and Warfare in the Islamic World* (London, 2014), 88, 98.

I (r. 306–37). Today, this is the location of Istanbul University. The Old Palace (Saray-ı Atik), as it came to be known after the construction of Topkapı, was, according to the available evidence, not a single edifice but a large collection of kiosks and palatial residences, with open spaces for gardens and hunting grounds, all contained within a massive rectangular wall; it thus functioned as a citadel in the middle of the old Byzantine city. Like the New Palace in Edirne, it featured a designated harem and a palatial privy chamber for the sultan, as well as council chambers for the business of government, kitchens, stables, a treasury, and, in keeping with its role as an urban citadel, lodgings for palace soldiery.[16] The harem was guarded by eunuchs, including African eunuchs, although exact numbers and proportions are impossible to come by. Rather ironically, no sultan ever resided permanently in this palace. Even Mehmed himself, in the four years between the foundation of this palace and that of Topkapı, moved back and forth between the Old Palace and the palace in Edirne.[17]

In 1458, Mehmed II launched a grandiose new palace at the confluence of the Bosphorus, the Golden Horn, and the Sea of Marmara, where the acropolis of the ancient city of Byzantion had been. This new palace came to be called Topkapı ("Cannon Gate") in the nineteenth century after the monumental Byzantine seaside gate, now lost, into the ancient acropolis; here, overlooking the point where the Bosphorus flows into the Golden Horn, Mehmed placed some forty cannon.[18] Like the Old Palace and the palace in Edirne, Topkapı consisted of multiple structures surrounded by gardens; a surrounding wall was added only in 1478.

Topkapı's layout was distinctive, though; when completed in the 1460s, it consisted of three courts that proceeded horizontally south to north (see Figure 3.1). The First, or Outer, Court, extended from the Bab-i Hümayun ("Imperial Portal") to the Orta Kapı ("Middle Gate") and was the most accessible to the public. In the Second Court, inside the Orta Kapı, the Janissaries and other units of palace soldiery mustered and the grand vizier presided over his governing council. Most secluded of all was the Third Court, which was separated from the Second by the Gate of Felicity (Babüssaade), which stood in front of the sultan's audience chamber. During Mehmed's reign, as Gülru Necipoğlu has shown, the sultan's privy chamber, backed by an open loggia, was located in the northeastern corner of the Third Court, with the dormitories of his pages nearby. (What came to be known as the Fourth

---

[16] Necipoğlu, *Architecture, Ceremonial, and Power*, 3–4, 93; Çiğdem Kafesçioğlu, *Constantinopolis/Istanbul: Cultural Encounter, Imperial Vision, and the Construction of the Ottoman Capital* (University Park, PA, 2009), 22–23.

[17] Kafesçioğlu, *Constantinopolis/Istanbul*, 23.

[18] Necipoğlu, *Architecture, Ceremonial, and Power*, 4–10, 13, 51, 200–201, 208, 221; Kafesçioğlu, *Constantinopolis/Istanbul*, 56–59, 60–66.

Figure 3.1 Plan of Topkapı Palace. From Robert Hillenbrand, *Islamic Architecture: Form, Funcation, and Meaning* (Edinburgh, 2000), 458. By permission of Edinburgh University Press. Labels added.

Court consisted of the gardens north of the Third Court; in later centuries, various sultans built kiosks there.) To the west of the privy chamber was a small, thoroughly enclosed harem, where the sultan's slave concubines lived.[19] Most of the remaining female members of the court, however, including the sultan's daughter and the mothers of his children, remained in Edirne or in the Old Palace,[20] which for the next seventy-five years would serve as the primary location of the imperial harem.

This division of male and female spaces into two sites separated by roughly three kilometers (just under two miles) was certainly unusual for an imperial dynasty. Yet there were precedents of a sort, even within the Ottoman dynasty itself: Orhan, after all, had left his wife in charge of Iznik while he relocated to Bursa. And of course, a sultan on campaign might be apart from his wives and concubines for many months, although imperial women occasionally accompanied the army for numerous stages of the march.[21] In later centuries, too, the wife of a provincial grandee might inhabit her own "harem house" separate from her husband's residence.[22]

This small harem in the new Topkapı was guarded by African eunuchs,[23] who would presumably have moved there from the Old Palace, along with the women whom they served. Their numbers were small during the decades immediately following Topkapı's construction: in 1475, the Venetian ambassador, known as the *bailo*, reported 25 eunuchs to watch over the 150 concubines who lived in the new palace (versus 250 women in the Old Palace at the time). And although most of the harem eunuchs may have been African, their chief was the white eunuch who controlled access to the Babüssaade and oversaw the training of the palace pages. This arrangement made sense given that, as Necipoğlu demonstrates, the Third Court was originally conceived as a training ground for the sultan's household slaves: on the one hand, pages; on the other, concubines.[24] Already by 1475 this chief white eunuch, known as the Kapı Ağası ("Agha of the Gate") or Babüssaade Ağası, outranked the chief of the harem eunuchs in the Old Palace.[25]

---

[19] Necipoğlu, *Architecture, Ceremonial, and Power*, 91–92, 159–61.

[20] M. Çağatay Uluçay, *Padişahların Kadınları ve Kızları* (Ankara, 1980; reprint, 1985, 1992), 18–21.

[21] E.g., Abdurrahman Abdi Pasha, "Abdurrahman Abdi Paşa Vekayi'name'si: Tahlil ve Metin Tenkidi, 1058–1053/1648–1682," ed. Fahri Çetin Derin, unpublished Ph.D. dissertation, Istanbul University, 1993, 163; Silahdar Fındıklılı Mehmed Agha, *Silahdar Tarihi* (Istanbul, 1928), I: 573–74, 717; II: 6, 566–67; Betül İpşirli Argıt, *Rabia Gülnuş Emetullah Sultan, 1640–1715* (Istanbul, 2014), 89.

[22] Hathaway, *Politics of Households*, 126.

[23] Necipoğlu, *Architecture, Ceremonial, and Power*, 162.

[24] Ibid., 161; Ottaviano Bon, in *Relazioni di ambasciatori veneti al Senato*, ed. Luigi Firpo, vol. 13: *Costantinopoli (1590–1793)* (Turin, 1984), 78, 80–81; Carlier de Pinon, *Relation du voyage en Orient*, 333.

[25] Necipoğlu, *Architecture, Ceremonial, and Power*, 160; cf. Carlier de Pinon, *Relation du voyage en Orient*, 196 and 335–37 n. 1.

Topkapı's original spatial and functional conception, in other words, reinforced the division of the Ottoman palace eunuchs into mutually exclusive groups of harem eunuchs and page-training eunuchs, a division that already existed in the New Palace in Edirne. Ultimately, this division would become synonymous with the division between African and white eunuchs. At this early date, however, the ethnoregional distinction between the two corps of eunuchs was not yet absolute: in particular, eunuchs from the Balkans and Anatolia still served in the harem. This sort of mixing was predictable at a time when the harem and Third Court eunuchs were linked by their shared responsibility for household slaves-in-training, and by the head white eunuch's supervision of both. This connection would erode in the course of the sixteenth century, with the transfer of the imperial women to Topkapı and the concomitant expansion of the harem.

Hürrem Moves into Topkapı (ca. 1530)

If the conquest of Constantinople and the construction of Topkapı Palace mark a turning point in the history of Ottoman palace eunuchs, then an equally significant turning point occurred during the sixteenth century, when women of the imperial family first moved into Topkapı's harem, which formerly had been reserved for slave concubines. The catalyst for this relocation was Hürrem Sultan (ca. 1502–58), the wife of Süleyman I. Known in western Europe as Roxelana, perhaps because of her vaguely "Russian" origins, she came to the Ottoman court as a slave concubine herself, probably from what is now Ukraine. Stories abound as to how she captured Süleyman's heart, so that he made her his sole legal wife and even abandoned his concubines out of devotion to her.[26]

Given the sultan's intense attachment to his wife, it seems only natural that she should have moved from the Old Palace, which by now was well established as a "harem house" for imperial women, to Topkapı, where she could live in proximity to her husband. Gülru Necipoğlu's research has effectively debunked the long-held belief that a fire in Hürrem's Old Palace apartments in 1541 prompted her removal to Topkapı, ostensibly only until such time as her quarters could be restored.[27] Already in 1534, the Venetian *bailo* reported Hürrem's presence in the new palace, implying that her relocation was a calculated strategy rather than a temporary expedient that unexpectedly became permanent.

Hürrem moved to Topkapı with a sizable entourage, including 100 female attendants[28] and a number of eunuchs, who, in keeping with the continuing

---

[26] Peirce, *Imperial Harem*, 58–60, 61–63.
[27] Necipoğlu, *Architecture, Ceremonial, and* Power, 163; Peirce, *Imperial Harem*, 62.
[28] Necipoğlu, *Architecture, Ceremonial, and Power*, 163; Peirce, *Imperial Harem*, 62.

ethnoregional fluidity among the harem eunuchs, were apparently a mix of Africans and non-Africans.[29] Even so, these new harem eunuchs were still outnumbered by the white eunuchs who guarded the Third Court. Under Süleyman's successor, Selim II (his second son by Hürrem), only eighteen eunuchs guarded the harem, as compared to thirty-five overseeing the Third Court.[30] Notwithstanding, the Topkapı harem had now became a locus of imperial authority rather than simply a preparatory facility for concubines. Correspondingly, the eunuchs who served in this harem were no longer simply the guardians and instructors of concubines but, at least potentially, adjuncts of imperial power. In these changed circumstances, it was no longer entirely logical for the Chief Threshold Eunuch, the Kapı Ağası, to hold authority over the harem eunuchs, even though he continued to do so for several more decades.

Once installed in Topkapı Palace, Hürrem Sultan did not move out, except perhaps for medical care toward the end of her life.[31] Unlike most mothers of princes during this period, she did not accompany her three surviving able-bodied sons to the governorships that, following long-standing Ottoman custom, they assumed in the Anatolian provinces in order to learn statecraft, although she did visit occasionally.[32] She had unquestionably set a precedent: henceforth the wives and favorite concubines of the sultan resided and gave birth at Topkapı; their young children lived with them in the harem. Under Murad III (r. 1574–95), Topkapı became the residence not only of the sultan's favorite concubines but of his mother, as well.

To accommodate its steadily increasing numbers of residents, the harem expanded radically in the last decades of the sixteenth century, metamorphosing from the modest enclosure west of the sultan's privy chamber to a vast complex of apartments, dormitories, and reception chambers to one side of the palace's Third Court.[33] Some 1,200 women now inhabited the harem, and the number of harem eunuchs expanded accordingly, rising from tens to several hundred.[34] This demand for eunuchs was fed by a new supply: with the Ottoman conquests of Egypt, northern Sudan, and the Somali coast, accomplished under Süleyman and his father, African eunuchs were readily available as never before. These two concurrent developments would ultimately seal a racial/spatial distinction between African harem eunuchs and white Third Court eunuchs that had been taking shape gradually since Topkapı's founding.

---

[29] Penzer, *The Harem*, 135.   [30] Necipoğlu, *Architecture, Ceremonial, and Power*, 163.
[31] Peirce, *Imperial Harem*, 63.
[32] Ibid., 60–61. Her sons were born before she moved to Topkapı.
[33] Necipoğlu, *Architecture, Ceremonial, and Power*, 164–74.   [34] Penzer, *The Harem*, 132.

Black Harem Eunuchs and White Threshold Eunuchs

The harem was now entirely separate from the Third Court, with an entrance just to the west of the grand vizier's council chamber in the northwest corner of the Second Court. Correspondingly, the eunuchs who served it came to be even further differentiated from the eunuchs who trained the pages of the Third Court and stood guard before the sultan's audience chamber. Beginning with Süleyman's reign, we can speak of a corps of mostly (though not yet entirely) African harem eunuchs that was utterly distinct from the parallel corps of white threshold eunuchs. Spatially, the African and white eunuchs were associated with two separate sections of the palace – the harem and the Third Court, respectively – but, more specifically, they were associated with two different thresholds: the white eunuchs with the Babüssaade, or "Gate of Felicity," the threshold in front of the sultan's audience chamber that separated the Second Court from the Third Court, and the mainly African eunuchs with the threshold marking the entrance to the harem, known euphemistically as the Darüssaade (Dar al-Sa'ada in Arabic), or "Abode of Felicity." That is to say, each corps guarded the boundary between the more public space of the Second Court and a highly restricted space:[35] the Third Court, restricted to the sultan and his pages, and the harem, restricted to the women of the palace and their young children (as well as the sultan when he chose to visit).

Eunuch Hierarchies. Within each corps of eunuchs, a strict hierarchy obtained, parallel to the hierarchy among the pages of the sultan's privy chamber, on the one hand, and among the harem women, on the other. In all these hierarchies, seniority, based on age and experience, was key. The Kapı Ağası would have worked his way up the hierarchy of threshold eunuchs, perhaps serving as chief palace treasurer (*hazinedar başı*) and even head of the sultan's privy chamber (*hass oda başı*) before becoming Chief Threshold Eunuch.[36] Likewise, the head of the harem eunuchs would have been a mature adult, perhaps in his fifties or sixties, who had entered harem service decades earlier and risen through the ranks.[37] His career might well have included a stint in the Old Palace, where the widows, daughters, and unmarried sisters of previous sultans now lived. At Topkapı, he presided over a hierarchy of younger and less seasoned eunuchs whose ranks included his eventual successor. Specific ranks within the harem eunuch hierarchy are difficult to determine for the sixteenth century; a more regularized hierarchy becomes apparent in the late seventeenth century, as later chapters will explain.

[35] Marmon, *Eunuchs and Sacred Boundaries*, 3–30.
[36] Penzer, *The Harem*, 120–21; Uzunçarşılı, *Saray Teşkilatı*, 340–42, 354–57; Necipoğlu, *Architecture, Ceremonial, and Power*, 102, 113–14, 118–19, 134–35.
[37] Uzunçarşılı, *Saray Teşkilatı*, 174.

This age-based hierarchy was designed not simply to reward years of loyal service but to ensure that harem eunuchs were thoroughly trained and had learned the lessons of experience before they rose to positions of significant authority. When we consider that the main purpose of the imperial harem was to control dynastic reproduction, the importance of this sort of training becomes more readily apparent. Leslie Peirce's research has demonstrated that the harem was not the "sultan's playpen," as contemporary European stereotypes would have it. It more closely resembled a women's dormitory in which a tiny selection of concubines was prepared for impregnation by the sultan; these chosen few were ideally limited to one son apiece.[38] In such circumstances, the sexuality of all the young women in the harem had to be carefully controlled, and this task fell to the senior women, above all the sultan's mother, and to the harem eunuchs. A young, inexperienced eunuch could not be expected to shoulder this responsibility, nor to cultivate the complex web of alliances with the senior harem women necessary to carry it out. We can regard this function of the harem eunuchs as a sort of indirect parallel to the manner in which the more senior threshold eunuchs prevented illicit sexual contact among the palace pages in training – and, by extension, to the manner in which eunuchs in the Mamluk Sultanate prevented sexual abuse of raw recruits by older mamluks.

Rivalry. Competition between the harem and threshold eunuchs was perhaps inevitable. Equally inevitable was the object of this competition: access to the sultan. Despite his frequent absences from Topkapı on campaign against the Habsburgs, Süleyman had cultivated an already existing tradition of sultanic seclusion within the palace.[39] When he was in residence, he was usually invisible to his subjects, except on those Fridays when he rode out to public noontime prayers. Even the grand vizier – with the exception of Ibrahim Pasha (term 1523–36), who was unusually close to Süleyman[40] – and the highest-ranking officers of the imperial Janissaries would have had trouble getting his ear, for he was almost always cloistered in the Third Court or in the harem. In fact, we can think of the Ottoman sultans for much of the sixteenth century as moving unevenly between these two locations whenever they were in the palace. In the first location, the pages and the Third Court eunuchs held a monopoly on contact with the sultan; in the second, the imperial women and the harem eunuchs enjoyed this privilege. However frequently the sultan might visit the harem while in residence at Topkapı, the fact that he "lived" and, at least until the reign of Selim II (1566–74), slept in his privy chamber balanced

---

[38] Peirce, *Imperial Harem*, 3–10, 42–45.
[39] Ibid., 10–12, 172–77; Necipoğlu, *Architecture, Ceremonial, and Power*, 23.
[40] Ebru Turan, "The Sultan's Favorite: Ibrahim Paşa and the Making of the Ottoman Universal Sovereignty," unpublished Ph.D. dissertation, University of Chicago, 2007.

the influence of the Third Court and the harem, and thus of the two populations of eunuchs who inhabited these spaces.

Murad III Moves into the Harem

This balance was upset when Sultan Murad III (r. 1574–95) established his living quarters inside the harem. Murad was deeply devoted to his mother, the formidable Venetian Nurbanu Sultan, who, following recent precedent, lived in the Topkapı harem. She was one of the first people whom Murad saw after his enthronement in 1574.[41] She was soon joined in the harem by Murad's favorite concubine, Safiye Sultan,[42] an equally formidable woman who, although she was Albanian, had been raised in a Venetian milieu owing to the Venetian occupation of Dalmatia (now southwestern Croatia) and large parts of what is now the Greek mainland, where Albanian populations were concentrated. She therefore continued Nurbanu's practice of patronizing a circle of Venetian courtiers and encouraging friendly ties with the Republic of Venice itself.[43]

Rather ironically, this Venetian solidarity gave these two women who made the harem such a bastion of political influence a durable connection to the *threshold* eunuchs. Both Nurbanu's and Safiye's coteries included the powerful Kapı Ağası Gazanfer Agha, a Venetian who, during the reign of Süleyman I, had been captured by corsairs, along with his brother, mother, and two sisters. His mother managed to ransom herself and her daughters; Gazanfer and his brother, however, were taken into palace service, where they became boon companions to the future Sultan Selim II. When Selim ascended the throne on Süleyman's death, according to a famous story, Gazanfer and his brother, Cafer, voluntarily underwent castration so that they could remain close to him, for no uncastrated male outside the imperial family would be allowed such close contact with the sultan. While the story holds that Cafer did not survive the operation, Maria Pia Pedani's research has shown that he not only survived but rose to become *hass oda başı* under Murad III. Gazanfer, meanwhile, had become Kapı Ağası, and when his brother died, in 1582, he took over the post of *hass oda başı*, as well.[44] Ultimately, Gazanfer's mother, one of his sisters, and one of the latter's two sons joined him at Topkapı. The sister in particular served as a key intermediary between the Venetian ambassador and the Ottoman court.[45]

[41] Necipoğlu, *Architecture, Ceremonial, and Power*, 164; Benjamin Arbel, "Nur Banu (c. 1530–1583): A Venetian Sultana?," *Turcica* 24 (1992): 241–59.
[42] Maria Pia Pedani, "Safiye's Household and Venetian Diplomacy," *Turcica* 32 (2000): 17–19, for evidence that Murad ultimately married Safiye.
[43] Ibid., 11–12, 16; Peirce, *Imperial Harem*, 94, 222–24.
[44] Pedani, "Safiye's Household," 14–15.   [45] Ibid., 21, 25–27.

While Nurbanu's and Safiye's closeness to the Kapı Ağası, who headed the corps of threshold, as opposed to harem, eunuchs, might seem a bit counter-intuitive, the Venetian cultural milieu in which both they and Gazanfer had been raised apparently transcended the spatial distance imposed by their respective positions within the palace. The fact that the third-ranking threshold eunuch, known as the *saray ağası* (literally, "commander of the palace"),[46] was a native of the Venetian-ruled city of Zara (today Zadar) in Dalmatia and also belonged to Safiye's circle reinforces this impression.[47] Moreover, Gazanfer, as Kapı Ağası, technically held authority over the harem eunuchs for at least the first several years of Murad's reign.

All of this might seem to indicate that the threshold eunuchs' position grew stronger, not weaker, under Murad III as a result of this Venetian connection. Yet the fact that a regional-cultural bond existed between Nurbanu and Safiye, on the one hand, and between Gazanfer and other threshold eunuchs, on the other, did not mean that the two imperial women did *not* cultivate ties to the harem eunuchs during their years in Topkapı's harem. Nor did it mean that the sultan himself favored the threshold eunuchs over the harem eunuchs. On the contrary, Murad enjoyed a close relationship with the head of the harem eunuchs, Habeshi ("Abyssinian") Mehmed Agha, the principal subject of Chapter 4. This, com-bined with his attachment to Safiye and Nurbanu, may be one reason why, shortly after ascending the throne, he chose to reside inside the harem. His father, Selim II, had already begun to sleep in the harem rather than in the sultanic privy chamber in the Third Court.[48] Murad had a lavish bedchamber constructed inside the harem; today, it is a highlight of harem tours. And whereas the royal bed of his predecessors had been guarded by four palace pages, Murad's bed was watched by rotating teams of elderly women.[49] To accommodate the waking hours that he spent in the harem, Murad ordered the construction of a domed reception hall, completed in 1585; next to it, a new royal bath was erected.[50]

In general, the harem expanded during Murad's reign, both in physical extent and in number of residents.[51] The sultan had spacious new apartments built for his mother and for Safiye; each of his approximately forty other concubines likewise enjoyed her own quarters.[52] Meanwhile, prospective concubines in training, as well as female servants in the harem, now numbered some 1,200;[53] the ranks of the latter included everyone from the *kâhya*, or *kethüda, kadını,* a sort of harem household manager,[54] to tutors, cooks, laundresses, seamstresses, wet-nurses, and bath attendants. These increased numbers were due not only to the unprecedented numbers of concubines under

---

[46] Uzunçarşılı, *Saray Teşkilatı*, 356–57.   [47] Pedani, "Safiye's Household," 20–21.
[48] Necipoğlu, *Architecture, Ceremonial, and Power*, 163.   [49] Ibid., 170–71.
[50] Ibid., 172–73.   [51] Ibid., 23, 164–65, 173–74.   [52] Ibid., 164–65.
[53] Penzer, *The Harem*, 132.   [54] Pedani, "Safiye's Household," 23–24.

Murad but also to the continual presence of the sultan himself, whose needs, while he was in the harem, had to be supplied by female servants and eunuchs. Accordingly, the number of harem eunuchs peaked under Murad, at perhaps 300–400.[55] They now outnumbered the threshold eunuchs by roughly ten to one.

Murad's presence in the harem meant that harem eunuchs had unprecedented access to the sultan, to complement the access they already enjoyed to the increasingly influential imperial women. In these circumstances, and despite the continuing influence of Gazanfer and other threshold eunuchs, the head of the harem eunuchs was well positioned to outstrip the Kapı Ağası in influence. This was exactly what happened some fourteen years into Murad's reign, as the next chapter will demonstrate.

---

[55] Penzer, *The Harem*, 132. I find Penzer's figure of 600–800 unreasonably high, particularly in view of the above-cited 1475 estimate of 25 eunuchs for 150 harem women, and Ignatius Mouradgea d'Ohsson's estimate of 200 eunuchs in the late eighteenth century: *Tableau général de l'Empire othoman* (Paris, 1787–1820), VII: 54.

4 The Creation of the Office of Chief Harem Eunuch and the Career of Habeshi Mehmed Agha

As we saw in Chapter 3, Murad III, who took the throne on the death of his father, Selim II, in 1574, was the first Ottoman sultan to reside in the harem of Topkapı Palace, as opposed to just sleeping there or visiting occasionally. Since, in addition, he did not usually lead military campaigns in person, the way all his predecessors had done, but preferred to delegate this duty to his grand viziers – setting an influential precedent – he had a great deal of time to spend in the harem. His removal to the harem was part of a larger pattern of sultanic seclusion that, as we have seen, was already at work during the reign of his grandfather, Süleyman I. Murad took this tendency to seclusion to its logical extreme, rarely leaving the palace at all and, even when he was in residence, sequestering himself in the part of it that was most difficult to access.

Murad's preference for the harem took him away from the white eunuchs and non-eunuch pages who staffed the "male harem" of the Third Court, known as the Enderun, and allowed the harem to displace the Third Court as a locus of political authority. Palace political factions now formed within the harem (see Table 4.1), attracting members from within the harem and from the Third Court as opportunity dictated. Even the Kapı Ağası, who had once supervised the entire palace household, now had to join one of the harem factions in order to retain his influence. This new reality created a tension between the harem and the Third Court that would persist until at least the early eighteenth century.

Such a palace faction, usually called *taraf* (literally, "side") in Ottoman sources,[1] comprised a network of patron–client ties supplemented by family connections. This was a fairly transient type of faction, its existence limited to the life or career of its leader – in this case, the sultan's mother or favorite concubine or, in the absence of such a strong female figure, the Chief Harem Eunuch himself. It was not an immutable, monolithic bloc with an unassailable corporate identity featuring public symbols and rituals, as in the case of

---

[1] E.g., Mustafa Naima, *Tarih-i Naima*, ed. Mehmed İpşirli (Ankara, 2007), III: 1325, 1333.

Table 4.1 *Major officers of the harem and Third Court during the reign of Murad III*[a]

Harem		Third Court	
		Chief Threshold Eunuch (Kapı Ağası) *Gazanfer*	
Sultan's Mother *Nurbanu (Murad III)* *Safiye (Mehmed III)*	Chief Harem Eunuch *Habeshi Mehmed*	**Gate of Felicity (Babüssaade)**	**Privy Chamber (Hass Oda)**
		Palace Treasurer (Hazinedar Başı)	Privy Chamber Head (Hass Oda Başı)
	Companions (Musahibs) *Habeshi Mehmed*	Palace Head (Saray Ağası)	Sword-Bearer (Silahdar)
			Valet (Çuhadar)
		Boys of the Threshold (Kapı Oğlanı) *Habeshi Mehmed*	Stirrup-Holder (Rikabdar)
			Pages *Ferhad* *Nasuh*

[a] Italics indicate individuals named in the chapter.

society-wide political factions in many pre- and early modern societies.[2] This brand of factional politics was just becoming dominant when Habeshi Mehmed Agha entered Topkapı Palace, and he would come to be one of its most adept practitioners.

Before Murad moved into the harem, the head of the harem eunuchs held a subordinate position in the Third Court hierarchy, below the Kapı Ağası, and therefore did not always merit the attention of court chroniclers or European observers. As a result, we know frustratingly little about the various harem eunuch heads before Murad's reign, even down to their names. In contrast, we can identify several prominent Kapı Ağaları and other key threshold eunuchs before and during Murad's reign, and even locate key monuments that they commissioned.[3] No such fund of information exists for the harem eunuchs during this period.

[2] Jane Hathaway, *A Tale of Two Factions: Myth, Memory, and Identity in Ottoman Egypt and Yemen* (Albany, NY, 2003), especially chapter 2.

[3] E.g., Hillary Sumner-Boyd and John Freely, *Strolling through Istanbul: The Classic Guide to the City*, revised ed. (London, 2010 [1972]), 32, 415; Emine Fetvacı, *Picturing History at the Ottoman Court* (Bloomington, IN, 2013), 49, 53; Gülru Necipoğlu, *The Age of Sinan: Architectural Culture in the Ottoman Empire* (London, 2005), 489–90.

All this changed dramatically with Murad's appointment of Habeshi ("Abyssinian") Mehmed Agha as head of the harem eunuchs in 1574, and his de facto creation of the office of Chief Harem Eunuch (Darüssaade Ağası) in 1588, when he made Habeshi Mehmed superintendent of the imperial pious foundations for Mecca and Medina. This chapter examines Habeshi Mehmed's background and career, as well as the precedents that he set for future Chief Eunuchs. What soon becomes clear is that his outsized authority was, to no small extent, a product of the wealth and influence that he had amassed before assuming the office; in other words, his personal power worked in conjunction with the institutional power that the office gave him.

Habeshi Mehmed Agha's Early Career

Ironically, in view of how important he was to become, relatively little of certainty is known about Habeshi Mehmed's background. We do have a remarkable account, supposedly related by the eunuch himself, of his enslavement. The story appears in the margin of a famous treatise on the merits of Ethiopians, composed by a rare Ethiopian member of the Ottoman ulema. It implies that Habeshi Mehmed was born a Muslim, since "the children of the Abyssinians accepted Islam in the time of the Prophet." Unlike most Ethiopian eunuchs, according to this tale, he was enslaved by Europeans. A Frankish commercial vessel, the story claims, called at Habesh, and the merchant, "after filling his ship to the brim with Habeshi merchandise, purchased me and two other eunuchs and started for Frengistan." The ship had been at sea for a week when it was suddenly overtaken and attacked by a Muslim vessel.

A great battle lasted from morning until the afternoon prayer time. The Muslims conquered our ship and were victorious. But that infidel Frank [merchant] was a courageous devil [literally, "a cursed brave one"], because he martyred the leader [shaykh] of the Muslims all by himself. But we could see that he had no strength left. He came to the lifeboat and with a great sigh sat down beside us. At that moment a [musket] ball flew across, struck him in the chest, and came out through his back, sending his soul to hell. The Muslims overcame the ship and divided everything hidden inside it. They took us and gave us to the governor of Egypt, and the governor of Egypt gave us to Selim Han son of Süleyman Han [i.e., Selim II, son of Süleyman I].[4]

This swash-buckling tale bears the marks of an origin legend. Art historian Emine Fetvacı suggests that the narrative of Habeshi Mehmed's purchase by a Frankish merchant may have been introduced to get around the fact that

---

[4] Ali b. Abdurrauf el-Habeşi, *Rafa'ilü'l-gubuş fi feza'ilü'l-Hubuş*, Istanbul, Süleymaniye Library, MS Fatih 4360, fol. 9b. I am grateful to Günhan Börekçi for procuring a copy of this manuscript for me.

castration violates Islamic law.[5] Even if we leave aside this rather fantastic account, though, Habeshi Mehmed was clearly one of a steadily increasing number of Ethiopian eunuchs entering Ottoman service in the wake of the Ottoman conquest of Egypt in 1517 and subsequent incursions into Sudan and the Horn of Africa. The one part of the tale that rings true is his presentation to the governor of Egypt in advance of his introduction to the palace. This sojourn in Egypt would have given him connections not only to the Ottoman governor but also to the province's grandees, many of whom were, in the late sixteenth century, closely tied to the imperial palace.[6]

As the story relates, Habeshi Mehmed entered the palace when the governor of Egypt presented him to the future Selim II, then still a prince.[7] Since Selim was born in 1524 and became sultan on his father Süleyman's death in 1566, this could have occurred at any time during the intervening forty-two years. If, however, we assume that Habeshi Mehmed was at least eighty years old at his death in January 1591 – for eunuchs who were not executed often lived to quite advanced ages – then the 1530s might seem a reasonable estimate, the more so as Selim would not yet have left the imperial palace to take up a provincial governorship in Anatolia, as was standard practice for Ottoman princes until the end of the sixteenth century. Once in the palace, Mehmed Agha was taken into the service of the Chief Threshold Eunuch, becoming one of the *kapı oğlanı* ("boys of the threshold") who massed around the Babüssaade.[8] This, again, was not atypical, for harem eunuchs in general were subordinate to the white eunuchs of the Third Court during this period. Years later, when Selim, now sultan, had the Chief Threshold Eunuch executed, he confiscated his property, including Habeshi Mehmed.

Although Habeshi Mehmed entered palace service under Selim II, he really made his mark during the reign of Selim's son Murad III. He was close to Murad's mother, the fearsome Venetian concubine Nurbanu Sultan, whose entourage he probably joined after he was "confiscated" by Selim II.[9] In that capacity, he would have had frequent contact with Prince Murad, whose attachment to his mother was noted in Chapter 3 – at least, that is, until Murad left for his princely governorate in the southwestern Anatolian city of Manisa. Following the precedent set by Hürrem Sultan, Nurbanu declined to accompany her son to his posting but remained in Topkapı Palace during the entire reign of Selim II (1566–74),[10] along with Habeshi Mehmed Agha. Instead, Gazanfer Agha, the future Chief Threshold Eunuch, traveled to Manisa with

---

[5] Fetvacı, *Picturing History*, 150.
[6] Hathaway, "The Mamluk-Breaker Who Was Really a *Kul*-Breaker," 97–102.
[7] Fetvacı, *Picturing History*, 150.
[8] Ibid.; el-Habeşi, *Rafa'ilü'l-gubuş*, fol. 9b; Peirce, *Imperial Harem*, 104.
[9] Necipoğlu, *Age of Sinan*, 498.   [10] Peirce, *Imperial Harem*, 55, 261.

Murad,[11] as if to prove that a sort of either/or choice already existed between the harem eunuchs and the eunuchs of the Third Court.

But even if he did not go to Manisa with Murad, Habeshi Mehmed must certainly have cultivated a relationship with the prince before his accession. This, plus his attachment to Nurbanu, made him a natural choice for Chief Harem Eunuch once Murad became sultan. Mustafa Safi, court chronicler to Sultan Ahmed I (r. 1603–17), describes Habeshi Mehmed as Murad's *musahib*, or boon companion, while his contemporary Hasan Beyzade refers to him as "the sultan's intimate" (*mukarreb-i padişah*).[12] At the time, it was still rare for a harem eunuch to occupy a position so close to the ruler; this development was a clear sign both of Murad's unprecedented attachment to the harem and of Habeshi Mehmed's influence with the sultan.

It was also rare for a Chief Eunuch's appointment to coincide with a sultan's accession. This may be yet another indication of Murad's intense interest in the harem, to the extent that he was not content to live with his father's choice of head eunuch but saw fit to appoint his own candidate, perhaps on his mother's advice, at the outset of his reign. Once he had become sultan, however, his favorite concubine, Safiye Sultan, joined his mother in the Topkapı harem. Despite their common Venetian cultural heritage, the two women did not get along but competed for Murad's preference.[13] This helps to explain why Safiye patronized Gazanfer Agha, who, as we will see below, quickly emerged as Habeshi Mehmed's rival.

In addition to the Chief Harem Eunuch's official residence, a suite of rooms just inside the entrance to Topkapı's harem, Habeshi Mehmed owned a palatial mansion, given to him by Murad III, near the Old Palace. As Fetvacı notes, maintaining a separate residence outside the palace was highly unusual for a harem eunuch.[14] This only provides further evidence of Habeshi Mehmed's unusual closeness to the sultan. As if to underline this connection, he served as Murad's representative (*vekil*) at the 1582 wedding of the *nişancı*, the bureaucrat who affixed the sultan's seal to official documents, to the daughter of one of Süleyman's grand viziers.[15]

And yet for the first several years of his tenure, Habeshi Mehmed, like everyone else at Murad's court, was overshadowed by the almost unimaginably powerful grand vizier Sokollu Mehmed Pasha. Originally a Bosnian Serb *devshirme* recruit, Sokollu was appointed grand vizier in 1565, just a year

[11] Uzunçarşılı, *Osmanlı Tarihi*, III, part 2, 44.
[12] Mustafa Safi, *Mustafa Safi'nin* Zübdetü't-Tevarih'*i*, ed. İbrahim Hakkı Çuhadar (Ankara, 2003), I: 248; Hasanbeyzade Ahmed Pasha, *Hasan Bey-zade Tarihi*, ed. Şevki Nezihi Aykut (Ankara, 2004), II: 338, 339.
[13] Peirce, *Imperial Harem*, 91, 94, 281; Uluçay, *Padişahların Kadınları ve Kızları*, 40, 43.
[14] Fetvacı, *Picturing History*, 152; Necipoğlu, *Age of Sinan*, 499.
[15] Selaniki Mustafa Efendi, *Selaniki Tarihi*, ed. Mehmet İpşirli (Istanbul, 1989), I: 131.

before the death of Süleyman I, and ended up running the Ottoman Empire in all but name until his assassination, at unknown hands, in 1579. He was playing this role when Habeshi Mehmed Agha became head of the harem eunuchs, yet the eunuch was not his client. On the contrary, Habeshi Mehmed's patroness, Nurbanu Sultan, was antagonistic toward Sokollu, as were her rivals Safiye Sultan and Gazanfer Agha.[16] Sokollu's murder left an enormous vacuum at the court that Nurbanu, Safiye, and the two eunuchs competed to fill. Habeshi Mehmed emerged triumphant in this competition, to judge from an extraordinary illuminated manuscript that he commissioned two years after the crime, in which he is portrayed as Sokollu's avenger who is, more to the point, firmly in charge in the palace. I will have more to say about this work, and about other manuscripts that Habeshi Mehmed commissioned, in Chapter 11.

The Evkafü'l-Haremeyn

What really cemented the Chief Harem Eunuch's authority, though, was control of the imperial pious foundations for the Muslim holy cities of Mecca and Medina, or Evkafü'l-Haremeyn. In 1588, Murad transferred supervision of these foundations from Gazanfer Agha, the powerful chief of the threshold eunuchs, to Habeshi Mehmed Agha.[17] This was an extraordinary move, especially when we consider the enormity of Gazanfer's influence: up to this point, he had supervised the sultan's household in general, including the harem. At the same time, Habeshi Mehmed began to be known as Aga-yı Darü's-sa'ade (literally, "agha of the Abode of Felicity"), the official title for the Chief Harem Eunuch. This signifies that the office of Chief Harem Eunuch was inextricably linked to the Evkaf.

These pious foundations require some explanation. Some form of charitable endowment to Mecca and Medina had existed virtually since the institution of the pious foundation, or endowment (Arabic, *waqf*; Turkish, *vakıf*), had come into being in roughly the ninth century CE. In such an endowment, the founder – usually a member of the ruling family, a powerful statesman, or a wealthy and influential religious official or merchant – earmarked the revenues from a piece of land or property, or from an urban operation such as customs, to the maintenance of a charitable or religious foundation, such as a mosque, soup kitchen, or madrasa.

---

[16] Uzunçarşılı, *Osmanlı Tarihi*, II: 552; III, part 1, 49–54; *EI²*, s.v. "Sokollu Mehmed Pasha," by Gilles Veinstein.
[17] Mustafa Güler, *Osmanlı Devlet'inde Haremeyn Vakıfları (XVI.–XVII. Yüzyıllar)* (Istanbul, 2002), 213–15; BOA, MD 62, no. 563, p. 249 (2 Receb 996/28 May 1588); Necipoğlu, *Age of Sinan*, 498; *TDVİA*, s.v. "Darüssaade," by Ülkü Altındağ.

Where Mecca and Medina were concerned, the Mamluk sultans had endowed revenues from lands and properties in their territories in Egypt and, to some extent, Syria to the construction and upkeep of mosques, madrasas, Qur'an schools, soup kitchens, hospitals, wells, and other public charitable foundations in Mecca and Medina and along the pilgrimage routes. In addition, and perhaps more significantly, these foundations earmarked specific villages in Egypt, above all Upper Egypt, to provide wheat and barley to the holy cities – since grain could not grow in the Hijaz. The Mamluk sultans of the fifteenth century set up the Deşişet-i Kubra, which translates roughly to "Big Grain," specifically to supply this need.[18] When the Ottomans began to conquer parts of southeastern Anatolia under Sultan Mehmed II, they took possession of some of these revenue-producing lands and started to remit *vakıf* revenues to Cairo.[19] Although this amounted to remitting revenues to the defeated party, it was not as ironic as it might at first seem, for earlier Ottoman sultans, notably Mehmed I (r. 1413–21), had already established their own foundations dedicated to Mecca and Medina.[20]

Following their conquest of Egypt in 1517, the Ottomans reinforced the massive Deşişet-i Kubra endowment while adding new endowments of their own: the Hassekiyye, founded by Süleyman I's wife Hürrem Sultan (so called because Hürrem was Süleyman's favorite, or *hasseki*); the Muradiyye, founded by Murad III (r. 1574–95) and sometimes known as the Deşişet-i Sughra, or "Little Grain"; and the Mehmediyye, founded by Mehmed IV (r. 1648–87).[21] In 1678, Mehmed IV's favorite, Rabia Gülnuş Emetullah Sultan, founded an additional endowment, later known as the Valide (sultan's mother) *vakıf*, centered on a hospital that she established in Mecca (this will be examined in Chapter 8). These, then, were the five principal pious foundations that made up the Ottoman-era Evkafü'l-Haremeyn, although when Habeshi Mehmed became head of the harem eunuchs, only the first two existed.

Apart from these "big five" foundations, more modest and narrowly focused endowments were established over the centuries, often by imperial women, to provide various services for Mecca or Medina; the Chief Harem Eunuch supervised these, as well. He even presided over imperial foundations that were unconnected to the holy cities. For example, Murad III's daughter, Ayşe Sultan (d. 1604), created endowments for a madrasa, a training academy for

[18] D'Ohsson, *Tableau général*, III: 223–24; Burckhardt, *Travels in Arabia*, 141; Doris Behrens-Abouseif, "Sultan Qaytbay's Foundation in Medina: The *Madrasah*, the *Ribat*, and the *Dashisha*," *Mamluk Studies Review* 2 (1998): 61–72; Güler, *Haremeyn Vakıfları*, 38.
[19] Yüksel Muslu, *Ottomans and Mamluks*, 160.   [20] Ibid., 105–6.
[21] *EI²*, s.v. "Wakf, II. In the Arab Lands, 1. Egypt," by Doris Behrens-Abouseif; Uzunçarşılı, *Osmanlı Devletinin Saray Teşkilatı*, 177–83; Güler, *Haremeyn Vakıfları*, 172–80; Jane Hathaway, "The Role of the Kızlar Ağası in 17th–18th Century Ottoman Egypt," *Studia Islamica* 75 (1992): 141–42.

Qur'an-school teachers, and Qur'an recitations at her tomb and that of her husband. Although the focus of all these foundations was Istanbul, the endowment deed stipulates that "whoever becomes Darüssaade Ağası" will serve as superintendent.[22]

The Mamluk-era Evkaf had drawn heavily on Egypt, which, after all, was the core of Mamluk territory; in addition, Egypt enjoyed a historical connection to the holy cities because of its relative proximity to them and the fact that it produced large amounts of grain. Under the Ottomans, Egypt remained central to the Evkafü'l-Haremeyn. Although revenues were now transmitted to Istanbul rather than to Cairo, a disproportionate quantity of endowed land was concentrated in Egypt.

What did supervision of the Evkaf entail? The superintendent, or *nazir*, had to make sure that revenues and grains from all the endowed lands, properties, and operations throughout the empire were delivered to Istanbul or directly to the holy cities each year. Given the preponderance of Egyptian lands endowed to the Evkaf, a superintendent with strong ties to Egypt was desirable. And given the fact that harem eunuchs often came to the palace by way of Egypt and cultivated ties with the province's governors and grandees, the Chief Harem Eunuch would seem to have been a natural candidate for superintendent.

Nevertheless, for some sixty-five years following the Ottoman conquest of Egypt and assumption of control of the Evkaf, the chief of the threshold eunuchs (Kapı Ağası or Babüssaade Ağası) held this position. To understand why, it helps to recall that until the late sixteenth century, the Chief Threshold Eunuch was the nominal head of the imperial household, and the Evkaf were essentially imperial household endowments: the personal endowments of various sultans. Yet Hürrem's endowment, along with that of Murad III's daughter, signaled that imperial women would henceforth play an important role in the expansion of the Evkaf, and in fact, later centuries saw a steady stream of endowments by sultanic favorites, sisters, and daughters alongside those endowed by the sultans themselves. Imperial women, moreover, occasionally made the pilgrimage to Mecca themselves, whereas the Ottoman sultans, like the Mughal emperors of India, never did, for reasons that have been debated over the years.[23] So the Evkaf, at least from the reign of Süleyman onward, had a certain natural connection to the imperial harem, and since the Chief Threshold Eunuch oversaw the harem, it made sense for him to oversee the Evkaf.

---

[22] Tülay Duran, *Tarihimizde Vakıf Kuran Kadınlar: Hanım Sultan Vakfiyyeleri* (Istanbul, 1990), 33–60; Uluçay, *Padişahların Kadınları ve Kızları*, 45.
[23] Suraiya Faroqhi, *Pilgrims and Sultans: The Hajj under the Ottomans* (London, 1994), 129.

In fact, when Murad named Habeshi Mehmed Agha *nazir* of the Evkafü'l-Haremeyn, he also removed the harem from the oversight of the Chief Threshold Eunuch. This helps to explain why Habeshi Mehmed assumed the title Darüssade Ağası, or "Agha of the Abode of Felicity," only when he became *nazir*. At the same time, the treasury of the Evkaf, where cash revenues from all over the Ottoman Empire were collected, was moved from the imperial treasury rooms at the back of the Third Court to the corridor just inside the harem entrance where the harem eunuchs' quarters were located.[24] Not long afterward, Habeshi Mehmed instituted the practice of holding weekly audiences at the entrance gate to the harem, located inside Topkapı's Second Court. He had the gate expanded for this purpose, as the inscription above the gate tells us, in a rare direct epigraphic reference to harem eunuch influence. Here, he discussed Evkaf-related issues.[25]

This restructuring of both the Evkaf and the harem administration dealt a severe blow to Gazanfer Agha, who saw these two sources of influence taken away from him at one fell swoop. Still, he must have sensed, from the time Murad III came to the throne in 1574, that his authority was waning. He could hardly have drawn any other conclusion from the sultan's closeness to Habeshi Mehmed or from his decision to move his residential quarters into the harem. Gazanfer, in any event, remained a force to be reckoned with. Playing on his Venetian roots, he nurtured his ties to Murad's favorite concubine, Safiye Sultan, while building up his own coterie of clients.[26] These included a number of African harem eunuchs – for, in his years overseeing the harem, he can hardly have avoided cultivating connections to some of these men. He thus attempted to ensure that future Chief Harem Eunuchs were appointed from among his own clients.[27] In other words, Gazanfer, chief of the eunuchs of the Third Court, crossed lines of imperial space and political influence in order to cultivate clients within the harem. This was a very canny way to retain his influence even while political authority was shifting increasingly to the harem.

Habeshi Mehmed Agha's Clients: Ferhad and Nasuh Pashas

But Habeshi Mehmed Agha could play that game, too. He had his own clients inside the Third Court – more specifically among the non-eunuch pages of the sultan's privy chamber, or *hass oda* – and he helped them to attain the highest offices in the Ottoman administration, up to and including that of grand vizier. The eighteenth-century statesman Ahmed Resmi Efendi, author of a

---

[24] D'Ohsson, *Tableau général*, II: 541; Necipoğlu, *Architecture, Ceremonial, and Power*, 180.
[25] Necipoğlu, *Architecture, Ceremonial, and Power*, 174; Fetvacı, *Picturing History*, 152.
[26] Pedani, "Safiye's Household and Venetian Diplomacy," 14–22.
[27] Ibid., 15; Penzer, *The Harem*, 50.

compendium of Chief Harem Eunuch biographies, notes that "most of the protégés who came out of his household became high-ranking viziers."[28] Particularly notable among these were the grand viziers Ferhad Pasha (terms 1591–92, 1595) and Nasuh Pasha (term 1611–14). A brief look at their careers helps to show what was at stake in the emerging game of clientage and counter-clientage.

Ferhad Pasha. An Albanian recruited to Ottoman service through the *devshirme*, the "collection" of boys for military and palace service, Ferhad had the dubious privilege of chaperoning the body of Süleyman I after the sultan's death while on campaign in Hungary in 1566. (Meanwhile, Sokollu, the grand vizier, kept the death secret until Selim II had taken the throne.) Later in his career, he served twice as commander of Ottoman forces combating the Safavids of Iran (1583 and 1586) before serving twice as grand vizier.[29]

The anti-Safavid duty, which was particularly unforgiving and dangerous, was a source of tension between Ferhad and Habeshi Mehmed Agha. Unpleasantly surprised by his second appointment, in 1586, Ferhad appealed, unsuccessfully, to Habeshi Mehmed to have the order rescinded.[30] This action strongly suggests that he was Habeshi Mehmed's client while underlining just how influential the Chief Harem Eunuch was, even before he assumed supervision of the imperial pious foundations. Habeshi Mehmed Agha must have known what he was doing, for in four years on campaign, Ferhad conquered the strategic fortress of Ganja in northwestern Azerbaijan from the Safavids and brokered a peace treaty that left the Ottomans in control of Azerbaijan until 1606.

Yet Ferhad Pasha ultimately fell victim to the ambitions of the palace faction led by Safiye Sultan, favorite concubine of Murad III and mother of his successor Mehmed III (r. 1595–1603). Habeshi Mehmed's death in 1591 and Murad's death in 1595 gave Safiye and her allies room to maneuver. It did not help matters that her faction included Habeshi Mehmed's arch-rival, the Chief Threshold Eunuch Gazanfer Agha, and Ferhad's arch-rival, Koca Sinan Pasha, a fellow Albanian and brilliant general who had traded the grand vizierate with Ferhad during the early 1590s. On Mehmed III's accession in early 1595, Ferhad was deposed and sentenced to death. He managed to take advantage of Sinan Pasha's own fall from grace and banishment from court to persuade Safiye Sultan to save his life by granting him permission to reside on his estate (*çiftlik*). This reprieve was short lived, however. Sinan Pasha was recalled to

---

[28] Ahmed Resmî Efendi, *Hamiletü'l-kübera*, ed. Ahmet Nezihi Turan (Istanbul, 2000), 45, 87.
[29] Ibrahim Peçevi, *Tarih-i Peçevi*, ed. Bekir Sıtkı Baykal (Ankara, 1981), II: 79–80, 98–100, 112–13, 153; Uzunçarşılı, *Osmanlı Tarihi*, III, part 2, 347–49; *EI*[2], s.v. "Ferhad Pasha," by V.J. Parry.
[30] Hasanbeyzade, *Hasan Bey-zade Tarihi*, II: 339; Naima, *Tarih-i Naima*, IV: 1924; Peçevi, *Tarih-i Peçevi*, II: 99 (which does not mention Habeshi Mehmed).

duty in August 1595 and connived to have Ferhad Pasha removed from his estate and transported to Yedikule prison at the end of Istanbul's Byzantine land walls, where he was executed in October 1595.[31]

Nasuh Pasha. Like Ferhad Pasha, Nasuh Pasha was a *devshirme* recruit, although historians disagree as to whether he was Albanian or Greek. Unlike Ferhad, however, he did not attain high office, and certainly not the grand vizierate, until after Habeshi Mehmed Agha's death. Rather, he enjoyed Habeshi Mehmed's patronage during the early part of his career, as a palace page. After being taken away from his family of origin, according to an account summarized by both François-Thomas Delbare and a frequently cited anonymous French letter, Nasuh was sold to Habeshi Mehmed and became his personal servant, living in his private residence near the Old Palace while the Chief Eunuch oversaw his education.[32] Only when Habeshi Mehmed recognized Nasuh's "perfidious and cruel nature"[33] did he present him to the palace. He used his influence to have Nasuh appointed to the corps of Zülüflü Baltacıs, or halberdiers with long sidelocks, whose barracks were located just outside the entrance to the harem as expanded by Murad III. (The sidelocks were supposed to prevent the halberdiers from gazing at the harem women.) In fact, Habeshi Mehmed Agha was responsible for renovating and expanding the Baltacıs' quarters in 1586–87.[34] Nasuh apparently used this proximity to the harem to cultivate a relationship with Safiye Sultan. Even as a very young man, Nasuh was adept at reading the political situation inside the palace, and he evidently realized that Safiye's faction was ascendant.

After Habeshi Mehmed's death in 1591, Nasuh "graduated" from palace service as an officer in the Müteferrika regiment, an elite corps of palace troops comprising, for the most part, the privileged sons of important statesmen.[35] With this rank, he served for nine years as governor (*voyvoda*) of the northern Anatolian district of Zile before returning to the palace and entering the *hass oda*. By this time, Mehmed III was on the throne, and his mother Safiye's influence was at its peak. The Chief Harem Eunuch during Mehmed III's reign was the former chief of Safiye's personal eunuch entourage, and he was utterly

---

[31] Peçevi, *Tarih-i Peçevi*, II: 156–58; Uzunçarşılı, *Osmanlı Tarihi*, III, part 2, 348–49; Fetvacı, *Picturing History*, 225, 230, 46; Hasanbeyzade, *Hasan Bey-zade Tarihi*, II: 374.

[32] François-Thomas Delbare, *Histoire des ministres-favoris, anciens et modernes* (Paris, 1820), 321; Anonymous, *Coppie d'une lettre escrite de Constantinople à un Gentil-homme François, contenant la trahison du Bascha Nassouf, sa mort estrange, & des grandes richesses qui luy ont esté trouees [sic]* (Paris, 1615), 4–5; *TDVİA*, s.v. "Nasuh Paşa," by Ömer İşbilir. I am grateful to Günhan Börekçi for bringing the French sources to my attention.

[33] *Coppie d'une lettre*, 4.

[34] Necipoğlu, *Architecture, Ceremonial, and Power*, 74, 174; Tommaso Alberti, *Viaggio a Costantinopoli di Tommaso Alberti (1620–1621), pubblicato da Alberto Bacchi della Lega* (Bologna, 1889), 49.

[35] Uzunçarşılı, *Saray Teşkilatı*, 428–31.

dominated by Safiye and Gazanfer. Even after Mehmed's death, Safiye remained influential at the court of her grandson Ahmed I (r. 1603–17).[36] With Safiye's support, Nasuh attained two choice positions in the outer palace service: *kapıcılar kethüdası*, or chief gatekeeper, and *küçük imrahor*, or assistant stablemaster.[37]

In 1603, following the massive uprising that resulted in Gazanfer Agha's execution, Nasuh left the palace for high-profile military commands that put him on the front lines against the Anatolian rebels known as Jelalis, on the one hand, and against the newly expansionist Safavids, under Shah Abbas I (r. 1589–1628), on the other.[38] He attained the grand vizierate in 1611, but he was so brutal and acquisitive, while not being particularly effective militarily, that his enemies sought any excuse to bring him down. In the end, they were able to use the treaty that he signed in 1612 with Shah Abbas, which recognized the Safavid reconquest of the Caucasus, claiming that Nasuh's peace overtures had allowed Abbas to pursue his aggression unchecked.[39] Nasuh was executed in November 1614.

With Ferhad and Nasuh, Habeshi Mehmed Agha extended his patronage network into the sultan's privy chamber, which was a potential rival to the harem as a site of political influence in the palace. Coopting *hass oda* pages enabled Habeshi Mehmed to circumvent the clientage networks forged by Gazanfer Agha, who supervised the entire Third Court, and his ally Safiye Sultan. At the same time, of course, Gazanfer, with Safiye's help, was forging his own alliances with specific harem eunuchs in order to counter Habeshi Mehmed's influence. What was happening, in other words, was that two factions had formed within Topkapı Palace's private space whose ties of clientage cut across the harem and the Third Court.

The careers of Ferhad and Nasuh Pashas, in any case, illustrate the changing balance of power between Nurbanu's and Safiye's factions in the wake of Habeshi Mehmed's death and the ascendancy of Safiye Sultan. Ferhad, patronized over most of his career by Habeshi Mehmed Agha, was consequently identified with Nurbanu's old faction and ultimately fell victim to the designs of members of Safiye's faction after his patron's death. Nasuh, in contrast, although he started out as Habeshi Mehmed's personal protégé, cultivated ties

---

[36] Pedani, "Safiye's Household and Venetian Diplomacy," 15; Peirce, *Imperial Harem*, 197, 210, 228.

[37] Delbare, *Histoire des ministres-favoris*, 322.

[38] Mustafa Safi, *Zübdetü't-tevarih*, II: 315–24; Rhoads Murphey, "Mustafa Safi's Version of the Kingly Virtues as Presented in His *Zübdetü't-tevarih*, or Annals of Sultan Ahmed, 1012–1023 A.H./1603–1614 A.D.," in *Frontiers of Ottoman Studies*, eds. Imber and Kiyotaki, I: 14, 24; Peçevi, *Tarih-i Peçevi*, II: 318–20; Delbare, *Histoire des ministres-favoris*, 322–37; *Coppie d'une lettre*, 4–5; *TDVİA*, s.v. "Nasuh Paşa," by İşbilir; Uzunçarşılı, *Osmanlı Tarihi*, III, part 1, 66–68, 103; part 2, 365–67; *EI²*, s.v. "Nasuh Pasha," by Franz Babinger.

[39] Delbare, *Histoire des ministres-favoris*, 328, 330–33.

to Safiye's faction just as that faction was becoming dominant. By the time of Nasuh's execution, though, the factional equation was changing again, as the next chapter will make clear.

Competition with Gazanfer: The Evidence of Mustafa Ali

During his tenure as Chief Harem Eunuch, Habeshi Mehmed Agha's main professional rivalry was with the Chief Threshold Eunuch Gazanfer Agha.[40] This was, in many respects, only natural since Habeshi Mehmed's ascendancy came largely at Gazanfer's expense. Certainly, Habeshi Mehmed's appointment as superintendent of the Evkafü'l-Haremeyn and independent head of the harem eunuchs was a blow to Gazanfer's influence. But over and above what these shifts in position meant for the two eunuchs themselves, they represented the consolidation of the harem's dominance over the Third Court as a seat of factional influence. This development carried major implications for the two eunuchs' respective clients. While the rivalry is not so explicit in the careers of Ferhad Pasha and Nasuh Pasha, it breaks through to the surface, with a vengeance, in the work of the well-known sixteenth-century bureaucrat and intellectual Mustafa Ali (1541–1600), a native of Gallipoli (Gelibolu) who occupied a number of key financial and administrative posts in Istanbul and in the Ottoman provinces in the course of a decades-long career. He was a client of Gazanfer Agha, whom he encountered while serving in the princely household of Selim II, and later of Murad III, in Manisa.[41]

For Gazanfer, Mustafa Ali composed his *Description of Cairo* (*Halatü'l-Kahire mine'l-'adati'z-zahire*), a lengthy rumination, in Ottoman Turkish, on Cairo, and Egypt more generally, based on his sojourn there in 1599, en route to what turned out to be his final administrative appointment, as governor (*sancak beyi*) of Jidda, the Red Sea port that served Mecca. Earlier in his career, in 1567, he had stayed briefly in Cairo while in the entourage of the vizier Lala Mustafa Pasha, who had been appointed to quell the rebellion of the Zaydi Shi'ite imam in Yemen.[42] Mustafa Ali clearly feels that conditions in Egypt have deteriorated markedly since his earlier sojourn and that African harem eunuchs bear much of the responsibility for the downturn. Toward the end of the *Description*, he inveighs against the increasing number of "aghas of Nubian or Ethiopian origin" who are retiring to Cairo with handsome pensions:

---

[40] Fetvacı, *Picturing History*, 194, 264.   [41] Ibid., 242.
[42] Cornell H. Fleischer, *Bureaucrat and Intellectual in the Ottoman Empire: The Historian Mustafa Ali (1541–1600)* (Princeton, NJ, 1986); Hathaway, *A Tale of Two* Factions, 85–86.

Now, at the zeal-containing time when this is written, that ilk has increased in the capital of Cairo and they help and assist each other. The lowest ones of them have obtained excellent salaries with assignments of barley [for their horses] and wheat. Some expert and unprejudiced senior persons tell us that from the time when Sultan Selim [I] succeeded in the conquest of Egypt until this moment, that is, until the days of the reign of Sultan Murad [III], there never were twenty or thirty eunuchs together in Egypt, and the most respected one of these, Mahmud Agha, the palace agha of the grand vizier Rüstem Pasha's [terms 1544–53, 1555–61] sultana [wife], came with a salary of seventy aspers per day and never rose enough in favor to reach a hundred. The others had [only] five or ten aspers. The total of the daily pay of all of them together was not more than three, four hundred aspers. Now, however, the black aghas cannot be counted any more. Those of the lowest rank have obtained salaries of forty, fifty aspers and abundant allowances of barley and wheat. Those of respected rank are not only given honor, all they might wish, but also come to Egypt with a daily pay of ten or twelve gold pieces. Afterwards, their honors are increased through the boundless mercy of the *beglerbegi*s [Ottoman governors] and they get hold of many, many salary raises through the indulgence and compliance of the fortunate ones who are grand viziers.[43]

Here, Mustafa Ali appears to be blaming this unfortunate situation on the Ottoman governors of Egypt who nurture the African harem eunuchs. In the passages immediately following this one, he seems to allude to Habeshi Mehmed:

But the truth is not one of them has reached the rank of an agha in the capital. As most of them have started [their careers] as *kapı oğlanı*, such a degree of being honored is much too much for them. In spite of that, they are not satisfied with it, and they have appropriated the Deşişe foundations as their sinecure and have squandered their revenues.[44]

Habeshi Mehmed, we recall, started out as one of the *kapı oğlanı*, or "boys of the threshold," subordinate to the threshold eunuchs. Eleven years before Mustafa Ali penned the *Description*, moreover, he had assumed the superintendency of the Holy Cities Pious Foundations, chief among which was the Deşişet-i Kubra, depriving Mustafa Ali's patron, Gazanfer, of this position.

Unquestionably the *Description* reflects the bitterness of an aging official who, as is well known, was continually frustrated in his attempts to garner the empire's highest administrative posts, above all that of grand vizier. On top of all this, he had witnessed the degradation of his patron's influence. In his *Book of Counsel for Sultans*, composed eighteen years earlier, by contrast, Mustafa Ali lists "the eunuchs, who clearly deserve it" among the recipients of pensions in Egypt and other provinces.[45] In one of many poems interspersed throughout

---

[43] Mustafa Ali, *Mustafa Ali's Description of Cairo of 1599*, 81–82.   [44] Ibid.

[45] Mustafa Ali, *Mustafa Ali's Counsel for Sultans of 1581: Edition, Translation, Notes*, ed. and trans. Andreas Tietze (Vienna, 1979–82), II: 39. I am grateful to Lisa Balabanlılar for bringing these passages to my attention.

this work, he likewise declares that "the Palace eunuchs are the only ones/That still show loyalty, grateful for [the sultan's] bread"[46] – but this probably refers to the threshold eunuchs, and Gazanfer in particular.

Mustafa Ali wrote his description of Cairo eight years after Habeshi Mehmed Agha's death, at a time when his patron Gazanfer Agha was riding rather high. Yet supervision of the Evkafü'l-Haremeyn never returned to the Chief Threshold Eunuch but remained the Chief Harem Eunuch's prerogative. Meanwhile, the number of African eunuchs exiled to Cairo at the end of their careers – a subject addressed in Chapter 8 – continued to grow apace. These underlying new realities inform Mustafa Ali's bitterness. Gazanfer may have outlived Habeshi Mehmed Agha and come to dominate the harem before his own death in 1603, but he could not undo the institutional changes that had propelled Habeshi Mehmed to such prominence in the first place.

Architectural Monuments

Gazanfer's Madrasa. Gazanfer's predicament is perhaps reflected in the limited number of architectural monuments he sponsored in Istanbul, as compared to an astonishing number of mammoth projects commissioned by Habeshi Mehmed Agha. To give him his due, Gazanfer commissioned a madrasa that is justifiably famous, not least because of its highly visible location. Designed by the chief architect Davud Agha (term 1588–98), the successor to the great Sinan, and built in 1596, it abuts the aqueduct built by the Roman emperor Valens (r. 364–78) in Istanbul's Saraçhane neighborhood, situated between the Golden Horn and the Sea of Marmara; the ancient Byzantine processional route passed right by the site, as did later Ottoman processional routes. The complex, which from 1989 to 2010 housed the Museum of Cartoons and Humor (presumably with no irony intended), includes Gazanfer Agha's tomb.[47] At the time of the madrasa's construction, the greater area, though largely Greek, contained a critical mass of Muslim residents, including the descendants of a population from the district of Aksaray in central Anatolia whom Mehmed II had forcibly relocated to Istanbul as part of his effort to repopulate the city in the wake of his conquest. (These refugees gave the name of their home district to a neighborhood just southwest of Gazanfer's complex.)

Habeshi Mehmed's Religious Complex in Çarşamba. By the time Gazanfer's madrasa was completed, though, Habeshi Mehmed Agha had

---

[46] Ibid., I: 34.
[47] *TDVİA*, s.v. "Gazanfer Ağa Medresesi," by Semavi Eyice; Fetvacı, *Picturing History*, 253–56. Today it is the Gazanfer Ağa Madrasa Educational and Cultural Center, which offers religious instruction and related services.

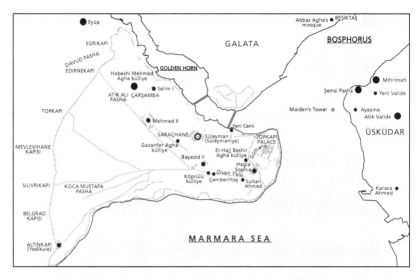

Map 4.1 Istanbul, showing neighborhoods where Chief Harem Eunuchs
endowed structures.

already left his mark on a part of Istanbul to the northwest of Saraçhane (see
Map 4.1). Here, in the neighborhood now known as Çarşamba, just south of
the Golden Horn, Davud Agha built a religious complex for him.[48] Erected in
1584–85, while Davud was still a deputy to Sinan, it comprises a Friday
mosque, a school for the study of sayings of the Prophet Muhammad
(*dar al-hadith*), a double bath (*hammam*), a fountain, and the eunuch's tomb,
along with a Sufi convent (*zaviye*), about which I will have more to say in
Chapter 9. Of these structures, the mosque, bath, and tomb are still standing.
The mosque is small but imposing, richly decorated with tiles from the western
Anatolian town of Iznik (the Byzantine Nicaea), long the center of Ottoman
tile manufacture (see Figure 4.1). Habeshi Mehmed's tomb, which stands to
one side of the mosque, has obviously suffered from clumsy restoration
attempts in the comparatively recent past; stuck to one external corner is what
looks like a bit of Byzantine-era *spolia*.

Necipoğlu has noted the mosque's location in a neighborhood very near the
Greek Orthodox patriarchate. In order to clear space for the complex, in fact,
Habeshi Mehmed Agha bought up the houses of the Greek Christians who

---

[48] Hafız Hüseyin Ayvansarayi, *The Garden of the Mosques: Hafız Hüseyin Ayvansarayî's Guide
to the Muslim Monuments of Ottoman Istanbul*, trans. and annotated by Howard Crane (Leiden,
2000), 218–19; Necipoğlu, *Age of Sinan*, 497–501.

Figure 4.1 Habeshi Mehmed Agha's mosque in Istanbul's Çarşamba district. Author's photos.

lived in the area.[49] The neighborhood had been a pivotal part of the old Byzantine capital: just down the hill was the palace of Blachernae, which the Byzantine emperors used from 1081 until the Ottoman conquest of Constantinople.[50] The construction of the mosque, *dar al-hadith*, and Sufi convent helped to rebrand the district as a site of state-sponsored Ottoman Sunni Islam. Meanwhile, the public bath catered to a growing Muslim population in what had been a heavily Greek Christian neighborhood.[51] It also produced revenue for the upkeep of the mosque, *dar al-hadith*, and Sufi convent, as did a number of shops and rooms that were to be rented to married couples.[52]

Habeshi Mehmed's complex was the third in a series of imperial complexes to change the religious complexion of the district: Mehmed the Conqueror built the Fatih ("Conqueror") complex to the southwest between 1463 and

[49] Necipoğlu, *Age of Sinan*, 499.
[50] John Julius Norwich, *A Short History of Byzantium* (New York, NY, 1997), 301, 304, 318, 380.
[51] Jane Hathaway, "Habeşi Mehmed Agha: The First Chief Harem Eunuch (Darüssaade Ağası) of the Ottoman Empire," in *The Islamic Scholarly Tradition: Studies in History, Law, and Thought in Honor of Professor Michael Allan Cook*, eds. Asad Q. Ahmed et al. (Leiden, 2011), 179–95; André Raymond, "Les bains publics au Caire à la fin du XVIIIe siècle," *Annales islamologiques* 8 (1969): 129–50.
[52] Necipoğlu, *Age of Sinan*, 499.

1470, while the mosque complex of Sultan Selim I was erected to the east in 1522.[53] The chronicler Selaniki Mustafa Efendi hints at the topographical connection among these three mosque complexes in his account of Habeshi Mehmed Agha's death, noting that prayers were recited for the eunuch in the harem section of the Fatih mosque before his body was removed to his tomb in Çarşamba for interment.[54]

Closer to Topkapı, along the processional route known as Divan Yolu, Habeshi Mehmed Agha founded a madrasa and two of the distinctive Qur'an school–fountain combinations known in Ottoman Turkish as *sebil-mekteb*. These will be discussed in Chapter 9. In combination with his complex in Çarşamba, these structures demonstrate that in the core part of Istanbul that had served as the Byzantine capital, Habeshi Mehmed endowed monuments that asserted the Ottoman and, more generally, the Sunni Muslim presence in the city. The siting of the individual foundations reflects a concern to assert this relatively new political and religious reality not only in the central areas that were now associated with the Ottoman dynasty (near Topkapı and the Old Palace) but also in the districts most closely associated with Byzantine authority and the power of the Greek Orthodox Church.

Structures in Üsküdar. Meanwhile, in the district of Üsküdar on the Asian side of the Bosphorus, Habeshi Mehmed's endowments added to a string of foundations established in the mid- to late sixteenth century on the waterfront and in the neighborhood just to the east by imperial women and courtiers. In the 1540s, Süleyman's daughter Mihrimah Sultan (1522–78) had commissioned a Friday mosque complex, designed by Sinan, along the Üsküdar waterfront; it was joined in 1580 by the mosque–tomb complex, also designed by Sinan and located just to the north, of Shemsi Ahmed Pasha (1492–1580), a veteran statesman who had served in the governing councils of Süleyman and Selim II before becoming grand vizier under Murad III.

Then, in 1583, Murad III's mother, Nurbanu, founded a massive religious complex, likewise designed by Sinan, on the crest of a hill sloping down to the waterfront. Now known as the Eski Valide or Atik Valide ("Old Sultan's Mother") complex to differentiate it from the Yeni Valide ("New Sultan's Mother") complex founded by the mother of Ahmed III in the early eighteenth century, it consisted of a Friday mosque, madrasa, library, soup kitchen, Sufi convent, Qur'an school, school for Qur'an-reciters (*dar al-qurra*), and hospital, with an associated public bath and caravanserai producing revenue for the upkeep of the charitable institutions.[55] Nurbanu named Habeshi Mehmed superintendent of this endowment; in this capacity, he enlarged her mosque after her death that same year and, to provide additional revenue for its

---

[53] Hathaway, "Habeşi Mehmed Agha," 189.   [54] Selaniki, *Selaniki Tarihi*, I: 229–30.
[55] https://archnet.org/resources, under "Iskele Camii," "Semsi Pasa," and "Atik Valide Külliyesi."

maintenance, endowed a garden that he owned near the complex and established several fountains nearby.[56]

These constructions all served to place the Ottoman stamp on a district of Istanbul that had not been part of the Byzantine capital but was of great strategic importance. During the thirteenth and early fourteenth centuries, the Byzantines had used Üsküdar as a defensive outpost from which to ward off attacks by the steadily advancing Ottomans. For the Ottomans, Üsküdar served as a staging area for the sultan's campaigns in the east, including the conquest of the Mamluk Sultanate and the seemingly endless expeditions against the Safavids. It was also the point of departure for the annual pilgrimage caravan to Mecca, which served to highlight the Ottoman sultan's status as custodian of the holy cities of Mecca and Medina. In short, the neighborhood played a not insignificant role in the dynasty's legitimacy. It was arguably of particular importance to the women of the imperial family, who, unlike the sultans, occasionally made the pilgrimage and who endowed numerous charitable works along the pilgrimage route and in the holy cities themselves. Meanwhile, Habeshi Mehmed's concern for the welfare of the holy cities, in connection with his supervision of the Evkafü'l-Haremeyn, would have enhanced the importance of Üsküdar in his eyes, as well.

Apart from his additions to the Atik Valide complex, Habeshi Mehmed Agha endowed a number of relatively modest structures inland from Üsküdar's waterfront, perhaps in an effort to provide services for a growing Muslim population in an area that was still relatively sparsely inhabited. Rather ironically, all of these edifices were razed during the first half of the twentieth century to accommodate neighborhood development. They included two mosques for daily prayer (Turkish, *mescid*; Arabic, *masjid*). One of these was attached to a Qur'an school. The other, which drew its revenue from a number of shops and a bread oven, was expanded into a Friday mosque by the immensely influential Chief Eunuch el-Hajj Beshir Agha in the early eighteenth century; even this, however, did not save it from destruction 200 years later. Near both his mosques Habeshi Mehmed endowed public fountains (Turkish singular, *çeşme*).[57]

İsmail Geçidi. Habeshi Mehmed's most grandiose pious endowment, though, was his project at İsmail Geçidi ("The Ford of Ismail"), today Izmail in southwestern Ukraine, situated in the Danube Delta near where the river flows into the Black Sea. Selim II had settled Nogay Tatars on this strategically valuable site in 1569 so as to secure it against encroachment by either the

---

[56] Necipoğlu, *Age of Sinan*, 499; Hathaway, "Habeşi Mehmed Agha," 189–91; www.uskudar.bel.tr/tr/main/erehber/tarihi-mekanlar/39.

[57] Ayvansarayi, *Garden of the Mosques*, 504–5, 515; Hathaway, "Habeşi Mehmed Agha," 189–90.

Habsburgs or the Russians. The surrounding countryside was a key grain-growing region that also supplied regular levies of soldiery to the Ottoman armies, both while the *devshirme* was in force and after it was abandoned. Although it was not in danger of falling into enemy hands until the Russo-Ottoman wars of the late eighteenth century, it played a critical role in provisioning Ottoman armies engaged against the Habsburgs and the Russians, and in provisioning the imperial capital.

İsmail Geçidi's chief attraction to Habeshi Mehmed was probably as a source of grain for the Evkafü'l-Haremeyn, to which it was endowed, and for Istanbul. This would explain why he petitioned Murad III to allow him to build a new settlement on the site so as to provide security for traffic along the Danube.[58] The new town, officially named Bağdad-ı Mehmedabad ("Mehmed's Town, the Gift of God") after its founder, centered on a fortified castle, inside which Habeshi Mehmed commissioned a Friday mosque. Following Habeshi Mehmed's death in 1591, funds from İsmail Geçidi's endowment were used to build a Qur'an school, a caravanserai, a public bath, and a number of shops to enhance the town's revenue-producing potential.[59] The endowment, meanwhile, remained under the supervision of the acting Chief Harem Eunuch.[60]

Habeshi Mehmed Agha's interest in İsmail Geçidi was, obviously, hardly a fluke. Rather, his constructions there contributed to commercial security in the region while, at the same time, helping to supply the endowments for which he was responsible. In fortifying the area, moreover, Habeshi Mehmed set a precedent. Some 150 years later, as Chapter 7 will explain, el-Hajj Beshir Agha would take a similar interest in the towns of Sulina, Romania, east of Ismail Geçidi in the Danube Delta, and Sistova (modern-day Svishtov, Bulgaria), located some 200 kilometers to the southwest, also along the Danube.[61]

In contrast to Gazanfer Agha, then, Habeshi Mehmed commissioned numerous charitable and economic projects at various locations in Istanbul and even, in the case of İsmail Geçidi, at a far remove from the imperial capital. Unquestionably, the Evkafü'l-Haremeyn enabled him to commission so lavishly, for most of these structures were endowed to the Evkaf. The properties associated with them produced revenue and provisions not only for these local charitable concerns but also for Mecca and Medina. So the difference in scope between Habeshi Mehmed's architectural patronage and that of Gazanfer Agha stems from the former's supervision of the Evkaf, which engendered the competition between the two eunuchs in the first place.

---

[58] Necipoğlu, *Age of Sinan*, 499.   [59] Ibid.   [60] Naima, *Tarih-i Naima*, III: 1442.
[61] Hathaway, *Beshir Agha*, 100.

Habeshi Mehmed's built legacy, which shaped Istanbul's urban topography and left a permanent mark on the Danube Delta, was appropriate to an empire in expansionist mode. The structures he commissioned in Istanbul catered to a growing Sunni Muslim population in parts of the city that had formerly been occupied entirely by Greek Christians or that had barely been occupied at all. His new settlement at İsmail Geçidi, meanwhile, brought Sunni Muslim infrastructure to a region where it had never before existed. Collectively, his architectural commissions projected the image of a powerful Sunni Muslim empire that was triumphantly expansionist yet well administered and protective of its subjects. The Chief Harem Eunuch, meanwhile, supported the dynasty, even stepping in to fill power vacuums such as the one created by Sokollu's assassination, and enabled it to fulfill these obligations. A more pointed version of this message would be conveyed by the painted images that memorialized the eunuch, as Chapter 11 will demonstrate.

Conclusion

Habeshi Mehmed Agha's career as Chief Harem Eunuch played out entirely under Murad III and virtually coincided with Murad's reign, minus some four years. In fact, his career was inextricably linked to Murad III's reign and the specific palace factions that existed at that time. Following the death of the extraordinarily powerful grand vizier Sokollu Mehmed Pasha in 1579, Habeshi Mehmed championed the emerging faction led by Murad III's mother, Nurbanu Sultan, against the faction led by Murad's favorite concubine, Safiye Sultan, and the Chief Threshold Eunuch Gazanfer Agha. At the same time, he acquired clients within the Third Court who ultimately rose to leadership positions in the Ottoman military-administrative hierarchy. His architectural patronage reflects these factional priorities to some degree but also projects an image of the Ottoman dynasty as a pious, even divinely ordained, line that provided justice and preserved societal stability while triumphantly expanding militarily.

From one standpoint, then, Habeshi Mehmed's distinctive career resulted from his success in playing the game of factional politics. But from a much broader perspective, it was the delayed result of the Ottoman conquest of Egypt and the Hijaz, which gave the Ottoman sultan custodianship of Islam's holy cities and the endowments that sustained them, along with unprecedented access to the East African slave trade routes along which eunuchs were imported into Ottoman lands. This is not to imply, however, that any harem eunuch, or any Ottoman courtier, could have acquired the specific combination of wealth, patronage ties, and influence, including connections in Egypt, that Habeshi Mehmed amassed. Had it not been for this combination, he might not have received supervision of the Evkafü'l-Haremeyn, which was the most lasting precedent he set during his tenure as Chief Harem Eunuch.

The other precedents that Habeshi Mehmed Agha set, above all that of the Chief Harem Eunuch's participation in court factionalism and his competition with the Chief Threshold Eunuch and the Third Court pages more generally, would have far-reaching implications during the crisis years of the early 1600s, when a series of youthful sultans, often heirless or with only underaged heirs, took the throne. This period of crisis is the subject of the next chapter.

5   The Crisis Years of the Seventeenth Century

Toward the end of the sixteenth century, the Ottoman Empire entered a multifaceted crisis that extended through the first half of the seventeenth century. This crisis was at once climatic, economic, demographic, military, and dynastic. Drought brought on by the Little Ice Age of the early seventeenth century devastated central Anatolia, the Ottoman Empire's breadbasket, and forced hundreds of thousands, if not millions, of peasants off their land.[1] Their plight was exacerbated by galloping inflation, which caused prices of agricultural commodities and finished goods alike to leap between 400 percent and 600 percent between 1489 and 1605.[2] Though quite a number of young male peasants had found employment as mercenary supplements to the Janissaries in the Long War (1593–1606) that the Ottomans were fighting against the Roman Catholic Habsburg Empire, they returned from their tours of duty to find their farms ruined by drought and inflation. They therefore put their matchlocks to good use holding up trade caravans and robbing travelers, or forming bandit gangs around mercenary strongmen. Thus, according to the conventional wisdom, these disgruntled mercenaries lay at the root of the infamous Jelali Rebellions, which engulfed Anatolia in chaos during these years.[3]

This chapter focuses on the dynastic component of the crisis, which directly affected the way that the Chief Harem Eunuch, and harem eunuchs generally, operated. Still, the dynastic crisis cannot be understood outside the context

---

[1] Sam White, *The Climate of Rebellion in the Early Modern Ottoman Empire* (Cambridge, 2011), especially part 2; Michael A. Cook, *Population Pressure in Rural Anatolia, 1450–1600* (London, 1972); Leila Erder and Suraiya Faroqhi, "Population Rise and Fall in Anatolia, 1550–1620," *Middle Eastern Studies* 15 (1979): 322–45.

[2] Ömer Lutfi Barkan, "The Price Revolution of the Sixteenth Century: A Turning Point in the Economic History of the Near East," trans. Justin McCarthy, *International Journal of Middle East Studies* 6 (1975): 3–28, especially 5–6, 9–12, 15–16, 22, 26; Şevket Pamuk, *A Monetary History of the Ottoman Empire* (Cambridge, 2000), chapter 7.

[3] Mustafa Akdağ, *Celali İsyanları (1550–1603)* (Ankara, 1963); William J. Griswold, *The Great Anatolian Rebellion, 1000–1020/1591–1611* (Berlin, 1983).

of the crisis as a whole, for it was intrexicably intertwined with the other elements of the crisis. Rampant inflation devastated the value of the imperial Janissaries' and cavalry's salaries, which they often received in debased coinage in any case. These fiscal woes, combined with the stresses of continuous military engagement against the Habsburgs and the Jelalis, contributed to an alarming upsurge in rebellions by these two regiments. Inflation likewise made the expanding harem, with its enormous contingent of eunuchs, prohibitively expensive to maintain. And since the Ottoman economy was increasingly monetized, inflation affected every sector, making all types of goods and services more costly. Monetization resulted in part from a surge in international trade, in which palace functionaries appointed to govern the Ottoman provinces were eager to engage, using hired mercenaries to police the trade routes. These governors thus gained a new source of non-palace-generated income, along with a new source of military manpower, that they could use to finance rebellion against the central authority.[4] Rebellious "Jelali governors" would become a looming threat to the Ottoman state by the mid-seventeenth century.

At the palace level, the dynastic crisis exacerbated some of the political trends that were already visible during the reign of Murad III. In particular, the harem was now unquestionably the main locus of political influence in the palace; rival political factions were now rooted in the harem, even if they drew adherents from other parts of the palace and society (Table 5.1). At the same time, the competition between these factions acquired a dangerous new military component as the two principal corps of palace soldiery backed opposing sides.

After exploring the nature of the dynastic crisis and the altered brands of factionalism to which it gave rise, this chapter examines the interplay of these types of factionalism in the careers of four key Chief Eunuchs of the crisis era. Osman Agha's career features an alliance between the Chief Harem Eunuch and the Chief Threshold Eunuch, despite ongoing friction between the corps of eunuchs whom they represented. The lengthy tenure of el-Hajj Mustafa Agha, which forms the chapter's centerpiece, illustrates how far the Chief Eunuch's patronage network could extend in the absence of factions headed by powerful harem women. Sünbül Agha's misadventures on the high seas point up the geopolitical hazards that could result from losing the game of factional politics. Finally, the brief but tumultuous run of Lala Süleyman Agha demonstrates the violence that had come to pervade harem-based factionalism by mid-century.

---

[4] Tezcan, *Second Ottoman Empire*, chapter 1 and 141–45.

Table 5.1 *Major officers of the harem and Third Court during the crisis era*[a]

Harem		Third Court	
		Chief Threshold Eunuch (Kapı Ağası) *Beyazi Mustafa (concurrently Chief Harem Eunuch) Malatyalı Ismail (concurrently Chief Harem Eunuch)*	
Sultan's Mother *Kösem (Murad IV, Ibrahim)* *Turhan (Mehmed IV)*	Chief Harem Eunuch *Server/Sünbül* Osman Abdurrezzak Cevher *El-Hajj Mustafa* Süleyman Idris *(Çaçu) Ibrahim* Sünbül *Taş Yatur Ali Lala Süleyman*	**Gate of Felicity (Babüssaade)** Palace Treasurer (Hazinedar Başı) Palace Head (Saray Ağası) Boys of the Threshold (Kapı Oğlanı)	**Privy Chamber (Hass Oda)** Privy Chamber Head (Hass Oda Başı) Sword-Bearer (Silahdar) *Siyavush* Valet (Çuhadar) Stirrup-Holder (Rikabdar) Pages *Gürcü Mehmed*

[a] Italics indicate individuals named in the chapter.

The Dynastic Crisis and the Harem

At the root of the dynastic crisis was a dearth of adult male heirs to the Ottoman throne. A sense of unease is evident during the reign of Murad III's son and successor, Mehmed III (r. 1595–1603). Unlike previous Ottoman sultans, Mehmed did not send his two sons, Ahmed and Mahmud, out to govern Anatolian provinces in order to learn statecraft.[5] Instead, they were raised in the harem, where their grandfather, we recall, had taken up residence. There, while still minors, they were educated by a tutor in a school constructed specially within the quarters of the African harem eunuchs.[6]

In June 1603, Sultan Mehmed had Prince Mahmud executed on suspicion of plotting to depose him.[7] Six months later, the sultan himself died, catapulting thirteen-year-old Ahmed onto the throne. Too young to have sired an heir, Ahmed came perilously close to succumbing to smallpox a few months later.[8]

---

[5] Peirce, *Imperial Harem*, 97–103; Günhan Börekçi, "Factions and Favorites at the Courts of Ahmed I (r. 1603–1617) and His Immediate Predecessors," unpublished Ph.D. dissertation, Ohio State University, 2010, 81–89; Fetvacı, *Picturing History*, 44.

[6] Necipoğlu, *Architecture, Ceremonial, and Power*, 164; Fetvacı, *Picturing History*, 34.

[7] Hasanbeyzade, *Hasan Bey-zade Tarihi*, III: 765; Naima, *Tarih-i Naima*, I: 228; Börekçi, "Factions and Favorites," 65–68.

[8] Börekçi, "Factions and Favorites," 83–84.

Had he died, the Ottoman male line would have come to an end. As it was, he survived to father three sons, each of whom later became sultan. This in itself indicated a critical change in succession procedure: the new sultan no longer executed his surviving brothers in order to prevent rebellion. Instead, sibling princes continued to reside in the Topkapı harem; once he had reached maturity, a prince moved into an apartment in a section at the rear of the harem complex known, appropriately, as the cage, or *kafes*. Here, his household was managed by a lower-ranking harem eunuch who functioned as a sort of combination butler and accountant.[9]

But the fortunes of Ahmed I's successors only exacerbated fears for the future of the Ottoman dynasty. For the next four decades, the Ottoman throne was occupied by minors, inexperienced twenty-somethings, and/or men of questionable mental competence. In this atmosphere, harem women and eunuchs filled the inevitable power vacuum at the Ottoman court, appointing, or at least endorsing, viziers and setting policy. Among the imperial women, Ahmed I's favorite concubine, Mahpeyker Kösem Sultan, the mother of Sultans Murad IV and Ibrahim, and the grandmother of Mehmed IV, is especially famous, or infamous, for wielding inordinate influence. But she, like the other women, operated in partnership with an increasingly influential corps of harem eunuchs, up to and including the Chief Harem Eunuch. In short, the crisis made the sultan's mother and the Chief Harem Eunuch more powerful than ever.

Palace Factionalism during the Crisis Years

Under the pressures generated by the crisis, factionalism among rival clientage networks within the palace intensified and grew more complex. We can identify four layers, or types, of factionalism at play during the crisis years. Most visible to court chroniclers and palace personnel was the competition between rival patronage networks rooted in the harem. The struggle between them was fiercest when they were headed by the sultan's mother and his wife or favorite concubine, as in the case of Nurbanu's and Safiye's factions, whose struggle informed the career of Habeshi Mehmed Agha and, as we will see below, resonated well after the deaths of two of the principal actors. Far more deadly was the competition between Mahpeyker Kösem, mentioned above, and Turhan, favorite of the mentally unstable Ibrahim and mother of Mehmed IV. In the absence of such influential women, the Chief Harem Eunuch's own patronage network might take center stage, as in the case of el-Hajj Mustafa Agha. The heads of these factions could cultivate clients from

---

[9] Bon, in *Relazioni di ambasciatori veneti al Senato*, XIII: 92; Penzer, *The Harem*, 128.

the harem, the Third Court, and outside the palace entirely, as Mustafa Agha's example will make clear.

During the crisis years, palace factionalism converged with a dangerous and far more dichotomous form of factionalism between the two principal corps of palace soldiery: the Janissaries and the imperial cavalry, or *sipahis*. Both regiments were *kapı kulları*, literally "servants of the gate," referring to the Orta Kapı, the grand, twin-towered gate separating Topkapı's First and Second courts. As such, they received a regular salary in cash, clothing, and provisions. (The imperial *sipahis*, unlike their counterparts in the Ottoman provinces, did not hold the grants of land revenue known as *tımars*.) Yet although these were both salaried regiments serving the sultan, they nurtured the same kind of competitive rivalry, sometimes degenerating into open hostility, toward each other that seems to characterize infantry and cavalry forces in a wide array of societies. The depth of their enmity meant that if the Janissaries supported one palace faction, the *sipahis* would almost inevitably support the other.

Exacerbating the interregimental struggle was a growing challenge to the palace *kullar* as a whole. Doubts about the *kullar*'s military effectiveness and efforts to supplement them with non-*kul* elements made the regiments restive and quick to resort to violence to protect their interests. The ultimate outcome of this development was young Sultan Osman II's murder by palace *kullar* in 1622.

Long before then, however, the two regiments of palace soldiery began to align themselves with competing palace factions based in the harem. By choosing sides in this fashion, they effectively militarized the palace factions, becoming a source of armed might that the leaders of the competing factions could use as leverage or threat. They thus introduced a dangerous uncertainty into the factional rivalry since, with the addition of deadly force, it could now spiral into armed confrontation at a moment's notice. The Chief Harem Eunuchs of the crisis years either sided with one or another regiment or tried to play them off against each other.

The rare occasions when the two regiments made common cause, however, put the Chief Harem Eunuchs in mortal danger. More than one Chief Eunuch fell victim to this violence, as will become clear below.

Opposition to the *kullar* generated a third kind of factionalism that Metin Kunt has described as ethnoregional, pitting "westerners" against "easterners."[10] "Westerners" in this context were the *kullar* themselves, who were largely, though not entirely, *devshirme* recruits from the Balkans and perhaps western Anatolia.[11] The Anatolian peasant mercenaries who sparked the Jelali

[10] Kunt, "Ethno-Regional (*Cins*) Solidarity."
[11] Uzunçarşılı, *Kapukulu Ocakları*, II: 146, 148, 152, 162–68.

rebellions represented an "eastern" alternative to the *kullar*, but so too did the mamluks from the Caucasus who were an increasingly popular source of palace pages. Many of the rebellious "Jelali governors" referenced above were of Caucasian, particularly Abkhazian, mamluk origin. Caucasian mamluk officals are increasingly visible among the clients of the crisis-era Chief Harem Eunuchs, above all el-Hajj Mustafa and Lala Süleyman Aghas. Competition between these "easterners" and the "western" *kullar* did not become obtrusive in palace circles until the middle of the seventeenth century. Still, in cultivating ties to "easterners," the Chief Eunuchs sought to avoid dependence on the increasingly tenuous good will of the *kullar*.

A similar sort of undercurrent to the friction between the harem factions and between the soldiery regiments was the sustained tension between the African and white eunuchs of Topkapı Palace and, by extension, between the spaces – the harem and the Third Court, including the *hass oda* – that they supervised. This fourth brand of factionalism was neither as dichotomous nor as violent as the rivalry of harem-based patronage networks or the clashes between Janissaries and *sipahi*s. As we have already seen in the case of Habeshi Mehmed's rivalry with Gazanfer Agha, harem and Third Court eunuchs habitually cultivated clients in each other's "territory." Still, the division between the two corps of eunuchs did generate real competition and even appears to have become something of a trope, a means of framing and understanding the spatial and occupational divisions in the private areas of the palace. This is evident in the verbiage of certain court chroniclers and intellectuals, such as Mustafa Ali, Selaniki, and Derviş Abdullah, who inveigh against African eunuchs, and others, such as the author of *Rafa'ilü'l-gubuş*, who extol their virtues (these writers were cited and/or discussed in Chapters 2 and 4). The black-white dichotomy was sealed for posterity in paintings, to be discussed in Chapter 11, depicting black and white eunuchs as two "sides" of the court, or one black and one white eunuch as a matched pair. These are the trappings of entrenched bilateral factionalism – identifying colors, rituals, stories – that I have delineated elsewhere.[12] Collectively, they may have comprised a sort of rhetorical bilateral factionalism that went well beyond the objective reality.

Like East-West factionalism, black-white factionalism almost never matched up exactly with the rivalry between harem factions or between the two regiments of palace soldiery. Thus, we cannot speak of a sultan's mother/harem eunuch/*sipahi*/easterner faction, for example, facing off against a sultan's favorite/Third Court eunuch/Janissary/westerner faction. Instead, the harem eunuch–Third Court eunuch competition remained in the background, informing but never completely determining the formation of palace factions. Yet it

---

[12] Hathaway, *A Tale of Two Factions*, 27–41.

did feed into a more general tension between the harem and the Third Court that implicated the personnel of both these parts of the palace. This tension was both racial and spatial. Racially, of course, it pitted the African harem eunuchs against the non-African Third Court pages. Spatially, it was a competition for the sultan's presence. The Third Court was obviously on the losing end of this spatial competition, especially during the reigns of underaged sultans who seldom left the harem at all. But this did not mean that the officials of the Third Court, including the Chief Threshold Eunuch and the officers of the *hass oda*, suddenly became insignificant. Certain *hass oda* officials might become grand viziers, which made them particularly desirable members of the palace factions. They might also try to assert themselves against the Chief Harem Eunuch and his allies. The historian Naima, writing in the early eighteenth century, clearly perceives a harem–*hass oda* rivalry;[13] his perceptions may reflect this underlying tension more than they do an actual episode of factionalism. His depiction of this rivalry taps into the sort of binaries that were available for descriptions of black versus white friction.

During the crisis years, then, we see the Chief Harem Eunuch participating, to varying degrees, in these four patterns of factionalism. Because of the addition of the palace soldiery to factional rivalries, the threat of violence was omnipresent. Two Chief Harem Eunuchs, one Chief Threshold Eunuch, and one sultan met violent ends – and this does not even count the Chief Eunuchs who died violently in exile or en route to exile. And the last Chief Eunuch to be considered in this chapter, Lala Süleyman Agha, supposedly murdered the mother of a sultan with his own hands.

Osman Agha, or the Gazanfer Interlude

In the wake of Habeshi Mehmed Agha's death in 1591, the status of the Chief Harem Eunuch became somewhat uncertain. After all, Habeshi Mehmed had acquired the supervision of the Evkafü'l-Haremeyn and the other perquisites of his office largely because of his personal influence. His exalted status was not automatically inherited by succeeding Chief Harem Eunuchs. Now that he was gone, in any case, the Chief Threshold Eunuch, Gazanfer Agha, asserted himself more generally at the expense of his late rival's immediate successors. The contemporary chronicler Selaniki Mustafa Efendi clearly regarded this as something of a victory for the white eunuchs and other pages of the Third Court. In his account, we read that the next Chief Eunuch, Server Agha, after occupying the post for roughly two years, was exiled to Egypt "for forbidding the pages [of the Third Court] from conducting business with the

---

[13] Naima, *Tarih-i Naima*, III: 1325, 1532–37.

'outside people'" – i.e., the "civilian" population of Istanbul – and confiscating their gains from this trade. The eighteenth-century Chief Harem Eunuch biographer Ahmed Resmi adds that Server was dismissed "because of his hostility and contentiousness" toward the white eunuchs of the Third Court.[14]

This is the first unequivocal indication we have of ongoing tension between the African and white eunuchs of Topkapı Palace, and we can probably assume that Gazanfer helped to stoke this tension. It seems telling that the next Darüssaade Ağası was a Bosnian *devshirme* recruit, Beyazi ("White") Mustafa, who had been posted to Yemen with a Bosnian contingent and, while there, forged a connection with the Ottoman governor, who, on his return to Istanbul, installed Mustafa in the palace corps of white eunuchs. A quarter-century later, Mustafa was named Chief Harem Eunuch, "contrary to custom," to quote Ahmed Resmi. With his appointment, Selaniki tells us, "the white aghas were ordered to control the black aghas by putting obstacles and difficulties [in their way]." After three years, however, he was removed from office because of blindness and failing health.[15]

The next Chief Harem Eunuch was Osman Agha, who, while African, was unquestionably part of Gazanfer's circle of allies. Like Gazanfer, he belonged to the coterie of Mehmed III's mother Safiye, having headed the eunuchs in her personal retinue before he became chief of the harem eunuchs.[16] Safiye and Gazanfer were now unconstrained by any remnant of the old faction of Nurbanu Sultan and her ally Habeshi Mehmed Agha. Even so, there seems to have been little question of Gazanfer's reacquiring supervision of the Evkafü'l-Haremeyn. On the contrary, Osman Agha appears to have expanded and consolidated the Chief Harem Eunuch's control of imperial pious foundations during his ten years in office. Selaniki links him to the Evkafü'l-Haremeyn the first time he mentions him: "Osman Agha, who had served in the superintendency of the pious foundations of Medina in the harem [and] attained the position of Chief Harem Eunuch."[17]

What occasions his appearance in Selaniki's chronicle at this juncture, at the beginning of Ramazan 1004/late April 1596, is his overhaul of the fiscal administration of both the Evkafü'l-Haremeyn and the sultanic foundations that were not connected to Mecca and Medina. Specifically, he consolidated the financial registers of all these foundations and placed them under a single accountant.[18] At the beginning of May 1598, Osman Agha received the

---

[14] Selaniki, *Selaniki Tarihi*, I: 281; Ahmed Resmi, *Hamiletü'l-kübera*, 46. Some sources list a Sünbül Agha who succeeded Server, but they appear to be the same person. See *Defter-i Ağayan-i Darüssaade*, Türk Tarih Kurumu Archives, MS Y 86, published as an appendix to *Hamiletü'l-kübera*, 164; Mehmed Süreyya, *Sicill-i Osmani* (Istanbul, 1308–15/1890–97; reprint, Westmead, Farnborough, Hampshire, UK, 1971), IV: 724ff.

[15] *Hamiletü'l-kübera*, 46; Selaniki, *Selaniki Tarihi*, I: 281; II: 568.   [16] *Hamiletü'l-kübera*, 46.

[17] Selaniki, *Selaniki Tarihi*, II: 594.   [18] Ibid., II: 594.

supervision of the endowments for the great sultanic religious complexes in Istanbul, including those of Mehmed the Conqueror, Bayezid II, Selim I, and Süleyman the Magnificent. He immediately replaced the *mütevelli*s, or overseers "on the spot," of these endowments with military officers who had won his personal trust.[19] Two years later, he named another such officer administrator (*emin*) of the mosque–soup kitchen complex that Safiye Sultan was launching at the port of Eminönü; in that capacity, he served as Safiye's agent (*vekil*) in all matters pertaining to the complex's endowment. This massive complex, now known as Yeni Cami ("New Mosque"), would be abandoned on Mehmed III's death in 1603, to be resurrected and brought to completion only in 1665.[20] As for the new administrator, he became Osman Agha's *kethüda*, or steward, and was also appointed *mütevelli* of the tombs of Selim II and Murad III near the great Ayasofya mosque in Istanbul.[21]

Selaniki, who served as an accountant in the pious foundations administration during these years, is a uniquely authoritative source on these changes. Still, his editorial comments on them should be taken with a grain of salt since he obviously took a dim view of Osman Agha and, from all appearances, of African harem eunuchs generally. Noting Habeshi Mehmed Agha's death in 1591, he remarks, "That black calamity has departed from this world!"[22] In his account of Osman Agha's appointment of new overseers to the sultanic foundations, he accuses the eunuch of awarding the positions to undeserving low-lifes in exchange for bribes, and turning over the offices frequently in order to increase his take. In these circumstances, he claims, the buildings that the endowments were designed to maintain fell into disrepair while the charitable works they supported struggled to survive.[23] Meanwhile, he describes the new administrator whom Osman had appointed to Safiye's mosque complex as uniquely unqualified for his new duties: illiterate, opinionated, devoid of business sense, heedless of the law.[24]

Although little is known about Selaniki's life and career, apart from what he divulges about his posts in the pious foundation accounts administration, we can probably conclude that he, rather like Mustafa Ali at about the same time, was profoundly uncomfortable with the Chief Harem Eunuch's steadily growing economic and political influence. He may have seen Osman Agha's attempts to fill the pious foundations administration with his protégés as a threat to his own employment, and more broadly as an effort by the Chief Eunuch to monopolize control of all imperial endowments.

---

[19] Ibid., II: 740, 741–42.
[20] Marc David Baer, "The Great Fire of 1660 and the Islamization of Christian and Jewish Space in Istanbul," *International Journal of Middle East Studies* 36 (2004): 166–70.
[21] Selaniki, *Selaniki Tarihi*, II: 849–50.   [22] Ibid., I: 229–30; Necipoğlu, *Age of Sinan*, 498.
[23] *Selaniki Tarihi*, II: 740, 741–42, and Mehmet İpşirli's introduction, I: xvi.
[24] Ibid., II: 849–50.

These changes seem to have occurred with the acquiescence, and perhaps even the encouragement, of Safiye Sultan and her ally Gazanfer Agha. So far from being any sort of rival to Gazanfer, and by extension to Safiye, Osman Agha was regarded by observers as a subordinate member of their team. Gazanfer's influence during the 1590s and the opening years of the seventeenth century can hardly be exaggerated. He engineered the appointments and depositions of a series of grand viziers during this period, going so far as to secure the execution of his fellow eunuch Hadım Hasan Pasha, who had held the office for only five months, in April 1598.[25] The Venetian *bailo* Agostino Nani reported in 1600 that Gazanfer and Safiye ran everything,[26] although other Venetian observers pointed to a broader clique of courtiers around the sultan's mother.[27]

Under Gazanfer, in other words, the Chief Threshold and Chief Harem Eunuchs cooperated, and even formed something of a team. Yet their cooperation did nothing to smooth over the antagonism between the imperial Janissaries, who tended to make common cause with their fellow *devshirme* recruits in the Third Court, and the *sipahi*s, or palace cavalry. Osman Agha, the Chief Harem Eunuch, adopted Gazanfer's and Safiye's preference for the Janissaries over the *sipahi*s. Already frustrated by their prolonged service in the struggle against the Habsburgs, the *sipahi*s instigated a series of rebellions during these years that took aim at Safiye's faction. In 1600, they succeeded in murdering Esperanza Malchi, Safiye's *kira*, the Jewish merchant woman who sold luxury goods to the harem. Having won Safiye's confidence, Malchi had come to wield a good deal of influence at court and had diverted revenues usually earmarked for the *sipahi*s to her own cronies in the palace.[28] As Selaniki explains,

The sergeant major (*çavuşbaşı*) [of the *sipahi*s] found the *kira*-woman, brought her out, put her on a pack horse, and brought her to the pasha's [grand vizier Damad Ibrahim Pasha] house. As she was getting off the horse, the *sipahi*s stabbed her, cut her to pieces, tied a rope to her feet, dragged her away, and left her corpse on the hippodrome. Then a huge group [of *sipahi*s] placed their hands on the holy Qur'an and swore that "Tomorrow we will bring all her children and relatives here."[29]

They did, in fact, succeed in murdering her older son; the younger one saved himself by converting to Islam.

---

[25] Hasanbeyzade, *Hasan Bey-zade Tarihi*, II: 374; III: 518–20, 537–39, 566–72, 690.
[26] Agostino Nani, in *Relazioni di ambasciatori veneti al Senato*, XIII: 37–39.
[27] Pedani, "Safiye's Household and Venetian Diplomacy," 15.
[28] Selaniki, *Selaniki Tarihi*, II: 854–56; Henry Lello, *The Report of Lello, Third English Ambassador to the Sublime Porte*, ed. Orhan Burian (Ankara, 1952), 5–7; Hasan Beyzade, *Hasan Bey-zade Tarihi*, III: 618; Baki Tezcan, "Searching for Osman," unpublished Ph.D. dissertation, Princeton University, 2001, 349; Börekçi, "Factions and Favorites," 48–50.
[29] Selaniki, *Selaniki Tarihi*, II: 855.

The following year, disgruntled *sipahi*s targeted Gazanfer himself, threatening Mehmed III with deposition unless he eliminated him. Gazanfer was saved at the last minute by the intercession of the grand vizier and his lieutenant.[30] In this instance, the rivalry between the Janissaries and the *sipahi*s worked to his advantage since neither corps was powerful enough by itself to bring him down.

In January 1603, though, the seemingly endless Austrian campaign combined with the central authority's mishandling of the Jelali rebellions to draw the two corps together. Soldiers returning from the Austrian front discovered that the Jelalis' ravages in Anatolia had reached unprecedented proportions, causing waves of displaced peasants to flee to Istanbul. They blamed a series of inept commanders of the armies confronting the Jelalis, notably Hadım ("the eunuch") Hüsrev Pasha, whose appointment they believed had been arranged by Gazanfer and Osman Aghas. Infuriated, they marched on the Babüssaade – the threshold in front of the sultan's audience chamber – then dragged Gazanfer and Osman out of the chamber and beheaded them, so that their heads rolled to the feet of the sultan "like a white and a black bead," as the seventeenth-century polymath Katib Çelebi later put it.[31]

Osman's successor, Abdurrezzak, another protégé of Safiye Sultan and Gazanfer Agha, was perhaps best known to Ottoman court chroniclers for his role in the execution of Mehmed III's son, Prince Mahmud, in 1603. According to Hasan Beyzade's version of events, he informed the sultan that a Sufi fortune-teller had predicted that the prince would accomplish great things when his father disappeared. This news prompted Mehmed to have the prince seized and strangled in June 1603.[32] Abdurrezzak himself was deposed when Sultan Ahmed I took the throne the following December; the new sultan perhaps regarded the eunuch as too much the tool of Safiye Sultan, whom he banished to the Old Palace at about the same time. Abdurrezzak was executed in November 1604.[33]

---

[30] Hasan Beyzade, *Hasan Bey-zade Tarihi*, III: 640–41; Nani, in *Relazioni di ambasciatori veneti al Senato*, XIII: 40; Pedani, "Safiye's Household and Venetian Diplomacy," 25; Tezcan, "Searching for Osman," 348; Börekçi, "Factions and Favorites," 51–53.

[31] Katib Çelebi, *Fezleke* (Istanbul, 1286–87/1869–71), I: 185–86. My thanks to Maria Pia Pedani for helping me find this reference. Also Hasan Beyzade, *Hasan Bey-zade Tarihi*, III: 682; Peçevi, *Tarih-i Peçevi*, II: 239–40; Naima, *Tarih-i Naima*, I: 216–17, 220; Ahmed Resmi, *Hamiletü'l-kübera*, 46–47; Pedani, "Safiye's Household and Venetian Diplomacy," 27; Börekçi, "Factions and Favorites," 27–41.

[32] Hasan Beyzade, *Hasan Bey-zade Tarihi*, III: 765; Mehmed bin Mehmed, "Mehmed bin Mehmed Er-Rumî (Edirneli)'nin *Nuhbetü't-tevarih ve'l-ahbar*'ı ile *Tarih-i Al-i Osman*'ının Metni ve Tahlilleri," ed. Abdurrahman Sağırlı, unpublished Ph.D. dissertation, Istanbul University, 2000, 595; Naima, *Tarih-i Naima*, I: 228; Börekçi, "Factions and Favorites," 65–66.

[33] Hasan Beyzade, *Hasan Bey-zade Tarihi*, III: 740; Naima, *Tarih-i Naima*, I: 265; Ahmed Resmi, *Hamiletü'l-kübera*, 47.

El-Hajj Mustafa Agha

Abdurrezzak was succeeded by Cevher (Jawhar) Agha, who held the office from the beginning of 1604 through the autumn of 1605[34] before being replaced by one of the most powerful Chief Eunuchs in Ottoman history, El-Hajj Mustafa Agha. Since making the pilgrimage to Mecca in 1602 – and thus acquiring the honorific title el-Hajj or Hajji, "pilgrim" – Mustafa Agha had been residing in Cairo. But in late 1604, he was recalled to the imperial capital. There, after a year as Ahmed I's boon companion (*musahib*), he rose to Chief Harem Eunuch, a post he would hold for the remainder of Ahmed's reign and beyond.[35] He would have appealed to Ahmed because he did not owe his position to either Safiye Sultan or Gazanfer Agha. Thus, he was able to fill the power vacuum left by Gazanfer's execution in 1603 and Safiye's banishment to the Old Palace in 1604. Small wonder that the Venetian *bailo* Cristoforo Valier reports that the status of the "Chisler Aga" "has grown so great and so commanding that in his manner, his clothing, and his duties he resembles a king, leaving no doubt which one is really the king."[36]

At the same time, Mustafa Agha's already established connections to Egypt and to the holy cities of Mecca and Medina probably made him an attractive candidate for the office of Chief Harem Eunuch since, lest we forget, the Chief Eunuch supervised the imperial pious foundations for the holy cities, which derived much of their revenue, and virtually all of the grain transmitted to Mecca and Medina each year, from Egypt. As Chapter 8 will demonstrate, Mustafa had a major hand in urban development in Cairo before, during, and after his tenure as Chief Harem Eunuch, while also endowing a key religious complex in Mecca. But his role in the expansion of the imperial capital's religious infrastructure was nearly as vast.

The Blue Mosque. In Istanbul, Mustafa Agha was instrumental in the construction of what is today perhaps the city's single most recognizable structure: the Mosque of Sultan Ahmed, popularly known as the Blue Mosque. In August 1609, Sultan Ahmed I launched this almost wildly ambitious project: the first mosque complex founded by an Ottoman sultan in the imperial capital since the days of his great-great-grandfather, Süleyman "the Magnificent,"

---

[34] Cevher is documented in Mustafa Safi, *Zübdetü't-tevarih*, I: 81; Topkapı Palace Archives, D 34, fol. 235a (14 Şaban 1012/17 January 1604); D 4124, p. 2 (mid-Muharrem 1014/ late May–early June 1605); D 2025, fols. 6b, 7a, 7b, 8a (1011–16/1603–8); E 7737/5 (11 Cemaziyelevvel 1013/ 5 October 1604); E 7737/7 (mid-Rebiülevvel 1014/late July–early August 1605); BOA, Maliyeden Müdevver D 169, p. 2 (1013/1604–5). I am grateful to Günhan Börekçi for bringing the archival documents to my attention. Several later sources list a Reyhan Agha, who, however, is not mentioned in contemporary sources.

[35] Mustafa Safi, *Zübdetü't-tevarih*, I: 80–81.

[36] Cristoforo Valier (term 1612–16), in *Relazioni di ambasciatori veneti al Senato*, XIII: 302–3.

whom Ahmed idolized.[37] The mosque was designed to be larger than Süley-man's mosque, with six minarets to the Süleymaniye's four. It was built by the court architect, Sedefkar Mehmed Agha, who had been trained by the legend-ary Sinan, at the southern end of Istanbul's hippodrome, facing the ancient mass of Ayasofya and, beyond it, Topkapı itself. Overlooking the confluence of the Bosphorus and the Sea of Marmara, it was almost as strategically located as the palace. Just to the north were a madrasa, a Qur'an school, a school for professional Qur'an-reciters (*dar al-qurra*), an insane asylum, a soup kitchen, a hostel for traveling dervishes (*tabhane*), and a public fountain; Sultan Ahmed was later entombed on the site.[38]

Mustafa Agha played a role in the erection of this mosque that was greater than any Chief Harem Eunuch had ever played in an imperial construction project. There was nothing novel in the Chief Harem Eunuch's supervising an imperial pious foundation: Osman Agha had taken charge of numerous sulta-nic endowments in addition to the Evkafü'l-Haremeyn, while Mustafa Agha himself, years later, served as supervisor and *mütevelli* of Yeni Cami, the mosque complex started by Safiye Sultan in 1600.[39] For the Chief Eunuch to supervise the endowment of a living sultan, however, was unprecedented. Mustafa Agha even appears to have had a role in the mosque's actual con-struction. Contemporary chroniclers Topçular Katibi Abdülkadir Efendi and Hasan Beyzade have Mustafa Agha working closely with the mosque's first director of construction from the project's inception.[40] Seven years later, Topçular Katibi describes Sedefkar Mehmed, the chief architect, working for Mustafa Agha, assisted by Idris Agha, a harem eunuch who had been appointed director of construction in 1025/1616.[41] (Idris Agha would become Chief Eunuch himself in 1624 and was probably Mustafa's protégé.) Mustafa is mentioned in an inscription on the mosque's exterior façade, on the side facing Topkapı, as the superintendent (*nazir*) of the mosque's construction (see Figure 5.1).[42] This marks the only time in Ottoman history that a Chief Harem Eunuch was included in the inscription of a sultanic mosque.

Osman II. In 1617, Ahmed I died of cholera at the age of twenty-seven. El-Hajj Mustafa Agha was in the harem when the sultan expired and informed the grand vizier of his demise. Since Ahmed's eldest son, Osman, was only

[37] Börekçi, "Factions and Favorites," 109.
[38] Ayvansarayi, *Garden of the Mosques*, 21–22; Zeynep Nayir, *Osmanlı Mimarlığında Sultan Ahmet Külliyesi ve Sonrası* (Istanbul, 1975); https://archnet.org/resources, under "Sultan Ahmet"; Evliya Çelebi, *Seyahatname*, I: 132.
[39] Topçular Katibi, *Topçular Katibi Tarihi*, I: 653–54.
[40] Ibid., I: 561; Hasan Beyzade, *Hasan Bey-zade Tarihi*, III: 884–85; Naima, *Tarih-i Naima*, II: 402.
[41] Topçular Katibi, *Topçular Katibi Tarihi*, I: 647–48.
[42] I am grateful to Günhan Börekçi for drawing my attention to this. For the text of the inscription, see www.ottomaninscriptions.com/verse.aspx?ref=list&bid=2974&hid=4616.

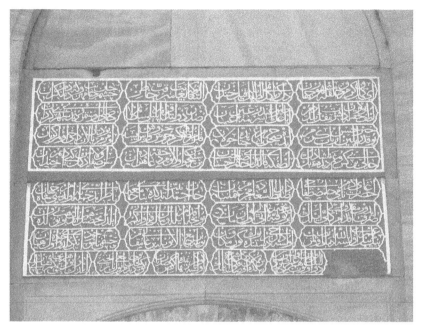

Figure 5.1 Inscription on the façade of the Sultan Ahmed Mosque, naming
el-Hajj Mustafa Agha as superintendent of the mosque's construction.
Photo by Günhan Börekçi.

fourteen years old, his younger brother Mustafa was dragged to the throne
from the *kafes* at the rear of the harem, where he had spent most of his twenty-
five years. Although el-Hajj Mustafa Agha was already close to Osman –
indeed, he had announced his birth in November 1604[43] – he helped to
engineer Sultan Mustafa's peaceful accession, even though he was aware that
Mustafa was of questionable mental ability or stability.

The narrative of what ensued has been explored thoroughly by Gabriel
Piterberg, Baki Tezcan, and others.[44] Sultan Mustafa's mental impairments
resulted in highly erratic behavior. El-Hajj Mustafa Agha was instrumental
in making Sultan Mustafa's infirmity publicly known and warning high officials of the danger of leaving him on the throne.[45] After three months of

---

[43] Naima, *Tarih-i Naima*, I: 289.
[44] Piterberg, *An Ottoman Tragedy*, especially 16–29, 82–85, 93–98, 108–9; Tezcan, "Looking for
Osman"; Baki Tezcan, "The 1622 Military Rebellion in Istanbul," in *Mutiny and Rebellion in
the Ottoman Empire*, ed. Jane Hathaway (Madison, WI, 2002), 25–27.
[45] Hasanbeyzade, *Hasan Bey-zade Tarihi*, III: 919; Naima, *Tarih-i Naima*, II: 440–41; Piterberg,
An Ottoman Tragedy, 15–16, 93–98.

his unpredictable conduct, el-Hajj Mustafa's faction deposed Mustafa and enthroned Osman. The new sultan, despite his youth, had a number of ideas for reforming the Ottoman administration, chiefly by increasing the sultan's autonomy and decreasing the influence of the *kullar*, overwhelmingly of *devshirme* origin, who had figured prominently in the military rebellions of the past few decades. By bringing Osman to the throne, Mustafa Agha implicitly gave his support to this agenda.

Before any of these reforms could be realized, though, Mustafa Agha was packed off to Egypt by the new grand vizier, İstanköylü Güzelce Ali Pasha ("Handsome Ali Pasha from İstanköy"), whose nickname referred to his first major posting, as governor of the Aegean island of İstanköy, today known as Kos. According to Naima, Güzelce Ali wormed his way into the young sultan's affections with lavish gifts, growing so close to him and, consequently, so powerful that he displaced Mustafa Agha, who had been so instrumental in Osman's accession. Ultimately Güzelce Ali "betrayed" the Chief Eunuch, auctioned off his property, and sent him to Cairo.[46] This was, from all appearances, part of a broader campaign against the Chief Eunuch's coterie, for Güzelce Ali did much the same to at least one of Mustafa Agha's clients around the same time.[47]

Despite all this, el-Hajj Mustafa was replaced as Chief Harem Eunuch by his own protégé, Süleyman Agha – a circumstance that attests to the extraordinary extent of Mustafa Agha's influence at court.[48] By 1620, he had been Chief Eunuch for some fifteen years and, from all appearances, had promoted and trained the entire top stratum of imperial harem eunuchs. Taking up where his predecessor had left off, Süleyman Agha supported the sultan's reformist agenda. Osman II sought to resurrect the activist, publicly visible sultanate of Süleyman the Magnificent's day, when the ruler had executed his brothers on assuming the throne and led the imperial armies in person. Accordingly, Osman commanded the Ottoman army in the spectacularly unsuccessful 1621 campaign against Hotin in what is now western Ukraine – where roughly a third of the army, some 40,000 soldiers, were killed – and ordered the execution of his brother Mehmed, albeit he spared his two other brothers, both sons of Ahmed I's favorite concubine Kösem Sultan.

Young Osman was also intent on curbing the power of the *kullar*. The army that had covered itself with shame at Hotin was composed overwhelmingly of such types. Meanwhile, the imperial capital was an arena for the power plays

---

[46] Naima, *Tarih-i Naima*, II: 450–51; Hasan Beyzade, *Hasan Bey-zade Tarihi*, III: 926; Piterberg, *An Ottoman Tragedy*, 16, 97.
[47] Tezcan, "1622 Military Rebellion," 32–33.
[48] Topçular Katibi, *Topçular Katibi Tarihi*, II: 701–2; Derviş Abdullah, *Risale-i teberdariye*, fols. 55b–58a.

of pages, soldiery, and viziers of *devshirme* origin, who had cultivated a pronounced ethnoregional and status solidarity. Osman therefore considered recruiting an army of paid mercenaries from among the Muslim subjects of Anatolia to supplement the imperial Janissary corps, which was heavily dominated by *devshirme* recruits. He likewise entertained the notion of moving the Ottoman capital to the Asiatic part of the empire, far outside the region from which most *kullar* came: to Bursa, to Damascus, perhaps even to Cairo, where the power of the *kullar* had been broken by the Ottoman governor between 1607 and 1611.[49] Not only did Süleyman Agha support these measures; he, along with the sultan's tutor, is thought to have incited the sultan against the *kullar*, whose military effectiveness he believed had deteriorated – and who could argue with him after Hotin?[50] The soldiers also believed that he had persuaded Osman to move the capital to Cairo.[51] (Given the ties binding the office of Chief Harem Eunuch to Egypt, their assumptions are not surprising.)

In essence, the youthful sultan sought to repress the *kullar* with the active support of his Chief Harem Eunuch. In May 1622, sensing a growing threat, the palace soldiery, supported by Sultan Mustafa's mother and Kösem Sultan, who wanted her own children to take the throne, staged a counter-coup. They invaded the harem and released Mustafa from the *kafes*. In an attempt to appease the rebels, Osman II sacrificed Dilaver Pasha, his then–grand vizier, and Süleyman Agha, the luckless replacement Chief Harem Eunuch. But the *kullar* insisted on reenthroning Sultan Mustafa. As for Osman, aged only seventeen, he was imprisoned in Yedikule, then forthwith strangled, largely through the efforts of Sultan Mustafa's mother and the new grand vizier.[52] The tension between harem and threshold eunuchs, while it did not define this upheaval, clearly affected its outcome. The rank-and-file harem eunuchs regarded the Chief Threshold Eunuch as responsible for Süleyman Agha's execution. In revenge, they tore him limb from limb.[53]

Return to the Palace. Under the circumstances, it comes as little surprise that the restored Sultan Mustafa's courtiers were suspicious of the African harem eunuchs – who, after all, had lynched the chief officer of the Third Court. During Mustafa's brief second reign, the offices of Chief Harem Eunuch and Chief Threshold Eunuch were combined as a means of limiting the harem eunuchs' influence, and the resulting super-post was held by a

---

[49] Piterberg, *An Ottoman Tragedy*, 22–25; Tezcan, "1622 Military Rebellion," 26–27; Hathaway, "The 'Mamluk-Breaker' Who Was Really a *Kul* Breaker," 97, 99–102, 105.

[50] Piterberg, *An Ottoman Tragedy*, 22–24, 83–84, 108–9; Topçular Katibi, *Topçular Katibi Tarihi*, II: 706, 711, 723, 726, 740–41.

[51] Peçevi, *Tarih-i Peçevi*, II: 355.

[52] Ibid., II: 354–63; Hasan Beyzade, *Hasan Bey-zade Tarihi*, III: 940–42, 945; Piterberg, *An Ottoman Tragedy*, 25–28; Tezcan, "1622 Military Rebellion," 27, 28.

[53] Naima, *Tarih-i Naima*, II: 495.

member of the corps of threshold eunuchs: Ismail Agha, a *devshirme* recruit from Malatya in southeastern Anatolia. He was the last white eunuch ever to supervise the harem. His main claim to fame is the mosque complex, still standing, that he endowed in Üsküdar.[54]

The deposition of Osman II had not, in any case, solved the problem of Mustafa's mental instability, which plagued his second reign no less than it had his first. He was again deposed after an additional year and a half on the throne. His successor, Murad IV (r. 1623–40), succeeded, to a large degree, in curbing the power of the *kullar* in the way that his late half-brother had envisioned. An early sign of the new order was the recall, once again, of Mustafa Agha from Cairo to resume the post of Chief Harem Eunuch.[55] This time, he retained the office until his death in July 1624. By now, Ahmed I's favorite concubine, Kösem Sultan, had come into her own as one of the most ambitious sultan's mothers in Ottoman history. She and Mustafa Agha had been on opposite sides of the Osman II affair, but now, with Kösem's own son on the throne, they began to function as allies. They represented a sort of parallel to the partnership of Safiye Sultan and Gazanfer Agha a quarter-century earlier.

Protégés and Enemies. Like Habeshi Mehmed Agha before him, Mustafa Agha cultivated a number of clients and protégés, many of whom attained important military and administrative positions, up to and including that of grand vizier. However, his pool of clients reflected the ethnoregional tensions, and by extension the East-West factional competition, of the times, for they included not only the *devshirme* recruits who had dominated the Ottoman military administration before Ahmed I, but also mamluks from the Caucasus, who for the moment seemed to offer a less rebellious alternative to the *kullar*.

Nasuh Pasha. Rather ironically, a profound antagonism took shape between Mustafa Agha and one of Habeshi Mehmed's most influential clients, Nasuh Pasha. As we saw in Chapter 4, Nasuh's career flourished long after Habeshi Mehmed's death; in fact, he attained most of the influential positions that he held while Mustafa Agha was Chief Harem Eunuch. Yet he accomplished all this in part because he cultivated ties to Safiye Sultan, Ahmed I's grandmother. Both Ahmed and his Chief Eunuch were inclined to be suspicious of Safiye's clients. Nonetheless, Nasuh grew quite close to the sultan, marrying his young daughter a few months after becoming grand vizier in 1611. Naima, writing nearly a century later, gives the impression that Nasuh Pasha and Mustafa Agha competed for the sultan's trust, and that Nasuh resented the eunuch's prominent role in the construction of the sultan's mosque.[56] Hasan Beyzade,

---

[54] Ayvansarayi, *Garden of the Mosques*, 510; www.uskudar.bel.tr/tr/main/erehber/camiiler/8/aga-camii-malatyali-ismail-aga-camii/14.
[55] Naima, *Tarih-i Naima*, II: 536–37.   [56] Ibid., II: 402.

who was present at Ahmed I's court, claims that "the mufti [the highest religious official]. . . and the Darüssaade Ağası suspected the . . . vizier of plotting and malice, and so each of them, confirmed in his fear and suspicion, . . . believed that [Nasuh] was going to betray the Sultan of the Horizons." They therefore, as Chapter 4 points out, seized on his peace overtures to the Safavids to secure his execution for fraternizing with the enemy.[57]

Kemankeş Ali Pasha. Apart from Nasuh Pasha, Mustafa Agha's main rivals, along with his key protégés, emerged during the second phase of his career, following his return to the palace in the aftermath of Osman II's murder in 1622. In something of a departure from the pattern set by Habeshi Mehmed, Mustafa Agha competed directly with several grand viziers for access to the sultan. The ugly episode with Güzelce Ali Pasha, which resulted in Mustafa's deposition and exile to Egypt in 1620, appears to have taught the eunuch a lesson. Three years later, Murad IV's first grand vizier, Kemankeş Ali Pasha, brought Mustafa Agha back from Egypt and reinstated him as Chief Harem Eunuch, even though he had been warned that Mustafa would not be obedient to him, as Naima recounts:

His clerk at the time, Kabasakal (Bushy Beard) Ali Agha, who was a well-meaning yet insolent man, . . . reproached the pasha: "Why are you having Mustafa Agha brought back? He is too ungovernable and independent. He will not obey you or submit to your orders. Someone like him, who is accustomed to deposing and appointing viziers, will not be afraid of you."[58]

Kemankeş Ali was, in fact, executed shortly after Mustafa Agha's return to the palace, but the reasons are more complex than one Chief Eunuch's "disobedience." He had essentially clawed his way to the grand vizierate, making many enemies in the process, including several powerful rival viziers and the Chief Mufti. But his worst mistake was allowing the Safavid shah Abbas to capture Baghdad in 1624, then hiding the fact from the twelve-year-old sultan Murad IV and, more importantly, from his mother, the fearsome Kösem Sultan. During these years, as Nasuh Pasha had discovered, any hint of appeasing Shah Abbas was grounds for execution. Following the new pattern described above, Kösem combined with Mustafa Agha to have the vizier deposed and strangled.[59]

Governors of Egypt. Otherwise, Mustafa Agha played the familiar game of promoting his clients, who comprised roughly equal numbers of *devshirme* recruits and mamluks, to choice vizierial positions and, when possible, to the grand vizierate. He was particularly concerned with the governorship of

[57] Hasan Beyzade, *Hasan Bey-zade Tarihi*, III: 886–88; Naima, *Tarih-i Naima*, II: 415.
[58] Naima, *Tarih-i Naima*, II: 536–37; Ahmed Resmi, *Hamiletü'l-kübera*, 48.
[59] Hasan Beyzade, *Hasan Bey-zade Tarihi*, III: 980–87; Uzunçarşılı, *Osmanlı Tarihi*, III, part 2, 379.

Egypt – hardly surprising, given the years he had spent there and, of course, the province's ongoing contributions to the Evkafü'l-Haremeyn. While he was living in Cairo, just before his first appointment as Chief Harem Eunuch, his protégé and fellow eunuch Gürcü ("Georgian") Mehmed Agha, became governor of Egypt; he remained in that post from September 1604 through July 1605. He had begun his career as Mustafa Agha's *sarraj* (literally, "saddler"), the equivalent of a bodyguard – a post that strongly suggests that he was the Chief Eunuch's personal mamluk.[60] He rose to the grand vizierate in September 1622 but was executed some five months later, probably as part of a general backlash against the administration of the deposed Osman II.[61]

A later governor of Egypt, Tabanı Yassı ("Flat Foot") Mehmed Pasha, whose term ran from 1628 to 1630, had entered Mustafa Agha's service on arriving in Istanbul with the *devshirme* from his homeland, Drama, in what is now northeastern Greece; the Chief Eunuch had initially installed the young Albanian in the Müteferrika, an elite regiment of palace soldiery.[62] He, too, served as grand vizier, in this case from 1632 to 1637. Meanwhile other viziers, in the words of Naima, "fought over powerful vizier and *defterdar* positions, laid out bribes, and gained their positions with the intercession of the Chief Eunuch Mustafa Agha and the protection of the grand viziers."[63]

Melek Ahmed Pasha. Tabanı Yassı's career trajectory attests that Mustafa Agha's clients continued to exert influence in Ottoman administrative circles well after the Chief Eunuch's death in 1624. Even one of Mehmed IV's (r. 1648–87) early grand viziers, Melek Ahmed Pasha, who held the post for three weeks in August 1651, had started out as Mustafa Agha's protégé. The son of a mamluk from Abkhazia, in what is now northwestern Georgia, Melek Ahmed was born in Istanbul but sent back to Abkhazia to be raised in the customs of his ancestral country, a common practice among peoples of the northern Caucasus. After this good Abkhazian upbringing, he was presented to the court of Ahmed I along with his female cousin. While his cousin was married off to the sultan's chief goldsmith and later became the mother of the famous traveler Evliya Çelebi, Melek Ahmed entered the palace pages' school at Galatasaray through Mustafa Agha's efforts.[64] In addition to his remarkably brief tenure as grand vizier, he held a number of important governorships and military commands, and married one of Ahmed I's daughters.[65]

---

[60] Hathaway, *Politics of Households*, 55, 57–58, 63.

[61] Naima, *Tarih-i Naima*, II: 603–4; Uzunçarşılı, *Osmanlı Tarihi*, III, part 2, 402.

[62] Naima, *Tarih-i Naima*, II: 635.   [63] Ibid., IV: 1642, also II: 376–77.

[64] Silahdar, *Silahdar Tarihi*, I: 256–57; Robert Dankoff, trans., *The Intimate Life of an Ottoman Statesman: Melek Ahmed Pasha (1599–1662) as Portrayed in Evliya Çelebi's Book of Travels*, historical introduction by Rhoads Murphey (Albany, NY, 1991), 5 (Murphey), 49.

[65] Dankoff, trans., *Intimate Life of an Ottoman Statesman*, passim.

The Khan of the Crimea. Mustafa Agha's office-bestowing powers may occasionally have extended beyond even the grand vizierate. In 1624, Mehmed III Giray, a member of the powerful Tatar family that monopolized the khanate of the Crimea under Ottoman suzerainty, claimed that his brother Janibek had unfairly obtained the khanate through Mustafa Agha's influence.[66] Like other members of his family, Mehmed Giray took advantage of the factional rivalry within the palace, winning the support of a former grand vizier who was Mustafa Agha's enemy for his appointment. His khanate lasted a tumultuous four years before he was killed in combat with Russian Cossack forces who had invaded the Crimea.[67]

The Crimean khan and the Tatar cavalry he could muster were critical to Ottoman military efforts against the Habsburgs and the Russians. The Tatars were likewise instrumental in conducting slave raids in the Ukrainian steppe and in the Caucasus to supply the imperial court and the Ottoman provinces with mamluks, who were an increasingly important pool of manpower throughout the empire at just this time. These features alone would perhaps suffice to explain why Mustafa Agha cared about the ruler of such a far-away satellite state. In addition, though, the khan's territory abutted the region of the eastern Danube where İsmail Geçidi, the settlement endowed by Habeshi Mehmed Agha and maintained by his successors, was located and where grain, much of it destined for Istanbul, was shipped across the Black Sea. This sensitive location made stability in the Crimea a top priority for the Chief Eunuch and helps to explain why he attached importance to the Tatar khan who administered it.

The Chief Harem Eunuch's Public Visibility. During Mustafa Agha's tenure, the Chief Harem Eunuch began to be more publicly visible than he had ever been before. The first Chief Eunuch, Habeshi Mehmed Agha, we recall, had inaugurated the practice of holding a weekly public audience at the harem gate to discuss questions related to imperial pious endowments. Mustafa Agha, for his part, regularly participated in imperial processions in Istanbul and in the former capital of Edirne, which served the sultans as a forward base against the Habsburgs and, during the seventeenth century, as a veritable second capital.

The chronicler Topçular Katibi, a military man who was well attuned to the importance of such processions for the projection of imperial authority, reports that Mustafa Agha led the harem aghas in the procession in Istanbul that celebrated the betrothal of Nasuh Pasha to the daughter of Ahmed I in February 1612. In this procession, intriguingly, the harem eunuchs and the threshold eunuchs paired off, so that a black and a white eunuch rode together

---

[66] Naima, *Tarih-i Naima*, II: 563–64.   [67] Uzunçarşılı, *Osmanlı Tarihi*, III, part 2, 10–12.

on horseback.[68] Although this may not have been the first time this color-coordinated pairing of eunuchs had occurred in a procession, it became a pattern in later years, demonstrating that the identification of black eunuchs with the harem and white eunuchs with the Babüssaade was now codified, even though a white eunuch would briefly head both harem and Babüssaade ten years later. The chronicler reports Mustafa Agha leading the other harem eunuchs in a similar procession in Edirne in 1614.[69] It was now likewise common for harem eunuchs to participate in processions seeing off conquering armies and celebrating landmark military victories, as in the case of the Eğri campaign in 1596 and, on the Safavid front, the expedition to Tabriz in 1612, the conquest of Revan in 1636, and the reconquest of Baghdad in 1638.[70]

Mustafa Agha's Death and Tomb. El-Hajj Mustafa Agha died in office in mid-July 1624. Although his age at the time of death is unknown, he was presumably elderly, like most Chief Harem Eunuchs, perhaps in his seventies or even eighties. Even in death, he set a notable precedent, for he was buried next to the tomb of the Prophet Muhammad's standard-bearer Abu Ayyub al-Ansari (Ebu Eyyub el-Ensari), which stood at the epicenter of a growing cemetery located outside Istanbul's land walls. (More will be said about this cemetery, and about el-Hajj Mustafa Agha's tomb, in Chapter 11.)

The site took on new prominence with Ahmed I's accession, when the new sultan visited the tomb and was girded with the sword of the Prophet Muhammad, or another sword of great religio-historical significance, by either the Chief Mufti or a descendant of Shaykh Edebali, the Sufi adept whose daughter married Osman, the founder of the Ottoman dynasty. From then on, every new sultan until the end of the empire, with one exception, went through a similar ceremony.[71] This choice of burial place was part of Mustafa Agha's heightened public visibility, not unlike his participation in processions.

Idris Agha. After his second, permanent departure from the palace, el-Hajj Mustafa Agha was smoothly succeeded by his protégé Idris Agha, who had worked closely with him on the Sultan Ahmed Mosque. In the same way that Mustafa Agha had been Ahmed I's Chief Harem Eunuch, so Idris was Murad IV's. He was deposed when Sultan Ibrahim came to the throne in 1640, and died soon afterward. According to Ahmed Resmi Efendi, "because [he] did not

---

[68] Topçular Katibi, *Topçular Katibi Tarihi*, I: 596–98, 601 n., 622–23; II: 1023, 1025, 1076; Mustafa Safi, *Zübdetü't-tevarih*, I: 138–39; Mehmed bin Mehmed, *Nuhbe*, 244; Naima, *Tarih-i Naima*, II: 93.

[69] Topçular Katibi, *Topçular Katibi Tarihi*, I: 617.

[70] Ibid., I: 145, 607; II: 892, 1023, 1025, 1072–73, 1076.

[71] Mustafa Safi, *Zübdetü't-tevarih*, I: 15–16; Cemal Kafadar, "Eyüp'te Kılıç Kuşanma Törenleri," in *Eyüp: Dün, Bugün (Sempozyum, 11–12 Aralık 1993)*, ed. Tülay Artan (Istanbul, 1994), 54–55; Tezcan, *Second Ottoman Empire*, 121 and n. 31; Piterberg, *An Ottoman Tragedy*, 10–11; Douglas S. Brookes, "Of Swords and Tombs: Symbolism in the Ottoman Accession Ritual," *Turkish Studies Association Bulletin* 17, 2 (1993): 1–22.

interfere without permission in affairs outside the harem, his character and conduct are not depicted by the chroniclers of events."[72] But the eighteenth-century chronicler's remarks seem rather disingenuous since, after all, Idris had been director of construction on the Blue Mosque.

Following on Mustafa's twenty years in office and Idris's sixteen, the terms of the next several Chief Harem Eunuchs seem almost pathetically short. Until Yusuf Agha toward the end of the seventeenth century, no single Chief Eunuch would serve for more than five years. This by no means indicates, however, that these short-term Chief Eunuchs lacked influence, as the following examples will demonstrate.

Sünbül Agha

The Chief Harem Eunuch Sünbül Agha, who held office from 1640 to 1644 – that is, during the first half of Sultan Ibrahim's reign – is supposed to have inspired the Ottoman conquest of Crete from Venice, but by accident, not because of any policy that he pursued. Following his deposition in April 1644, he was, like several of his predecessors, placed onboard a ship headed to Egypt. The vessel stopped briefly in Rhodes, off the southwest Anatolian coast, and when it reembarked, it was attacked by pirates of the Knights of St. John of Malta (who had been the Knights of Rhodes until Süleyman I expelled them from that island in 1522). As Katib Çelebi, who knew a thing or two about naval warfare, tells it:

As it was approaching the island of Kerpe [Karpathos, between Rhodes and Crete], effeminate infidels suddenly appeared. [The ship] at once drew away, but [the infidels] gave chase and turned their cannon on the ship, so that the agha and the people on the ship had to stand and fight. In the course of the battle, the agha and the captain were martyred; the other warriors fell in battle; the rest were taken captive.[73]

The Knights then steered the hijacked ship to Crete, where they presented one of Sünbül's horses, along with other spoils, to the island's Venetian governor. "The news gradually spread through Istanbul," Katib Çelebi continues, "and when the harem eunuchs brought it to the royal hearing, it resulted in the preparation of the navy, the commencement of the Crete campaign, and the conquest of numerous lands."[74]

Of course, the Ottoman conquest of Crete from the Venetians was not nearly so neat as Katib Çelebi makes it sound. Instead, it was a twenty-five-year

---

[72] *Hamiletü'l-kübera*, 50; Derviş Abdullah, *Risale-i teberdariye*, fol. 58a.
[73] Katib Çelebi, *Fezleke*, II: 234; Topkapı Archive, E 8211 (ca. 1054/1644–45); E 7884/2 (undated); Paul Rycaut, *A History of the Turkish Empire from the Year 1623 to the Year 1677* (London, 1680), 13–15.
[74] Katib Çelebi, *Fezleke*, II: 234.

ordeal. Despite early successes elsewhere on the island, the Ottomans simply could not dislodge the Venetians from the capital of Candia (modern-day Iraklion). Only in 1669, under grand vizier Köprülü Fazıl Ahmed Pasha, were Ottoman forces able to overcome Venetian resistance and take Candia's seaside fortress.[75] Crete would remain Ottoman territory until 1913.

Sünbül's exile is popularly held to have inaugurated the custom of exiling deposed Chief Harem Eunuchs to Egypt.[76] An Egyptian exile certainly became increasingly common following Sünbül's martyrdom, although as we have already seen, el-Hajj Mustafa Agha spent years in Cairo, both before his initial tenure as Chief Eunuch and afterward. In addition, Sünbül's successor, Taş Yatur Ali Agha (term 1644–45), was brought back from Cairo to take up the office.[77] Meanwhile, lower-ranking harem eunuchs had apparently been exiled to Cairo since well before Sünbül's ordeal. The pattern of Egyptian exile at the end of a term as Chief Eunuch would, in any case, continue until the late eighteenth century.

Lala Süleyman Agha

Lala ("Tutor") Süleyman Agha, also known as Uzun ("Tall") Süleyman, held the post of Chief Harem Eunuch for only ten months, September 1651 through July 1652, yet he had a huge impact on palace politics. After his deposition, he became a leading personality in Cairo's local politics and was even involved in an international incident that will be described in Chapter 8. Initially, much of his influence within the palace derived from the position he held before his appointment as Chief Eunuch: that of head of the entourage of eunuchs who surrounded Turhan Sultan, the mother of Sultan Mehmed IV, who had acceded to the throne in 1648 at the age of seven.

Only twenty-one herself at the time, Turhan was considered too young and inexperienced to act as regent to the young sultan, and so the grand vizier's governing council asked the boy's grandmother, the formidable Kösem Sultan, to fill this role. Kösem, we recall, was no stranger to palace politics, having participated in the enthronement and subsequent deposition of Osman II, the son of one of her rivals. She was only too happy to dominate the court once again. But whereas a quarter of a century earlier, she had allied herself with el-Hajj Mustafa Agha, she was now firmly ensconced at the head of her own faction, which included the imperial Janissaries and the eunuchs and pages of the Third Court. Turhan, in contrast, had Lala Süleyman Agha and the other harem eunuchs firmly on her side. The court historian Naima, writing some six decades later, portrays the enmity between the two women as the latest

---

[75] Naima, *Tarih-i Naima*, III: 1011–12, 1028; Ahmed Resmi, *Hamiletü'l-kübera*, 51–53.
[76] Uzunçarşılı, *Saray Teşkilatı*, 174–75, 180.   [77] Naima, *Tarih-i Naima*, III: 1011–12.

incarnation of a chronic rivalry between the harem eunuchs, on one hand, and the threshold eunuchs and *hass oda* pages, on the other.[78] Tellingly, though, contemporary chroniclers do not frame it in this way. They may have seen the conflict as yet another example of the *kullar* struggling to protect their interests by retaining their influence with the sultan through his grandmother.

After a few years of domination by her mother-in-law, Turhan began to chafe against Kösem's control. The wily Kösem therefore conspired with the Janissaries to kill both Turhan and her son, whom they intended to replace with the son of one of Sultan Ibrahim's other concubines. Lala Süleyman apparently learned of this plot and warned Turhan, who joined with him and the other harem eunuchs in a counter-scheme to eliminate Kösem. On the critical night, 3 September 1651, a band of African eunuchs attacked Kösem and chased her through the harem. As N.M. Penzer describes it:

[Turhan] Sultan was awakened, and an oath of allegiance was taken to serve and defend the young [Mehmed], who was still but a child. The mufti declared by a *fetva* that [Kösem] must die, and a decree was drawn up by the [grand vizier] and signed by the trembling hand of the young sultan. It was now the hour of [Turhan's] triumph, and a search was made in [Kösem's] suite without result. At last the wretched old woman was discovered hidden in a clothes-chest and dragged out to her death. Every atom of respect was forgotten in the terrible scene that followed. Her earrings and bracelets were torn off her, the money she scattered on the ground as a bait was ignored, her rich robes were torn in a thousand pieces, and, in spite of all the orders her oppressors had received to respect the body of the sultan's grandmother, the hapless woman was stripped of her clothes and dragged by the feet naked to the gate of the harem ... There she was strangled, and her partisans were killed later.[79]

The various chroniclers' accounts differ in their details. Some have Lala Süleyman Agha himself strangling Kösem with her braids.[80] Among the harem eunuchs, four were instrumental to the plot to kill Kösem: Lala Süleyman, naturally, plus Hoca Reyhan Agha; Lala, or Hajji, Ibrahim Agha; and one Ali Agha about whom little is known. Hoca Reyhan was a companion (*musahib*) of Turhan known for his piety and his learning in Islamic theology and law, as well as secular literature;[81] Lala Ibrahim would succeed Süleyman as the head eunuch of Turhan's entourage. Although neither of them ever became Chief Harem Eunuch, both had bright futures within the palace, as will become clear below, in the case of Lala Ibrahim, and in Chapter 9, in the case of Hoca Reyhan.

Grand Vizier–Maker. Even before his appointment as Chief Harem Eunuch, which occurred within a few weeks of Kösem's murder, Lala Süleyman was

[78] Ibid., III: 1325, 1532–37.   [79] Penzer, *The Harem*, 191–92.
[80] Naima, *Tarih-i Naima*, III: 1327–28, 1342; Abdurrahman Abdi, *Vekayiname*, 29–33.
[81] Naima, *Tarih-i Naima*, IV: 1576–77.

able to make and break at least two grand viziers – both of them, in keeping with the post-Osman II preference for "easterners," mamluks from the Caucasus: Abaza ("Abkhazian") Siyavush Pasha and Gürcü ("Georgian") Mehmed Pasha (not to be confused with his namesake, who was executed in 1622). When the grand vizier Melek Ahmed Pasha, the Abkhazian relative of Evliya Çelebi and one-time client of el-Hajj Mustafa Agha, was deposed in late August 1651, Lala Süleyman persuaded Turhan Sultan to appoint Siyavush Pasha over the Janissary agha, who was Kösem Sultan's preferred candidate – not surprisingly, given Kösem's ties to the Janissaries.[82]

Siyavush had started out as the mamluk and personal treasurer of his fellow Abkhazian Abaza Mehmed Pasha, who had infamously rebelled against Mustafa I following the execution of Osman II and had been executed himself some years later.[83] With his master gone, Siyavush was drafted into the corps of palace pages "because of his extraordinary beauty."[84] During Murad IV's reign, he rose steadily through the *hass oda* ranks, serving as the sultan's sword-bearer (*silahdar*) before becoming a vizier. He then served a less-than-stellar term as grand admiral and held several important provincial governorships. This career trajectory alone would have made him a candidate for the grand vizierate, even without Lala Süleyman's endorsement. But in supporting him, Lala Süleyman was pursuing the strategy of his most influential Chief Harem Eunuch predecessors by cultivating clients who had come up through the *hass oda*.

Having become grand vizier with Lala Süleyman's blessing, though, Siyavush had to put up with his interference, which he quickly grew to resent. Only a few weeks into his tenure, he is said to have exclaimed, in a fit of pique, "What kind of vizierate is this, when I am dominated and ruled by an African?"[85] Shortly thereafter, Lala Süleyman confronted him and threatened to "break his mouth" if he refused to hand over the grand vizier's seal.[86] He proceeded to imprison Siyavush in Yedikule.

Lala Süleyman's role in the selection of Siyavush's replacement is depicted differently by the two primary chroniclers of court appointments under Mehmed IV, Abdurrahman Abdi Pasha, who was the sultan's official chronicler, and Mustafa Naima, the "Köprülüs' historian," who compiled his account in the early eighteenth century. To replace Siyavush, Lala Süleyman, now ensconced as Chief Harem Eunuch, either chose (Naima) or accepted (Abdurrahman Abdi) the octogenarian Gürcü Mehmed Pasha, who had launched

---

[82] Ibid., III: 1321–22.
[83] Gabriel Piterberg, "The Alleged Rebellion of Abaza Mehmed Pasha: Historiography and the State in the Seventeenth Century," in *Mutiny and Rebellion in the Ottoman Empire*, ed. Hathaway, 15; Silahdar, *Silahdar Tarihi*, I: 61.
[84] Uzunçarşılı, *Osmanlı Tarihi*, III, part 2, 400.   [85] Naima, *Tarih-i Naima*, III: 1365.
[86] Ibid., III: 1368; Abdurrahman Abdi, *Vekayiname*, 33; Silahdar, *Silahdar Tarihi*, I: 62.

his career in the early years of the seventeenth century with the help of his then-patron, the great admiral Koca Sinan Pasha, sometime protégé of Safiye Sultan. He pursued a trajectory similar to Siyavush Pasha's, climbing through the *hass oda* ranks, then holding numerous provincial governorships.

To secure his appointment as grand vizier, though, Gürcü Mehmed had to counter a move by Turhan Sultan's steward (*kethüda*), the threshold eunuch Mimar ("the Architect") Kasım Agha, to put forward Köprülü Mehmed Pasha, who five years later would transform the grand vizierate. By Naima's account, Lala Süleyman managed to discredit Kasım Agha, who was exiled to Cyprus while Köprülü Mehmed was appointed governor of the backwater district of Köstendil in far western Bulgaria. Abdurrahman Abdi, in contrast, holds Gürcü Mehmed himself responsible for Kasim Agha's exile and Köprülü Mehmed's rustication; Lala Süleyman, in his account, is an ally of Kasim Agha who promotes Köprülü Mehmed's career.[87] If we try to distill patterns of patronage from these partisan narratives, we can see Turhan beginning to assert herself through her network of clients, and both Turhan and Lala Süleyman trying to use their connections in the *hass oda* to control the grand vizierate.

Whether he was Lala Süleyman Agha's protégé or not, Gürcü Mehmed as grand vizier was, by all accounts, merely the tool of Turhan Sultan and her coterie of harem eunuchs.[88] His inefficacy seemingly made Lala Süleyman nostalgic for Siyavush Pasha; after only a few months, he conspired with the Chief Mufti and the head of the community of descendants of the Prophet to depose Gürcü Mehmed and reinstate Siyavush so that Süleyman could manipulate him again. Here, then, he was turning to allies within Istanbul's community of ulema and other religious luminaries to pursue his agenda. He was unsuccessful, though, for the new chief of Turhan's eunuch entourage, the same Lala Ibrahim Agha who had joined Süleyman in the murder of Kösem, advised her to select the new grand vizier herself. Rejecting Süleyman's preference, she chose the then-governor of Egypt, Tarhuncu Ahmed Pasha.[89] Turhan, in other words, had finally thrown off Lala Süleyman's influence and emerged as a power in her own right, and head of her own harem faction. This was clearly a turning point since a few months later, Süleyman Agha was deposed as Chief Eunuch and exiled to Egypt.[90]

Career Resuscitator. During his brief tenure as Chief Harem Eunuch, Lala Süleyman Agha became a magnet for ambitious office-seekers – particularly, it seemed, those who had been deposed from one position and were seeking to

---

[87] Naima, *Tarih-i Naima*, III: 1367–68, 1372, 1392, 1399, 1421–22, 1550; Abdurrahman Abdi, *Vekayiname*, 34.
[88] Uzunçarşılı, *Osmanlı Tarihi*, III, part 2, 402.   [89] Naima, *Tarih-i Naima*, III: 1342, 1399.
[90] Ibid., III: 1411; Abdurrahman Abdi, *Vekayiname*, 36.

rebound professionally. Their ambition (or desperation) coalesced perfectly with the eunuch's agenda. Thus, in early 1652, the former Chief Financial Officer (*baş defterdar*) Ibrahim Pasha was reappointed to the post with Lala Süleyman's help after paying 200 purses of silver coins (singular, *akçe*) to an undisclosed government official (possibly Lala Süleyman himself). When he died not long afterward, the eunuch assisted another deposed *defterdar*, Emin Pasha, in reobtaining the post. (Meanwhile, the 200 purses of silver that Ibrahim Pasha had forfeited were found and confiscated.)[91]

Members of not only the military-administrative hierarchy but the judicial hierarchy, as well, turned to Lala Süleyman for career rehabilitation, affirming his links to members of the ulema, noted above. Shortly before Gürcü Mehmed Pasha became grand vizier in 1651, Şami ("Damascene") Nu'man Efendi, the deposed chief judge of the city of Kayseri in central Anatolia, cultivated a tie of clientage (*intisab*) with Lala Süleyman, who interceded with his ally Chief Mufti to ensure that Şami Nu'man obtained the high-profile post of chief judge of Edirne.[92]

But ultimately, this habit of resuscitating the careers of his protégés led to Lala Süleyman's downfall – or at least to his deposition. Later that same year, he interceded with the recently appointed grand vizier Tarhuncu Ahmed Pasha to have yet another of his clients, the deposed head of the palace gate-keepers (*kapıcılar kethüdası*), one Bıyıklı ("moustachioed") Mehmed, appointed governor of Egypt. Lala Süleyman was already out of favor with Tarhuncu Ahmed – whose appointment, we recall, he had opposed – and with Tarhuncu's patron, Turhan Sultan, who at this point was obviously weary of bending to his will. Tarhuncu Ahmed now asked Turhan to depose the Chief Eunuch, which she did. Like Sünbül Agha and others among his predecessors, he was exiled to Egypt.[93]

Conclusion

The prolonged and multifaceted crisis that began during the reign of Murad III and stretched into the reign of Mehmed IV more than fifty years later served to reinforce certain key trends in the Chief Harem Eunuch's manner of functioning. Like Habeshi Mehmed Agha, the Chief Eunuchs of the crisis era, often in combination with the sultan's mother or favorite concubine, headed vast patronage networks-cum-factions that might include future grand viziers and other high officials. Now, however, the competition between rival harem-based factions was more intransigent and violent than it had ever been. This occurred in part because the Ottoman dynasty was under threat. Rebellious

---

[91] Naima, *Tarih-i Naima*, III: 1380–81.   [92] Ibid., III: 1372, also III: 1390, 1399.
[93] Ibid., III: 1409–11.

mercenaries and governors threatened to march on Istanbul even as inflation and drought drove palace expenditures to unsustainable heights. Inside the palace, the enthronement of Sultan Ahmed I in 1603 kicked off nearly half a century of underage or mentally challenged rulers, one of whom, the unfortunate Osman II, was even murdered, becoming the first regicide in Ottoman history. The harem filled the vacuum that these "deficient" sultans created, becoming the chief locus of palace politics and thus of political factionalism. As the harem eunuchs' influence increased, tension with the white eunuchs of the Third Court inevitably resulted, leading to an ongoing friction that exacerbated the existing factional differences.

At the same time, the threat of violent conflict increased exponentially when the palace Janissaries and cavalry joined the factional competition, throwing their support to rival harem-based factions. At a time when the utility and even the existence of palace *kullar* were being questioned, and more and more non-*kul* "easterners" were entering palace service, these two rival *kapıkulu* regiments added a volatile and unpredictable element to factional competition. The addition of deadly force to factional rivalry played a role in the murders of Osman and Gazanfer Aghas in 1603, Sultan Osman II in 1622, and Kösem Sultan in 1651.

By the time Lala Süleyman Agha took office in 1651, violence had become a normative part of factional politics, even inside the residential sections of the palace. As we have seen, Süleyman physically threatened at least one grand vizier. During his tenure, the two corps of palace soldiery did not even have to come together to provoke violence within the harem. Kösem's murder was carried out by the harem eunuchs themselves, and despite the Janissaries' attempts to defend the aging matriarch. In some respects, we can see this pervasive threat of violence as the logical corollary of the intersection, over several decades, of harem-based factionalism, militarization, ethnoregional rivalries, and friction between harem and Third Court eunuchs. These four types of factionalism reinforced each other, creating a well-nigh unbearable tension within the palace.

This perhaps makes it all the more remarkable that the Köprülü family of grand viziers, who first came to power in the late 1650s, would succeed, to a large extent, in vanquishing this intransigent factional rivalry by placing members of their own household in the harem, the *hass oda*, and the military and administrative hierarchy. The effect of their efforts on the Chief Harem Eunuch's office is the subject of the next chapter.

6   Yusuf Agha and the Köprülü Reforms

Lala Süleyman's tenure exemplifies the tumult of the mid-seventeenth century, with rebellious Jelali governors still a threat, the campaign in Crete bogged down, and the dynastic crisis as yet unresolved. By 1651, the year of Kösem Sultan's murder, palace factionalism had reached a dangerous new peak, with the partisans of Kösem and those of Turhan on the brink of armed conflict. Their antagonism threatened the safety of the young sultan, Mehmed IV, who was still only ten years old. Ironically, the two harem-based factions found it increasingly difficult to depend on the support of the regiments of palace soldiery that had backed them over the past few decades (see Table 6.1). Fully aware of their power to make or break a ruler, and increasingly roiled by the ethnoregional frictions described in Chapter 5, the Janissaries and *sipahi*s now resembled a mob of deadly unpredictability, capable at a moment's notice of slaughtering each other, banding together to exterminate enemies in the palace, or running amok in the streets of Istanbul.

This was the backdrop for the appointment of Köprülü Mehmed Pasha as grand vizier. He founded a veritable grand vizier dynasty that monopolized the administration of the Ottoman Empire from 1656 through the 1683 Vienna debacle, and continued to wield authority well into the eighteenth century. Ottomanist scholarship has traditionally portrayed the Köprülüs as "saviors" who, with brutal efficiency, (temporarily) rescued the empire from dynastic turmoil and military annihilation.[1] While this image is not entirely inaccurate, the reality, like most realities, is more complicated, and the fortunes of the Chief Harem Eunuchs during the "Köprülü era" reflect this complexity.

The first Köprülü grand vizier, Köprülü Mehmed Pasha (term 1656–61), and his son and successor, Fazıl Ahmed Pasha (1661–76), pursued a strategy of filling government offices of all kinds, both in Istanbul and in the Ottoman provinces, with members of their own administrative household. This type of household, which combined a kinship network with a conglomeration of

---

[1] Uzunçarşılı, *Osmanlı Tarihi*, III, part 1, 367–433; Norman Itzkowitz, *Ottoman Empire and Islamic Tradition* (Chicago, IL, 1972), 77–85; Stanford J. Shaw and Ezel Kural Shaw, *History of the Ottoman Empire and Modern Turkey* (Cambridge, 1976–77), I: 207–15.

Table 6.1 *Major officers of the harem and Third Court in the late seventeenth century*[a]

Harem		Third Court	
		Chief Threshold Eunuch (Kapı Ağası)	
		Bosnian Ahmed Agha	
Sultan's Mother	Chief Harem	**Gate of Felicity**	**Privy Chamber (Hass**
Turhan (Mehmed IV)	Eunuch	**(Babüssaade)**	**Oda)**
Saliha Dilaşub	*Behram*		
(Süleyman II)	*Dilaver*	Palace Treasurer	Privy Chamber Head
Muazzez (Ahmed II)	*Solak Mehmed*	(Hazinedar Başı)	(Hass Oda Başı)
Gülnuş Emetullah	*Musli*		
(Ahmed III)	*Abbas*	Palace Head (Saray	Sword-Bearer (Silahdar)
	Yusuf	Ağası)	*Çorlulu Ali*
	Hazinedar Ali		
	Mustafa	Boys of the	Valet (Çuhadar)
	Karagöz Gedai	Threshold (Kapı	
	Ahmed	Oğlanı)	Stirrup-Holder (Rikabdar)
		Musli	
	Harem Treasurer		Pages
	(Hazinedar-i		
	Şehriyari)		
	Solak Mehmed		
	Yusuf		
	Hazinedar Ali		

[a] Italics indicate individuals named in the chapter.

patron–client ties, became common among high Ottoman officials toward the middle of the sixteenth century. In two now-classic studies, Metin Kunt noted the importance of these households to both the central and provincial administration between 1550 and 1650, while Rifaat Abou-El-Haj labeled them "vizier and pasha households."[2] Such a household was modeled on the sultan's household in the imperial palace yet, ironically, gave these men a base of operations separate from the imperial household. Along with the harem-based factions, it was thus a key sign of what I have called "decentralization at the center," a hallmark of Ottoman political culture in the seventeenth century.[3]

[2] Metin Kunt, *The Sultan's Servants: The Transformation of Ottoman Provincial Government, 1550–1650* (New York, NY, 1983); Rifaat A. Abou-El-Haj, "The Ottoman Vezir and Paşa Households, 1683–1703: A Preliminary Report," *Journal of the American Oriental Society* 94 (1974): 438–47.

[3] Hathaway, *Arab Lands under Ottoman Rule*, 8, 11–12.

In essence, then, the sultan's household was now one player in a game that also included his mother's and his favorite concubine's households and those of the grand vizier and other key officials. The Köprülüs' genius lay in cultivating such a comprehensive network of patronage ties that their household served as a pool of manpower for positions in all branches of palace service and at all levels of the Ottoman administration empire-wide. The sheer extent of their household allowed them to put their stamp on the Ottoman administration in a way that few previous grand viziers had, and helps to explain the relative stability and continuity of the era during which they dominated the grand vizierate.

Where the Chief Harem Eunuch was concerned, though, the Köprülüs were not always able to impose members of their household, in particular because Turhan Sultan, the mother of Mehmed IV, had her own favorite candidates for the post who usually came out of her own entourage. In some cases, Chief Eunuchs who did not come from the Köprülüs' circle acted directly contrary to the grand viziers' interests – and were sometimes deposed or imprisoned as a result.

But over and above individual appointments to the office of Chief Harem Eunuch, the Köprülüs succeeded in putting in place a new Chief Harem Eunuch career trajectory that arguably gave the grand vizier greater leverage over the office of Chief Eunuch and the revenues that it controlled. The critical element in this new trajectory was the office of harem treasurer, which now became a virtual prerequisite for the post of Chief Harem Eunuch. In addition, though, the Köprülüs oversaw a more pronounced and sustained engagement of the Chief Harem Eunuch, both while in office and after leaving office, with Egypt and the Hijaz. In some respects, this was a revival of the pattern established more than half a century earlier by el-Hajj Mustafa Agha, yet it also reflected the priorities of the Köprülü grand viziers. The array of ties that bound the Chief Harem Eunuch to Egypt form the focus of Chapter 8. Here, though, we consider his links to the Hijaz through the office of Şeyhü'l-Harem, or chief of the eunuchs who guarded the Prophet Muhammad's tomb. The Köprülü agenda incorporated this office by making it a conduit for former Chief Harem Eunuchs.

This chapter opens by demonstrating the severity of the palace divisions during the 1650s, which created an unsustainable climate of violence and intimidation within the palace. We then proceed to Köprülü Mehmed Pasha's appointment as grand vizier, which was designed to resolve this horrific situation, and the effects of his reformist policies on the Chief Harem Eunuch's career trajectory. However, we do not discount variations to that trajectory following Köprülü Mehmed's death in 1661. Finally, we consider the career of the long-serving Chief Harem Eunuch Yusuf Agha (term 1671–87), who, while not a Köprülü client, in many ways exemplifies their reforms.

Behram Agha and the Çınar Vak'ası

With the murder of her detested mother-in-law, Kösem, in 1651, and the deposition of Kösem's increasingly controlling alleged murderer, Lala Süleyman Agha, in 1652, Turhan Sultan, the mother of Mehmed IV, had rid herself of two tormentors. This, however, did not mean that her son's position on the throne was suddenly secure. After all, Topkapı Palace was still full of Janissaries and Third Court pages who had supported Kösem and who regarded Mehmed IV and his brothers as mere tools of Turhan and her harem faction.

Mustafa Naima, the court historian whose narrative is thought to be highly favorable to the Köprülüs, saw a toxic antagonism between the harem eunuchs and the functionaries of the Third Court, particularly the *hass oda*, that chronicles contemporary with the events do not emphasize. He relates how, in October 1654, Lala Süleyman's successor, Behram Agha, and his fellow harem eunuch Hoca Reyhan Agha, one of the eunuchs implicated in the murder of Kösem, feared that the *hass oda* pages, eunuchs and otherwise, would use a traditional entertainment for 'Id al-Adha (Kurban Bayramı in Turkish), the holiday marking the completion of the *hajj*, as an excuse to strike at the young sultan and his brothers. (Naima's wording implies that the non-eunuch pages would rape the sultan.) By Naima's account, Turhan was oddly unsuspecting. "Hey Agha," the chronicler has her saying to Behram, "this is the night of the Bayram, and my lion [that is, the sultan] is still a minor. It's an ancient custom [*kanun-i kadim*] for him to watch the [*hass oda*] aghas' games and displays tonight, so let him watch them for half the night; then we'll call him into the harem." But the wary Behram disobeyed her and summoned the sultan to the harem, pretending that he was acting on Turhan's orders.

This turn of events made the *hass oda* pages apopleptic. "You oppressor! You tyrant!" they screamed at Behram, according to Naima. "Don't you know that it's the custom, since ancient times, for holiday entertainments to take place in the *hass oda*?"[4] After attempting to stab him, they formally accused him of conspiring against the sultan and the princes himself. In despair, Behram begged Turhan and her son to manumit him and let him go to Egypt.

Naima may well have wished to convey the impression of a palace divided against itself, foreshadowing the bloody chaos to come, which Köprülü Mehmed Pasha would quell. He may also have chosen to portray Turhan as naïve and in need of a protector. And yet his story is at least plausible in light of earlier friction between harem eunuchs and Third Court pages, and above all in light of the violence that had engulfed the harem just a few years before. In Naima's narrative, the role of neutral third party in the conflict was taken by

---

[4] Naima, *Tarih-i Naima*, III: 1532–36.

the empire's supreme religious official, the Chief Mufti, or Şeyhü'l-Islam, even though in the recent past, this same official had been firmly allied with the Chief Harem Eunuch, siding with el-Hajj Mustafa Agha, then Lala Süleyman Agha, and even issuing a *fetva* condoning Kösem Sultan's murder. On this occasion, the mufti interceded to make peace between the two factions, and Behram Agha remained in office.[5]

Ironically, the mufti's intervention cost Behram his life two years later, in March 1656, when one of the most cataclysmic military rebellions in Ottoman history erupted, known to posterity as the Çınar Vak'ası, or "Plane Tree Incident." As in 1603, the imperial Janissaries and *sipahi*s joined forces over a common grievance, arrears in their pay. While the rival harem-based factions could easily play the two corps of soldiery off against each other, they were helpless against the brute force of the two combined. The soldiers besieged the palace, demanding the heads of the leaders of both the harem and the Third Court, whom they held collectively responsible for withholding their salaries. Terrified, Turhan Sultan and fifteen-year-old Sultan Mehmed sacrificed them all.

As the court chronicler Abdurrahman Abdi Pasha recounts, "The Darüssaade Ağası Behram Agha and the Kapı Ağası [Chief Threshold Eunuch "Bosnian"] Ahmed Agha were at once chained up from head to toe and delivered into the hands of those unbelievers," after which "they hung the two murdered men from the plane tree on the hippodrome." Several other harem and threshold eunuchs managed to escape, but not for long. "The aghas who had fled and hidden were also taken captive," Abdurrahman Abdi continues, "and after they killed them, the rebels hung them from the plane tree on the hippodrome ... This is the decree of all-knowing God." With these gruesome additions, the plane tree now resembled the mythical Waq-Waq tree, whose branches terminate in human bodies, causing some later chroniclers to refer to the rebellion with the alliterative phrase Vak'a-ı Vakvakiyye, or "the Waq-Waq Incident."[6]

This chaotic bloodbath would have deeply traumatized the youthful sultan and his mother. Turhan's desire to prevent such upheavals – at all costs – led her to offer the grand vizierate to Köprülü Mehmed Pasha and to accept the rather stringent conditions upon which he insisted.

Köprülü Mehmed Pasha

The new grand vizier was an Albanian *devshirme* recruit who was known as Köprülü because of an early posting in the north central Anatolian town

---

[5] Ibid., III: 1537–38; Ahmed Resmi, *Hamiletü'l-kübera*, 57.
[6] Aburrahman Abdi, *Vekayiname*, 73–74; Naima, *Tarih-i Naima*, IV: 1654–55, 1721, 1752.

of Köprü, site of a prominent bridge (*köprü* in Turkish). By 1656, he was some eighty years old and a veteran of numerous minor provincial governor-ships, including the one to which, as we saw in Chapter 5, Lala Süleyman Agha had more or less banished him after rejecting him as a candidate for grand vizier in 1651. But now, five years later, his very lack of clientage ties to dominant palace insiders made him an attractive candidate for grand vizier. He accepted the grand vizierate only after Turhan Sultan agreed to a number of conditions, among them virtually no court interference in his decisions and appointments, and a residence-cum-office complex for the grand vizier outside Topkapı Palace.[7]

A grand vizierial residence separate from the imperial palace was nothing new. Nearly 150 years earlier, after all, Ibrahim Pasha, the famously powerful grand vizier of Süleyman I, had built his own palace – today the Museum of Turkish and Islamic Arts – on the western edge of Istanbul's hippodrome. Succeeding grand viziers likewise lived outside the palace. But the idea of separating the chancery from the palace had first appeared only in 1649, when Kara Murad Pasha was grand vizier.[8] By relocating the space in which he performed the duties of his office, the grand vizier physically removed himself from the sultan's household and established his own household in his own space outside the palace. Perhaps more importantly, he distanced himself from the spaces in which the rivalries of the palace factions played out and could thus, at least in theory, transcend their intractable conflicts – although this might be challenging if he were himself a product of the *hass oda*, as many seventeenth-century grand viziers were. He could then compete with the leaders of both palace factions for influence. (For the Köprülüs, as we shall see, this strategy succeeded to a large degree.)

Köprülü Mehmed Pasha's new residence would be the germ of the Bab-i Ali, or "Sublime Porte," located just southwest of Topkapı. Ultimately, the name of the residence would become synonymous with the imperial govern-ment, an indication of how far-reaching this change was.

Köprülü Mehmed's accomplishments as grand vizier were impressive. He won the support of the imperial Janissaries with a combination of dire threats and timely salary payments, then used them to crush a cavalry rebellion in 1657; here, he was following the ordinarily foolproof strategy of dividing the imperial Janissaries and *sipahi*s against each other. Meanwhile, he reinvigor-ated the Ottoman military efforts against both Venice and the Habsburgs, punishing military failure with execution in several cases. He scored his first major military success with the reconquest of Bozca Ada (Tenedos) from Venice in 1657.

---

[7] Naima, *Tarih-i Naima*, IV: 1700–1701.
[8] Tülay Artan, "The Making of the Sublime Porte near the Alay Köşkü and a Tour of a Grand Vizierial Palace at Süleymaniye," *Turcica* 43 (2011): 145–206, especially 150, 182–91.

But Köprülü Mehmed's reforms went far beyond the military to encompass general administrative reform. In this realm, he sought to eliminate corruption throughout the Ottoman military and administrative hierarchies, including lower-ranking viziers, provincial and district governors, military officers, employees of the chancery and the financial bureaucracy, and even palace personnel. He did this to a large extent by appointing members of his own household to these positions. The reach of the Köprülü household extended even to the harem eunuchs, and to the eunuch and non-eunuch pages of the *hass oda* and the rest of the Third Court. Cultivating clients in all these critical spaces helped the grand vizier to lay old palace factional rivalries to rest.

Inevitably, these changes affected the office of Chief Harem Eunuch itself. Köprülü Mehmed had formed a bond with the harem treasurer (*hazinedar-i şehriyari*) Solak ("Left-Handed") Mehmed Agha, who had brought him a robe of honor when he regained Bozca Ada. In 1658, he asked Sultan Mehmed to depose the Chief Eunuch Dilaver Agha, whom he did not trust, and replace him with Solak Mehmed, who was also a favorite of Turhan Sultan. (Dilaver had assumed the post following Behram Agha's murder in the Plane Tree Incident.)[9] This was the first time that the harem treasurer had become Chief Harem Eunuch, and it set a lasting precedent.

We can easily see why this career trajectory would have appealed to Köprülü Mehmed, and to his sons, nephew, and grandson after him: in this way, the supervisor of the harem budget, including outlays for the sultan's mother and all the harem eunuchs, became supervisor of the Holy Cities Pious Foundations, whose revenues were collected in the harem. And if both the treasurer and the Chief Harem Eunuch were Köprülü clients, maximum Köprülü control of the imperial family's expenditures and endowments was theoretically assured. When we consider that the rampant growth of the harem population, both "inmates" and functionaries, and the corresponding growth of harem expenditures, were among the complaints of reform-minded Ottoman bureaucrats during the late sixteenth and early seventeenth centuries,[10] we sense that the Köprülüs encouraged the harem treasurer–Chief Eunuch track as a means of reining in the harem.

After Köprülü Mehmed

Still, we should not regard Köprülü Mehmed and the other members of his family who held the grand vizierate as omnipotent, nor should we assume that the sultan and his mother unquestioningly supported every action that they

---

[9] Abdurrahman Abdi, *Vekayiname*, 99–100; Naima, *Tarih-i Naima*, III: 1653; IV: 1697, 1749–50, 1755, 1759, 1774; Silahdar, *Silahdar Tarihi*, I: 99, 101, 117.

[10] Koçi Bey, *Risaleler*, 103–7; Peirce, *Imperial Harem*, 179–80, 183–85.

took. A personality as strong as Turhan Sultan was not going to sit idly by and allow the grand vizier to dictate personnel appointments with no input from her. And while she may well have found the grizzled octogenarian Köprülü Mehmed intimidating, his son Fazıl Ahmed, who succeeded him following his death in 1661, was more of a peer. Perhaps it is no surprise, then, that in 1663, Turhan sent Köprülü Mehmed's client Solak Mehmed Agha to Egypt and replaced him with a eunuch from her personal entourage, the Baş Kapı Oğlanı ("Head of the Young Men of the [Third Court] Gate") Musli Agha.[11]

Musli was a frail man who, according to Abdurrahman Abdi Pasha, spent most of his five-year tenure on his sickbed.[12] He was apparently "shadowed" throughout this period by the head eunuch of Turhan's entourage (Valide Baş Ağası) Abbas Agha, who succeeded him when Musli died in 1668.[13] Ironically, Abbas's own term was shorter than that of the sickly Musli. He was exiled to Cairo in 1671, leaving a mosque and a public fountain, both still extant, in the neighborhood of Beşiktaş on the European side of the Bosphorus, and taking with him his impressive library, including a number of costly illuminated Qur'ans and important exegetical works.[14] His vigorous commercial activities in Egypt will be covered in Chapter 8.

Yusuf Agha

In the wake of Abbas Agha's exile, the harem treasurer Yusuf Agha ascended to the post of Chief Harem Eunuch. The manner of his appointment mirrors that of Solak Mehmed Agha, thirteen years before, closely enough to point up the importance of this career trajectory to the Köprülü agenda. Ironically, in view of all this, Yusuf did not start out as a Köprülü client at all. Instead, he, like his predecessors Musli and Abbas Aghas (and also Hoca Reyhan Agha), was the eunuch companion (*musahib*) of Mehmed IV's mother Turhan. Since he was only sixty-five or so at the time of his deposition in 1687, he would presumably have entered the Topkapı harem around 1640. He was Turhan's

---

[11] Abdurrahman Abdi, *Vekayiname*, 363; Uzunçarşılı, *Saray Teşkilatı*, 174, 357, 34–35.

[12] Abdurrahman Abdi, *Vekayiname*, 185, 249, 250; Silahdar, *Silahdar Tarihi*, I: 256, 391.

[13] Abdurrahman Abdi, *Vekayiname*, 249–50; Silahdar, *Silahdar Tarihi*, I: 473.

[14] Jane Hathaway, "The Wealth and Influence of an Exiled Ottoman Eunuch in Egypt: The *Waqf* Inventory of Abbas Agha," *Journal of the Economic and Social History of the Orient* 37 (1994): 295, 297, 308–9; Hathaway, *Politics of Households*, 142–43 and n. 15; Topkapı Archive D 7657 (undated), D 8786/2 (1108–9/1697–98), E 11691 (1 Şaban 1108/22 February 1697), E 7833/2–3 (1 Ramazan 1079/1 February 1669), E 7833/7 (31 Rebiülevvel 1081/17 August 1670), E 7844/1–3 (1 Receb 1077/27 December 1666), E 7844/4–5 (1 Rebiülevvel 1080/29 July 1669), E 7926 (1 Şaban 1080/24 December 1669), E 7833/4 (11 Ramazan 1080/1 February 1670), E 7920/2 (1 Cemaziyelahir 1080/26 October 1669); BOA, MD 110, no. 49 (mid-Zilkade 1108/4 June 1697), no. 288 (mid-Cemaziyelevvel 1108/9 December 1696), no. 559 (30 Rebiülevvel 1109/15 October 1697); Ayvansarayi, *Garden of the Mosques*, 418.

musahib by 1655, when he and the older eunuch Hoca Reyhan Agha, along with "the other *musahibs*," delivered an imperial order to the vizier İbşir Mustafa Pasha.[15] In 1667, Yusuf, already harem treasurer, stood in for the dying Musli Agha at the marriage of Fatma Sultan, daughter of Ahmed I, to Yusuf Pasha, the governor of Silistre.[16] (In royal weddings of this sort, the Chief Harem Eunuch commonly served as the bride's representative, or *vekil*.)

Yusuf appears to have been briefly demoted from the treasurer's office, but he was reinstated in 1669, replacing a eunuch who was battling a lengthy illness.[17] (His career seems to have benefited noticeably from the ill-health of certain senior harem eunuchs.) His reappointment occurred just after he had delivered congratulatory gifts to grand vizier Köprülü Fazıl Ahmed Pasha, who had at long last conquered the Cretan capital of Candia. The grand vizier's father, Köprülü Mehmed, had promoted Solak Mehmed Agha to Chief Harem Eunuch after just such a "conquest acknowledgment" mission in 1657. But Köprülü Fazıl Ahmed's capture of Crete was even more momentous than his father's conquest of Tenedos since the siege of Candia had dragged on for a quarter of a century and since, with the acquisition of Crete, the Ottomans had all but expelled Venice and the Knights of St. John from the eastern Mediterranean. Symbolically, the arrival of a high-ranking harem eunuch to acknowledge the victory avenged Sünbül Agha's martyrdom, which, as noted in Chapter 5, had supposedly triggered the Ottoman attempt to conquer Crete.

These eunuch emissaries who delivered gifts after major conquests must have been very carefully chosen, although the selection mechanism is mysterious. Certainly, a close companion of the sultan's mother would have been a strong candidate, but someone who had or could easily win the favor of the grand vizier and his army was also desirable. Choosing the right eunuch to lead the mission was essential since he would presumably be encamped alongside the grand vizier for several weeks, during which raucous festivities would take place and the victorious Ottoman troops would receive various bonuses while piling up spoils of war. Under the circumstances, one of his duties might be escorting select female captives from among the conquered population to Istanbul or Edirne to enter the imperial harem.[18]

The experiences of Solak Mehmed Agha and, thirteen years later, Yusuf Agha suggest that the Köprülü grand viziers saw these missions as an opportunity to test the eunuch leaders' trustworthiness and compatibility. At the same time, the missions offered the grand viziers a chance to coopt eunuchs who belonged to the sultan's entourage or that of his mother. Like Solak

---

[15] Naima, *Tarih-i Naima*, IV: 1574; Abdurrahman Abdi, *Vekayiname*, 60.
[16] Abdurrahman Abdi, *Vekayiname*, 232.   [17] Ibid., 276, 282.
[18] Gülnuş Emetullah Sultan, Mehmed IV's favorite concubine, was originally a Cretan captive (see below).

Mehmed, Yusuf apparently passed the test, for he was not only reinstated as harem treasurer but promoted to Chief Harem Eunuch two years later. Both these appointments probably occurred with the grand vizier's approval, if not on his express orders.

Public Visibility. A congratulatory gift mission was a public ritual, and the appointment of eunuch officials to lead it enhanced the public visibility of the Ottoman harem eunuchs overall, in keeping with the trend established by el-Hajj Mustafa Agha. Mustafa Agha, we recall, had been especially active in processions celebrating the "life cycle events" of imperial family members, and Yusuf followed and expanded upon this precedent, as well. In 1675, he proudly presided at Mehmed IV's lavish celebration (*şenlik*) in Edirne of his seven-year-old daughter Hatice Sultan's marriage to Musahib Mustafa Pasha, as well as the circumcisions of his two sons, the future Mustafa II (r. 1695–1703) and Ahmed III (r. 1703–30). Significantly, Yusuf marched in the circumcision procession next to his successor as harem treasurer, Hazinedar Ali Agha, on whose right marched the future Chief Mufti Feyzullah Efendi, who at the time was the princes' religious instructor.[19]

In his account of the wedding festivities, the chronicler Abdurrahman Abdi Pasha describes Yusuf dressing the viziers and the chief judges (s. *kadı 'asker*, or *kazasker*) of Rumelia and Anatolia "with his own hand" in sable furs sent to them by the sultan, after which the "best man," Defterdar Ahmed Pasha, personally dressed the Chief Eunuch in a fur sent by the bridegroom.[20] This is a level of intimacy that we might not expect to see between the Chief Harem Eunuch and uncastrated males other than the sultan and the imperial princes. On the other hand, it highlights the Chief Eunuch's role as mediator between the private realm of the imperial family and the public realm of Ottoman administrators.

Gülnuş Emetullah Sultan's Pious Foundation. By the time Yusuf Agha became Chief Harem Eunuch, Mehmed IV was finally a grown man with his own concubines. His favorite among these, Rabia Gülnuş Emetullah Sultan, had begun to come into her own as a force within the harem. A daughter of one of the great Venetian families of Rethymno, Crete – possibly the Barozzis[21] – she was captured as a small child by the admiral Deli Hüseyin

[19] Özdemir Nutku, *IV. Mehmet'in Edirne Şenliği (1675)* (Ankara, 1972; 2nd printing 1987), 42–48 and insert following p. 48; Abdurrahman Abdi, *Vekayiname*, 394ff., 312; Defterdar Sarı Mehmed Pasha, *Zübde-i Vekayiât*, ed. Abdülkadir Özcan (Ankara, 1995), 63.

[20] Abdurrahman Abdi, *Vekayiname*, 394–95; Defterdar Sarı Mehmed, *Zübde-i Vekayiât*, 66; Abdi Efendi, *Surname*, in *Osmanlı Saray Düğünleri ve Şenlikleri*, ed. Mehmet Arslan (Istanbul, 2008), V: 492, 505, 513, 524, 531. I am grateful to Sinem Erdoğan İşkorkutan for calling my attention to Arslan's editions of these *surnames*.

[21] Sieur de la Croix gave rise to the belief that her family name was Verzizzi, but no family of this name is documented among the Venetian nobility of Crete. In contrast, the Barozzis were one of

Pasha shortly after the Ottoman conquest of the city in 1646; Deli Hüseyin, who thought her exceptionally attractive, earmarked her for the sultan's harem. In 1664, she gave birth to Prince Mustafa, in 1673 to Prince Ahmed.

Being the mother of two princes enhanced Gülnuş Emetullah's standing in the harem relative to the sultan's still-powerful mother Turhan Sultan. Still, we do not hear of a rivalry between Gülnuş and Turhan that even remotely resembled the murderous competition between Turhan and Kösem a couple of decades earlier. Ostensibly, the only issue that divided them was whether Mehmed IV's half-brothers Süleyman and Ahmed, neither a son of Turhan, should succeed to the throne before Gülnuş's sons, and while Turhan opposed Gülnuş's idea of executing the half-brothers outright, she was not ready to kill or die to ensure their enthronement.[22] (A mark of Turhan's continuing authority is that her opinion prevailed, and both brothers lived to rule briefly.) In this far less fraught harem atmosphere, we should not be entirely surprised to learn, Gülnuş grew close to Yusuf Agha, Turhan's one-time companion, even years before Turhan's death in 1683.

A key indicator of the close relationship between Gülnuş and Yusuf Agha is the new pious foundation (*vakıf*) that Gülnuş founded in 1678 to provide for a hospital and soup kitchen in Mecca. The foundation deed specifies that "Yusuf Agha ibn Abdulmenan, currently Chief Harem Eunuch" will be the superintendent (*nazir ve mütevelli*) of the foundation. (Abdulmenan [literally, "servant of the benefactor," referring to God] is an example of the sort of elevated patronymic that harem eunuchs occasionally took on attaining high rank, in preference to the Abdullah patronymic common among elite slaves; it does not indicate that Yusuf's father was known, let alone a Muslim.) For this service, he received an annual salary of 21,600 *para*s, or Egyptian silver coins, and 40,000 *oka*s (roughly 49,250 kilograms, or more than 100 tons) of wheat.[23] He was to be succeeded by whoever held the office of Chief Eunuch.[24]

The deed describes in exhaustive detail the personnel for which the foundation provides: physicians, surgeons, bookkeepers, cleaners, lamp-lighters, a mortician, and a prayer leader for the hospital; gate-keepers, cooks, dishwashers, carriers of water and firewood, wheat-threshers and -grinders, bakers, and a carpenter for the soup kitchen. Vast quantities of provisions are likewise

---

the most influential Venetian notable families of Rethymno. See Juergen Schulz, *The New Palaces of Medieval Venice* (University Park, PA, 2004), 118ff. Cf. Sieur de la Croix, *Le Sérail des empereurs turcs: Relation manuscrite du sieur de la Croix à la fin du règne du sultan Mehmed IV*, ed. Corinne Thépaut-Cabasset (Paris, 2007), 165; Uluçay, *Padişahların Kadınları ve Kızları*, 66. See also İpşirli Argıt, *Rabia Gülnuş Emetullah Sultan*.

[22] Uluçay, *Padişahların Kadınları ve Kızları*, 66.

[23] For conversion of units of volume, see André Raymond, *Artisans et commerçants au Caire au XVIIIe siècle* (Damascus, 1973–74; reprint, Cairo, 1999), I: lvii.

[24] Duran, ed., *Tarihimizde Vakıf Kuran Kadınlar*, 134–35.

itemized: for the hospital, mattresses, quilts, pillows, soap, "drugs and syrups and pastes"; for the soup kitchen, rice, clarified butter, honey, chickpeas, and onions, in addition to wheat.[25] Apart from the quilts and pillows, most of these things were to come to Mecca from Egypt, in the same way that grain from Egyptian villages was transported to Mecca and Medina every year with the pilgrimage caravan. All of this meant that in order to oversee the endowment, Yusuf Agha had to have reliable ties to Egypt and to Mecca itself, including the Red Sea port of Jidda, through which goods were shipped, and a reliable network of agents and clients in both places. Chapter 8 will provide details of some of these ties. Suffice it to say here that he had the requisite connections and contacts by the time the endowment was established, and they grew stronger and more numerous as the years passed.

The Vienna Debacle. Yusuf was serving as Chief Harem Eunuch at the time of the disastrous Ottoman defeat at Vienna in 1683, when the besieging Ottoman forces were routed by reinforcements led by the Polish general Jan Sobieski, assisted by the torrential rains and impassable mud of the Middle European summer.[26] Rather uncharacteristically, he does not seem to have visited the encampment of the commander of the Vienna campaign, Grand Vizier Merzifonlu Kara Mustafa Pasha, the son-in-law of Köprülü Mehmed Pasha, with messages and robes of honor – but then again, there was no victory to celebrate.

Once Kara Mustafa had been routed and returned to Istanbul in disgrace, moreover, Yusuf appears to have been instrumental in his deposition and execution. This was more than just a matter of disgust over Kara Mustafa's poor battlefield performance. In this case, Yusuf was working with elements in the palace's outer service to bring Kara Mustafa down and replace him with a prominent member of the outer service administrative hierarchy. Specifically, according to the chronicler Silahdar Mehmed Agha, Yusuf aided the Chief Stable Master (Büyük Mir Ahor) Buşnak Sarı Süleyman ("Blond Süleyman the Bosnian") Agha in his quest to depose Kara Mustafa Pasha and claim the grand vizierate for himself. Remarkably, Sarı Süleyman was a protégé of the late Malatyalı Ismail Agha, a white eunuch who, as noted in Chapter 5, had held the posts of Chief Harem and Chief Threshold Eunuch simultaneously in the 1620s, during the brief second reign of Sultan Mustafa I.[27] He thus indirectly represented the pages of the Third Court, who seldom made common cause with harem eunuchs. The two corps of palace pages could, however, join forces against a common foe, which is what Kara Mustafa Pasha appears to have been in this instance.

---

[25] Ibid., 95–157, passim.
[26] Silahdar, *Silahdar Tarihi*, II: 85–96; Finkel, *Osman's Dream*, 284–88.
[27] Silahdar, *Silahdar Tarihi*, II: 293.

The Vienna disaster supplied the perfect pretext for Yusuf and Sarı Süleyman to persuade Mehmed IV to rid himself of his militarily challenged grand vizier. In December 1683, Kara Mustafa's severed head was delivered to Yusuf as he stood before the harem entrance; he himself carried it to the sultan.[28] Even so, Sarı Süleyman had to wait two years to be appointed grand vizier himself.

Deposition. Four years later, though, Yusuf and Sarı Süleyman received their come-uppance at the hands of the volatile palace soldiery. True, Köprülü Mehmed Pasha and his son had tamed the deadly antagonism between the imperial Janissaries and *sipahi*s. By 1687, though, both regiments of soldiery were strained to the breaking point by endless campaigns, particularly against the Habsburgs; insufficient provisions; and tardy pay. The threat of a joint revolt was thus ever present. In August 1687, a party of rebellious soldiers rose up against Buşnak Sarı Süleyman, who was now grand vizier, because of his failure against the Habsburgs. The rebels demanded the deposition of seventy Ottoman officials, including not only the grand vizier but also Yusuf Agha and the Chief Threshold Eunuch. While Sarı Süleyman was executed, Yusuf, apparently on the intercession of the future grand vizier Köprülü Fazıl Mustafa Pasha, younger brother of Fazıl Ahmed, was allowed to set out for exile in Egypt after paying 150,000 *kurush* to the imperial treasury. He was replaced by the harem treasurer Hazinedar Ali Agha, who had actually plotted with the rebels to depose Yusuf and seize his wealth.[29]

But the soldiers were not satisfied with this shuffling of office-holders. By the time Yusuf and his entourage reached Iznik/Nicaea in western Anatolia, the rebels had overthrown Mehmed IV himself and enthroned his brother Süleyman II, a son of Sultan Ibrahim's third-ranking concubine, Saliha Dilaşub Sultan, who was an enemy of Mehmed's mother Turhan and thus presumably felt little sympathy for Turhan's former companion.[30] Insisting that Yusuf had left for Egypt without "our" permission, a band of the rebels stopped his caravan and escorted the eunuch back to Istanbul, where they imprisoned him in Yedikule while his possessions in the capital were inventoried, preparatory to being confiscated. At the same time the new sultan ordered the governor of Egypt to confiscate Yusuf's properties in that province.[31]

In one stroke, then, Yusuf lost the possessions, including slaves, that would have assured a comfortable Egyptian retirement. The Turcophone Egyptian chronicler Mehmed ibn Yusuf al-Hallaq notes that even the house to which

---

[28] Ibid., II: 119–21, 123, 293.

[29] Defterdar Sarı Mehmed, *Zübde-i Vekayiât*, 249; Silahdar, *Silahdar Tarihi*, II: 296–98.

[30] Uluçay, *Padişahların Kadınları ve Kızları*, 59–60; Silahdar, *Silahdar Tarihi*, II: 484.

[31] Silahdar, *Silahdar Tarihi*, II: 277–80, 288–91, 296–98, 305–8, 368; Defterdar Sarı Mehmed, *Zübde-i Vekayiât*, 240–41, 249; BOA, MD 99, no. 381 (mid-Cemaziyelahir 1101/25 March 1690), no. 382 (same date).

the previous governor had been taken on being deposed belonged to Yusuf Agha and had to be sold.[32] Silahdar Mehmed Agha has Yusuf exclaiming, "I was the Chief Harem Eunuch. Now I'm just a ten-*kurush* African ['*Arab* in the text]!"[33] He was grudgingly given just enough of a stipend to live on, plus a "ruined village" for a pittance of additional revenue, and allowed to proceed to Cairo. By the time he arrived there, of course, he had no property, not even a house in which to live. Fortunately, one of his agents in Cairo managed to amass enough money to buy back Yusuf's house, which was located in a neighborhood that was the hub of elite residence in Cairo at the time.[34] Here the humiliated eunuch retreated.

While Süleyman II reigned, Yusuf lived as a virtual non-person in Cairo. His humble stipend would have been disbursed monthly from the imperial treasury through the Keşide regiment, a sort of "retirees'" regiment that existed only on paper.[35] He could not endow properties to pious foundations, either, a common means of generating revenue employed by virtually all exiled Chief Harem Eunuchs. Only private property (*mülk*) could be endowed as *vakıf*, and Yusuf had been stripped of all his private property before he arrived in Cairo. In order to found a new *vakıf*, he, or his agents, would have had to perform a transaction in one of Cairo's Muslim law courts to transform state (*miri*) property into private property,[36] and Süleyman II's administration would surely never have allowed him to do so. His existence during these years must have resembled a penurious form of house arrest, and we may wonder how often he actually left his old house during this period. Everyone in his elite neighborhood would have known who he was, and probably what had happened to him. We can only imagine that this was intensely frustrating to him. He was not a very elderly man by the standards of Chief Harem Eunuchs: roughly sixty-six at the time of his deposition, an age at which many Chief Eunuchs were at the height of their powers.

The Şeyhü'l-Harem

Redemption finally arrived four years later, in 1691, when Süleyman II died and the throne passed to his younger half-brother, Ahmed II. The new sultan

---

[32] Al-Hallaq, *Tarih-i Mısr-ı Kahire*, fol. 219a; Ahmed Çelebi, *Awdah al-isharat*, 181.

[33] Silahdar, *Silahdar Tarihi*, II: 307.

[34] Ahmed Çelebi, *Awdah al-isharat*, 182; André Raymond, "Essai de géographie des quartiers de residence aristocratique au Caire au XVIIIe siècle," *Journal of the Economic and Social History of the Orient* 3 (1963): 66, 67, 72–73, 75–78, 89.

[35] Hathaway, "Role of the Kızlar Ağası," 142.

[36] John Robert Barnes, *An Introduction to Religious Foundations in the Ottoman Empire* (Leiden, 1987); Daniel Crecelius, "The *Waqf* of Muhammad Bey Abu al-Dhahab in Cairo," *International Journal of Middle East Studies* 23, 1 (1991): 59–63.

was the son of Muazzez Sultan, Sultan Ibrahim's second concubine, who had died during a fire in the Old Palace in 1683 and who, in any case, did not share Dilaşub's hostility toward Mehmed IV, his mother, and his mother's inner circle.[37] Ahmed II had little trouble pardoning Yusuf Agha. In addition, the grand vizier at the time of Süleyman's death, Köprülü Fazıl Mustafa Pasha, who four years earlier had saved Yusuf from execution, probably had a hand in the eunuch's reprieve. Fazıl Mustafa Pasha did not trust Mustafa Agha, the Chief Harem Eunuch during most of Süleyman II's reign, and, even before the sultan's death, exiled him to Egypt with the acquiescence of other high government officials. He was replaced by the treasurer of the holy cities, Karagöz Gedai Ahmed Agha.[38]

Yusuf's property was now returned to him. Shortly thereafter, in an extraordinary move, he was appointed Şeyhü'l-Harem, or head of the corps of eunuchs – most of them former imperial harem eunuchs – who guarded the Prophet Muhammad's tomb in Medina. He seems to have held this post for roughly five years before returning to Cairo.[39] He set a precedent that would ultimately extend through the end of the Ottoman Empire.

The Tomb Eunuchs. Why was the Prophet Muhammad's tomb guarded by eunuchs? The institution of the eunuch guard has been exhaustively studied by Shaun Marmon.[40] To summarize briefly, the Zengid and Ayyubid dynasties, who controlled Mecca and Medina from the mid-twelfth through the mid-thirteenth century, instituted the guard as a means of shoring up Sunnism in Medina, which, at least since the Fatimids took over the region in the late tenth century, had been dominated by Ismaili and Zaydi Shi'ites. Shi'ite residents of the city heckled the Sunni preachers whom the Zengids and Ayyubids installed in the Prophet's Mosque. At the same time, they objected to the presence in the nearby tomb precinct of the graves of Abu Bakr and 'Umar ibn al-Khattab, whom Sunnis recognize as the first two caliphs, or successors to Muhammad as leader of the Muslim community, but who Shi'ites believe usurped the caliphate from 'Ali ibn Abi Talib; in the mid-nineteenth century, Sir Richard Francis Burton described Shi'ite pilgrims throwing rubbish and worse in the direction of Abu Bakr's and 'Umar's graves.[41] The Zengids and Ayyubids installed a "row of eunuchs" in front of the *minbar* – the structure from which

---

[37] Silahdar, *Silahdar Tarihi*, II: 273; Uluçay, *Padişahların Kadınları ve Kızları*, 60.

[38] Silahdar, *Silahdar Tarihi*, II: 501; Defterdar Sarı Mehmed, *Zübde-i Vekayiât*, 360–61; BOA, MD 99, no. 495 (mid-Receb 1101/23 April 1690).

[39] Silahdar, *Silahdar Tarihi*, II: 782–83; Defterdar Sarı Mehmed, *Zübde-i Vekayiât*, 385; BOA, MD 102, no. 751 (1 Receb 1103/18 March 1692); MD 104, no. 787 (1 Receb 1104/7 March 1693); MD 108, no. 242 (1 Cemaziyelahir 1107/6 January 1696).

[40] Marmon, *Eunuchs and Sacred Boundaries*, 31–77.

[41] Burton, *Personal Narrative*, I: 321 and n. 1.

the prayer leader delivers the oration at Friday noontime prayers – in the mosque and a eunuch guard around the tomb.

The Prophet's Mosque abuts his tomb: the original mosque was constructed next to the humble house that he inhabited after his migration to Medina in 622 CE. When Muhammad died in 632 CE, his youngest wife, Aisha, the daughter of Abu Bakr, buried him beneath the floor of the house, as was the custom. This was how Abu Bakr and 'Umar came to be buried in the tomb precinct since they, too, were buried under the floor of the Prophet's house when they died. The Umayyad caliph al-Walid (r. 705–15) transformed the mosque and the house into a religious complex, the germ of the modern-day mosque–mausoleum complex. As the centuries passed, visiting the Prophet's tomb came to be a popular ritual for Muslims, often combined with the *hajj* or with a personal pilgrimage (*'umra*) to Mecca outside of the *hajj* season.

As early as the eighth century, the Umayyads had built a barrier to keep visitors from stampeding toward the tomb and thus disrupting the site. Under the Zengids and Ayyubids, only members of the eunuch guard could actually enter the chamber housing the tomb. They entered the passageway outside the tomb chamber daily to sweep up and to light and extinguish the oil lamps that hung there. Once a year, on a night during the *hajj* season, they entered the tomb chamber itself to replace the ceremonial covering, known as the *kiswa*, over the tomb; a new covering was woven in Damascus each year and carried to Medina with the Damascus *hajj* caravan. (In the same fashion, a *kiswa* for the Ka'ba was woven in Alexandria each year and delivered by the Egyptian *hajj* caravan. But while the Ka'ba covering was black with a band of gold calligraphic Qur'an inscriptions, the tomb covering resembled other Muslim tomb coverings: green silk with bands of white Qur'anic calligraphy in a chevron pattern.)[42]

On a day-to-day basis, a portion of the eunuchs sat in the so-called eunuchs' porch on the tomb's northern façade so as to monitor the appearance and behavior of visitors. Many of them held long, thin wooden rods that they did not hesitate to use on visitors whose behavior they deemed disruptive or uncouth. They could, and did, physically expel anyone whose actions they found particularly irksome.[43] We do not know whether Yusuf took his turn on the eunuchs' porch, however.

And why eunuchs specifically, as opposed to uncastrated functionaries? For the same reason that empires had always employed them: they were the most loyal government officials available, with an unshakable allegiance to the regimes that employed them. But in the case of the Prophet's mosque and

---

[42] D'Ohsson, *Tableau général*, III: 302, 305–6; Burton, *Personal Narrative*, I: 321–22 n. 2.
[43] D'Ohsson, *Tableau général*, III: 305–6; Burckhardt, *Travels in Arabia*, 332–33; Burton, *Personal Narrative*, I: 316 n. 2, 372.

tomb, the utility of eunuchs went well beyond loyalty to the ruling power, drawing on some of the qualities discussed in Chapter 1. As Marmon eloquently explains, eunuchs were the logical occupants of the liminal space between the sacred space of the tomb and the public space outside the tomb precinct, just as they were the logical occupants of the similarly taboo space between the palace harem and the public space of Topkapı's Second Court. Most eunuchs employed by Muslim empires were male-gendered, but even so, as nonreproductive beings, they retained the "uncorrupted" status of children and were thus able to mediate between the purity of the tomb (or, in a palace setting, the women's quarters) and the pollution of the public arena.[44] Add to this the practical benefits of having no children or other family members to draw them away from service to the tomb or the mosque.

Under the Ottomans, the tomb eunuchs were, virtually without exception, former harem eunuchs. This helps to explain why all of them were African. Before the Ottoman Empire took control of the holy cities, the corps of tomb eunuchs had been far more diverse: in his account of Medina in the mid-fifteenth century, the Mamluk chronicler al-Sakhawi describes tomb eunuchs of Anatolian Greek, Ethiopian, West African, and Indian origin, with the Indians forming the largest single category.[45] The number of tomb eunuchs appears to have remained remarkably stable for several centuries: al-Sakhawi reports forty, the same number given by the Armenian dragoman Mouradgea d'Ohsson at the end of the eighteenth century and the Spaniard who traveled under the pseudonym Ali Bey al-Abbasi in 1806, while the Swiss Orientalist John Lewis Burckhardt, in 1814, has forty to fifty. By the time Richard Francis Burton visited in the 1850s, though, the number had jumped to 120.[46]

The title Şeyhü'l-Harem (Shaykh al-Haram) (literally, "leader of the holy sanctuary," referring to either Mecca or Medina) appears to have originated with the Ottomans in the decades after they acquired control of the holy cities from the Mamluk Sultanate. Under the Ottomans, there were two şeyhs: one for Mecca, one for Medina. Originally, neither office was identified with the chief of the tomb eunuchs. Naima mentions a Mevla or Molla Mehmed – obviously a member of the ulema – who served as Şeyhü'l-Harem in Medina toward the end of the sixteenth century, dying in 1591–92.[47] A year after Sultan Osman II's murder in 1622, his tutor, who had been in hiding, was

---

[44] Marmon, *Eunuchs and Sacred Boundaries*, 85–92.
[45] Al-Sakhawi, cited in Marmon, *Eunuchs and Sacred Boundaries*, 39. ˙
[46] Ibid.; d'Ohsson, *Tableau général*, III: 305; Ali Bey al-Abbasi (Domingo Badia y Leyblich), cited in F.E. Peters, *Mecca: A Literary History of the Muslim Holy Land* (Princeton, NJ, 1994), 263, 275, 283 (d'Ohsson and Ali Bey may be using al-Sakhawi's figure); Burckhardt, *Travels in Arabia*, 342; Burton, *Personal Narrative*, I: 372; BOA, MD 99, no. 281 (mid-Cemaziyelevvel 1101/23 February 1691).
[47] Naima, *Tarih-i Naima*, I: 55; d'Ohsson, *Tableau général*, III: 280.

appointed Şeyhü'l-Harem of Mecca on the intercession of Istanbul's ulema.[48] In the late sixteenth and early seventeenth centuries, then, the office in both holy cities seems to have been dominated by Muslim scholars. Nonetheless, by the late seventeenth century, Mecca's Şeyhü'l-Harem was always a bey of Egypt. In 1708, though, the Ottoman central authority began to appoint pashas to the office, no doubt as part of a broader effort to tighten control over the pilgrimage.[49]

As for the Şeyhü'l-Harem of Medina, Naima mentions a eunuch companion (*musahib*) of Murad IV, one Beshir Agha, taking up the post in 1644, during Sultan Ibrahim's reign; at the same time, he was appointed overseer in Egypt of one of the Evkafü'l-Haremeyn. Several years later, he was recalled to the palace to be the young Sultan Mehmed IV's calligraphy teacher.[50] His experience illustrates several developing trends in appointments to this office. First, the post was filled by a harem eunuch who held, or had previously held, the rank of sultan's companion, or *musahib*; it was not yet occupied by former or future Chief Harem Eunuchs. Second, the office was linked, explicitly or implicitly, to Egypt. In this particular case, it entailed supervision of operations in Egypt – primarily grain and revenue collection and transport – of one of the imperial endowments for Mecca and Medina, but these duties would always come under the ultimate authority of the acting Chief Harem Eunuch in Istanbul. Finally, the appointment of a calligrapher-eunuch could perhaps represent a nod to the earlier dominance of the office by ulema, though it was not uncommon for eunuchs to be calligraphers.

This custom of filling the post of Şeyhü'l-Harem with harem eunuchs who had served as sultans' companions continued well into the reign of Mehmed IV. In 1666, Abdurrahman Abdi reports that the sultan summoned Şeyhü'l-Harem Hajji Salih Agha back to Edirne to resume his post as companion; Mehmed had apparently missed his jokes (*lata'if*).[51] And while Yusuf Agha set a precedent by becoming the first former Chief Harem Eunuch to hold the post of Şeyhü'l-Harem of Medina, it was nearly a century before another Chief Eunuch followed this trajectory. During the nineteenth century, this career pattern became much more routine.[52]

A key benefit to the appointment of a former Chief Harem Eunuch as Şeyhü'l-Harem was that it linked eunuch networks in Istanbul, Cairo, and

---

[48] Naima, *Tarih-i Naima*, II: 508.
[49] Ahmad Katkhuda al-Damurdashi, *Al-Durra al-musana fi akhbar al-Kinana*, British Library, MS OR 1073–74, 99–101; Karl K. Barbir, *Ottoman Rule in Damascus, 1700–1758* (Princeton, NJ, 1980), 13–14, 51–56, and passim.
[50] Naima, *Tarih-i Naima*, III: 997; II: 825; III: 1253; BOA, MD 90, no. 436 (30 Şaban 1056/10 October 1646); MD 91, no. 447 (9 Şevval 1056/17 November 1646).
[51] Abdurrahman Abdi, *Vekayiname*, 196, 218.
[52] *Defter-i Ağayan-ı Darüssaade*, appendix to *Hamiletü'l-kübera*, 171–75.

Medina as never before. This not only facilitated the movement of eunuchs among these three cities; it also contributed to the palace's control over the Holy Cities Pious Foundations, and to palace influence over Cairo's and Medina's affairs. An intriguing question is the degree to which Yusuf Agha might have served as the grand vizier's eyes and ears in Medina. This may have been Köprülü Fazıl Mustafa Pasha's grand design before his untimely death at the Battle of Slankamen in northern Serbia in 1691.

Over the years, the presence of the corps of eunuchs at the Prophet's mosque and tomb had given rise to a eunuch quarter in Medina, known as Harat al-Aghawat ("Neighborhood of the Aghas"), just outside one of the gates of the tomb complex. Burckhardt, who scrutinized Mecca and Medina with characteristic thoroughness in 1814, describes the tomb eunuchs "liv[ing] together in one of the best quarters of Medina … [T]heir houses are said to be furnished in a more costly manner than any others in the town." The Şeyhü'l-Harem's "palace" stood slightly apart from the quarter, just southeast of the tomb and slightly to the west of Jannat al-Baqi' cemetery, where many luminaries of early Islam, including the Prophet's favorite wife Aisha, are buried.[53] For Yusuf Agha, it would presumably have made for a refreshing change of scene after four years of virtual house arrest in Cairo. Now Yusuf Agha was one of Medina's local notables. He would have enjoyed an extensive staff of servants and aides at the new house. Burckhardt even reports that the Şeyhü'l-Harem was one of the few people in Medina who kept horses.[54] This, after four excruciating years of ignominy, was real power again.

The accounts of Burckhardt and Burton provide a clue to the opportunities that the office of Şeyhü'l-Harem might have offered Yusuf for rebuilding his household. The Şeyhü'l-Harem, Burton tells us, was responsible for appointing all the tomb eunuchs who were subordinate to him. An administrative hierarchy existed among the tomb eunuchs that, to some degree, mimicked the eunuch hierarchy in the palace.[55] Directly below the Şeyhü'l-Harem was the chief treasurer of the mosque and tomb complex; if his post had fallen vacant, then Yusuf could have replaced him with one of his clients. Yet Yusuf served as Şeyhü'l-Harem for only five or six years, so he may have been able to make only a limited number of appointments. Most of the lower-ranking eunuchs at the Prophet's tomb during his tenure would have been a hodge-podge of appointees of a variety of şeyhs.

---

[53] Burckhardt, *Travels in Arabia*, 324, 342–43, and 320–21 (map); Burton, *Personal Narrative*, I, map between 392 and 393.

[54] Burckhardt, *Travels in Arabia*, 386.

[55] BOA, MD 99, nos. 281 (mid-Cemaziyelevvel 1101/23 February 1690), 303 (30 Cemaziyelevvel 1101/10 March 1690); MD 110, no. 817 (30 Cemaziyelahir 1109/12 January 1698); Burton, *Personal Narrative*, I: 371–72.

In stark contrast, by Burckhardt's account, the much smaller corps of eunuchs who guarded the Great Mosque in Mecca were true protégés of their chief: they were appointed while still minors and actually lived with the head of the Mecca eunuchs, who supervised their education "till they attain a sufficient age to allow of their living in private lodgings."[56] But the chief of the tomb eunuchs in Medina was a far more influential figure than his counterpart in Mecca, so perhaps the Köprülüs and other grand viziers wished to exercise a bit more control over his office, in the same way they sought to control the office of Chief Harem Eunuch. If so, they could do so by limiting the Şeyhü'l-Harem's term. This would prevent him from appointing large numbers of tomb eunuchs from among his own protégés, and thus turning the corps of tomb eunuchs into a bastion of his own influence. So appointment as Şeyhü'l-Harem was perhaps not the foolproof route to household reconstitution for which Yusuf had been hoping.

Yet there were other compensations. The Şeyhü'l-Harem and the rest of the adult tomb eunuchs were married "to black or Abyssinian slaves," in Burckhardt's words.[57] This appears to have been largely a symbolic perquisite, indicating the eunuch's "completion" after making "the *hijra* to God and his Prophet."[58] The sacred aura of service at the Prophet's tomb can hardly be overemphasized. Mouradgea d'Ohsson observed that many high officials volunteered to serve as tomb-sweepers alongside the eunuchs out of personal piety. He further claims that harem eunuchs who were "disgraced and relegated to Egypt" dreamed of ending their days in Medina.[59] But a wife could contribute significantly to household wealth by acquiring properties and investing in economic activities in her own right,[60] so her contribution to Yusuf's well-being may have been more than spiritual. Unfortunately, we know absolutely nothing about the wives of Medina's eunuchs, apart from the fact that they were apparently from East Africa; their activities are likewise a complete mystery.

Yusuf was Şeyhü'l-Harem until perhaps 1696 or 1697. After that, he appears in a 1702 list of Cairo-based overseers of Gülnuş Emetullah's pious foundation, to be discussed in Chapter 8. He then all but disappears from the historical record until his death in 1717. He was getting on by 1702 – roughly eighty years old, and presumably with the usual catalogue of eunuch health complaints: osteoporosis, chronic urinary tract infections, obesity or emaciation, and so on. The Cairene chronicler Ahmed Çelebi memorably places his report of Yusuf's death, at the age of ninety-six, just ahead of news that el-Hajj

---

[56] Burckhardt, *Travels in Arabia*, 116.   [57] Ibid., 343; Burton, *Personal Narrative*, I: 372.
[58] Al-Qalqashandi, cited in Marmon, *Eunuchs and Sacred Boundaries*, 59.
[59] D'Ohsson, *Tableau général*, III: 305–6.
[60] Hathaway, *Politics of Households*, 116–19, 126, 130.

Beshir Agha has been recalled from Cairo to Istanbul to take up the mantle of Chief Harem Eunuch.[61]

Despite his stints as Şeyhü'l-Harem and supervisor of Gülnuş Emetullah's pious foundation, Yusuf's estate was modest at best, and may even have been rather meager – again, this may have been in part an effect of his relatively brief term as Şeyhu'l-Harem. In 1725, the Egyptian chronicler Ahmed Kethüda (Ahmad Katkhuda) al-Damurdashi reports the mamluk of one of Yusuf's clients living in the eunuch's old house in Cairo, but this man was so poor that he had had to lease the house out, using the legal subterfuge of a ninety-year lease, which amounted to a de facto sale.[62] So far as the welfare of his clients was concerned, Yusuf's fall from grace back in 1687 seems to have dealt the eunuch's fortunes a permanent blow.

Conclusion

Historians of the Ottoman Empire tend to agree that the crisis of the seventeenth century ended not simply with the reforms of the Köprülü grand viziers but with a regularization of career definitions and patterns that dovetailed with the Köprülüs' agenda. This regularization occurred across a wide swath of the Ottoman Empire's administrative echelons: the religious establishment, the central and provincial government bureaucracies, and, of course, the military and administrative hierarchies.[63] We can certainly observe this kind of regularization in the office of Chief Harem Eunuch and the milieu within which he operated. The Köprülüs imposed a degree of predictability on the office that allowed them, and other grand viziers, to exercise greater leverage on the Chief Eunuch. More generally, the Köprülü agenda dovetailed with and took advantage of a number of administrative and demographic changes that were already at work in the Ottoman Empire when Köprülü Mehmed Pasha first became grand vizier in 1656.

Where palace politics were concerned, the Köprülü grand viziers unquestionably succeeded in their mission of curbing the ruinous conflict between palace factions, abetted by the corps of palace soldiery. By the time Köprülü Fazıl Mustafa Pasha, younger son of Köprülü Mehmed Pasha, became grand vizier in 1689, it was barely detectable. Köprülü Mehmed's and Köprülü Fazıl Ahmed's policy of packing the Ottoman administrative hierarchy with members of their own households played a key role in neutralizing the

---

[61] Ahmed Çelebi, *Awdah al-isharat*, 290.
[62] Al-Damurdashi, *Al-Durra al-musana*, 322; Hathaway, "Role of the Kızlar Ağası," 145.
[63] Madeline C. Zilfi, *The Politics of Piety: The Ottoman Ulema in the Post-Classical Age, 1600–1800* (Minneapolis, MN, 1988), chapters 5–6; Norman Itzkowitz, "Eighteenth-Century Ottoman Realities," *Studia Islamica* 16 (1962): 73–94.

competition. This was the epitome of vizier and pasha household political culture, for the Köprülü household took precedence not only over the imperial household but also over competing vizier and pasha households at the imperial center and in the provinces.

The broader Köprülü agenda also benefited from other factors that were part of the larger late seventeenth-century landscape. One of the most important of these was the separation of the grand vizier's base of operations from the palace. While the grand vizier's council chamber was still in its familiar place on the west side of Topkapı's Second Court, the chancery, over which the grand vizier presided, had moved outside the palace, to the site later known as Bab-i Ali. This meant that on a day-to-day basis, the grand vizier was physically removed from the contentious spaces within the palace where factional rivalry operated. The idea of a chancery outside the palace did not originate with the Köprülü grand viziers, but they made it a permanent feature of the office.

A further aid to the Köprülü agenda was the changing demographic composition of the Third Court page population. Following Osman II's murder by rebellious *kullar* of *devshirme* origin, the Ottoman palace turned to alternative recruitment methods to supplement, and ultimately to displace, the *devshirme*, in particular hiring Muslim-born mercenaries from Anatolia and purchasing mamluks from the Caucasus. These new elements diluted the ethnoregional solidarity of the palace pages, as well as the imperial Janissaries and other corps of palace soldiery. The corps of palace pages and soldiers alike were now likely to be internally divided into broad ethnoregional categories, specifically "westerners" from the Balkans and western Anatolia, who might still be recruited through the *devshirme*, and "easterners" from the Caucasus, who were usually mamluks. The growing diversity of palace personnel enabled the Köprülüs to use a "divide and conquer" strategy – or, on the other hand, to emphasize the common purpose of serving the sultan that, they insisted, came before ethnoregional solidarity.[64]

At the same time, the internal administrative hierarchy of the Third Court was changing. The Chief Threshold Eunuch (*Kapı Ağası*) was still important, and his appointment or deposition is duly noted by late seventeenth-century chroniclers.[65] Yet he was beginning to be upstaged by influential non-eunuch members of the *hass oda* administration, above all the *silahdar*, or sultan's sword-bearer. In the early eighteenth century, the reforming grand vizier Çorlulu Ali Pasha (who was not a Köprülü), himself the former *silahdar* to Sultan Mustafa II, gave the *silahdar* command of the Third Court in place of the white eunuchs. From this point until the abolition of the office of *silahdar*

---

[64] Kunt, "Ethno-Regional (*Cins*) Solidarity," 239.
[65] E.g., Abdurrahman Abdi, *Vekayiname*, 33, 101, 133, 170, 419; Naima, *Tarih-i Naima*, II: 898.

in 1830, the leaders of the harem and the Third Court were the Chief Harem Eunuch and, not the Chief Threshold Eunuch, but the *silahdar*.[66] This meant that there was less potential for direct competition between the Chief Harem Eunuch and the Chief Threshold Eunuch since they no longer held parallel offices of anything like equal authority. As for the *silahdar*, his ultimate goal was not supremacy within the palace's inner sanctum but an influential post outside it, up to and including that of grand vizier. In this context, it was at least possible for the leader of the harem and the leader of the Third Court to be allies.

The restive imperial Janissary and *sipahi* regiments posed a less predictable and more life-threatening challenge. The Köprülüs dealt with this challenge in part by using the traditional tactic of setting the two regiments against each other; in these cases, they usually favored the Janissaries. But they also set a new and lethal precedent by simply crushing rebellion or threats of rebellion with brutal, ruthless force. Köprülü Mehmed Pasha's and Köprülü Fazıl Ahmed Pasha's military successes, with the military bonuses and war booty that went with them, also helped to quiet the soldiery. Meanwhile, gradual abandonment of the *devshirme* had the same effect on the imperial Janissaries that it had on the Third Court, undercutting the regiment's ethnoregional solidarity and sense of entitlement. As cavalry became a less important component of imperial armies, moreover, the *sipahi*s became, as it were, permanently inferior to the Janissaries, making military confrontation between the two regiments an increasingly rare occurrence. By the early eighteenth century, military unrest in the capital was unlikely to come from the imperial Janissaries and *sipahi*s, and far more likely to be the work of the increasing numbers of mercenary troops.

Where the office of Chief Harem Eunuch was concerned, the Köprülüs sought more institutionalized control and, to that end, virtually imposed a career trajectory that led from harem treasurer to the top office. This progression had become the norm within fifteen years of Köprülü Mehmed Pasha's appointment as grand vizier, testifying to the efficacy of the Köprülü agenda in this regard. Among other things, this career path limited the influence of the sultan's mother since it decreased the chances that the head of her eunuch entourage would become Chief Eunuch. The harem treasurer might be a former boon companion to the sultan, but he was almost never a protégé of the sultan's mother. Nor was he the client of his predecessor as Chief Harem Eunuch. In essence, then, this career trajectory was a "divide and conquer" tactic similar to the tactics that the Köprülüs applied to the palace soldiery and the pages of the Third Court.

---

[66] D'Ohsson, *Tableau général*, VII: 58–61; Uzunçarşılı, *Saray Teşkilatı*, 341–46; Naima, *Tarih-i Naima*, II: 974; III: 1064–68.

In light of these considerations, Yusuf Agha makes a rather curious case study of the effects of the Köprülüs' measures. He was not the client of either Köprülü Mehmed or Köprülü Fazıl Ahmed Pasha. Instead, he seems to have been far more closely associated with Mehmed IV, and perhaps even more so with Turhan Sultan and Gülnuş Emetullah, although he was never Valide Baş Ağası to either of them. Nonetheless, the high and low points of his career coincide rather uncannily with those of the Köprülü grand viziers. Although he helped to bring down the Köprülü in-law Kara Mustafa Pasha, he himself was saved from utter disaster, in the aftermath of Mehmed IV's overthrow, by Köprülü Fazıl Mustafa's intercession with the rebels. His rehabilitation and appointment as Şeyhü'l-Harem likewise coincided with the enthronement of Ahmed II, Fazıl Mustafa's choice for the sultanate in preference to the sons of Mehmed IV, and Fazıl Mustafa's occupation of the grand vizierate. He returned to Egypt, and, as we shall see in Chapter 8, assumed the status of a sort of honorary provincial grandee during the reign of Mustafa II, who had thrown off the "Köprülü yoke" and attempted to assert himself as a warrior sultan.[67] Similarly, this phase of his career appears to end around the time of Ahmed III's accession in 1703, although of course, Yusuf was also an old man by then and, we have to assume, slowing down somewhat.

Notwithstanding, the evidence linking Yusuf Agha to the Köprülüs' reforming agenda is circumstantial at best. Unlike Solak Mehmed Agha, he was not their client; unlike Dilaver and Mustafa Aghas, he was not expelled by them from the capital. It may be safest to regard him as a palace stalwart whose own agenda not infrequently coincided with that of the Köprülüs. In the end, he outlived all but one of the Köprülü grand viziers, as well as Turhan Sultan, Gülnuş Emetullah, and Mehmed IV.

By the time of Yusuf's death in 1717, the Ottoman Empire had pulled out of its prolonged crisis, thanks in no small part to the Köprülüs themselves. The economy was growing again, and the socioeconomic elite were enjoying an unprecedented surge in trade with western Europe. These were the conditions in which el-Hajj Beshir Agha, who, as Ahmed Çelebi reminds us, became Chief Eunuch just after Yusuf's death, would set an indelible stamp on the office.

---

[67] Rifaat A. Abou-El-Haj, *The 1703 Rebellion and the Structure of Ottoman Politics* (Leiden, 1984), 34, 42, 47, 49, 53.

7   A New Paradigm
El-Hajj Beshir Agha and His Successors

As we saw in Chapter 6, the Ottoman Empire by the last years of the seventeenth century was beginning to pull out of the wrenching crisis that had gripped it for so many decades. What did an empire look like that had recovered from such a severe crisis? Most obviously, things were calmer. Bands of mercenaries – whether demobilized soldiers, peasants driven from the land by drought and inflation, or some combination of the two – no longer roamed the countryside. Bands of militant students, despairing of gainful employment in the ranks of the ulema, no longer terrorized the cities. Meanwhile, the agricultural, military, bureaucratic, and ulema professions had become more regular, characterized by far more generational continuity: in other words, sons succeeded fathers in these lines of work, drastically curtailing career possibilities for those hoping to enter a profession from outside but increasing the social stability that came from having such predictable career trajectories.

Greater stability characterized the palace, as well. The competition between the harem functionaries and those of the Third Court had quieted now that the *hass oda* was dominated by non-eunuch officers who could hope to become grand vizier (Table 7.1). As we saw in Chapter 6, the Chief Eunuch now sought to control the grand vizierate by channeling clients into the *hass oda*. But the 1699 Treaty of Karlowitz, which ended the Ottoman-Habsburg struggle ignited by the failed siege of Vienna, ushered in a period of greater diplomacy in which grand viziers came increasingly from the imperial bureaucracy rather than from the palace page system. This limited the Chief Eunuch's opportunities to channel palace clients into the office. During the eighteenth century, as a result, the grand vizier emerged as the Chief Eunuch's principal rival.

Where the imperial family was concerned, the post-crisis era featured less seclusion from the sultan's subjects. Following the long reign of Mehmed IV, a series of grown men took the throne. While they had all been raised in the harem and were, to varying degrees, influenced by a series of Chief Eunuchs, they at least represented the dynasty publicly, appearing regularly at public Friday prayers and participating in public spectacles. After 1703, furthermore, for reasons that will be explained below, they were back in Istanbul after

129

Table 7.1 *Major officers of the harem and Third Court in the early to mid-eighteenth century*

Harem		Third Court	
		Sword-Bearer (Silahdar) *Çorlulu Ali* *Damad Ali*	
Sultan's Mother	Chief Harem Eunuch	**Gate of Felicity**	**Privy Chamber**
Gülnuş	*Yapraksız Ali*	**(Babüssaade)**	**(Hass Oda)**
Emetullah	*Solak Nezir*		
(Mustafa II,	*Küçük Abdurrahman*	Chief Threshold	Valet (Çuhadar)
Ahmed III)	*Uzun Süleyman*	Eunuch (Kapı Ağası)	
Saliha (Mahmud I)	*Mercan*		Stirrup-Holder
	El-Hajj Beshir	Palace Treasurer	(Rikabdar)
	Moralı Beshir	(Hazinedar Başı)	
	Ebu'l-Vukuf Ahmed		Privy Chamber Head
		Palace Head (Saray	(Hass Oda Başı)
	Harem Treasurer	Ağası)	
	(Hazinedar-i Şehriyari)		
	Solak Nezir	Boys of the	
	Hafiz Mehmed	Threshold (Kapı	
	El-Hajj Beshir	Oğlanı)	
	Moralı Beshir		
	Süleyman		
	Ebu'l-Vukuf Ahmed		
	Companions (Musahibs)		
	Solak Nezir		
	Hafiz Mehmed		
	El-Hajj Beshir		

a Italics indicate individuals named in the chapter.

decades in Edirne, favorite haunt of Mehmed IV. The court's return to the imperial capital triggered a boom in the construction of pleasure palaces and outdoor pavilions in previously sparsely populated areas of Istanbul. Here, the sultan presided over increasingly lavish entertainments, taking advantage of expanding trade in luxury goods with western Europe.

Less seclusion and greater connectedness are likewise dominant motifs in the conduct of the Chief Harem Eunuch during the post-crisis era. In Istanbul, he took the lead in planning, executing, and presiding over the imperial entertainments that became so visible during the eighteenth century. And if he did not become more connected to the mass of Ottoman subjects, he did cultivate sustained relationships outside the imperial capital: with the increasingly influential notables of the Ottoman provinces, with the holy cities of Mecca and Medina, and with the commercial and diplomatic agents of the European powers. These new tendencies built on older patterns that were already established features of the Chief Eunuch's career by the end of the seventeenth century: stints in Egypt before and after appointment as Chief Eunuch, appointment to head the tomb eunuchs in Medina, and the career trajectory of harem treasurer to Chief Eunuch.

All these tendencies reached their epitome in the twenty-nine-year tenure of el-Hajj Beshir Agha, which forms the centerpiece of this chapter. They persisted in the careers of his successors, two of whom are profiled here. We can therefore say that el-Hajj Beshir Agha introduced a new paradigm to the career of Chief Harem Eunuch that lasted until the end of the eighteenth century. What the careers of Beshir's successors reveal, though, is that Beshir's career is somewhat exceptional. While the paradigm persisted, some of its features had negative consequences for later Chief Eunuchs. In this sense, el-Hajj Beshir Agha broke the mold.

This chapter begins with the careers of two Chief Eunuchs who set the stage for el-Hajj Beshir's ascendancy. Solak Nezir Agha was intimately involved with the crisis that brought the Ottoman court back to Istanbul. Uzun Süleyman Agha, meanwhile, was el-Hajj Beshir's direct superior during the early part of his career. Their careers provide context for his own. In addition, his career was, to different degrees, intertwined with theirs. We then turn to el-Hajj Beshir and his successor, Moralı Beshir, and how their careers reflect the new cosmopolitanism and "public sociability" of the eighteenth-century Ottoman court. A final section examines the increasing enmeshment of provincial notables, particularly those connected to the pilgrimage, with the Chief Eunuch, focusing on el-Hajj Beshir and another of his successors.

Solak Nezir Agha (1701–1703) and the Edirne Vak'ası

One tendency of the crisis years that did not become normative in the eighteenth century was the Chief Harem Eunuch's alliances with high-ranking members of the Ottoman ulema, particularly the Chief Mufti, or Şeyhü'l-Islam. In Chapter 6, we observed the mufti intervening to protect the Chief Eunuch from the *hass oda* pages. El-Hajj Mustafa Agha and Lala Süleyman Agha even combined with the Chief Mufti – and, in Lala Süleyman's case, the Nakibü'l-Eşraf, or head of the descendants of the Prophet – to bring down troublesome grand viziers. By the reign of Ahmed III (1703–30), this sort of strategic partnership was no longer a reliable option, largely because the office of Şeyhü'l-Islam had been tarnished by the 1703 Edirne Incident (Edirne Vak'ası), which was triggered by the excesses of the nepotistic mufti Feyzullah Efendi. While it is not clear that Feyzullah was allied with the Chief Eunuch of his day, Solak Nezir Agha, the latter suffered from guilt by association, to the extent that the mufti's downfall triggered his own, as well as that of Sultan Mustafa II (r. 1695–1703).

Nezir Agha was probably known as Solak, "left-handed," to distinguish him from an earlier Nezir Agha, known as Kaba ("coarse" or "rude"), who had served as Chief Harem Eunuch from 1691 to 1694. Following the pattern established by el-Hajj Mustafa Agha and other seventeenth-century Chief Eunuchs, Solak Nezir assumed high office in the palace eunuch hierarchy only after living in exile in Cairo for several years. His rehabilitation began in May 1695, when the newly enthroned sultan, Mustafa II, brought his former tutor, Yapraksız Ali Agha, the patron of el-Hajj Beshir Agha, back to Edirne from Cairo to serve as Chief Harem Eunuch. (He was probably called Yapraksız, "leafless," because he lacked eyelashes, perhaps an aftereffect of the hormonal deficiencies that resulted from castration.)[1] With him came six other previously exiled harem eunuchs, including Solak Nezir. Solak Nezir was appointed harem treasurer, following the pattern set by Yusuf Agha and taken by three of the seven intervening Chief Eunuchs. In addition, Nezir and the others had apparently been brought back to serve as boon companions to Mustafa II: they all held the title *musahib*, and the chronicler Silahdar Mehmed Agha tells us that they hunted with the sultan, who apparently shared his father Mehmed IV's obsession with the chase. Meanwhile, Nezir's predecessor in the treasurer post was himself packed off to Cairo.[2]

As harem treasurer, Nezir took on some of the roles traditionally reserved for the Chief Eunuch, reinforcing the impression that the treasurership was now the standard precursor to the top office. In July 1695, two months after returning from Egypt, he received a fur for slaughtering sacrifices alongside the sultan during celebrations for 'Id al-Adha, the "sacrifice holiday" marking completion of the *hajj* to Mecca every year.[3] September found him delivering an imperial order (*hatt-ı hümayun*), with gifts, to the grand vizier.[4] When Mustafa II's son, the future Mahmud I, was born in August 1696, Nezir, rather than Yapraksız Ali, distributed and received celebratory gifts.[5] The pattern was repeated two and a half years later, when the future Osman III was born.[6] Yapraksız Ali, on the other hand, personally delivered greetings and gifts to the campaigning sultan from his mother, Gülnuş Emetullah.[7] We might conclude that while Yapraksız Ali was closer to Gülnuş, Nezir was closer to Mustafa II, even though Yapraksız Ali had been the sultan's tutor.

---

[1] According to Professor Harriet Blitzer, to whom I owe many thanks, this is the meaning of the equivalent term in modern Greek.
[2] Silahdar Fındıklılı Mehmed Agha, *Nusretname*, ed. İsmet Parmaksızoğlu (Istanbul, 1962), I: 27, 30, 189; Defterdar Sarı Mehmed, *Zübde-i Vekayiât*, 526.
[3] Silahdar, *Nusretname*, I: 46.   [4] Ibid., I: 95–96.   [5] Ibid., I: 170, 193.   [6] Ibid., I: 353.
[7] Ibid., I: 109, 208, 209.

Toward the end of 1700, Mustafa II raised Solak Nezir to Chief Harem Eunuch. Yapraksız Ali Agha was sent back to Egypt, while Hafız Mehmed Agha, one of the six *musahib*s who had returned from Egypt with Nezir, became harem treasurer. As Chief Eunuch, Nezir remained close to the sultan, hunting with him in the woods around Edirne on occasion.[8] In May 1702, he gave a banquet to mark the beginning of the six-year-old Prince Mahmud's studies.[9]

Feyzullah Efendi. Unfortunately for Nezir Agha, his tenure as Chief Eunuch dovetailed with the career of the notorious Chief Mufti Feyzullah Efendi (1639–1703). Feyzullah's career, like Nezir's, reflects the regularization of Ottoman society in the wake of the seventeenth-century crisis. During the eighteenth century, the ulema, perhaps more than any other occupational group, embraced the hereditary principle whereby sons followed their fathers into ulema careers, and often into the same positions.[10] Feyzullah, however, took this pattern to extremes, installing blood relatives and in-laws alike in choice slots in the ulema hierarchy.

A native of the northeastern Anatolian city of Erzurum, Feyzullah studied with his fellow Erzurumlu, Vani Mehmed Efendi, leader of the puritanical Kadızadeli movement (to be discussed in Chapter 9), who had married his cousin. When Vani, at the invitation of new grand vizier Köprülü Fazıl Ahmed Pasha, moved to Edirne in 1662 to become Mehmed IV's personal preacher, Feyzullah accompanied him and married his daughter. His status as Vani's son-in-law paved the way for his appointment as tutor to the future sultans Mustafa II and Ahmed III in 1669. On the other hand, his relations with their father, Mehmed IV, were fractious at best; at one point, Gülnuş Emetullah was obliged to intervene to save him from the sultan's wrath.[11]

Feyzullah's distance from Mehmed IV perhaps explains how he was able to escape unscathed from the 1683 Vienna debacle, which led to his father-in-law's banishment from the imperial capital. Like Nezir Agha, again, he came into his own once Mustafa II, his former pupil, took the throne in 1695. He ascended to the post of Chief Mufti, then parlayed the office into a position of impregnable power, essentially choosing Mustafa's grand viziers and appointing his own four sons to influential and lucrative judgeships even though they had not undergone the rigorous training necessary to fill such prominent posts.[12] At his urging, the sultan even issued an unprecedented

---

[8] Ibid., II: 44.   [9] Ibid., II: 81–82.
[10] Zilfi, *Politics of Piety*, chapters 5–6, 215–20; Silahdar, *Nusretname*, II: 140–84; Michael Nizri, *Ottoman High Politics and the Ulema Household* (New York, NY, 2014).
[11] Silahdar, *Silahdar Tarihi*, II: 242; İpşirli Argıt, *Rabia Gülnuş Emetullah Sultan*, 93; Nizri, *Ottoman High Politics*, 34–35; Topkapı Archives, E 79/19 (ca. 1701).
[12] Abou-El-Haj, *1703 Rebellion*, 50, 57; Silahdar, *Nusretname*, II: 140–84.

imperial order stipulating that Feyzullah's eldest son, Fethullah, would succeed him as Chief Mufti.

Yet not without reason had Gülnuş Emetullah warned Mustafa II that he would have to choose between Feyzullah and the throne.[13] Blaming the Chief Mufti for the Ottoman Empire's humiliating territorial concessions to the Habsburgs in the 1699 Treaty of Karlowitz, a combination of imperial Janissaries and Istanbul guildsmen rebelled in August 1703 and marched to Edirne in an uprising that has gone down in history as the "Edirne Incident." They succeeded in deposing Mustafa II in favor of his younger brother Ahmed III, who had also been Feyzullah's pupil. The new sultan was obliged to return his court to Istanbul, for one of the rebels' complaints had been that the sultan was never present in the imperial capital. As for Feyzullah and his sons, they attempted to return to their hometown, Erzurum, but were captured by the rebels and imprisoned in Edirne. After torturing them for three days in a vain attempt to discover the location of their fortune, the rebels hanged Feyzullah, cut off his head, and threw his corpse into the Tunca River, which runs to the south of the city.[14]

Like Nezir Agha, then, Feyzullah Efendi was close to Mustafa II, while he was arguably closer than Nezir to Gülnuş Emetullah. And yet as closely as the mufti's career paralleled that of the Chief Eunuch, we cannot be sure that they were allies, though it seems likely. As noted above, there was certainly precedent for the Chief Eunuch making common cause with the mufti. And in general terms, no member of the ulema could get so close to the sultan, let alone his mother, without having an alliance of sorts with the Chief Harem Eunuch.

As Mustafa II's close confidant, Nezir Agha accompanied the deposed sultan and his sons to Istanbul, where they were all imprisoned in the *kafes* of Topkapı Palace.[15] Later, Nezir and two of his lieutenants were transferred to Kapuarası ("Between the Gates"), a bleak prison inside the gate between Topkapı Palace's First and Second courts that served as a holding cell for those awaiting execution. This, Silahdar tells us, echoed by Defterdar Sarı Mehmed Pasha, was their punishment for their "unlawful behavior" during Mustafa II's reign, that is, their interference in politics in a manner parallel to Feyzullah's.[16] Meanwhile, Ahmed III arrested four of the harem eunuchs who had returned from Cairo with Nezir eight years earlier and reexiled them to Egypt.

---

[13] Abou-El-Haj, *1703 Rebellion*, 51.
[14] Ibid., 80; Silahdar, *Nusretname*, II: 192–95; Topkapı Archive E 79/18.
[15] Silahdar, *Nusretname*, II: 187.
[16] Ibid., II: 160–61, 189; Defterdar Sarı Mehmed, *Zübde-i Vekayiât*, 817.

A few months later, Nezir was removed from the palace and imprisoned in the infamous Yedikule fortress, along with Feyzullah's eldest son Fethullah, who had been head of the descendants of the Prophet (Nakibü'l-Eşraf). (This joint incarceration points to Nezir's closeness to Feyzullah's family.) Fethullah was hanged there; his brothers were banished to Famagusta on Cyprus. As for Nezir, he was exiled not to Cairo but to Lemnos, the large Aegean island off the northwestern coast of Anatolia.[17] This was a bad sign since, for a Chief Eunuch, Aegean exile, as opposed to exile to Cairo, usually preceded execution. And sure enough, as Defterdar Sarı Mehmed sarcastically reports, "after a few days had passed, a fortunate imperial order was issued and sent, and by the exemplary means of the sword he was done to death."[18]

Uzun Süleyman Agha

Nezir's replacement as Chief Harem Eunuch was Küçük ("Little" or "Younger") Abdurrahman Agha, who was not the harem treasurer but chief of the eunuchs who served the women of the Old Palace, indicating that he was closer to the sultan's mother than Nezir had been.[19] Gülnuş Emetullah may, in fact, have been trying to assert herself within the harem eunuch hierarchy by promoting her own candidates for Chief Eunuch while bypassing, or even undermining, the office of harem treasurer. When Küçük Abdurrahman was deposed less than a year later, he was exiled to Egypt along with the harem treasurer, thus preventing the latter from succeeding him.

In the absence of the harem treasurer, the new Chief Harem Eunuch was, predictably, another eunuch close to the sultan's mother: Uzun ("Tall") Süleyman Agha, the head of Gülnuş Emetullah's personal entourage of eunuchs.[20] Once in office, Uzun Süleyman performed the usual tasks associated with the Chief Harem Eunuch, such as participating in the funeral of deposed sultan Mustafa II in December 1703 and acting as the bride's representative (*vekil*) at the wedding of Ahmed III's daughter in spring 1706.[21] He also surely had a hand, though just how is not clear, in the construction of Gülnuş Emetullah Sultan's imposing mosque complex in Üsküdar on the Asian side of the Bosphorus. The mosque was completed in spring 1711 after two and a half years of effort; Uzun Süleyman attended the opening ceremony.[22] Today, the mosque is known as the Yeni Valide Camii ("New Sultan's Mother Mosque") to distinguish it from the mosque of Nurbanu Sultan, the mother of Murad III,

---

[17] Silahdar, *Nusretname*, II: 189, 196–97, 201.
[18] Defterdar Sarı Mehmed, *Zübde-i Vekayiât*, 823.   [19] Silahdar, *Nusretname*, II: 192.
[20] Ibid., II: 213; Defterdar Sarı Mehmed, *Zübde-i Vekayiât*, 843.
[21] Defterdar Sarı Mehmed, *Zübde-i Vekayiât*, 836; Silahdar, *Nusretname*, II: 209, 250–51.
[22] Silahdar, *Nusretname*, II: 246, 269; İpşirli Argıt, *Rabia Gülnuş Emetullah Sultan*, 182–86; Topkapı Archive E 79/26.

also located in Üsküdar. Gülnuş Emetullah is buried at the mosque's northern edge, in an open tomb surrounded by rosebushes.

While attending to these ceremonial duties, Uzun Süleyman Agha wasted little time in bringing his influence to bear on the selection of grand viziers, perhaps setting an example for el-Hajj Beshir Agha. In fact, his tenure began with the deposition of his adversary Damad Hasan Pasha, a close ally of the deposed harem treasurer, and the appointment of Kalaylıkoz Hajji Ahmed Pasha, with whom Uzun Süleyman was more compatible. The new grand vizier even arrived in Istanbul on Uzun Süleyman's boat.[23] In the course of his nine-year tenure as Chief Eunuch, Uzun Süleyman took the seal of authority from three more grand viziers. Small wonder that the venomously anti–harem eunuch author Derviş Abdullah Efendi laments, "For nine years the black aghas ran things."[24]

Ironically, Uzun Süleyman's last deposition of a grand vizier, in 1712, brought to the office the formidable Silahdar Damad Ali Pasha, who held the post from April 1713 until his death at the battle of Peterwardein in what is now northern Serbia in August 1716. Damad Ali took a dim view of Uzun Süleyman's machinations and attempted to block the importation of African eunuchs into Ottoman territory entirely. He also replaced the African eunuch Şeyhü'l-Harem in Medina with a former grand vizier and upheld his predecessor Çorlulu Ali Pasha's decision, noted in Chapter 6, to make the white eunuchs of the Third Court subordinate to the *silahdar*, or sword-bearer.[25]

So hostile was Damad Ali Pasha toward Uzun Süleyman and his circle, in fact, that he engineered the eunuch's deposition in June 1713. Like his predecessor, Uzun Süleyman was exiled along with the harem treasurer, el-Hajj Beshir Agha, who attained the post in 1706 (and may briefly have held it in the mid-1690s).[26] Lacking the 1,000 purses demanded of them by the sultan's gate-keepers, the two eunuchs were imprisoned in the sultan's private garden until their property could be sold. They were then sent to Cyprus.[27] The curse of the Aegean islands held true for Uzun Süleyman just as it had for Nezir Agha: he was executed in Famagusta in May 1715.[28] El-Hajj Beshir, however, was allowed to continue to Cairo. This dispensation was a sign that the grand vizier did not regard him as Uzun Süleyman's "partner," whatever else he may have had against him.

---

[23] Silahdar, *Nusretname*, II: 215; Mehmed Raşid, *Tarih-i Raşid* (Istanbul, 1282/1865), IV: 242; Ahmed Resmi, *Hamiletü'l-kübera*, 62.

[24] Silahdar, *Nusretname*, II: 229, 262, 288; Derviş Abdullah, *Risale-i teberdariye*, fol. 65b.

[25] Derviş Abdullah, *Risale-i teberdariye*, fol. 66b.   [26] *Silahdar Tarihi*, II: 745.

[27] Silahdar, *Nusretname*, II: 295, 306; Derviş Abdullah, *Risale-i teberdariye*, fol. 66b; d'Ohsson, *Tableau général*, VII: 58–60; Mehmed Raşid, *Tarih-i Raşid*, III: 224, Topkapı Palace Archive, E 153/3 (1125–26/1713–14).

[28] Silahdar, *Nusretname*, II: 332.

El-Hajj Beshir Agha

El-Hajj Beshir's sojourn in Cairo was not his first. Archival evidence also indicates that he paid brief visits as *musahib*, then as harem treasurer, between 1703 and 1708.[29] Before he entered the imperial harem, furthermore, he apparently cultivated a bond to one of Cairo's notable households, as Chapter 8 will demonstrate.

This time, in any case, his stay in the city was quite brief, perhaps only a few months. During it, he lived in the harem eunuch quarter that had taken shape near Cairo's citadel, in a house located next-door to a residence belonging to the late Uzun Süleyman Agha, with whom he had been exiled to Cyprus. Under the circumstances, it can hardly be a coincidence that this house had most recently been occupied by one Kıbrıslı, or "the Cypriot."[30] In fact, Beshir may have been plotting out this latest Cairene phase of his career before Uzun Süleyman's death.

Şeyhü'l-Harem in Medina. Sometime in 1715, Beshir Agha was dispatched from Cairo to Medina to take up the post of Şeyhü'l-Harem, the head of the corps of eunuchs who guarded the Prophet Muhammad's mosque and tomb there. As we saw in Chapter 6, this office had been held by a harem eunuch since at least the early seventeenth century, although Yusuf Agha, in 1691, was the first deposed Chief Harem Eunuch to occupy it. El-Hajj Beshir, for his part, became the only harem eunuch ever to hold the office *before* promotion to Chief Harem Eunuch. The appointment was part of a continuing improvement in his fortunes, beginning with his relocation from Cyprus to Egypt.

Beshir's experience as Chief Tomb Eunuch was probably much like that of Yusuf Agha twenty years earlier, albeit far briefer. Although he stayed in Medina for only a year at most, he felt a sufficient connection to the city to endow both a madrasa and a *dar al-hadith*, or school for the study of the sayings of the Prophet, there over twenty years later. We will examine these in Chapter 9.

Return to Istanbul. In November 1716, el-Hajj Beshir took advantage of his relative proximity to Mecca to make the pilgrimage. This was not his first *hajj*; he had earned the title el-Hajj, or Hacı in Turkish, when he accompanied the *daye kadın*, the wet-nurse to an Ottoman prince, on pilgrimage from Istanbul in 1706.[31] While in Mecca, he received word that he had been

[29] BOA, MD 114, no. 425 (end Zilkade 1114/16 April 1703); MD 115, no. 1012 (mid-Zilkade 1118/17 February 1707); MD 115, no. 2155 (mid-Zilkade 1119/6 February 1708).

[30] Hamza Abd al-Aziz Badr and Daniel Crecelius, "The *Awqaf* of al-Hajj Bashir Agha in Cairo," *Annales Islamologiques* 27 (1993): 296.

[31] Topkapı Archive E 2429/6 (29 Muharrem 1118/12 May 1706); Ayvansarayi, *Garden of the Mosques*, 55.

appointed Chief Harem Eunuch, replacing the deposed Mercan Agha, who had held office for only a few months in 1717. He returned to Istanbul after stopping briefly in Cairo, where, as Chapter 8 will explain, he left an agent building a *sebil-mekteb*, a Qur'an school over a public fountain. He must have expected that he would return to Cairo eventually – unaware, obviously, that he was embarking on an unprecedented twenty-nine-year career as Chief Harem Eunuch and that he would be one of the rare holders of that post to die in office.

By the time el-Hajj Beshir returned to Istanbul, Gülnuş Emetullah Sultan, the mother of reigning sultan Ahmed III, was dead.[32] Yet her death did not have a negative effect on his career, for, unlike Yusuf Agha or Uzun Süleyman Agha, he was not her protégé. Instead, his main connection to the imperial family was the sultan himself; Beshir had served as his boon companion (*musahib*) before becoming harem treasurer. This, too, reflects a new early eighteenth-century reality: the sultans of the era were mature adults when they took the throne; while their mothers had molded them and dominated their upbringings, they themselves determined the character of their reigns and the inner circle of confidants who surrounded them. Of the imperial mothers of the era, only Gülnuş Emetullah came anywhere close to wielding the influence of Kösem and Turhan during the previous century.

Nevşehirli Ibrahim Pasha and the "Tulip Era" (1718–1730). A little more than a year after Beshir's installation as Chief Harem Eunuch, Ahmed III appointed one of Ottoman history's longest-serving and most influential grand viziers, Nevşehirli Ibrahim Pasha, who had married the sultan's daughter Fatma, widow of the martyred grand vizier Silahdar Damad Ali Pasha, the previous year.[33] (Damad Ali, we recall, had exiled el-Hajj Beshir to Cyprus with Uzun Süleyman Agha.) Damad Ibrahim was a powerful personality who had exerted immense influence over Ahmed III since the latter was a prince. His appointment followed the fall of Belgrade to the Habsburgs by only a few months, and one of his first noteworthy acts, in July 1718, was to sign the Treaty of Passarowitz, which formally stripped the Ottoman Empire of a good part of its Balkan territory while recognizing its gains against Venice in the Morea.[34]

In the aftermath of this new territorial humiliation, Ibrahim Pasha pursued a policy of peace. He is best known, of course, for presiding over what the early

---

[32] Silahdar, *Nusretname*, II: 336; Mehmed Raşid, *Tarih-i Raşid*, III: 165; İpşirli Argıt, *Rabia Gülnuş Emetullah*, 199.

[33] Silahdar, *Nusretname*, II: 380; Mehmed Raşid, *Tarih-i Raşid*, V: 20–102; d'Ohsson, *Tableau général*, VII: 449–50.

[34] Rhoads Murphey, "Twists and Turns in the Diplomatic Dialogue: The Politics of Peace-Making in the Early Eighteenth Century," in *The Peace of Passarowitz, 1718*, eds. Charles Ingrao et al. (West Lafayette, IN, 2011), 73–91.

twentieth-century historian Ahmet Refik (1881–1937) christened the Tulip Era (Lale Devri): a peaceful period of elite cultural flowering and consumption of western European luxury goods, notably clocks and mirrors. During the twelve years of Ibrahim's grand vizierate, Ahmed III hosted lavish entertainments at the Aynalıkavak pleasure pavilion on the northern shore of the Golden Horn and oversaw the construction of the lavish Sadabad summer palace at Kağıthane, northeast of the Golden Horn.[35]

The Çırağan Entertainments. El-Hajj Beshir Agha played a critical part in the signature entertainments of Nevşehirli Ibrahim's tenure: the so-called Çırağan Eğlenceleri (literally, "Lantern Entertainments"), which took place in Istanbul every spring to celebrate the blooming of the tulips. This sort of entertainment captured the spirit of the "Tulip Era" like no other. It was ostensibly a private entertainment for the imperial household, and above all the imperial women, held in late March or early April and completely unconnected to the Muslim religious calendar or to such "life cycle" events as weddings and circumcisions.

Festivities took place well outside Topkapı Palace, at one of the pleasure pavilions that had begun to spring up along the Golden Horn and, increasingly, along the western shore of the Bosphorus in the wake of the court's enforced return to Istanbul from Edirne in 1703.[36] (Some of these structures, particularly on the Golden Horn, were renovations and expansions of earlier palaces.) Nevşehirli Ibrahim Pasha had a palace built in the northern district of Beşiktaş specifically for his wife, the sultan's daughter, to enjoy these entertainments with other palace women. Known as the Sahil Sarayı, or Coastal Palace, it stood on the approximate spot where the Çırağan Palace – whose name, naturally, harks back to these entertainments – was built in the nineteenth century.

Much of the planning for the Çırağan festivities fell, from all appearances, to el-Hajj Beshir Agha and his successors as Chief Harem Eunuch – hardly a surprise, since the celebrations centered on the palace women. The eunuchs faced a formidable task, for the entertainments stretched over several days and ran from morning or afternoon through the evening. Court historian Mehmed Raşid Efendi, echoed by his successor Ismail Asım Efendi, a.k.a. Küçükçele-bizade, describes how the harem women amused themselves: "During daylight hours," he says, "they passed the time in delightful music and conversation (*saz ve söz*), jokes and games; and at night, they enjoyed the lanterns and the

---

[35] Ahmet Refik (Altınay), *Lale Devri, 1130–1143* (Istanbul, 1331 [1915]); *TDVİA*, s.v. "Lale Devri," by Abdülkadir Özcan; Can Erimtan, *Ottomans Facing West? The Origins of the Tulip Age and Its Development in Modern Turkey* (London, 2008).

[36] Shirine Hamadeh, *The City's Pleasures: Istanbul in the Eighteenth Century* (Seattle, WA, 2008), 18–19, 25–30, 59–62, 65–75, 101–8, 113, 135–36, 229–35, 236; d'Ohsson, *Tableau général*, VII: 83, 144.

tulip beds."[37] Quantities of food and (presumably non-alcoholic) drink were consumed, and court poets recited panegyric odes penned for the occasion. We get some idea of the festive atmosphere from the compositions of the famous eighteenth-century poet Nedim (1681–1730), many of whose poems celebrate the Çırağan entertainments held at the new Sadabad palace at Kağıthane, north of the Golden Horn. One of his most famous poems goes this way:

> Let us visit Sadabad, my swaying Cypress, let us go!
> For a while we'll stroll beside the pool, and then another while
> Off we'll go to view the palace, moved to marvel by its style;
> Now we'll sing a ballad, now with dainty verse the hours beguile.
> Let us visit Sadabad, my swaying Cypress, let us go![38]

The festival culminated in the distribution of gifts – again, presumably organized by the Chief Harem Eunuch – according to rank. Popular memory fastened on the feature that gave the festivities the name Çırağan: the darkness of evening was illuminated by tiny candles that moved through the shadows, borne on the backs of turtles or placed inside eggshells and seashells and set to float in the water channels that ran through Sadabad and similar pleasure sites.[39]

While the Çırağan entertainments are strongly associated with Nevşehirli Ibrahim Pasha, the grand vizier's violent deposition in 1730, to be discussed below, did not put an end to them. On the contrary, according to the French merchant Jean-Claude Flachat, who supplied luxury goods to the Ottoman court during the late 1740s and early 1750s, these sorts of festivities enjoyed unprecedented popularity during the reign of Mahmud I (1730–54). Flachat even describes a few innovations to the Çırağan ritual during this sultan's reign: toward the end of the festival, he tells us, the sultan selected a "favorite" from among the assembled women, although whether this amounted to choosing her for his bed is unclear; afterward, the Chief Eunuch distributed jewels and costly textiles as gifts. In the evening, after the private women's party had ended, the sultan hosted his officials at a musical performance.[40]

A parallel winter entertainment, the *helva sohbetleri* ("helva gatherings"), even made its debut under Mahmud. This was a private indoor spectacle at which the confection known as helva, made from semolina paste and quantities of sugar, was prepared while harem women and Third Court pages watched

---

[37] Mehmed Raşid, *Tarih-i Raşid*, V: 205–6; İsmail Asım, *Tarih-i İsmail Asım Efendi* (Istanbul, 1282/1865), 456–59, 556–57.

[38] Nermin Menemencioğlu, ed., with Fahir İz, *The Penguin Book of Turkish Verse* (Hammondsworth, 1978), 113–14; *TDVİA*, s.v. "Sadabad," by Banu Bilgicioğlu.

[39] Mehmed Raşid, *Tarih-i Raşid*, V: 205; İsmail Asım, *Tarih-i İsmail Asım Efendi*, 457–58; *EI*[2], s.v. "Čiraghan," by Tahsin Öz; *TDVİA*, s.v. "Çırağan," by Selda Ertuğrul.

[40] Jean-Claude Flachat, *Observations sur le commerce et sur les arts d'une partie de l'Europe, de l'Asie, de l'Afrique et même des Indes orientales* (Lyon, 1766), II: 19ff., 27–29, 163.

from gender-segregated spaces. One feature that marks the *helva sohbetleri* as an eighteenth-century phenomenon is that they were jointly organized by the Chief Harem Eunuch and the *silahdar*, the non-eunuch official who was now his counterpart in the Third Court.[41] Such cooperation between the harem and the Third Court would have been unlikely a century earlier.

These new, relatively small-scale entertainments reflect several new "eighteenth-century realities" of Ottoman court life and of the topography of the imperial capital, as Shirine Hamadeh has pointed out.[42] Although these were, ostensibly, private festivities restricted to the imperial family, they took place in locations considerably removed from Topkapı Palace. They also tended to occur out of doors, in gardens and garden pavilions. In these locations, the public could not only glimpse the imperial family and their circle of intimates but even inhabit the fringes of the same public spaces. In this sense, the sultan and his household, including the Chief Harem Eunuch, became less secluded from and more connected to the public than they had been during the seventeenth century, and arguably during the sixteenth century, as well. Meanwhile, the public garden spaces in which these entertainments could be staged multiplied and moved north of the Golden Horn and up the Bosphorus. This expansion resulted from the growth of the city's population in the wake of the court's return from Edirne and the post-crisis recovery of the Ottoman economy, but also from the emergence of this new culture of public sociability.[43] As master of ceremonies, the Chief Harem Eunuch became more of a public figure than ever before, even as he continued to police the boundary between public and private.

Nor was this sort of entertainment, with its accompanying consumption of luxury goods, limited to the imperial capital. In the Ottoman provinces, grandees imported luxury goods directly from European suppliers and engaged European craftsmen to build and decorate their mansions. Generally, these provincial elites sponsored a provincial culture of public sociability that drew on and contributed to its counterpart in the imperial capital.[44] This sort of cultural symbiosis mirrored the economic and military symbiosis between the central government and provincial notables during the eighteenth century.

---

[41] Hamadeh, *City's Pleasures*, 53; Mehmet Ali Beyhan, "Amusements in the Ottoman Palace in the Early Nineteenth Century," in *Celebration, Entertainment, and Theatre in the Ottoman World*, eds. Suraiya Faroqhi and Arzu Öztürkmen (London, 2014), 229.

[42] Hamadeh, *City's Pleasures*, 54–55, 101, 113–15, 135–36.

[43] James Grehan, "Smoking and 'Early Modern' Sociability: The Great Tobacco Debate in the Ottoman Middle East (Seventeenth to Eighteenth Centuries)," *American Historical Review* 111, 5 (2006): 1352–77.

[44] Filiz Yenişehirlioğlu, "Architectural Patronage of *Ayan* Families in Anatolia," in *Provincial Elites in the Ottoman Empire*, ed. Antonis Anastasopoulos (Rethmyno, 2005), 321–39; al-Jabarti, *'Aja'ib al-athar*, I: 217–18, 231–32.

The Patrona Halil Rebellion. Notwithstanding the influence that he obviously wielded at the Ottoman court during his first thirteen years as Chief Eunuch – manifested in his organization of these lavish entertainments – el-Hajj Beshir Agha was probably subordinate to Nevşehirli Ibrahim Pasha during this period. We do not read of him affecting administrative appointments or Ottoman foreign policy during these years. All of this changed in the early autumn of 1730, when Ahmed III was overthrown and Ibrahim Pasha killed in the cataclysmic rebellion led by the naval mercenary known as Patrona ("Boss") Halil. As has been widely remarked, this revolt – more of a revolution, really – stemmed from long-standing dissatisfaction with the peace policy pursued by Ahmed III and Nevşehirli Ibrahim, as well as frustration with rampant inflation and lax payment of military salaries at a time when the sultan and his grand vizier were spending huge sums on conspicuous consumption.

The igniting spark was, rather ironically, mobilization for a campaign against Iran, which was in turmoil following the collapse of the Safavid empire in 1722. Ottoman inability to stop the advances of the Safavid revivalist Nadir Shah, to be discussed below, inspired Patrona Halil to lead a band of mercenaries who refused the deployment.[45] Marching on the palace, the rebels demanded the execution of Nevşehirli Ibrahim Pasha. At this point, el-Hajj Beshir Agha sprang into action, wresting the grand vizier's seal of office from him by force.[46] But the rebels insisted that the sultan himself step down in favor of his nephew Mahmud, son of Mustafa II, who took the throne in October 1730 as Mahmud I. The rebels were, in truth, in the grip of a hysterical, bloodthirsty rage. There is no other way to explain the gruesome, mocking fashion in which they expressed their outrage at the wasteful extravagance of the Çırağan entertainments, at least according to the chronicle of Destari Salih: sticking candles in the gouged-out eyes of Nevşehirli Ibrahim, his lieutenant (*kethüda*), and the grand admiral, then thrusting them in the faces of appalled courtiers while crying "This is your Çırağan!"[47]

Patrona Halil and his rebels controlled the capital and all administrative appointments for roughly two months. Then, in late November 1730, a species

---

[45] M. Münir Aktepe, *Patrona İsyanı, 1730* (Istanbul, 1958); Subhi Efendi, *Subhi Efendi Tarihi*, in *Tarih-i Sami ve Şakir ve Subhi* (Istanbul, 1198/1783), 1–13, 21–24, 26, 43; Şemdanizade Fındıklılı Süleyman Efendi, *Şem'dani-zade Fındıklılı Süleyman Efendi Tarihi: Mür'i't-tevarih*, ed. M. Münir Aktepe (Istanbul, 1976), I: 6–16; Abdi Efendi, *Abdi Tarihi: 1730 Patrona İhtilali Hakkında bir Eser*, ed. Faik Reşit Unat (Ankara, 1943), 26–27, 28–42; Fariba Zarinebaf, *Crime and Punishment in Istanbul, 1700–1800* (Berkeley, CA, 2010), 54–59.

[46] Şemdanizade, *Şemdanizade Tarihi*, I: 10.

[47] Destari Salih Efendi, *Destari Salih Tarihi: Patrona Halil Ayaklanması Hakkında bir Kaynak*, ed. Bekir Sıtkı Baykal (Ankara, 1962), 19; Avner Wishnitzer, "Into the Dark: Power, Light, and Nocturnal Life in Eighteenth-Century Istanbul," *International Journal of Middle East Studies* 46, 3 (2014): 520–23, 525–26.

of counter-coup took shape. Both the chronicler Şemdanizade Fındıklılı Süleyman Efendi and the anti-eunuch polemicist Derviş Abdullah credit the counter-coup to the future grand vizier Kabakulak Ibrahim Agha, *kethüda* of former grand vizier and governor of Egypt Nişancı Mehmed Pasha and close ally of el-Hajj Beshir.[48] Ostensibly at Kabakulak's urging, Sultan Mahmud and his top administrators summoned Patrona Halil and his supporters to a meeting at Topkapı to discuss their demands for administrative office. In an oft-repeated instance – almost a trope, in fact – of wily administrators and military commanders tricking gullible opponents, the rebels accepted the invitation and dutifully arrived at the palace, only to be separated from each other and summarily killed. Authority was thus restored to the hands of the new sultan and his officials.[49]

Particularly striking in all of this is the fact that el-Hajj Beshir Agha seems to have been almost wholly unaffected by the rebellion and its aftermath. The rebels never demanded his ouster, let alone his execution, in marked contrast to the experience of earlier Chief Eunuchs caught up in serious rebellions. This indicates that the rebels did not consider him a crony or protégé of Nevşehirli Ibrahim Pasha and, further, that they did not feel that the harem women had played a role in shaping state policy during Ibrahim Pasha's tenure as grand vizier. They surely knew, in addition, that he was a confidant of Prince Mahmud, whom they wanted enthroned. Beshir's links to the merchants in Istanbul's bazaars, to whom the rebels likewise enjoyed ties, may also have worked in his favor. Beshir himself, of course, did his part to distance himself from the unpopular Nevşehirli Ibrahim by withdrawing the grand vizier's seal from him, a gesture worthy of his predecessors at the height of the seventeenth-century crisis. The fact that the leader of the counter-coup was his ally speaks to his ability to manipulate the aftermath of the rebellion to his own advantage.

The Reign of Mahmud I. While el-Hajj Beshir Agha was probably not terribly close to Sultan Ahmed III, he was something of a mentor to his nephew, who was a young man in his twenties, living in Topkapı Palace's *kafes*, during the early years of Beshir's tenure. He was also close to Mahmud's mother, Saliha Sultan.[50] Not surprisingly, then, his influence over Mahmud, once the latter took the throne, was many times greater than his influence over Ahmed III, to say nothing of Nevşehirli Ibrahim Pasha. During Mahmud's reign, Beshir acted as a veritable vizier-maker, essentially dictating the sultan's

---

[48] Şemdanizade, *Şemdanizade Tarihi*, I: 16, 19; Derviş Abdullah, *Risale-i teberdariye*, fols. 67a–b.

[49] Şemdanizade, *Şemdanizade Tarihi*, I: 17–21; Abdi, *Abdi Tarihi*, 55–60; Zarinebaf, *Crime and Punishment*, 59. The most famous example of this phenomenon is Mehmed Ali Pasha's massacre of Egypt's mamluks after inviting them to a military parade at Cairo's citadel in 1811.

[50] Şemdanizade, *Şemdanizade Tarihi*, I: 24; Uluçay, *Padişahların Kadınların ve Kızları*, 73.

appointment and deposition of roughly a dozen grand viziers. Mahmud himself, no doubt with his uncle's deposition in mind, was reluctant to allow his grand viziers free rein and relied on Beshir Agha to check their authority.[51]

Nadir Shah. Most of Mahmud's grand viziers concurred with the sultan's rather aggressive foreign policy, which stood in marked contrast to the generally peaceable policies of his predecessor. To be sure, the Ottoman Empire under Mahmud I faced new external threats, above all in the form of the Safavid revivalist Nadir Shah. After the Safavid empire succumbed to Afghan forces in 1722, Nadir, a warlord in northeastern Iran, pledged fealty to the son of the last Safavid shah and began retaking territory from the Afghans. He was so successful that by 1730, he had burst into Ottoman-controlled territory in Azerbaijan and taken Hamadan and Tabriz. This incursion was what prompted the Ottoman mobilization that in turn triggered the Patrona Halil rebellion. From Azerbaijan, Nadir moved into Ottoman Iraq, besieging Baghdad in 1733 and Mosul in 1736, the same year that he abandoned the "Safavid resurrection" pretense and declared himself shah.[52] He seemed unstoppable, invading Central Asia, the Caucasus, and even, in 1738, India, where he famously demanded that the Mughal emperor give him the Peacock Throne as the price of his withdrawal (he did).

Through it all, however, Nadir maintained that he was willing to make peace with the Ottomans if *they* would recognize the Twelver Shi'ism to which he adhered as a fifth Sunni legal rite (*mezhep* or *madhhab*), the so-called Ja'fari rite, after Ja'far al-Sadiq (d. 765 CE), the sixth Shi'ite imam, known for articulating many of the sect's core doctrines. More than simply a theological formality, this measure would officially recognize Twelver Shi'ism as a legitimate branch of Ottoman Islam. How much daily realities on the ground would have changed is unclear, for while Ottoman jurisconsults officially condemned all branches of Shi'ism as heretical, the state had historically accommodated significant Shi'ite populations over a wide swath of territory.[53] At the least, though, Twelver Shi'ites might have been summoned to their mosques by a public Shi'ite call to prayer such as is not heard even in today's Turkey.

Negotiations over this issue dragged on for years, led on the Ottoman side by the *reisü'l-küttab*, or "chief scribe." From 1741 to 1744, this post was held by the energetic future grand vizier Raghib Mehmed Efendi, who did not like the idea of a Ja'fari rite but was willing to accept it as a matter

---

[51] Şemdanizade, *Şemdanizade Tarihi*, I: 29.

[52] İsmail Asım, *Tarih-i İsmail Asım Efendi*, 450–52, 459–60; Abdi, *Abdi Tarihi*, 9–24, 27–28; Hathaway, *Arab Lands under Ottoman Rule*, 95, 97; Holt, *Egypt and the Fertile Crescent*, 144–46.

[53] Stefan Winter, *The Shi'ites of Lebanon under Ottoman Rule, 1516–1788* (Cambridge, 2010), 17–30.

of "necessity" (*zarura*), stressing the advisability of making peace with Iran when the Ottomans were at war with Russia and, before 1739, with the Habsburgs.[54] El-Hajj Beshir Agha, however, was not so conciliatory. According to the chronicler Şemdanizade, who was, admittedly, a fan of Raghib Mehmed, Beshir insisted that "while I am alive, I will not allow this false fifth rite to be added to the four [true] rites."[55] Beshir Agha's consistent frustration of Raghib's diplomatic efforts may have contributed to the latter's antipathy toward Beshir's successors as Chief Eunuch.

Only after Beshir Agha's death in 1746 was a treaty finally signed that, while not recognizing the Ja'fari rite, did allow Iranian pilgrims to make the *hajj* to Ottoman-controlled Mecca while giving Nadir Shah control of the Shi'ite shrine city of Najaf in southern Iraq.[56] The following June, however, he was stabbed to death by one of his own officers, who feared the shah's increasingly capricious executions of his underlings. This unexpected intervention caused his state to collapse. The succeeding Zand (1750–94) and Qajar (1794–1924) dynasties focused much of their attention on quelling internal opposition, on the one hand, and confronting the expansionist Russian empire, on the other. Never again would Iran pose a significant military threat to the Ottomans.

El-Hajj Beshir Agha's Pious Foundations. When he wasn't bringing his considerable weight to bear on administrative appointments and foreign policy, el-Hajj Beshir Agha continued his habit, already well established during his brief time in Cairo and Medina, of endowing religious, charitable, and educational foundations. These left a lasting architectural imprint on the cities where he lived. Their geographical range more or less corresponds to that of the Ottoman Empire itself: from present-day Romania to present-day Iraq, from Bulgaria to Egypt. His Egyptian foundations will be discussed in Chapter 8. Here, we concentrate on the foundations that he endowed in the imperial capital and along the Danube River. The Danube foundations may not be as lavish or high-profile as certain of Beshir's foundations in Istanbul or in other Ottoman provinces, but they point up the critical importance that Chief Harem Eunuchs attached to this river, which was an economic lifeline of the empire.

In Istanbul. Once he became Chief Harem Eunuch, el-Hajj Beshir was able to focus his attention on the imperial capital. Admittedly, very few of his endowments in the city date from the period before the Patrona Halil rebellion. In subsequent years, however, and above all in the seven years before his

---

[54] Ernest S. Tucker, *Nadir Shah's Quest for Legitimacy in Post-Safavid Iran* (Gainesville, FL, 2006), 114–15; Henning Sievert, *Zwischen arabischer Provinz und Hoher Pforte: Beziehungen, Bildung und Politik des osmanischen Bürokraten Ragib Mehmed Paşa (st. 1763)* (Würzburg, 2008), 102–22.

[55] Şemdanizade, *Şemdanizade Tarihi*, I: 123, also I: 61, 103–4, 106–7, 113, 114, 120.

[56] Ibid., I: 119–21.

death, he lavished attention on an array of neighborhoods within the city. A lengthy compilation of numerous *vakıf*s that Beshir endowed late in life, now housed in Istanbul's Süleymaniye Library, shows that he made three major waves of endowments during his last seven years: in January 1739, October 1740, and October 1745, less than a year before he died. One of his last projects, the impressive religious complex, or *külliye*, in Gülhane, just south of Topkapı Palace, was endowed in 1745 and will be discussed in Chapter 9. Even his far more modest projects, however, were extensive enough to revitalize key parts of Istanbul.

Many of the endowed properties comprise not high-minded religious and charitable foundations but the mundane structures that provided revenue for such worthy endeavors, notably a large number of *menzil*s, or residential buildings, which could consist of anything from rented bachelor rooms to mansion-equivalents. According to the *vakıf* compilation, Beshir constructed five *menzil*s and restored seven in 1739. These were concentrated along the European shore of the Bosphorus, in and just south of the neighborhood of Beşiktaş, on the one hand, and in the vicinity of the Koca Mustafa Pasha neighborhood, north of the Sea of Marmara, on the other.[57]

A surge in religious and charitable foundations along the western coast of the Bosphorus, north of the old Byzantine Constantinople, is noticeable beginning in the late seventeenth century. More broadly, the European shore of the Bosphorus, in addition to the northern shore of the Golden Horn nearby, was becoming increasingly popular with members of the Ottoman court as a site for new construction. During the early eighteenth century, both these locations began to sprout summer residences and pleasure pavilions, as noted above; in addition, the western side of the Bosphorus became a preferred venue for mosques, tombs, public fountains, and, on the evidence of Beshir Agha's *vakıf* compilation, housing of various kinds.

In contrast, the Koca Mustafa Pasha neighborhood lies decidedly within the old city, although considerably west of the old city center, where the covered bazaar, Ayasofya, the hippodrome, and the Mosque of Sultan Ahmed are located. Its namesake was a grand vizier under Bayezid II and Selim I who constructed a mosque on the site of a Byzantine monastery to the east of the Yedikule fortress in the old Byzantine city walls.

In the early eighteenth century, this neighborhood was not as heavily populated as the old Greek quarter where Habeshi Mehmed Agha had built his mosque complex some 150 years earlier. Yet Beshir's endowments indicate that the quarter's population was growing, moving onto agricultural land and requiring the amenities of an established urban district. Hence the rebuilt

---

[57] Istanbul, Süleymaniye Library, MS Hacı Beşir Ağa 682.

public bath near Koca Mustafa's mosque, bordered by gardens; two restored baths, with shops and a public oven, in the nearby Davud Pasha quarter; a *menzil* in the same neighborhood, amid peach orchards; and a farmhouse-like *menzil* at the nearby Silivri Gate in the old land walls, complete with a stable, water wheel, and orchard.[58] All this infrastructural development tallied nicely with Beshir Agha's attention, detailed in Chapter 9, to the tomb of a Sufi saint buried in the neighborhood.

On the Danube. Ordinarily, Beshir Agha's economic foundations supported religious and charitable endowments in the same city or region. This was the norm for Muslim pious endowments and explains why in many Ottoman cities, and certainly in the imperial capital, mosques and madrasas stand cheek-by-jowl with covered bazaars, baths, and similar revenue-producing operations. In the provinces of Damascus, Aleppo, and Antioch, in contrast, Beshir endowed enormous swaths of land planted in olive and mulberry trees. These were guaranteed money-makers that could be used to fund endowments anywhere. In particular, Beshir's *dar al-hadith* in Medina drew heavily on lands near Damascus, as stipulated in the *vakif* compilation.[59]

Along the Danube River, though, Beshir Agha endowed a major religious-educational complex and several unrelated commercial ventures, virtually none of which survives. These projects underline how important the Danube was to him, and to Chief Eunuchs generally. It was, after all, a major transportation artery connecting what the Ottomans had historically regarded as their heartland to the Black Sea, the "Ottoman lake" through which huge quantities of goods, above all wheat, moved from the Danube Delta to Istanbul. The Danube had long been a bone of contention between the Ottomans and their longtime rivals, the Habsburgs. By the time el-Hajj Beshir Agha took office, the Ottomans had lost two major Danubian cities, Budapest and Belgrade, to the Habsburgs, although they regained Belgrade through military victories, followed by canny negotiation, in 1739.[60] Meanwhile, the Russian empire had become a serious threat to the eastern reaches of the Danube, including the delta.

Beshir Agha's Danubian endowments seem designed to confront these new challenges while building, sometimes literally, on previous riverfront projects. At Svishtov, on what is now the border between Bulgaria and Romania, he founded a madrasa, with a substantial library, that will be discussed in Chapter 9. To support this establishment, he endowed several coffeehouses and a

---

[58] Ibid., fols. 6a, 11a–b, 12a–b, 13a.   [59] Ibid., fols. 12b–23b, 24b, 52b–68b, 69b–75b.
[60] Virginia H. Aksan, *An Ottoman Statesman in War and Peace: Ahmed Resmi Efendi, 1700–1783* (Leiden, 1995), 8–9, 19, 25, 129–30, 196, and 8 n. 23; d'Ohsson, *Tableau général,* VII: 457, 462.

paçahane, a shop selling sheep trotters.[61] We can perhaps imagine the madrasa students and teachers going out for coffee and eating trotter soup after sundown during Ramadan, although the soup-consumers may also have included soldiers and other urban "riff-raff" since trotter soup, like tripe (*işkembe*) soup, heavily laced with vinegar, is a popular hangover remedy.

But most of Beshir's endowment efforts on the Danube were concentrated in the river's delta. Here, we recall, the first Chief Harem Eunuch, Habeshi Mehmed Agha, had founded a fortified town at İsmail Geçidi, on the northern Kiliya branch of the Danube in Bessarabia, now in Ukraine. At the time, the Russian empire was just beginning to flex its muscles as a regional power. In the same locale, Beshir Agha commissioned an array of what we might call commercial support facilities: two caravanserais (singular, *han*), two oil storehouses, two barbershops, one with a coffeehouse attached, tanneries, and an astonishing thirty-two wheat storehouses; this last item underlines this region's importance to the Ottomans as a source of grain.[62] These structures can only have helped to maintain and extend the facilities put in place under Habeshi Mehmed Agha's direction. Northeastward along the same branch of the river, he arranged a similar, if smaller, constellation of commercial facilities in Kiliya: caravanserai, storehouses, trotter-shop, coffeehouse, even a shop selling the fermented wheat beverage known as boza (there was, after all, no shortage of wheat from which to brew it); once again, the target consumers were probably soldiers, who benefited from the drink's energy-giving carbohydrate load. To oversee it all, he commissioned what the *vakıf* compilation calls an *ihtisabhane*, a residence for the supervisor of public markets, or *muhtasib*.[63]

Still, the pièce de resistance of all this Danube Delta development was Beshir Agha's lighthouse at Sulina (Sünne), today the easternmost point in Romania. Here, where grain-bearing ships entered the Black Sea, bound for Istanbul, Beshir commissioned a fortified lighthouse "because the Sünne strait is difficult to navigate, and most of the loaded ships sink and perish in the dark nights."[64] The fortress, mounted with cannon, was manned by seventeen soldiers – all local recruits, apparently – commanded by the brother of the endowment's local supervisor (*mütevelli*); the post of commander was

---

[61] Süleymaniye Library, MS Hacı Beşir Ağa 682, fol. 104b; İsmet Kayaoğlu, "Beşir Ağa Vakfı," *Belgeler* 15, 2 (1981–86): 84–85.
[62] Süleymaniye Library, MS Hacı Beşir Ağa 682, fols. 88a–92a.   [63] Ibid., fols. 92a–94a.
[64] Kayaoğlu, "Beşir Ağa Vakfı," *Belgeler* 11, 15 (1981–86): 77–87; Tahsin Gemil, "Vakifuri otomane fondate pe teritoriul Românei (sec. XV–XIII)," in *Fațetele istoriei: existențe, identități, dinamici – Omagiu academicianului Ștefan Ștefănescu*, eds. Tudor Teoteoi et al. (Bucharest, 2000), 196–97. I am grateful to Dr. Catalina Hunt for drawing my attention to both these publications and for translating the relevant parts of Gemil's article. I am also indebted to Mr. Valentin Lavric of Sulina, Romania, for drawing my attention to the lighthouse in the first place.

hereditary in this family, which must have dominated the area's local notables. The endowment also provided for three lighthouse-lighters and a supply of olive oil for fuel, as well as four storehouses, four granaries, and six barges. Clearly, the intent of this project was to facilitate grain shipment from the Danube to the Black Sea, and to protect it from shipwreck and Russian aggression.

Income for this endowment came not only from the commercial structures in Sulina but from sources across the entire Danube Delta. In addition, the endowment supported other ventures besides the lighthouse and fortress. Most notable among these was a soup kitchen (*imaret*) serving the poor of Sulina, perhaps another attempt by the nonagenarian eunuch to ensure his legacy through good works. At the same time, the endowment helped to restore and to assign new revenues to properties associated with earlier endowments, near Sulina and far away, founded by Beshir Agha and founded by others. These included Beshir's library at Svishtov; a Friday mosque founded by a Türkmen chieftain in the district of Milas in southwestern Anatolia; a soup kitchen in Istanbul's Atik Ali Pasha quarter, east of Edirnekapı; and a public fountain in İsmail Geçidi founded by el-Hajj Ismail Agha, the late supervisor (*mütevelli*) of Habeshi Mehmed Agha's endowment there.[65]

In other words, a single *vakıf* could be used to intervene in completely separate endowments; a separate endowment deed was not necessary. This presumably made it easier for Beshir Agha and his agents to handle the enormous number of endowments he founded across Ottoman territory while also maintaining the structures endowed by his predecessors as Chief Harem Eunuch. It also facilitated Beshir's agenda of renewing and further developing key parts of Istanbul.

El-Hajj Beshir's Death. El-Hajj Beshir Agha died on 2 June 1746 (13 Cemaziyelevvel 1159), aged somewhere in the vicinity of ninety. By this time, according to the Russian diplomat Adrian Nepluev, who was resident in Istanbul between 1745 and 1750, he was deaf and paralyzed on the left side after suffering a stroke two months earlier. (Ahmed Resmi Efendi, the collector of Chief Eunuch biographies, explains that "because of advanced age and the girth of his body, he was afflicted by accidents and misfortunes.")[66] In view of his condition, he did not join the "imperial migration" (*göç-i hümayun*) of the court from Topkapı to summer quarters on the northern shore of the Golden

[65] Kayaoğlu, "Beşir Ağa Vakfı," 83–84.
[66] Ahmed Resmi, *Hamiletü'l-kübera*, 63; Adrian Ivanovich Nepluev, *Relation*, Archive of the Foreign Policy of the Russian Empire, Fund 89: Relations of Russia with Turkey, File 2, p. 311, 18 May 1746 (Julian); File 6, pp. 7–8, 5 July 1746 (Julian). I am extremely grateful to Professors Mikhail Meyer and Svetlana Kirillina of the Institute for African and Asian Studies, Moscow State University, for, respectively, making this archival material available to me and translating it into English.

Horn, or at some nearby location. Instead, he was transported to Bahariye, his pavilion on the southern bank of the Golden Horn just outside the Eyüp district, where his tomb had already been prepared, and there he died.[67] His body was transported the short distance to Eyüp, outside the Byzantine land walls, for burial in a specially constructed tomb next to that of Abu Ayyub al-Ansari, the Prophet Muhammad's standard-bearer, for whom the quarter is named (I shall have more to say about this tomb in Chapter 11).

Moralı Beshir Agha

On the very day of el-Hajj Beshir's death, Nepluev relates, the thirty-three-year-old harem treasurer, Moralı Hafız Beshir Agha, took his place as Chief Harem Eunuch. (His sobriquet derived from one of his early masters, the tax collector, or *muhassil*, of the Morea [Mora in Turkish], the central region of Greece.) This, according to Nepluev, was the last thing that el-Hajj Beshir wanted. Moralı Beshir was no friend of el-Hajj Beshir – nor of anyone else, by Nepluev's account; he had few supporters, the Russian asserts, because he was "too young, short-tempered, and greedy for money."[68] On regaining consciousness after his stroke, in fact, el-Hajj Beshir had tried to prevent the younger eunuch's succession, urging the sultan to appoint one of three alternative candidates from among the population of current and former harem eunuchs while warning against choosing Moralı Beshir, who he felt was "unsuitable."[69]

Here, once again, we see the effect, and perhaps the aim, of the career trajectory of harem treasurer to Chief Eunuch. It was not the case that the Chief Eunuch could engineer the appointment of his own protégé to the treasurer position and thus, in effect, choose his own successor. Rather, the harem treasurer came from a rival patronage network and thus served as a check on the Chief Eunuch's influence.

Not surprisingly, in light of such opposition to his appointment, one of Moralı Beshir's first acts on taking office was to exile all of these eunuch alsorans to Egypt. He likewise dispatched the Chief Mufti Pirizade Efendi, whom Nepluev describes as el-Hajj Beshir's ally, to Mecca. Yet the next Chief Mufti, Mehmed Emin Efendi, combined with Grand Vizier Seyyid Hasan Pasha to limit Moralı Beshir's influence by decreeing that scholar-officials could not consult with the harem eunuchs.[70] This ruling prevented any alliance between

---

[67] Ahmed Resmi, *Hamiletü'l-kübera*, 63.
[68] Nepluev, *Relation*, File 2, p. 311, 18 May 1746 (Julian). [69] Ibid.
[70] Nepluev, *Relation*, File 6, pp. 7–8, 5 July 1746 (Julian); Aleksei Andreevich Veshyakov (Russian resident in Istanbul 1734–36, 1739–45), letter to the Russian ambassador in Berlin, Archive of the Foreign Policy of the Russian Empire, Fund 89: Relations of Russia with Turkey, File 4, p. 388 obverse, 7 December 1745 (Julian).

the Chief Eunuch and the senior Ottoman ulema, above all the Chief Mufti, reinforcing the effects of the Edirne Incident half a century earlier.

Despite all this, Moralı Beshir appears to have been a genuine ally of Mahmud I. How else to explain the trust that the sultan placed in him when he instructed him to supervise the construction of the Mahmudiyye madrasa in Cairo, the first sultanic madrasa to be erected in an Ottoman province in more than 200 years? This was the first time that a Chief Eunuch had performed such a function since el-Hajj Mustafa Agha directed the construction of the Mosque of Sultan Ahmed in the early seventeenth century (see Chapter 5). I will have more to say about this edifice in Chapter 9.

European Luxury Goods and Jean-Claude Flachat. While confrontation with Russia continued during Moralı Beshir's six-year tenure, the Habsburg and Iranian fronts remained quiet in the wake of the 1739 Treaty of Belgrade and the 1746 treaty with Nadir Shah. At the same time, relations with France and England remained cordial, while Ottoman trade with these two countries, as with the Italian city-states, boomed as more and more European luxury goods found their way into Ottoman territory. Renewal of the Capitulations with France in 1740 facilitated this trend.[71] As early as the 1690s, an inventory of the personal effects of the Chief Eunuchs Uzun Ismail (term 1691–92) and Kaba Nezir Agha (term 1692–94) after their deaths shows numerous gold-encrusted and bejeweled French clocks, a fad that continued well into the eighteenth century.[72] Moralı Beshir shared his predecessors' concern with the high-end trade from France, and this helps to explain why the prolific French merchant Jean-Claude Flachat paints a picture of Moralı Beshir that is diametrically opposed to Nepluev's negative portrayal.

Flachat had joined the entourage of the ambassador of Naples to the Porte and, in this capacity, supplied jewels and other luxury items to Moralı Beshir and to the harem treasurer, Süleyman Agha, who passed them on to the grand vizier and the sultan. After the French ambassador denied him a passport to continue traveling with the Neopolitan delegation, citing the dangers, Flachat remained in Istanbul for upward of fifteen years.[73] With no official employment in the foreign diplomatic establishment, he managed to obtain the post of Chief Merchant (*bazargan başı*) to the court, displacing an Armenian Christian merchant named Hagop or Ya'qub (i.e., Jacob), whom Flachat more or less dismisses as dealing only in "common" merchandise. Flachat, in contrast, continued to supply Moralı Beshir with luxury goods, even while his appointment drew the resentment of indigenous and fellow European merchants alike.[74] He claims that Moralı Beshir imparted his taste for jewels, European

---

[71] Flachat, *Observations*, I: 518ff.   [72] Topkapı Palace Archive, D 7244/2 (1106/1694–95).
[73] Flachat, *Observations*, I: 384, 409ff.
[74] Ibid., II: 153, 156, 160; d'Ohsson, *Tableau général*, VII: 7, 22.

furniture, and the like to the sultan. Early on, Flachat had made a major impression on the court with some automatons that he had had constructed – the sort of mechanical figures that were all the rage in Europe in the mid- to late eighteenth century – which fascinated the harem women and provided Flachat with an entrée to Moralı Beshir, to whom he became rather close.[75]

This closeness comes across in Flachat's enthusiastic description of the Chief Eunuch. "One rarely found among [the eunuchs]," he writes,

one who had, like him, an open forehead, a well-made nose, large, fiery eyes, a small mouth, rosy lips, dazzlingly white teeth, a perfectly proportioned neck with no wrinkles, fine arms and legs, and all the rest of the body supple and free, more fat than thin. His tone of voice reflected the gentility of his manners; it was insinuating, clear, and sonorous.[76]

These were, admittedly, rather back-handed compliments, praising Moralı Beshir for not fitting the negative stereotypes of African eunuchs' appearance and comportment. To Flachat, he seemed a cultivated intellectual: a fluent writer and talented calligrapher who, like his predecessor, amassed an impressive library of classic works in Arabic, Persian, and Turkish, in which he read for hours each day.[77]

According to Flachat, Moralı Beshir, like Habeshi Mehmed Agha close to 200 years earlier, had his own palace near Topkapı, outfitted with "the richest things that manufacturers could produce, the greatest things that the arts could achieve."[78] He shared it with the harem treasurer Süleyman Agha, who, by Flachat's account, kept his own harem there.[79] (Having essentially purged the harem eunuch hierarchy on taking office, Moralı Beshir was apparently able to clear the way for a harem treasurer who was his protégé and confidant.) By the Frenchman's account, Moralı Beshir also built "palaces," more properly kiosks or pavilions, in Beşiktaş and at a site called "Ağa Bahçesi" ("Agha's Garden"), and added rooms to Topkapı; asked to provide furnishings for all of these, Flachat arranged with Süleyman Agha to import them from France.[80]

Downfall and Execution. Ultimately, according to Flachat, the chief eunuch biographer Ahmed Resmi Efendi, and the chronicler Şemdanizade, Moralı Beshir was brought down by his clients. (Şemdanizade has him selling offices and ensuring that only his protégés became grand vizier.) "The Turks who were in his service, or whom he honored with his protection," Flachat

---

[75] Flachat, *Observations*, I: 501, 505–6; II: 163; also II: 10, 176–77, 180–81, 207, 213–14, 216, 218.
[76] Ibid., II: 127–28.   [77] Ibid., II: 128–29; Ahmed Resmi, *Hamiletü'l-kübera*, 72.
[78] Flachat, *Observations*, II: 133–34.   [79] Ibid., II: 136.
[80] Ibid., II: 153–55, 159, 232, 261–70.

writes, "were not like him. They were tyrants who exploited the provinces; they did not respect anyone."[81] Both he and Ahmed Resmi relate a jarring episode in which a gang of the Chief Eunuch's young Georgian "footmen" (singular, *çuhadar*, literally "bearer of cloth"), returning from a military expedition in Anatolia, rampaged through Üsküdar, knocking off the turban of the district's mullah, a grave insult. Although he promised to execute them, Moralı Beshir simply sent them out on another campaign, whereupon they occupied, then tore down, the mullah's house. In the following weeks, they set fires all over Istanbul.

The new grand vizier, Köse Bahir Mustafa Pasha, despite being a client of the Chief Eunuch, was sufficiently worried about these abuses, as well as the sheer extent of Moralı Beshir's power, to request a *fetva* from the Chief Mufti authorizing his execution. Moralı Beshir expected to be sent on his way to Egypt, like so many deposed Chief Eunuchs before him. Instead, he was imprisoned and executed in the Kız Kulesi (Maiden's Tower) in the middle of the Bosphorus, across from Üsküdar, home of the aggrieved mullah, on 12 July 1752. According to a *Register of Chief Harem Eunuchs* (*Defter-i Ağayan-ı Darüsaade*) prepared at the end of the nineteenth century, he was buried in Üsküdar's Doğancılar quarter, although I have not been able to locate his grave. Süleyman the treasurer and Hagop the Chief Merchant were beheaded, Hagop after lengthy torture designed to compel him to divulge the location of suspected hidden wealth; his brother, a former Chief Merchant, was also killed, and the brothers' bodies were mutilated by a mob. Moralı Beshir's clients in the provinces were proscribed or executed.[82]

For all his overreaching and the excesses of his clients, Moralı Beshir Agha did build on several key precedents established by el-Hajj Beshir. Admittedly, he was not as successful as his predecessor (or his predecessor's predecessors) at channeling his clients into the grand vizierate or at cultivating alliances with the Chief Mufti, despite his efforts. His foreign policy interventions, meanwhile, focused on commercial relations with the European powers. In part because of this emphasis, he succeeded in replicating el-Hajj Beshir's patronage of court entertainments featuring imported luxury goods. His attention to

---

[81] Ibid., II: 132; Ahmed Resmi, *Hamiletü'l-kübera*, 72–73; Şemdanizade, *Şemdanizade Tarihi*, I: 164–65; Henning Sievert, "Der schwarze Obereunuch Moralı Beşir Ağa in den Augen von Ahmed Resmi Efendi," in *Islamwissenschaft als Kuturwissenschaft*, vol. 1: *Historische Anthropologie: Ansätze und Möglichkeiten*, eds. Stephan Conermann and Syrinx von Hees (Hamburg, 2007), 345–78.

[82] Flachat, *Observations*, I: 151; II: 138–48; Ahmed Resmi, *Hamiletü'l-kübera*, 72–74; Şemdanizade, *Şemdanizade Tarihi*, I: 166–68; II: 2, 76; Ayvansarayi, *Garden of the Mosques*, 416–17; *Defter-i Ağayan-i Darüssaade*, appendix to *Hamiletü'l-kübera*, 170.

luxury goods was part of a broader concern with commerce, and more particularly with the worry-free transit of staple and luxury goods to the palace – a concern that, as we have seen, el-Hajj Beshir Agha unquestionably shared. In order to facilitate this commerce, both Beshirs forged alliances with merchants, including foreign merchants, and local notables of various kinds.

Damascus and the *Hajj* Caravan

Patronage of provincial notables cannot be overemphasized as part of the new Chief Eunuch paradigm that el-Hajj Beshir Agha represented. Ever since Habeshi Mehmed Agha, of course, the Chief Harem Eunuch had needed clients in the Ottoman provinces to carry out revenue and grain collection for the Evkafü'l-Haremeyn. In the eighteenth century, though, the number of Chief Eunuch clients in the provinces increased dramatically, as did their visibility in Ottoman chronicles and archival documents. The increase stemmed in part from the growing importance during these years of provincial notables, known as *ayan*, empire-wide. But the reinforcement of the Chief Harem Eunuch's connection to Medina through the office of Şeyhü'l-Harem also played a role, as did changes in the administration of the pilgrimage to Mecca.

Changes in the *hajj* administration help to explain the interest of el-Hajj Beshir and his successors in the notables of the province of Damascus, which encompassed central and southern Syria and present-day Lebanon, Jordan, Israel, and the Palestinian territories. As a result of an administrative reorganization in 1708, spearheaded by the reform-minded grand vizier Çorlulu Ali Pasha, the governor of Damascus began to lead the annual Syrian pilgrimage caravan in person. This meant that he spent several months of every year on the road and that he bore personal responsibility for organizing and equipping the pilgrimage caravan. This was a period of considerable tribal migration in the Arabian peninsula, Greater Syria, and Iraq, which made the pilgrimage route that much less secure, particularly in time of drought or other climatic challenges; these considerations no doubt figured in the decision to put the governor in charge of the caravan.[83] But to be effective at the new task, the governor had to be able to cultivate ties to the various Bedouin populations along the route.

For much of the eighteenth century, the governorship of Damascus was dominated by the 'Azm family, who are classic examples of local notables as defined by the late Albert Hourani – that is to say, they originated in an Ottoman province and built up a power base there that did not depend for its

[83] Barbir, *Ottoman Rule in Damascus*, 103–7 and chapter 3; Hathaway, *Arab Lands under Ottoman Rule*, 87–90, 183–84.

existence on the Ottoman palace.[84] They were apparently an old Arab family who emerged in the vicinity of Hama when the Mamluk Sultanate ruled the region. By the 1720s, they had come to monopolize the governorship of Damascus, as well as the governorships of several other districts in Greater Syria, including Aleppo, Hama, and Tripoli in Lebanon. They purchased these governorships as enormous life-tenure tax farms.[85]

In 1743, one of el-Hajj Beshir Agha's clients, the Damascene notable Fethi Efendi, who at the time was chief financial administrator, or *defterdar*, of the province of Damascus, attempted to wrest the governorship from the 'Azms' grasp. He started by confiscating the estate of Süleyman Pasha al-'Azm, who had died in office. When Süleyman's nephew, the powerful Es'ad Pasha al-'Azm, succeeded him as governor, Fethi set out to undermine him so as to win the governorship for himself. His scheme might have worked if el-Hajj Beshir had not died in June 1746, leaving Fethi defenseless against Es'ad Pasha, who now persuaded his own clients in Istanbul to press for Fethi's execution for corrupt practices. In the end, Fethi was hanged. Meanwhile, Es'ad Pasha grew richer and richer from trade conducted during the pilgrimage, and dotted Damascus with his charitable foundations, a number of which are still standing.

Es'ad Pasha al-'Azm was still governor of Damascus eleven years later, when the Chief Harem Eunuch Ebu'l-Vukuf (sometimes rendered Ebukoff) Ahmed Agha (term 1755–57) championed yet another alternative provincial notable against him. The notable in question was one Mekkizade Hüseyin Pasha, or Hüseyin Pasha ibn al-Makki ("son of the Meccan"), who, despite his sobriquet, came from a family with deep roots in Gaza. Ebu'l-Vukuf managed to see to it that Mekkizade was appointed governor of Damascus, and thus commander of the Damascene pilgrimage caravan, in 1757, replacing Es'ad al-'Azm.

This was a challenging time for the Damascus caravan since southern Syria was in the second year of a severe drought, and the Bedouin tribes of the region were increasingly unable to conduct their normal exchange of livestock for agricultural products, textiles, and manufactured goods. The Gaza-oriented Mekkizade lacked the connections with the tribes that the 'Azms had forged. He dutifully led the pilgrims to Mecca in August 1757 and completed the *hajj*, but on the way back, disaster struck. As the caravan neared Damascus, a massive force of Bedouin raiders fell upon it, slaughtering 20,000 pilgrims

---

[84] Albert Hourani, "Ottoman Reform and the Politics of Notables," in *Beginnings of Modernization in the Middle East in the Nineteenth Century*, eds. William R. Polk and Richard L. Chambers (Chicago, IL, 1968), 41–68.

[85] Hathaway, *Arab Lands under Ottoman Rule*, 88.

indiscriminately and stranding the rest, naked, in the desert. To quote the chronicle of the Damascene barber known as al-Budayri:

> The news came to Damascus that the Bedouin had attacked the *hajj* [caravan] and plundered it, stolen the possessions of both women and men, and their clothing ... On Thursday, the 25th of Safar, some of the Damascus Janissaries arrived from the pilgrimage route, along with the pilgrims riding two or three to a mount. They were in the last stage of privation ... They reported that behind them was a large group of pilgrims, and with them the women and children with the princess [the sister of Sultan Osman III, who had made the *hajj* that year], barefoot and naked ... The things that had been done to the pilgrims the servants of hell would not have done, for they reported that [the Bedouin] would strip a man and search [for valuables] under his armpits and buttocks, and in his mouth and under his testicles, and if he were fat or had a pot belly, they would rip open his pot belly if it were big. It was reported that they split stomachs and pot-bellies and inserted their hands in the anuses of women and men and searched the vaginas of women ...
>
> Then the pilgrims remained [in the desert] for four days, hungry and thirsty, with no water and no provisions, and some of them died of hunger, thirst, cold, and heat, and that was after drinking each other's urine.[86]

Mekkizade survived this horror, only to flee to his family stronghold in Gaza. Furious decrees from the newly enthroned Sultan Mustafa III (r. 1757–74) ordered him to return to Damascus immediately to sort out the aftermath, aid the pitiable survivors, and coordinate a retaliatory expedition. Rather surprisingly, he was not executed but instead deposed and permanently rusticated to his Gaza base. The grand vizier, Raghib Mehmed Pasha, who, as *reisü'l-küttab*, had led the negotiations with Nadir Shah, deposed Ebu'l-Vukuf, who had arranged Mekkizade's ill-advised appointment, and ordered the execution of Es'ad Pasha al-'Azm, whom he suspected of organizing the Bedouin attack in an effort to get his old post back.[87] Ebu'l-Vukuf took the familiar path to exile in Egypt, only to be executed, on Raghib Pasha's orders, at Çanakkale on the Dardanelles en route.[88]

The fact that a Chief Harem Eunuch could fall because of a provincial incident, even one involving the *hajj* caravan, further reflects the paradigm

---

[86] Ahmad al-Budayri al-Hallaq, *Hawadith Dimashq al-yawmiyya, 1154–1175 h./1741–1762*, ed. Ahmad 'Izzat Abd al-Karim, condensed by Muhammad Sa'id al-Qasimi (Cairo, 1959), 207–8. I am grateful for Professor Dana Sajdi's insights on the original manuscript of this text; see her monograph *The Barber of Damascus: Nouveau Literacy in the Eighteenth-Century Ottoman Levant* (Stanford, CA, 2013).

[87] Barbir, *Ottoman Rule in Damascus*, 30, 178; Hathaway, *Arab Lands under Ottoman Rule*, 89–90; Şemdanizade, *Şemdanizade Tarihi*, II: 13–14; Norman Itzkowitz, "Mehmed Raghip Paşa: The Making of an Ottoman Grand Vizier," unpublished Ph.D. dissertation, Princeton University 1958, 150–54; BOA, MD 160, No. 1 (8 Rebiülevvel 1171/20 November 1757).

[88] Şemdanizade, *Şemdanizade Tarihi*, II: 14; Barbir, *Ottoman Rule in Damascus*, 178.

shift in the way the office of Chief Eunuch operated in the post-seventeenth-century-crisis Ottoman Empire. Provincial notables such as Es'ad Pasha al-'Azm, Fethi Efendi, and Mekkizade Hüseyin Pasha – to say nothing of the family of lighthouse-keepers in the Danube Delta – all of whom came from long-established provincial families and none of whom had been trained in the palace, now had a visible effect on decision-making and key appointments at the imperial center. Meanwhile, the pilgrimage itself had assumed paramount importance in the projection of Ottoman imperial authority (not to mention religious legitimacy) at a time when the empire's territorial expansion had ceased and relations with competing geopolitical powers were more and more frequently mediated through diplomacy. All of this meant that in order to sustain his influence at the imperial center while retaining control over the pilgrimage, which was vital to the Evkafü'l-Haremeyn, the Chief Harem Eunuch had to cultivate these provincial notables, in Damascus no less than in Egypt (the subject of Chapter 8).

At the same time, the heightened political importance of the pilgrimage, combined with its ongoing economic importance, helps to explain why the Chief Eunuch's career trajectory of post-deposition appointment as chief of Medina's tomb eunuchs, first followed by Yusuf Agha in 1691, had become the norm a century later. In fact, two deposed Chief Eunuchs, Cevher Mehmed Agha (terms 1772–74, 1779–83) and Sarıkçı ("Turban-Bearer") Beshir Agha (term 1774–79), were dispatched directly to Medina on leaving office, with no stop in Cairo.[89]

Conclusion

The careers of el-Hajj Beshir Agha and his successors, as well as his immediate predecessors, embody the new realities of Ottoman court life, society, center–periphery relations, and geopolitics in the first half of the eighteenth century. We have just seen how the Chief Harem Eunuch could not ignore the steadily increasing influence of provincial notables and, as a result, sometimes got caught in the web of provincial politics. In addition, the Ottoman Empire's changing geopolitical status had a number of interlocking implications for the Chief Eunuch. While the empire was still almost constantly at war or contemplating the threat of war, more and more of its interactions with foreign powers were peaceful: booming trade with France, England, and the Italian city-states; diplomacy with the Habsburgs, Russia, and even Iran.

---

[89] On his initial deposition, Cevher went to Cairo, then Medina, before being reinstated as Chief Eunuch. On his second and final deposition, he went straight to Medina.

Flourishing trade with western Europe, particularly in luxury goods, during the early eighteenth century fueled the so-called Tulip Era, to which el-Hajj Beshir Agha contributed. Of more lasting consequence, Chief Harem Eunuchs now had formidable ties to European merchants, of whom Jean-Claude Flachat, friend and fan of Moralı Beshir Agha, is merely the most verbose example. European merchants supplied the Ottoman court with luxury merchandise, which the Chief Eunuch distributed at outdoor garden parties, held in a steadily expanding array of public gathering places where at least a portion of the public might glimpse the new consumer goods, stoking their own demand for them. Consumerism and conspicuous consumption were, in turn, signs of the Ottoman economy's recovery from the long, drawn-out crisis. Similarly, this expanded trade aided the rise of local notables who now traded directly with the European powers, not seeking Istanbul's mediation.

Meanwhile, diplomacy was promoted by a new breed of bureaucrats, led by the *reisü'l-küttab*, or "chief scribe," who by the mid-eighteenth century had become a sort of proto-foreign minister. More and more frequently, the *reisü'l-küttab* and other bureaucrats trained in the grand vizier's chancery or in the finance administration ascended to the grand vizierate. Raghib Mehmed Pasha was the supreme example of one of these "efendis-turned-pashas," to use Norman Itzkowitz's term,[90] but he was not the first or only one. Because they did not come from the palace, these bureaucrat grand viziers were harder for the Chief Eunuch to coopt as clients.

By the 1750s, a pattern had emerged of the grand vizier opposing the Chief Harem Eunuch in his policy preferences and attempting to restrict the Chief Eunuch's overall influence. As we have seen, the reformist grand vizier Silahdar Damad Ali Pasha – who was not a bureaucrat, as it happened – in the early eighteenth century tried to ban the importation of African eunuchs into Ottoman territory altogether. A few decades later, Raghib Mehmed Pasha, as *reisü'l-küttab*, led negotiations with Nadir Shah that el-Hajj Beshir Agha vehemently opposed. As grand vizier, Raghib deposed (and ultimately executed) Ebu'l-Vukuf Ahmed Agha for promoting Mekkizade Hüseyin Pasha as governor of Damascus and thus indirectly triggering the horrific 1757 *hajj* caravan attack. Perhaps not coincidentally, an imperial order condemning the castration of male African slaves imported into Ottoman territory reached the governor and chief judge of Egypt a little more than a year later.[91] Raghib's contention with these two opinionated Chief Eunuchs combined multiple elements of the new eighteenth-century paradigm: an efendi-turned-pasha

---

[90] Itzkowitz, "Eighteenth-Century Ottoman Realities," 86.
[91] BOA, Mühimme-i Mısır, vol. 7, No. 545 (1 Cemaziyelevvel 1172/30 December 1758).

advocating diplomacy while the Chief Eunuch favored war, and struggling to curb the influence of local notables whom the Chief Eunuch patronized. By the time of Raghib's grand vizierate – and arguably by the time of Damad Ali's – the main political rivalry at court was no longer between rival harem factions, or between the harem and the Third Court, but between the harem and the grand vizier.

An inescapable part of the new Chief Eunuch paradigm was his ever-increasing ties to Egypt, which arguably occupied a place of importance in the Chief Eunuch's career unmatched by any other province, even the Hijaz. Chapter 8 explores these ties and their consequences.

8   Exile and the Kingdom
The Chief Harem Eunuch and Egypt

Although the Chief Harem Eunuch lived in Istanbul during his tenure in office, Egypt was constantly on his mind and, in fact, lurked constantly in the background. It could hardly have been otherwise. In many cases, Egypt bookended the Chief Eunuch's life and career: he was castrated and commenced his service in Egypt; he returned to Egypt upon his deposition, and, like as not, died there. And as we have seen, stints in Egypt in between initial enslavement and retirement were not terribly unusual and had become fairly common by the end of the seventeenth century, as el-Hajj Beshir's experience shows.

In sum, a stream of deposed Chief Harem Eunuchs, as well as lower-ranking eunuchs in temporary or permanent exile, arrived in Cairo from the early seventeenth century until Mehmed Ali Pasha took over Egypt in the early nineteenth century. Not surprisingly, they tended to congregate in the same neighborhoods in Cairo, even exchanging houses in some cases. By at least the mid-seventeenth century, as a result, Cairo had acquired an identifiable population of African eunuchs who sometimes acted as a cohesive interest group and were regarded as such by the greater populace.

This chapter treats the Chief Harem Eunuch's relationship with Egypt throughout his life and career, beginning with his immediate post-enslavement presence in the province. We then turn to his dealings with Egypt while in office, particularly in connection with the Evkafü'l-Haremeyn, and his efforts to navigate the maze of Egypt's "politics of notables" so as to ensure the timely collection of Evkaf revenues and grain. In this context, we examine the Chief Eunuch's permanent agent (*vekil*) in Cairo. Finally, we consider the Chief Eunuch's exile to Cairo, the clients necessary to make exile productive and even profitable, and the various projects that exiled Chief Eunuchs undertook, along with their effects on Egypt.

Egypt's Political Situation

We cannot begin this task, though, without explaining Egypt's distinctive situation as an Ottoman province, which helped to determine the character of the Chief Eunuch's dealings with Egypt's grandees. After the Ottomans

160

conquered it from the Mamluk Sultanate in 1517, Egypt became the empire's largest province and the biggest revenue-producer. Administratively, it was, in some respects, a mirror image of Istanbul itself: the provincial governor, appointed from Istanbul, had a governing council, or *divan*, and commanded seven regiments of Ottoman soldiery. Meanwhile, Egypt's thirteen subprovinces were administered by *sancak beyi*s, in the manner of subprovincial districts elsewhere in the Ottoman domains (although certain lower-ranking subprovincial governors held the old Mamluk title *kashif*).

During the sixteenth century, most of the soldiers and *sancak beyi*s were palace-trained *devshirme* recruits, so that by 1600 Egypt, like Istanbul, had something of a "*kul* problem." A massive rebellion by Egypt's soldiery in 1609 was brutally suppressed by the governor Öküz Mehmed Pasha, who came to be known, appropriately, as *Kul Kıran*, or "the *kul*-breaker." Afterward, as in Istanbul, mamluks from the Caucasus became an attractive alternative source of manpower. By the late seventeenth century, Egypt's grandees were importing their own mamluks, bypassing the imperial palace, and channeling them, and other clients, into the regiments of soldiery and the ranks of the *sancak beyi*s. In this way, Egypt's grandees, like grandees in other Ottoman provinces, became increasingly "localized."

Every year, Egypt dispatched one of the two official Ottoman pilgrimage caravans to Mecca (the other, as we have seen, came from Damascus). But whereas the governor of Damascus, beginning in 1708, led the Syrian pilgrimage caravan, Egypt's was commanded by one of the *sancak beyi*s, who received the title *emirü'l-hac* (*amir al-hajj* in Arabic). This was one of the two most important (and lucrative) administrative positions in the province, along with that of *defterdar*, or chief financial administrator, an office also held by a *sancak beyi*. The acting Chief Harem Eunuch was, understandably, concerned with the reliability of Egypt's pilgrimage commander, who delivered the all-important grain, along with cash and many other sorts of provisions, to the holy cities each year.

But this was not the only thing the Chief Harem Eunuch had to worry about where Egypt was concerned. His main headache was no doubt Egypt's distinctive political culture, the context in which all these military and administrative appointments took place. In Egypt, as in other provinces and in the imperial capital, high-ranking administrators formed households, consisting of their families and clients. In Egypt, such clients comprised mainly soldiers and *sancak beyi*s.

But in the early seventeenth century, these households coalesced into two rival factions, the Faqaris (a.k.a. Zülfıkarlıs) and the Qasimis, whose conflicts stretched into the 1730s and frequently gave rise to violent upheavals. These were not relatively short-lived factions of convenience, comparable to the palace harem factions, but deeply entrenched factions of astonishing longevity, with their own dichomotous traditions, symbols, colors, and origin myths, not unlike the Guelphs and Ghibellines of medieval Italy or the Hatfields and McCoys of the antebellum United States. At times, the Ottoman governor sought to divide the subprovincial governorships and the posts of pilgrimage commander and *defterdar* between the two factions. The Chief Harem Eunuch seemed to patronize both, although occasionally we can faintly perceive a slight preference for one or the other. By the mid-eighteenth century, in any case, the two factions had been displaced by the powerful Kazdağlı household, originally a Faqari household that emerged within Egypt's Janissary regiment during the seventeenth century but that gradually came to dominate not only the regiments of soldiery but also the rank of *sancak beyi*. In this way, the Kazdağlıs managed to overcome the endemic friction between the regiments and the *sancak beyi*s, which historically had only exacerbated the confrontation between the Faqari and Qasimi factions.[1]

We might not think that this culture of factions, and of soldiers versus beys, could have much of an effect on the immediate post-castration life of an African eunuch in Egypt. But as the following discussion will show, it could, and did.

Early Connections to Egypt

Egypt was the place where most Ottoman harem eunuchs became eunuchs. As we have already seen, Asyut district in Upper Egypt was the site of a veritable castration "factory" housed in a Coptic monastery. After castration, most new eunuchs were transported to Cairo and sold in that city's vast slave market. Relatively few, however, were purchased directly by the imperial palace, although we have no concrete figures. Instead, most were bought by the Ottoman governor and his retinue, or by wealthy provincial grandees, above all the military and administrative elite, and installed in their households. The heads of these households later presented eunuchs to the Ottoman palace. In effect, these households served as a sort of "finishing school" for African harem eunuchs: way stations where they learned Ottoman Turkish, received a basic Muslim education, and became acquainted with the rudiments of Ottoman political realities.

We might think that we can easily see why a governor of Egypt would present a eunuch to the Ottoman palace. He hoped, we assume, that the eunuch would ultimately become Chief Eunuch and, in that lofty position, would remember the governor in whose household his career began. Yet his rise

---

[1] Hathaway, *Politics of Households*; Hathaway, *A Tale of Two Factions*; Hathaway, *Arab Lands under Ottoman Rule*, 83–87, 98–105; Hathaway, "The 'Mamluk Breaker' Who Was Really a *Kul* Breaker."

would take decades; after all, Chief Eunuch was an office that a eunuch usually assumed in late middle age. By that time, the governor in question would probably be dead. A more plausible explanation is simply that the governor wished to curry favor with the sultan and his entourage in the hope of obtaining choice postings (although governor of Egypt was itself a highly desirable office) and other preferments.

Provincial grandee households, on the other hand, could afford to take the long view. In Egypt, some of the most prominent households seem to have regarded East African eunuchs as a sound investment. This trend is particularly noticeable among the households of the Faqari faction, above all the Kazdağlı household, which in the course of the eighteenth century came to dominate the entire province. As we saw in Chapter 2, the French pharmacist Charles Jacques Poncet, on the way back to Cairo from Ethiopia, witnessed a young Ethiopian slave boy being seized by Egypt's Janissaries for their commander, the Janissary *kethüda* Mustafa al-Kazdağlı, founder of the household.[2] (Before 1754, the head of the Kazdağlı household usually held the rank of *kethüda*, technically lieutenant commander, of the Janissary regiment.) Mustafa Kethüda at the time ran Egypt in all but name, in collaboration with two other Faqari chieftains: his patron, Hasan Agha, the commander of Egypt's Gönüllüyan (Volunteers) regiment, and Hasan Agha's son-in-law, the *defterdar* Ismail Bey.[3]

Ismail Bey was ostensibly the patron of the most famous harem eunuch in Ottoman history, the legendary el-Hajj Beshir Agha. The Egyptian chronicler Ahmed Kethüda al-Damurdashi recounts a scene in 1733 when the sultan's ruling council made recommendations for the top administrative positions in Egypt. "And for *defterdar*," the Chief Harem Eunuch, who would have been el-Hajj Beshir, is supposed to have said, "the son of *sayyidi* ('my master'), Mehmed Bey Ismail."[4] He was recommending Ismail Bey's son, Mehmed Bey, who indeed became *defterdar*, but more strikingly, he is apparently acknowledging Ismail Bey as his "master" (*sayyid*), using a term for "master" that was sometimes encountered among elite slaves, or mamluks.[5] It is certainly conceivable that Beshir Agha was at some point a member of Ismail Bey's household, which may have entailed living and being educated in his residential compound. If so, then Ismail Bey may have engineered Beshir's entry into the imperial palace.

More substantive evidence of Faqari, and more specifically Kazdağlı, patronage of African harem eunuchs comes from the probate inventory of Osman

[2] Foster, ed., *Red Sea and Adjacent Countries*, xxix; Bruce, *Travels*, III: 92.
[3] Al-Damurdashi, *Al-Durra al-musana*, 101; Hathaway, *Politics of Households*, 65–70.
[4] Al-Damurdashi, *Al-Durra al-musana*, 407; Hathaway, "Role of the Kızlar Ağası," 154.
[5] David Ayalon, *L'esclavage du mamelouk* (Jerusalem, 1951), 25ff.

Kethüda al-Kazdağlı, a Georgian mamluk by origin, who was head of the Kazdağlı household from roughly 1716 through 1736. These two decades marked the household's emergence as the major player in Egypt's commercial and political life. Osman's estate inventory, compiled after his 1736 murder in a carefully orchestrated massacre at the home of Egypt's *defterdar*, has been studied by Michel Tuchscherer. It lists twelve of his "followers" (*tawabi'*), including "Bashir Agha Dar al-Sa'ada," or Beshir the imperial harem eunuch.[6]

This could not have been el-Hajj Beshir, who by 1736 had been Chief Harem Eunuch for nearly twenty years, probably longer than Osman Kethüda had been in Egypt. Following el-Hajj Beshir's death in 1746, there were four more Chief Eunuchs named Beshir; in fact, the name had become quite a popular one for harem eunuchs, no doubt because of el-Hajj Beshir's remarkable success and longevity. Osman Kethüda's Beshir may conceivably have been the third of these, known as Hazinedar Beshir, who was Chief Eunuch from 1752 to 1755, although he would have been well along in his progress up the palace eunuch hierarchy by the time of Osman's death.[7] A more likely candidate is the fifth and last Beshir Agha, known as Sarıkçı ("Turban-Bearer") Beshir, who was Chief Eunuch from 1774 to 1779 and who, following the growing trend among Chief Eunuchs, was sent to Medina to lead the tomb eunuchs on his deposition.

One or another of these Beshir Aghas in the latter half of the eighteenth century owned a house on the banks of Birkat al-Azbakiyya, a pond northwest of Cairo's citadel that had recently become the hub of elite residence. Tellingly, the house was next-door to the residence of Ibrahim Kethüda al-Kazdağlı, who all but ran Egypt from 1748 to 1754; his house was later occupied by Mehmed Bey Abu al-Dhahab, the client of the famous Ali Bey al-Kabir, who in turn was Ibrahim Kethüda's client.[8]

These examples of Egypt's grandees' cultivating ties with future Chief Harem Eunuchs all involve patronage by leaders of the Kazdağlı household and (in the case of Ismail Bey) its closest allies. We may conclude that the Kazdağlıs pursued a deliberate agenda of linking themselves to eunuchs of the imperial harem at fairly early stages of the eunuchs' careers, with the ultimate aim of forging a solid network of ties to eunuchs at all ranks of the palace hierarchy, up to and very much including the acting Chief Harem Eunuch. This strategy would have allowed them to take advantage of opportunities that arose when one of their client eunuchs was promoted to an

---

[6] Michel Tuchscherer, "Le Pèlerinage de l'émir Sulaymân Ğâwiš al-Qazduġlî, sirdâr de la caravane de la Mekke en 1739," *Annales islamologiques* 24 (1988): 157 n. 10; Hathaway, *Politics of Households*, 74–79.

[7] Hathaway, *Politics of Households*, 160–62.

[8] Raymond, "Essai de géographie," 66, 73–75, 77, 80–81, 100; Hathaway, *Politics of Households*, 162–63.

influential position at the palace. By cultivating ties to numerous eunuchs, though, they could avoid disaster if a particular eunuch fell from imperial favor. This seems a more sensible strategy than throwing in one's lot with a single eunuch, no matter how powerful, as Fethi the Defterdar and Mekkizade Hüseyin Pasha had done in Damascus. For the eunuchs, meanwhile, a connection to the Kazdağlıs or some other influential Egyptian household offered an opportunity to become acquainted with the network of alliances and counter-alliances among Egypt's grandees at a given time. This information could prove invaluable when it came to choosing agents or assigning the tax farms of lands endowed to the Evkafü'l-Haremeyn.

Egypt and the Evkafü'l-Haremeyn

While in office, of course, the Chief Harem Eunuch supervised the imperial pious foundations for Mecca and Medina, known in Ottoman Turkish as Evkafü'l-Haremeyn, which were described in Chapter 4. Numerous Egyptian villages were endowed to the Evkaf for the express purpose of supplying grain to the holy cities. It was the Chief Harem Eunuch's responsibility to ensure that the grain made it to Mecca and Medina with the Egyptian pilgrimage caravan every year. Naturally, he could not leave his post in Istanbul and tour the Egyptian countryside, overseeing the grain harvest, the loading of Nile boats with the produce, and its transport to Cairo to be loaded onto camels for the trek to Suez (see Map 8.1), then onto Indian ships – specifically provided for by the endowments – for the voyage to Jidda, Mecca's port. Instead, these duties had to be farmed out – in essence, sold – to people on the spot.

Naturally, the only people wealthy enough to purchase these rights were, with a few exceptions, provincial grandees. At a local auction, a grandee offered a purchase price based on the value of grain that he estimated the village would produce in a fiscal year. He paid this price to the imperial treasury up front, then sent one of his clients to collect the grain, along with other revenues, while he remained in Cairo. The client had a free hand in collecting, so long as he amassed the equivalent of the purchase price; any amount that he collected above this price constituted the tax-farmer's profit on his investment.[9]

Tax farming, or *iltizam*, became widespread in the Ottoman Empire in the course of the seventeenth century. In 1695, the government of Sultan Mustafa II introduced the life-tenure tax farm, known in Ottoman Turkish as *malikane*, as a fiscal reform measure;[10] the effect in Egypt was to make the competition

---

[9] Hathaway, *Arab Lands under Ottoman Rule*, 171–72.
[10] Ariel Salzmann, "An Ancien Régime Revisited: 'Privatization' and Political Economy in the Eighteenth-Century Ottoman Empire," *Politics and Society* 21, 4 (1993): 400–402.

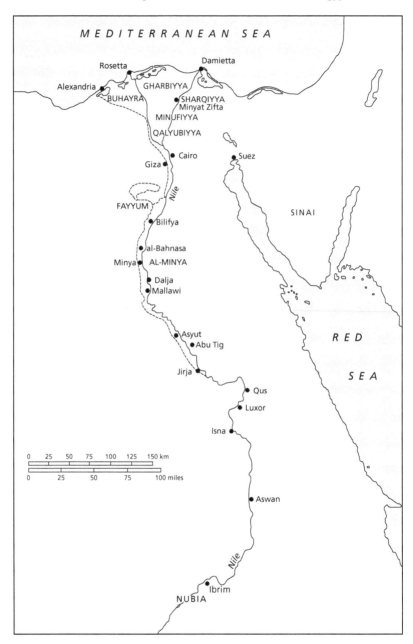

Map 8.1 Egypt, showing subprovinces.

among provincial grandees for the tax farms of Evkaf villages all the fiercer. In this atmosphere, Egypt's grandees cultivated ties to the acting Chief Harem Eunuch so as to improve their chances of acquiring these lucrative tax farms. Correspondingly, the Chief Eunuch tried to ensure that grandees with whom he had strong relationships received preference for these revenue grants. The end result was a network of reciprocal influence that spread throughout the Egyptian countryside.

A telling example of such a network involves the rural conglomerate established by Hasan Agha Bilifya, the Gönüllüyan commander mentioned above who essentially ran Egypt, along with his son-in-law Ismail Bey and client Mustafa Kethüda al-Kazdağlı, toward the end of the seventeenth century. Hasan Agha, an elderly commander of Anatolian Greek origin who had probably come to Egypt in the early decades of the seventeenth century, derived his sobriquet from his lengthy tenure as tax-farmer of Bilifya, a village in al-Bahnasa subprovince (today part of al-Minya province) in Middle Egypt that was endowed to the Evkafü'l-Haremeyn. In the course of his career, he added several more *vakıf* villages, all located in al-Bahnasa, to Bilifya, creating for himself a sort of endowed redoubt in the subprovince. He himself, from all appearances, almost never traveled to visit his holdings but enjoyed them from Cairo as a dependable source of revenue. On his death in 1704, his mamluk Mustafa Bey, also known as Bilifya, inherited the cluster of tax farms.[11] Well into the twentieth century, al-Bahnasa boasted a village populated by the descendants of "Turkish mamluks," indicating that members of, if not the heads of, the Bilifya household settled in the region.[12]

Hasan Agha's tax farm cluster would not have been possible without the cooperation of one or more of the Chief Harem Eunuchs of the late seventeenth century. Unfortunately, we have no evidence of his connection to any specific Chief Eunuch, although his son-in-law's purported ties to el-Hajj Beshir Agha are certainly suggestive. The situation is arguably a bit more clear-cut with somewhat later grandees. In particular, el-Hajj Beshir Agha seemed to have had a soft spot for the young firebrand Ismail Bey ibn Ivaz Bey, a wildly popular Qasimi chieftain whom the Ottoman government suspected of harboring dreams of rebellion.

The son of the Circassian Qasimi leader Ivaz Bey, who was assassinated in Egypt's 1711 faction-driven civil war, Ismail was intensely resented not only by leaders of the rival Faqari faction but also by a Qasimi subfaction led by Çerkes ("Circassian") Mehmed Bey, the mamluk of Ivaz's Bosnian comrade-in-arms Ibrahim Bey Abu Shanab. Evkaf villages featured prominently in

[11] Hathaway, "Role of the Kızlar Ağası," 153–55; Hathaway, *Politics of Households*, 156–60; Hathaway, "Wealth and Influence," 304 n. 50.
[12] Personal observation of Professor Abd al-Wahhab Bakr, Cairo, April 1989.

Ismail's conflicts with rival grandees. In 1719, Ismail and Çerkes Mehmed came close to armed conflict over an Evkaf village in Gharbiyya subprovince in the western Nile Delta.[13]

Three years after this confrontation, however, el-Hajj Beshir Agha allegedly interceded with the sultan to secure an imperial pardon for Ismail Bey. According to the Egyptian chronicler Ahmed Çelebi, el-Hajj Beshir combined with the grand vezir Nevşehirli Ibrahim Pasha to persuade Sultan Ahmed III of Ismail's loyalty. Admittedly, this seems somewhat unlikely, given the lack of hard evidence of alliance or cooperation between the two. (On the contrary, as we saw in Chapter 7, Beshir Agha wrenched the grand vizier's seal away from Ibrahim Pasha at the height of the Patrona Halil rebellion, clearing the way for his execution.)

In Ahmed Çelebi's elaborately detailed account – much of it no doubt embellished for dramatic effect – the governor's secretary reads the imperial rescript before a large gathering of officials at Kara Meydan, the square outside Cairo's citadel, and drapes Ismail Bey in a fur sent specially from the palace. "It had never before happened that a rescript was read at Kara Meydan," the chronicler insists, "and the sultan had never sent a fur to one of the beys of Egypt." (As Ismail's arch-enemy Çerkes Mehmed Bey observed all this, "his face turned white as cotton.") Ahmed Çelebi then reconstructs the scene in which Beshir Agha and Ibrahim Pasha appeal to the sultan, who finally relents: "I am pardoning him for your sake, you two."[14] We should probably regard this narrative as evidence that on the Egyptian provincial scene, Ismail Bey ibn Ivaz was regarded as someone with a special connection to el-Hajj Beshir Agha and, through him, to the sultan. This in itself speaks to el-Hajj Beshir's influence, and that of the Chief Harem Eunuch more generally, in Egypt.

Apart from the tax farms of villages endowed to the Evkafü'l-Haremeyn, provincial grandees could also compete for the province-wide supervision of the individual endowments. For while the Chief Eunuch oversaw the Evkaf from Istanbul, he required "on site" supervisors, who usually went by the title *mütevelli* (*mutawalli* in Arabic), although primary sources sometimes use this title interchangeably with *nazir*, the post of overall supervisor. Under the reforming Köprülü grand viziers, the provincial administration of the endowments underwent a fundamental transformation. In 1670, grand vizier Köprülü

---

[13] Ahmed Çelebi, *Awdah al-isharat*, 295; BOA, Mühimme-i Mısır, vol. 3, nos. 560 (1138/1725–26), 603 (1138/1725–26); vol. 4, no. 8 (1139/1726–27); Hathaway, "Role of the Kızlar Ağası," 156; André Raymond, "Une 'révolution' au Caire sous les mamelouks: La crise de 1123/1711," *Annales islamologiques* 6 (1966): 95–120; Holt, *Egypt and the Fertile Crescent*, 88–90; Hathaway, *Politics of Households*, 70, 71–74; Hathaway, *A Tale of Two Factions*, 138–39.

[14] Ahmed Çelebi, *Awdah al-isharat*, 343–44, 468.

Fazıl Ahmed Pasha appointed his lieutenant, Kara Ibrahim Pasha, governor of Egypt and dispatched him to Cairo with orders to remove the beys who held the *mütevelli*-ships of the Deşişet-i Kubra, the Mehmediyye, the Muradiyye (here called the Haremeyn), and the Hassekiyye *vakıf*s and replace them with, respectively, the Janissary agha, the Janissary *kethüda*, the Janissary *baş çavuş* (technically third in command of the regiment), and the *kethüda* of the Azeban corps, an elite regiment that was smaller than the Janissaries but occasionally competed with them for influence.[15]

This move had the effect of attaching the positions to discrete offices that, at least in theory, rotated regularly, so that no one provincial grandee could monopolize the supervision of a given *vakıf*. It also gave the governor of Egypt a greater measure of control over provincial *vakıf* administration, for the Janissary agha and *baş çavuş* during the seventeenth century usually came to Cairo from the imperial palace and were closely connected to the governor's council, or *divan*; governors who founded *vakıf*s in Egypt often appointed the Janissary agha to supervise them.[16] Also noticeable is a certain factional balance in the apportionment of *mütevelli*-ships, for while the Janissary regiment was controlled by the Faqaris, the Azeban corps was something of a Qasimi stronghold.

All this changed in 1691 as a result of the machinations of the Faqari chieftain Ibrahim Bey ibn Zülfikar Bey. Seeking to deprive the regimental officers of revenue and, hence, of influence, Ibrahim Bey conspired with the Ottoman governor to transfer the Evkaf *mütevelli*-ships to specific beys: the Deşişet-i Kubra to Ibrahim Bey himself, who at the time was pilgrimage commander; the Mehmediyye to Murad Bey the *defterdar*; the Muradiyye/ Haremeyn to Ismail Bey, son-in-law of Hasan Agha Bilifya; and the Hassekiyye to Abdullah Bey.[17] Except for Murad Bey, all were Faqaris, and after several months, Ismail Bey took Murad's place as supervisor of the Mehmediyye *vakıf*, becoming local supervisor of two major imperial foundations. This startling transformation coincided roughly with the enthronement of Ahmed II, the death in battle of the grand vizier Köprülü Fazıl Mustafa Pasha, and the appointment of Kaba Nezir Agha as Chief Eunuch.

In 1699, Sultan Mustafa II, perhaps at the urging of grand vizier Amcazade Köprülü Hüseyin Pasha, issued a rescript ordering the return of the *mütevelli* positions to Janissary and Azeban officers. His move came in response to a

---

[15] Al-Hallaq, *Tarih-i Mısr-ı Kahire*, fols. 204a–b; anonymous, *Akhbar al-nuwwab min dawlat Al 'Uthman min hin istawala 'alayha al-sultan Salim Khan*, Topkapı Palace Library, MS Hazine 1623, fol. 33b; Ahmed Çelebi, *Awdah al-isharat*, 171; Hathaway, *Politics of Households*, 148–50.

[16] Hathaway, *Politics of Households*, 149 and n. 40.

[17] Al-Hallaq, *Tarih-i Mısr-ı Kahire*, fol. 226a; anonymous, *Akhbar al-nuwwab*, fol. 42a; Ahmed Çelebi, *Awdah al-isharat*, 187; Hathaway, *Politics of Households*, 152–53.

petition by indignant regimental commanders that illustrated the growing tension between officers and beys in Egypt. Regardless, his efforts to roll back the changes failed.[18] By this time, rather ironically, Ibrahim Bey ibn Zülfikar was dead of the plague, and Kaba Nezir Agha was in exile in Cairo.

The Vekil-i Darüssaade

This intense competition over local supervision of the Evkaf, to say nothing of the unseemly squabbles over the tax farms of particular endowed villages, illustrates the considerable challenges to effective administration of these enormous foundations by the late seventeenth century. Around the same time, not surprisingly, the Chief Harem Eunuch began to employ a permanent agent (*vekil*) who was based in Cairo and who could oversee the annual collection of revenues and shipments of grain. This official came to be known as Vekil-i Darüssaade, or "agent of the harem," underlining the fact that he served the interests of the office of Chief Harem Eunuch, not the personal interests of the acting Chief Eunuch, though he might be closely attached to him. He was not a *mütevelli* or tax-farmer and thus did not have a stake in the competition for revenues. But he *was* a local grandee who knew the lay of the land, literally and figuratively, and could navigate the inter- and intrafactional rivalries that might hamper proper functioning of the Evkaf.

No doubt the most visible Vekil-i Darüssaade during the late seventeenth and early eighteenth centuries was Mustafa Bey, known as Kızlar because he was the protégé of the Kızlar Ağası Yusuf Agha. He enters the archival record in 1677, when he is cited as Yusuf's *vekil* in the deed for a fountain and caravanserai (Arabic, *wakala*) that Yusuf had purchased, then endowed, in Cairo in 1677.[19] At that point, he was the agha, or commander, of Egypt's Müteferrika regiment, one of two mixed cavalry and infantry regiments (the other being the Çavuşan) that were attached to the governor's administrative council. In the late seventeenth century, this regiment was filled almost exclusively from the imperial palace, so it is quite possible that Yusuf sent Mustafa to Egypt from Istanbul or Edirne.

---

[18] Topkapı Palace Archive, E 5211/12 (mid-Zilkade 1110/June 1699); Hathaway, *Politics of Households*, 152–53.

[19] André Raymond, "The *Sabil* of Yusuf Agha Dar al-Sa'ada (1088/1677) According to Its *Waqf* Document," in *The Cairo Heritage: Essays in Honor of Laila Ali Ibrahim*, ed. Doris Behrens-Abouseif (Cairo, 2003), 225–26; I am grateful to the late Professor Raymond for sending me a copy of this article. See also BOA, MD 99, no. 491 (mid-Receb 1101/23 April 1690); Stanford J. Shaw, *The Financial and Administrative Organization and Development of Ottoman Egypt, 1517–1798* (Princeton, NJ, 1962), 192–94; Hathaway, *Politics of Households*, 32–33, 37–38, 40, 42, 65, 144, 177.

Members of the Müteferrika and Çavuşan had received preference for promotion to *sancak beyi* in two sultanic orders of 1564 and 1576,[20] so it is not terribly surprising that Mustafa was eventually made a bey. As Mustafa Bey, he appears in Egyptian chronicles in 1687, when he held the office of *kaymakam* (Arabic, *qa'im maqam*), or stand-in for a deposed governor. Before his death, around 1730, he served once more as *kaymakam*, once as *defterdar*, and, most significantly, once as governor of the enormous Upper Egyptian province of Jirja, the veritable breadbasket of the province.[21] Although he seems to be a member of the Faqari faction, close to the factional leadership and occasionally present at their war councils, it is hard to be entirely certain; toward the beginning of his chronicle, al-Damurdashi lists him among the members of both the Faqari and Qasimi factions.[22] We can hazard the guess that Yusuf Agha, who was Chief Eunuch from 1671 to 1687, sent Mustafa to Egypt early in his tenure, perhaps with the specific intention that he serve as *vekil*.[23]

Regardless, Mustafa Bey continued as *vekil* of the Chief Harem Eunuch long after Yusuf was deposed and even after Yusuf's death in 1717. In 1729, not long before his own death, he helped to resolve the latest episode of intra-Qasimi friction, when Abdurrahman Bey, the tax-farmer of Dalja village in Ushmunayn subprovince and a follower of Ismail Bey ibn Ivaz, was betrayed by followers of Çerkes Mehmed Bey and forced to flee to Istanbul. At the imperial court, he met el-Hajj Beshir Agha, who appointed Mustafa Bey Kızlar, identified as his *vekil*, to administer Abdurrahman's lands in Ushmunayn while Abdurrahman himself remained in the imperial capital. Sultan Ahmed III issued an imperial order prohibiting any challenge to Abdurrahman Bey's control of these lands.[24] Here, the Vekil-i Darüssaade was taking direct action to make sure that the delivery of grains from Evkafü'l-Haremeyn villages would not be disrupted.

The death of the Chief Harem Eunuch was the situation that really tested the Vekil-i Darüssaade's mettle, as el-Hajj Beshir Agha's demise in June 1746 amply attests. By this time, the Vekil-i Darüssaade was one Osman Agha, possibly the commander of the Müteferrika regiment. To him fell the mammoth task of wrapping up the superannuated eunuch's affairs. Since Beshir

---

[20] BOA, MD 6, no. 487 (Cemaziyelevvel 572/December 1564), and 29, no. 9 (1 Ramazan 984/ 21 November 1576); Hathaway, *Politics of Households*, 11, 37, 65, 82 n. 120, 174, 177.

[21] Al-Hallaq, *Tarih-i Mısr-ı Kahire*, fols. 219a, 223b; anonymous, *Akhbar al-nuwwab*, fol. 41a; al-Damurdashi, *Al-Durra al-musana*, 58–59, 322; al-Jabarti, *'Aja'ib al-athar*, I: 133; BOA, MD 110, no. 2610 (30 Cemaziyelahir 1110/2 January 1699).

[22] Al-Damurdashi, *Al-Durra al-musana*, 5; al-Jabarti, *'Aja'ib al-athar*, I: 26.

[23] Al-Hallaq, *Tarih-i Mısr-ı Kahire*, fol. 219b; BOA, MD 99, no. 491 (mid-Receb 1101/23 April 1690).

[24] Al-Damurdashi, *Al-Durra al-musana*, 293; BOA, Mühimme-i Mısır, vol. 4, no. 217 (1142/ 1729–30); Hathaway, "Role of the Kızlar Ağası," 156–57.

Agha left no heirs, any part of his estate that he had not endowed as *vakıf* could be confiscated by the imperial treasury. This meant that every such property had to be inventoried and assigned a price so that it could be sold at auction. In Egypt alone, el-Hajj Beshir left scores of clients and massive amounts of land and urban properties. He had managed to endow most of these properties, including his enormous collections of books, to his personal *vakıf*s, however, so that relatively little remained for the treasury. Osman Agha's work, documented by a paper trail in the Ottoman archives and likewise mentioned in provincial chronicles, consisted largely of collecting surplus revenues (*fa'iz*) and undelivered grain from the grandees who held the tax farms of Egypt's many Evkafü'l-Haremeyn villages.[25]

By this time, el-Hajj Beshir's preferred provincial grandees in Egypt were members of the Qatamish household, which, while part of the Faqari faction, offered an alternative to the growing dominance of the Kazdağlı household. The single greatest concentration of surplus revenues and grain was in the possession of Ibrahim Bey Qatamish, who occupied the post of *shaykh al-balad*, roughly equivalent to "mayor" of Cairo, the most powerful beylical office by the mid-eighteenth century. This made Ibrahim Bey a target of Egypt's three so-called *sipahi* (salaried cavalry) regiments, who were on the point of rebelling because they had not received their grain and fodder rations that year. As the chronicler al-Damurdashi recounts, Osman Agha approached Ibrahim Bey and asked, "What will the soldiers eat if you don't release the grain?" To this, Ibrahim Bey memorably retorted, at least according to al-Damurdashi, "The soldiers can eat my shit!"[26] Osman Agha handled the volatile situation diplomatically, chiding Ibrahim for his outburst and persuading him to allow a delegation of officers to appraise his grain so that Osman Agha could purchase it with the Chief Eunuch's funds.[27]

Osman Agha may have been able to coax Ibrahim Bey Qatamish into compliance, but he could not save the Qatamish household from destruction once its leading advocate in the imperial palace was dead. El-Hajj Beshir's death came at a time, too, when other Egyptian grandees were complaining loudly and long to the governor of Egypt, the famous future grand vizier Raghib Mehmed Pasha, about Qatamish misdeeds. Even the sultan of Morocco chimed in, outraged over the mistreatment of Moroccan pilgrims by the mamluks of Ibrahim's comrade-in-arms, the *emirü'l-hacc* Halil

---

[25] Hathaway, *Politics of Households*, 91; Hathaway, *Beshir Agha*, 82–83; BOA, Mühimme-i Mısır, vol. 6, nos. 318, 319, 341, 342 (all 1159/1746); vol. 7, nos. 35 (1 Ramazan 1165/12 July 1752), 36 (same date), 44 (1 Zilkade 1165/9 September 1752).

[26] Al-Damurdashi, *Al-Durra al-musana*, 528–31; Topkapı Palace Archive, E 5215/27–28 (early Ramazan 1160/early September 1747); BOA, Mühimme-i Mısır, vol. 6, no. 426 (1161/1748).

[27] Al-Damurdashi, *Al-Durra al-musana*, 530–31.

Bey Qatamish.[28] No sooner had the grain issue been resolved than an imperial order arrived from Istanbul, authorizing Raghib Pasha to "cut" the Qatamish household – literally. Ibrahim, Halil, and their comrade Ömer Bey were all beheaded.[29] (We are left to imagine Raghib Pasha's satisfaction at the collapse of a household patronized by his old nemesis Beshir Agha.) Osman Agha, however, remained in Egypt long after el-Hajj Beshir Agha's estate was settled. A *vakıf* account dated 1166–67/1753–54 describes him as the tax-farmer of Daljamun village in Minufiyya subprovince, which would imply that he was entrenched among Egypt's military-administrative cadre.[30]

Generally speaking, then, the Vekil-i Darüssaade was not a eunuch and not a transplant from the imperial palace, unless he had spent years in Egypt and firmly implanted himself in the province's household and factional political culture. He was usually a military-administrative grandee, either a bey or a high regimental officer, someone who inspired respect among other grandees. Yet he was not a provincial "chieftain" with a large household and scores of clients – that is, not someone who had an independent financial and political base separate from the Chief Eunuch's patronage. Choosing an effective *vekil* was, in other words, a delicate balancing act. In Mustafa Bey and Osman Agha, in any case, the Chief Harem Eunuch seems to have achieved this balance.

Exile

Naturally, the practice of exiling Chief Harem Eunuchs to Egypt following their removal from office provided the most reliable connection between that province and the Chief Eunuch. Practically from the time the office of Darüs-saade Ağası originated, its occupants knew that they stood a good chance of relocating to Cairo at the end of their careers, and perhaps dying there. Already at the end of the sixteenth century, as we saw in Chapter 4, the famous intellectual Mustafa Ali deplored what, to him, seemed a plague of exiled African eunuchs in Cairo, who, by his account, "cannot be counted any more." "Those of the lowest rank," he complained, "have obtained salaries of forty, fifty aspers and abundant allowances of barley and wheat. Those of respected rank are not only given honor … but also come to Egypt with a daily pay of … ten or twelve gold pieces."[31] (Since Mustafa Ali's patron was Gazanfer

---

[28] Ibid., 525; al-Jabarti, *'Aja'ib al-athar*, I: 198–200.
[29] Al-Damurdashi, *Al-Durra al-musana*, 531–33; Hathaway, *Politics of Households*, 91–92; BOA, Mühimme-i Mısır, vol. 6, no. 583 (1163/1750).
[30] Topkapı Palace Archive, D 5599.
[31] Mustafa Ali, *Mustafa Ali's Description of Cairo*, 81–82.

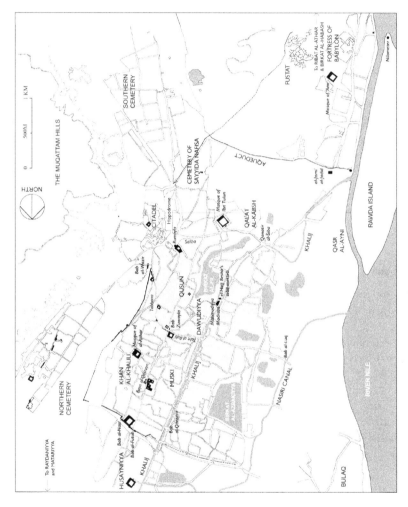

Map 8.2 Cairo, showing neighborhoods where harem eunuchs were active. Map drawn by Nicholas Warner, based on his map in Doris Behrens-Abouseif, *Cairo of the Mamluks: A History of the Architecture and Its Culture* (London, 2007), 52–53. By permission of Nicholas Warner.

Agha, the Venetian Chief Threshold Eunuch, his antagonism toward African harem eunuchs is hardly surprising.)

The pension that Mustafa Ali described came from imperial revenues earmarked for Egypt, known as the *mal-i Misri* ("Egyptian money"), the tribute that Egypt remitted to Istanbul every year.[32] These pensions were paid out in the form of "salaries" to the Keşide "regiment," a legal fiction that encompassed all retirees in Egypt who were on the imperial treasury's payroll.[33] Faced with the likelihood of exile to Cairo, acting Chief Eunuchs set about acquiring the things they would need in exile: houses, clients, and income sources to supplement their pensions.

Houses. In the same way that today, a well-to-do professional might purchase a "retirement home" in a distant state or province, or even in another country, years before actually retiring, so the Chief Harem Eunuch, in anticipation of exile to Cairo, usually acquired a large residence there while still in office. Within Cairo, the harem eunuchs tended to live in one concentrated area of the city, a fact that no doubt compounded their influence (see Map 8.2). The area in question was the general vicinity of Birkat al-Fil ("Elephant Pool"), the pond below Cairo's citadel whose name derived from its shape, which resembled the head and trunk of an elephant. (This pond and Birkat al-Azbakiyya to the northwest were paved over in the mid-nineteenth century.) As André Raymond has pointed out, this neighborhood had become the hub of elite residence by 1650.[34]

Birkat al-Fil was exceptionally well located: just west of the citadel, where the governor resided and presided over his administrative council four times a week, and where the barracks of the garrison troops resident in Cairo, above all the Janissaries and Azeban, were located.[35] The neighborhood was in close proximity to a major *shari'a* court of the Hanafi rite at Qusun, where the eunuchs, or their representatives, registered pious endowment deeds and where their estates might be surveyed if they died in Cairo, as was often the case.[36] Directly north was Bab Zuwayla, the southern gate of the Fatimid city of al-Qahira that led into the major thoroughfare known as Bayn al-Qasrayn, site of the bustling Khan al-Khalili bazaar and the venerable al-Azhar mosque/madrasa. Not coincidentally, the highest officers of these regiments, as well as

---

[32] Naima, *Tarih-i Naima*, III: 1391–92.

[33] Shaw, *Financial and Administrative Organization*, 202; Hathaway, "Role of the Kızlar Ağası," 142; Hathaway, *Politics of Households*, 141.

[34] Raymond, "Essai de géographie," 65–67, 72–73, 75–78.

[35] Ibid.; Ömer Lutfi Barkan, ed., "Kanunname-i Mısır," in *XV ve XVıncı Asırlarda Osmanlı İmparatorluğunda Ziraî Ekonominin Hukuki ve Mali Esasları*, ed. Barkan (Istanbul, 1943), vol. 1: *Kanunlar*, 357–58, 378.

[36] Jane Hathaway, "Exiled Harem Eunuchs as Proponents of the Hanafi *Madhhab* in Egypt," *Annales islamologiques* 37 (2003): 193.

several prominent *sancak beyi*s, acquired residences around and near Birkat al-Fil, as well. This made it all the easier for the exiled eunuchs to cultivate ties of patronage with them.

A snapshot of Birkat al-Fil and vicinity in the early eighteenth century reveals the residences of at least eight former Chief Harem Eunuchs: the house of Abbas Agha (term 1667–71) on the southern shore, abutted to the south by the house of Hazinedar Ali Agha (term 1687), previously occupied by Mehmed Agha (term 1649–51); the house of el-Hajj Mustafa Agha (terms 1605–20, 1623–24) just north of the pond; the house of Yusuf Agha (term 1671–87), previously inhabited by Taş Yatur Ali Agha (term 1644–45), just to the southeast of the pond, near the house of Uzun Süleyman Agha (term 1704–13), which was next-door to that of el-Hajj Beshir Agha (term 1717–46), his fellow exile on Cyprus[37] – and these are only the houses whose locations can be determined through chronicles and *shari'a* court records, nor do they include the houses of lower-ranking harem eunuchs.

This sort of residential continuity resulted in part from eunuchs' passing their houses down to their clients, in part from the accumulation of a stock of houses that circulated among "generations" of exiled harem eunuchs as the decades passed. The fact that a eunuch could endow his personal residence as *vakıf* no doubt facilitated the circulation of these houses since it kept them off the open real estate market and out of the hands of the imperial treasury – except in the rare instances when the treasury seized all of a deposed eunuch's property, as happened to Yusuf Agha, whose agent, as we saw in Chapter 6, had to buy his house back from the governor.

Among all these eunuch residences near Birkat al-Fil, perhaps the most intriguing is the house occupied by Hazinedar Ali Agha (and previously by Mehmed Agha), for in a court case concerning Abbas Agha's house, which bordered it on the north, it is called, in Arabic, *sukn qasr al-aghawat*, which translates roughly to "the residence [known as] castle of the eunuchs."[38] The Arabic word *qasr*, root of the English "castle," is a bit ambiguous. It could indeed mean a castle, that is, a fortified structure, although such a thing would have been somewhat unusual in this neighborhood. It could also connote a luxurious compound, not unlike certain European overseas research institutes, where numerous exiled eunuchs could live. El-Hajj Beshir Agha's home, which is called *qasr* in an endowment deed prepared in a Cairene court, fits this description: a two-story affair, it boasted several storerooms, a stable,

[37] Raymond, "Essai de géographie," 66, 76–77; Topkapı Palace Archive, E 7900 (24 Ramazan 1076/29 March 1666); Hathaway, "Wealth and Influence," 296, 302, 304–5; Evliya Çelebi, *Seyahatname*, X: 156.

[38] Topkapı Palace Archive, E 7900 (24 Ramazan 1076/29 March 1666); Hathaway, "Wealth and Influence," 305.

reception areas, several different types of residential units, and even three shops. *Sukn qasr al-aghawat* could have been a sort of "designated eunuch house," perhaps a place for deposed eunuchs newly arrived in Cairo to reside while they got their bearings and their agents located a permanent place for them to live. Such a structure might also have provided a home for younger, less wealthy harem eunuchs who were exiled to Egypt relatively early in their careers. Tellingly, a nearby street was known as Darb al-Aghawat, roughly equivalent to "Eunuch Lane."[39]

A eunuch's house in Cairo was not simply a place to live, then. El-Hajj Beshir Agha's *qasr* produced revenue from which the eunuch could benefit wherever he was, throughout his life. After Beshir's death, the endowment deed specifies, these revenues were to go to the oldest of his manumitted slaves, and then, when his slaves had all died off, to the Evkafü'l-Haremeyn.[40] Certain of his manumitted slaves may have lived in the house after his death, in the way that a mamluk of Yusuf Agha's agent Mustafa Bey Kızlar lived in his house not far away. Clearly, such a house provided a physical and economic haven not only for the exiled harem eunuch but for his slaves and other clients, as well. The proximity of the various eunuchs' houses, meanwhile, allowed for a form of solidarity among the eunuch residents. Since the exiled eunuchs were neighbors, economic cooperation and financial aid were possible, as was the exchange of servants. Younger eunuchs could help an elderly eunuch out, and vice versa. Public displays of eunuch solidarity were even possible, such as the protest that capped the "Habesh incident," discussed below.

In the latter half of the eighteenth century, though, Birkat al-Azbakiyya, a pool to the northwest named for the fifteenth-century Mamluk general Özbek (Azbak), displaced Birkat al-Fil as the hub of elite residence in Cairo. The heads of the Kazdağlı household had already established themselves there by the 1720s, and by 1750, the southwest bank of the pond in particular was filling up with the houses of the "new" elite: Kazdağlı chiefs, the heads of the allied Jalfi household, and the Sharaybi family, wealthy coffee and spice merchants.[41] Here, not far from the home of Osman Kethüda al-Kazdağlı, the Janissary officer under whose leadership the Kazdağlıs, in the 1720s, became an impregnable force in Egypt's political and economic life, stood the home of one Beshir Agha.[42] This could conceivably have been the same Beshir Agha who appeared in Osman Kethüda's estate inventory, discussed above. As noted above, this Beshir may have been Sarıkçı Beshir Agha, the

[39] Ahmed Çelebi, *Awdah al-isharat*, 187; Hathaway, "Wealth and Influence," 305 n. 54.
[40] Badr and Crecelius, "The *Awqaf* of al-Hajj Bashir Agha in Cairo," 293 and n. 11, 294, 296, 299, 303, 304.
[41] Raymond, "Essai de géographie," 73–75, 80–81, 85–103; Doris Behrens-Abouseif, *Azbakiyya and Its Environs from Azbak to Ismail, 1476–1879* (Cairo, 1985), 55ff.
[42] Raymond, "Essai de géographie," 66, 77–78, 81, 100.

last Chief Harem Eunuch named Beshir, who came to Cairo in the 1780s after serving as head of the tomb eunuchs in Medina. Alternatively, the homeowner may have been Hazinedar Beshir (term 1752–55), who was exiled to Cairo on his deposition and died there in 1759. This seems particularly plausible because the house stood next-door to that of the powerful Ibrahim Kethüda al-Kazdağlı, who had recently died when Hazinedar Beshir arrived in Cairo.[43]

Clients. Apart from the Vekil-i Darüssaade, the acting Chief Harem Eunuch appears to have had relatively few clients in Egypt who rose to positions of great prominence in Egypt's political hierarchy. The few who did occupy such positions, though, wielded considerable influence. During the seventeenth century, the Ottoman governor of Egypt was not infrequently the Chief Eunuch's client. Hamza Pasha (term 1683–87), for example, was the *yazıcı* (scribe) of Yusuf Agha and, in that capacity, registered charitable donations to Mecca and Medina. When he was deposed, the chronicler al-Hallaq notes, he was taken down from the citadel to Yusuf's house, but a few months later, when Yusuf himself was deposed and stripped of all his property, the house was sold by Hamza's successor as governor (although one of Yusuf's clients later managed to buy it back).[44] The immensely influential el-Hajj Mustafa Agha, in the early seventeenth century, patronized several governors of Egypt, as we would expect in view of his extensive sojourns in the province before, in between, and after his two terms as Chief Eunuch.[45]

At the same time, the Vekil-i Darüssaade was not necessarily limited to *vekil* work but could function as a "normal" member of Egypt's household- and faction-based political culture. Yusuf Agha's mamluk Mustafa Bey Kızlar, for the most prominent example, was apparently allied with the Faqari faction, though he does not seem to have joined the household of any of the faction's leaders. In the course of his career as an Egyptian grandee, as we saw above, he served in three critical posts: *kaymakam*, or stand-in for a deposed Ottoman governor; *defterdar*, or chief financial officer; and governor of the enormous Upper Egyptian subprovince of Jirja.[46] At the time, this last office was matched only by that of pilgrimage commander in its administrative importance since Jirja was a major source of Egypt's land tax revenue and played a major role in producing the grain that the *hajj* caravan transported to the holy cities every year. Although this position obviously linked Mustafa Bey to the pilgrimage, he himself was never pilgrimage commander, an office that would have removed him from Egypt for several months of the year and thus would

---

[43] Hathaway, *Politics of Households*, 161–63; BOA, Mühimme-i Mısır, vol. 7, no. 236 (1 Zilhicce 1168/7 September 1755).

[44] Al-Hallaq, *Tarih-i Mısr-ı Kahire*, fols. 219a–b.

[45] D'Ohsson, *Tableau général*, II: 363, 368; VII: 32.

[46] Hathaway, "Wealth and Influence," 304 n. 49; Raymond, "*Sabil* of Yusuf Agha," 227.

have hindered his ability to keep an eye on revenue-collection for the Evkafü'l-Haremeyn. In contrast, *kaymakam* was an office tailor-made for him since his connection to Yusuf Agha arguably made him a known and trusted quantity in the imperial palace.

When Yusuf Agha's property was sold, his *vekil* in Cairo, one Ahmed Agha, managed to amass enough money to buy back his house.[47] This was probably the future Ahmed Bey Minufiyya, whose name derived from the fact that after being promoted to *sancak beyi*, he governed the subprovince of Minufiyya in the Nile Delta. Unlike Mustafa Bey, Ahmed Bey was apparently never Vekil-i Darüssaade, the official agent of the Evkafü'l-Haremeyn, but instead Yusuf Agha's personal *vekil*, although the lines between the two positions could be quite blurry. Whereas Mustafa Bey Kızlar ostensibly belonged to the Faqari faction, Ahmed Bey was apparently affiliated with the Qasimis; his master, it appears, had taken the politically sensible tack of patronizing both sides in the incessant struggle.

There is uncertainty about Ahmed Bey's factional affiliation, too, though, for al-Jabarti lists an Ahmed Bey Kızlar immediately after Mustafa Bey Kızlar in his roster of *Faqari* beys at the beginning of the twelfth *hijri* century – even though he lists Ahmed Bey Minufiyya separately as a Qasimi.[48] Like Mustafa Bey, Ahmed was never heavily involved in the factional conflict, although he would have been present for a number of confrontations between the Qasimis and Faqaris since he seems to have deputized an agent to govern Minufiyya while he remained in Cairo; this was not an unusual tactic for a subprovincial governor, and was probably necessary for one working for a retired Chief Eunuch in the provincial capital. Although he may have served once as pilgrimage commander, he was never governor of Jirja or *defterdar*. Otherwise, he receives mention in the chronicles mainly for his role in commanding a force sent to protect the Aegean islands of Chios and Rhodes from Venetian pirate attacks in 1695. He died peacefully in Jidda, where he was probably governor, in 1696 or 1697.[49]

Neither Ahmed Bey nor Mustafa Bey seems to have left much of a lasting mark on Egypt, though of course each of them, like all other *sancak beyi*s, had his own clients, including mamluks. Yet there is next to no trace of these clients in archival or narrative sources. Al-Damurdashi reports one of Mustafa Bey Kızlar's former mamluks living in Yusuf Agha's old house,

---

[47] Ahmed Çelebi, *Awdah al-isharat*, 181–82.   [48] Al-Jabarti, *'Aja'ib al-athar*, I: 26.

[49] Hathaway, *Politics of Households*, 145–46 and n. 23, 151, 154; al-Hallaq, *Tarih-i Mısr-ı Kahire*, fols. 229b–230a; Ahmed Çelebi, *Awdah al-isharat*, 192; al-Damurdashi, *Al-Durra al-musana*, 5, 17–19, 30, 52, 85; al-Jabarti, *'Aja'ib al-athar*, I: 29, 111; Silahdar, *Silahdar Tarihi*, II: 783.

but, as noted above, poverty forced him to lease it out so that he effectively became a tenant in his own property.[50]

In most cases, the Chief Eunuch acquired clients in Egypt during one or more sojourns there before he became Chief Eunuch. Their main purpose was to assist the Eunuch in various enterprises, including commercial ventures of the sort to be discussed below. The great el-Hajj Beshir Agha had at least two clients who fit this description: Hasan Agha and Abdullah "al-Fahl," literally "stallion," connoting an uncastrated mamluk. The endowment deed for el-Hajj Beshir's *sebil-mekteb* in Cairo, mentioned in Chapter 7, notes that Hasan Agha was an officer in Egypt's Çavuşan corps, which, along with the Müteferrika, was particularly close to the Ottoman governor's council.[51] Both men were active during the eunuch's brief stay in Cairo and Medina in between exile on Cyprus and appointment as Chief Harem Eunuch. Hasan Agha acquired Beshir's house at Birkat al-Fil for him shortly before he arrived in Cairo from Cyprus in 1716. One of the two of them took the lead in building the *sebil-mekteb*, which still stands in Cairo's Darb al-Gamamiz neighborhood, across from where Beshir's house used to be.[52]

A third client of el-Hajj Beshir, Mehmed Agha, provides an example of how the Chief Harem Eunuch was able to engage with Egypt's most powerful grandee households and, at the same time, with the actual villages that supplied grain to Mecca and Medina. According to the Egyptian chronicler al-Jabarti, this Mehmed Agha, presumably an officer in one of Egypt's regiments in the early eighteenth century, was the mamluk of "Bashir Agha al-Kızlar," who is unmistakably el-Hajj Beshir. He once performed a service for one Mansur al-Zataharci ("the linseed oil-maker," from a mistranscription of *zayt har*, literally, "hot oil"), who held the tax farm of Sinjalf, an Evkafü'l-Haremeyn village in Minufiyya subprovince, north of Cairo.[53] To seal the bond of friendship between them, Mehmed Agha arranged for the marriage of his mamluk, Hasan, the *kethüda* of Egypt's Azeban regiment, to Mansur's daughter, who was known as al-Sitt al-Jalfiyya, "the [Sin]Jalfi lady"; she bestowed her name, Jalfi, on the powerful household that her new husband founded, which for much of the eighteenth century functioned as a loyal subordinate to the Kazdağlıs. Linseed, or flax-seed, oil, was a popular fuel oil in Ottoman

---

[50] Al-Damurdashi, *Al-Durra al-musana*, 322; Hathaway, *Politics of Households*, 145; Hathaway, "Role of the Kızlar Ağası," 148.

[51] Ahmed Çelebi, *Awdah al-isharat*, 290; Badr and Crecelius, "*Awqaf* of al-Hajj Bashir Agha in Cairo," 293–94, 297, 293 n. 11; Shaw, *Financial and Administrative Organization*, 194–96; Hathaway, "Wealth and Influence," 294 n. 5; 305 and n. 53.

[52] Badr and Crecelius, "*Awqaf* of al-Hajj Bashir Agha in Cairo," 294; Ahmed Çelebi, *Awdah al-isharat*, 290; BOA, Mühimme-i Mısır, vol. 5, no. 522 (1153/1740–41).

[53] Al-Jabarti, *'Aja'ib al-athar*, I: 194; Hathaway, *Politics of Households*, 53–54; Nelly Hanna, *Artisan Entrepreneurs in Cairo and Early-Modern Capitalism (1600–1800)* (Syracuse, NY, 2014), 214 n. 3; BOA, Mühimme-i Mısır, vol. 4, no. 514 (1145/1732–33); vol. 5, no. 44 (1146/1733–34); vol. 5, no. 56 (1146/1733–34).

Egypt, and since flax grew plentifully in the Egyptian countryside,[54] selling it was a reliable source of income. In fact, the linseed oil trade appears to have been the economic foundation of the Jalfi household.[55]

The Jalfi household's connection with the Chief Harem Eunuch did not end there, however. Several decades later, the daughter of the then-head of the Jalfi household, the Azeban *kethüda* Rıdvan, cemented the household's alliance with the Kazdağlıs by marrying Ismail Bey the Younger (al-Saghir in Arabic), a client of the Janissary commander Ibrahim Kethüda al-Kazdağlı. The groom had a rather unusual background. He was one of five brothers, four of whom had migrated from Istanbul to Cairo and joined Ibrahim Kethüda's household after being clients of "Bashir Agha Kızlar" – in this case, not el-Hajj Beshir, who had died in 1746, but almost certainly his successor, Moralı Beshir.[56] Moralı Beshir's execution in 1752, described in Chapter 7, like the deposition of Yusuf Agha in 1687 and the death of el-Hajj Beshir in 1746, presumably triggered a purge of his clients that prompted the brothers' flight to Cairo. Clearly, the Chief Eunuch's clients needed to have a "Plan B" for the time when their patron was no longer in power.

In this case, Moralı Beshir's clients were able to take refuge in a provincial household – the Kazdağlı household – that had historically nurtured ties to the Chief Eunuch and other harem eunuchs. Ismail Bey the Younger went a step farther, using a marriage alliance to reinforce the bond between the Kazdağlıs and the Jalfi household, which had a historical link to el-Hajj Beshir Agha. Collectively, the experiences of el-Hajj Beshir's and Moralı Beshir's clients demonstrate that marriage alliances were an important mechanism of integrating clients of an "outside" patron – namely, the Chief Eunuch – into the provincial household culture. If the Chief Eunuch died or fell from favor, this sort of alliance could be a life-saver.

Yusuf Agha and the Valide Sultan *Vakıf*: An Exiled Chief Harem Eunuch as an Honorary Provincial Grandee

Could, or would, an exiled Chief Harem Eunuch act as his own *vekil*? That is, could he not only do his own location-scouting and *vakıf*-endowing, but even engage *directly* in Egypt's politics of factions and households? The answer appears to be no, except in the case of Yusuf Agha, and more specifically in the case of the pious foundation established in 1678 by Gülnuş Emetullah Sultan, the favorite concubine of Mehmed IV and mother of Mustafa II and Ahmed III,

---

[54] S.D. Goitein, *A Mediterranean Society*, vol. 1: *Economic Foundations* (Berkeley, CA, 1967), 104–5, 224–28, 455–57 n. 61.

[55] Hanna, *Artisan Entrepreneurs*, 108–27.

[56] Al-Jabarti, *'Aja'ib al-athar*, II: 21–22; Hathaway, *Politics of Households*, 111 and n. 7; Şemdanizade, *Şemdanizade Tarihi*, I: 169.

to support a hospital and soup kitchen in Mecca. As we saw in Chapter 6, Gülnuş Sultan's elaborate endowment deed specifically names Yusuf, who at the time was still acting Chief Eunuch, as the *nazir*, or superintendent, of this foundation. (This, then, was another imperial foundation for him to supervise, in addition to the existing Evkafü'l-Haremeyn.) But after Yusuf's deposition, this foundation would give Yusuf a seemingly unique opportunity to function as a sort of honorary Egyptian grandee.

As Chapter 6 pointed out, Gülnuş's hospital and kitchen received grain from four specific villages in Egypt, in addition to the Nile port of Bulaq. The four villages were Mallawi (rendered Menlawi in the deed) in al-Minya sub-province in Middle Egypt, and Birma, Tataya, and al-Ja'fariyya in the Nile Delta subprovince of Gharbiyya.[57] Why these particular villages? Mallawi, at least, was already endowed to the Evkafü'l-Haremeyn. Meanwhile, Gharbiyya subprovince, located between the Rosetta and Damietta branches of the Nile, was full of villages endowed to these foundations, though Birma, Tataya, and al-Ja'fariyya do not seem to have been among them – a fact that may have made them more attractive as sources of grain for this new foundation. The grain was to be shipped to Bulaq, the river port serving Cairo, then carried overland to Suez, from where it would be shipped to Mecca's Red Sea port of Jidda.

Baskets, sacks, and boxes in which to transport provisions are carefully itemized in the endowment deed, as are rents for pack animals for the Bulaq to Suez and Jidda to Mecca stretches. Even the guards, bankers, scribes, and other functionaries on the docks and in the warehouses at Bulaq, Suez, Jidda, and Mecca itself are specified.[58] The only elements not mentioned in the deed – and their absence is noticeable amid the welter of detail on all the foundation's other components – are the ships to carry the provisions down the Nile and across the Red Sea. These, however, are specified in a series of income and expenditure registers related to this endowment, housed in the Topkapı Palace archives. Eschewing the lumbering Suez-built vessels of dubious seaworthiness that habitually plied the Red Sea route, Gülnuş Emetullah's foundation rented Indian ships, sturdy dhows that had long been employed in the Red Sea coffee trade.[59] Meanwhile, the foundation funded the construction of Nile boats to ferry provisions from Mallawi to Bulaq.[60]

---

[57] Duran, ed., *Tarihimizde Vakıf Kuran Kadınlar*, 152–53; Hathaway, *Politics of Households*, 150 and n. 41.

[58] Duran, ed., *Tarihimizde Vakıf Kuran Kadınlar*, 148–53, 136–45; Evliya Çelebi, *Seyahatname*, X: 159–60.

[59] Topkapı Palace Archive, E 33/9 (1093/1682), 33/14 (1094/1683), 33/19 (1111/1699–1700), 33/22 (1113/1701–2), 33/23 (1116/1704–5); Hathaway, *Arab Lands under Ottoman Rule*, 158–59.

[60] Topkapı Palace Archive, E 33/18 (1111/1699–1700), E 33/19 (1111/1699–1700), E 33/20 (1108/1696–97), E 33/21 (1112/1700–1701), E 33/22 (1113/1701–2).

No one could imagine Gülnuş Emetullah poring over a map of Egypt, trying to figure out which villages to endow to her foundation. Presumably, she would have relied on Yusuf Agha, the foundation superintendent, to identify the most promising villages. Yusuf in turn would have relied on his Vekil-i Darüssaade, Mustafa Bey Kızlar, who at the time may still have been agha of the Müteferrika regiment.

Ordinarily, in the case of imperial endowments to the holy cities, a local or day-to-day Egyptian supervisor, usually holding the title *mütevelli*, was appointed from among Egypt's regimental officers or beys. This official is not specified in the endowment deed. However, the foundation's accounts from the 1690s and early 1700s in the Topkapı archives name a series of pilgrimage commanders belonging to the Faqari faction, although they use the title *nazir*, which was occasionally used interchangeably with *mütevelli*. Curiously, though, Yusuf Agha himself is listed as *nazir* in 1108–10/1696–99, 1112/1700–1701, and 1113/1701–2.[61] By this time, he was no longer Chief Harem Eunuch, so he cannot have been *nazir* of the foundation in that capacity. We can conclude only that he was alternating with these Faqari beys in the post of *mütevelli*, and perhaps even competing with them for it. The year 1696 was roughly when he returned to Cairo from his stint as Şeyhü'l-Harem, or head of the tomb eunuchs in Medina, so, even though his stipend from the provincial treasury had been reinstated following his imperial pardon, he may well have been looking for supplemental income – seeking, perhaps, to reassemble the properties and the slaves and other clients that he had amassed in Cairo before his deposition. Regardless, he was effectively functioning as an "honorary" provincial grandee, something completely unheard-of for an exiled Chief Harem Eunuch.

This experiment, which would not be repeated, probably attests to Yusuf's still rather anomalous position in exile, and perhaps to the still rather uncertain status of the local Evkafü'l-Haremeyn supervisory positions following Ibrahim Bey ibn Zülfikar's restructuring in 1691. Yusuf was apparently still suffering from the aftereffects of his deposition and the seizure of his property. This helps to explain why his clients in Egypt, and their clients in turn, never seem to have become as wealthy and prominent as those of, for example, el-Hajj Beshir Agha. Gülnuş's foundation, which had augmented his career as Chief Harem Eunuch, now gave him a way to take advantage of the revenue sources available to provincial grandees during his long years in exile.

---

[61] Hathaway, *Politics of Households*, 150 and n. 42; Topkapı Palace Archive, E 33/20 (1108/ 1696–97), E 33/21 (1112/1700–1701), E 33/22 (1113/1701–2), and E 33/37 (1108–10/ 1696–99); E 33/16, E 33/18, E 33/19 (all 1111/1699–1700) (former *nazir*); E 33/31 (1123–25/1711–13), E 153/5 (1127/1715), E 79/27 (undated) (Ismail Bey ibn Ivaz as *nazir*).

Economic Infrastructure and Enterprises

Ordinarily, the economic agenda of an acting or exiled Chief Harem Eunuch was carried out, in Egypt as in other Ottoman provinces, by his clients, who took the initiative in forging alliances with strategically placed locals. If we return to the alliance between Mehmed Agha, the client of el-Hajj Beshir Agha, and Mansur al-Zataharcı, the linseed oil merchant, we see the client of an acting Chief Harem Eunuch taking advantage of an established provincial economic enterprise that would yield revenue without fail. Mehmed's patron, el-Hajj Beshir Agha, pursued a similar strategy in Syria, as we saw in Chapter 7, endowing hectare after hectare of land planted with olive and mulberry trees. Generally speaking, investing in reliably profitable enterprises and building the infrastructure to support them were standard strategies of Chief Eunuchs, both acting and exiled. Egypt was the most likely site for this kind of investment, both because it was so closely connected to the Evkafü'l-Haremeyn and because it was the standard site of Chief Eunuch exile.

Urban Development under Osman and Davud Aghas. In fact, a good bit of Cairo's commercial development during the Ottoman era seems to have stemmed from Chief Harem Eunuch initiatives. Less than a generation after the Chief Harem Eunuch assumed supervision of the Evkafü'l-Haremeyn, Osman Agha, who was murdered alongside the Chief Threshold Eunuch Gazanfer Agha in the 1603 palace soldiery rebellion, spearheaded several major urban development projects in Cairo. Outside Cairo's northwestern gate Bab al-Luq, he founded a large commercial complex consisting of a caravanserai (*wakala*), a slaughterhouse, two tanneries, mills, a bakery, a coffeehouse, stables, storerooms, and wells. Revenues from all these operations funded the construction of a mosque for daily prayers (*masjid*) on the southwestern edge of Cairo, which also drew revenues from a village in Minufiyya subprovince. Doris Behrens-Abouseif, who has studied the mosque's endowment deed, notes that the eunuch had intended his tomb to adjoin the mosque[62] – a clear indication that he had expected to be exiled to Cairo and to live out his days there. Construction of the mosque was overseen locally by the harem eunuch Davud Agha, acting as Osman's *vekil* and *mütevelli* of his endowment, who purchased the tanneries located in the area and demolished them to make way for the new structure. At the same time, Davud led two additional development projects in the same general vicinity, one of which formed the core of the neighborhood now known as Dawudiyya.[63] Exiled harem eunuchs, including Davud Agha

---

[62] Doris Behrens-Abouseif, *Egypt's Adjustment to Ottoman Rule: Institutions, Waqf, and Architecture (16th and 17th Centuries)* (Leiden, 1994), 173–77, 208–11.

[63] Ibid., 173–74, 207–8.

himself, already resided in this area, which bordered what would later become the eunuch quarter described above.

The relocation of tanneries, which, because of their disagreeable smell, were ordinarily located on the outskirts of cities, indicates that Osman's and Davud's projects had the effect of extending Cairo's boundaries, contributing to an overall pattern of growth during the Ottoman period.[64] After Osman's murder, though, Mehmed III's powerful mother, Safiye, appropriated his endowment on the grounds that the eunuch had never been manumitted and therefore had no legal right to endow a pious foundation. She appointed his successor, Abdurrezzak Agha (term 1603–4), as superintendent, a responsibility that was now to be associated with the office of Chief Harem Eunuch.[65] The mosque, which was finally completed in 1610, came to be known as the Malika Safiya mosque. Architecturally, the structure follows classical Ottoman mosque style, apart from Mamluk-style panels of polychrome marble in the *mihrab*, the niche showing the direction of Mecca.[66]

El-Hajj Mustafa Agha. Osman and Davud Aghas may have left a large mark on Cairo, but their successor Mustafa Agha's impact on the city, and on Egypt at large, in the early seventeenth century surpassed that of any Chief Eunuch up to that time. A lengthy Arabic endowment deed housed in Egypt's Ministry of Pious Endowments lists a vast number of his residential and commercial properties in Cairo, as well as lands and commercial operations in a number of Egyptian subprovinces.[67] Properties in Cairo are concentrated in the district of Saliba, just north of Dawudiyya; this is also the site of the eunuch's house, which he cannily endowed to his Cairene *vakıf*. There is also a commercial complex near the Muski, located north of the Fatimid gate Bab Zuwayla, close by the great mosque/madrasa of al-Azhar and the Khan al-Khalili bazaar. This pattern strongly suggests that Mustafa Agha sought to extend the urban development projects that Davud and Osman had initiated a number of years earlier. His projects must have had a profound effect on this central zone of Cairo, restoring residential and commercial

---

[64] Ibid., 175; André Raymond, "Le déplacement des tanneries à Alep, au Caire et à Tunis à l'époque ottomane: un 'indicateur' de croissance urbaine," *Revue du monde musulman et de la Méditerranée* 55–56 (1990): 34–43.

[65] Behrens-Abouseif, *Egypt's Adjustment to Ottoman Rule*, 176, 210.

[66] https://archnet.org/resources, under "Masjid al-Malika Safiyya"; Caroline Williams, *Islamic Monuments in Cairo: The Practical Guide*, new revised ed. (Cairo, 2008), 131–32; Doris Behrens-Abouseif, *Islamic Architecture in Cairo: An Introduction* (Leiden, 1989; new ed. Cairo, 1993), 162–63.

[67] Cairo, Wizarat al-Awqaf, No. 302/51 (dated 15 Zilhicce (Dhu'l-Hijja) 1032/10 October 1623). I am grateful to Professor Muhammad Husam al-Din Ismail Abd al-Fattah for providing me with a copy of this document.

infrastructure from the late Mamluk era while adding new infrastructure where little had existed before.[68]

Mustafa Agha's commercial endowments, apart from the complex near the Muski, were concentrated in three critical ports: the Nile port of Bulaq and the Mediterranean ports of Damietta and Rosetta, where the eastern arm of the Nile joins the ocean. In each of these three locations, he founded or added to a *wakala*, the sort of "urban caravanserai" that had proliferated in Cairo since the Fatimid era. (The Rosetta *wakala* had been erected by the governor Öküz Mehmed Pasha, who served from 1607 to 1611.)[69] In such a structure, merchants could store commodities before shipping them into or out of the city; they could also lodge there themselves and keep their animals there, even using the *wakala* as a sort of office.[70]

Like their medieval predecessors, these *wakala*s accommodated merchants dealing in specific commodities. Mustafa's endowment deed specifies that the Damietta *wakala* was used primarily for the storage and sale of flax, which had been grown throughout the Egyptian countryside since Pharaonic times and which, naturally, sustained Egypt's production of linen.[71] In a sign of the times, however, this *wakala* boasted a coffeehouse, as did the structure at Rosetta; in addition, the Rosetta *wakala* seems to have been dedicated to the trade in Yemeni coffee, which had arrived in Egypt in the late fifteenth century and had become a prized item of commerce in both the Red Sea and the Mediterranean.[72] The governor Hafız Ahmed Pasha (term 1591–95) had built *wakala*–coffeehouse combinations at both Bulaq and Rosetta only a few years earlier.[73]

Flax and coffee *wakala*s were nothing unusual in the early seventeenth century. But Mustafa's third *wakala* was a complete departure from the ordinary; here, the eunuch provided for eleven storehouses for colocasia (*kolkas* or *kilkas* in Arabic), a.k.a. taro or "elephant ear," a plant of South and Southeast Asian origin that was introduced to Egypt during the Pharaonic era. Its root is used in stews and soups in a variety of Asian, African, and Middle Eastern cuisines. I have not encountered a reference to stocks of taro

---

[68] André Raymond, "The Residential Districts of Cairo's Elite in the Mamluk and Ottoman Periods (Fourteenth to Eighteenth Centuries)," in *The Mamluks in Egyptian Politics and Society*, eds. Thomas Philipp and Ulrich Haarmann (Cambridge, 1998), 210–20.

[69] Wizarat al-Awqaf, No. 302/51, p. 31, line 5; BOA, Maliyeden Müdevver 7816 (1066–70/ 1655–59).

[70] Goitein, *A Mediterranean Society*, I: 186–92.   [71] Ibid., I: 224–28, 455–57 n. 61.

[72] Hathaway, *Politics of Households*, chapter 7; Jane Hathaway, "The Ottomans and the Yemeni Coffee Trade," in *The Ottomans and Trade*, eds. Ebru Boyar and Kate Fleet, *Oriente Moderno* 25, 1 (2006): 161–71.

[73] Muhammad 'Abd al-Mu'ti al-Ishaqi, *Akhbar al-uwal fi man tasarrafa fi Misr al-Qahira min arbab al-duwal* (Bulaq, 1304/1886–87), 160; Ahmed Çelebi, *Awdah al-isharat*, 123.

anywhere else. Possibly this stock originated in Egypt's subprovinces and was destined for shipment to Cairo. The traveler Evliya Çelebi, in his account of the cuisine of Egypt, describes "*kurkas*" as poor people's food,[74] so it seems unlikely that it would have been shipped outside Egypt unless as emergency food aid for other Ottoman provinces in crisis – although it bears remembering that central Anatolia was suffering devastating drought at just this time.[75] It may also have been intended as emergency food for Cairo in case of need. If so, then Mustafa Agha played a role not unlike that of the biblical and Qur'anic Joseph, who stored up grain in preparation for seven years of famine (Gen. 41–42; Qur'an 12:43–57).

Mustafa Agha also endowed land in the subprovinces of Giza, Qalyubiyya, Minufiyya, and Gharbiyya. Apart from Giza, which is just south of Cairo proper, these subprovinces lie along the route leading from Cairo down the Nile to the Mediterranean. Along with the *wakala*s in Rosetta and Damietta, these locations point to a desire on the Chief Eunuch's part to develop Egypt's trade through its Mediterranean ports, perhaps above all in commodities such as flax and coffee.

This pious endowment deed names Mustafa Agha as superintendent (*nazir*) of his own foundation and the redoubtable Davud Agha as *mütevelli* and agent (*vekil*), and stipulates that Davud will succeed Mustafa Agha as superintendent of the overall endowment. Davud's role in Mustafa Agha's enterprise is thus similar to the role he played in Osman Agha's undertakings, underlining the continuity in these two Chief Harem Eunuchs' activities in Cairo. Davud Agha may, in fact, have functioned as a precursor to the Vekil-i Darüssaade, the Chief Harem Eunuch's permanent agent in Cairo, who, as we have seen, would occupy a prominent place among Egypt's notables by the late seventeenth century.

Abbas Agha. Abbas Agha, who was exiled to Egypt in 1671 after only four years as Chief Eunuch, followed el-Hajj Mustafa's lead in investing heavily in flax. An inventory of his estate, prepared after his death in Cairo sometime in the mid-1690s, shows that he endowed a large *wakala* at the Nile port of Bulaq. This was almost certainly devoted to flax, as was a similar structure in Cairo's Gamaliyya neighborhood; here, merchants could store and sell the raw product. Yet Abbas apparently went beyond Mustafa Agha's efforts by investing in the production of finished linen cloth – and not only in Cairo but in the countryside, where flax grew and cloth was woven. His estate inventory lists four establishments where flax was retted, or soaked before weaving, in a village in the western Nile Delta subprovince of Gharbiyya, as well as three

---

[74] Evliya Çelebi, *Seyahatname*, X: 270, 459.   [75] White, *Climate of Rebellion*, 140–62.

fulling mills and a dyehouse in Gamaliyya, site of his above-mentioned flax *wakala*.[76] These endowments suggest a rather comprehensive interest in the linen industry, from flax fiber to fulled and dyed cloth, ready to sell.

Abbas took a similar approach to his investments in the coffee trade, which in the late seventeenth century was booming in Egypt. The Janissary officers who controlled Egypt's Mediterranean and Red Sea port customs, as well as the Indian ships that carried the beans from Mocha to Jidda and Suez, were growing rich beyond imagining from customs duties.[77] Abbas Agha's estate inventory features an extraordinary "coffee complex" in the town of Minyat Zifta in Gharbiyya. The eunuch held the tax farm of this town, which, since the Middle Ages, had been a key node in the distribution of trade items from Cairo through the countryside. Five hundred years earlier, in fact, it had been a site for the transshipment of raw silk fiber, at the time a widely traded item.[78] At Abbas Agha's establishment, coffee beans were ground at what the inventory describes as a "coffee-pounding place," while patrons enjoyed the brewed beverage at a coffeehouse. What distinguishes this establishment from Abbas's linen-making facility is that coffee, unlike flax, did not grow in Egypt. Rather, the beans would have come to Minyat Zifta with small-scale traveling merchants who purchased them in Cairo after they were imported from Yemen, then transshipped from Suez. In other words, Abbas's establishment helped to spread coffee through the Egyptian countryside, much as imported silk fiber had spread half a millennium earlier.

Abbas Agha's measures to promote the processing of and trade in both coffee and linen parallel the commercial projects of el-Hajj Mustafa Agha in Egypt fifty years before and those of el-Hajj Beshir Agha in the Danube Delta seventy years afterward. All three Chief Eunuchs sought to stimulate regional trade, whether within an Ottoman province or between that province and the imperial capital. The key difference was that Abbas established his enterprises after his exile to Egypt, whereas Mustafa and Beshir undertook theirs while still in office. We might therefore assume that all profits went to Abbas personally. However, where the Chief Eunuch was concerned, the distinction between imperial endowments for the holy cities and personal endowments

---

[76] Topkapı Palace Archive, D 7657 (undated); Hathaway, "Wealth and Influence," 302–3, 305; Hathaway, *Politics of Households*, 142; Hathaway, "Role of the Kızlar Ağası," 144.

[77] Hathaway, *Politics of Households*, 134–38; Hathaway, "The Ottomans and the Yemeni Coffee Trade," 161–71.

[78] Hathaway, "Wealth and Influence of an Exiled Eunuch," 302, 307; Hathaway, *Politics of Households*, 142; Hathaway, "Role of the Kızlar Ağası," 144; Evliya Çelebi, *Seyahatname*, X: 385; Goitein, *A Mediterranean Society*, I: 101–4, 203, 217, 222–24, 264; vol. 2: *The Community* (Berkeley, CA, 1971), 44–50; Jane Hathaway, "A Twelfth-Century Partnership in Silk-Trading in the Egyptian Delta: A Geniza Study," *Journal of the Middle East Studies Society at Columbia University* 2, 1 (1988): 23–37.

was often rather blurry. Mustafa and Beshir and their entourages unquestionably profited from their endowments connected to the Evkafü'l-Haremeyn; at the same time, the holy cities were the beneficiaries of Mustafa's and Beshir's personal endowments (and probably Abbas's, as well) for their endowment deeds named the poor of the holy cities as beneficiaries when their clients' lines of descent died out.[79]

Exiled Harem Eunuch Solidarity

In his 1599 *Description of Cairo*, the Ottoman bureaucrat and intellectual Mustafa Ali, as we saw above, was already lamenting that the exiled harem eunuchs in Cairo "cannot be counted any more." By the middle of the following century, according to the chronicler Naima, some thirty exiled harem eunuchs were living in the city – concentrated, as we have seen, in the vicinity of Birkat al-Fil. If they were living in a common neighborhood and exchanging houses, the exiled harem eunuchs must have felt a high degree of shared identity, and perhaps even solidarity. They must also have been recognized as a discrete population by other residents of Cairo. Their physical appearance alone would have made them stand out. Emasculation would have deprived them of facial hair – in a society in which most free adult males wore beards – and made them unusually tall and long-limbed, with a tendency toward either obesity or unusual thinness. In addition, most of them were originally from Ethiopia and vicinity, with the distinctive skin color and facial features of the populations of the Horn of Africa. If a stranger to Cairo had stumbled into the Birkat al-Fil area by accident, he would soon have realized that this was no ordinary neighborhood.

Yet what made this neighborhood potentially "threatening" to observers such as Mustafa Ali was precisely that it was *not* a "self-segregated" eunuch quarter but that the eunuchs lived there along with Egypt's most important provincial administrators and grandees. In a certain sense, Birkat al-Fil in the seventeenth century mirrored Topkapı Palace during the same period, with the rulers screened off by African harem eunuchs, or even Baghdad in the ninth century CE, with the caliph's palace surrounded by his African eunuchs' dwellings.

Naima's chronicle gives us a sense of the size and visibility of Cairo's exiled eunuch community by the mid-seventeenth century that is even more visceral than Mustafa Ali's 1599 account. In 1065/1654 occurred what Naima calls the "Abyssinia Incident" (Habeş Vak'ası), which, while centered on the remote province of Habesh in the Horn of Africa, came to involve Cairo's eunuchs.

---

[79] Wizarat al-Awqaf, No. 302/51, p. 43, lines 1–2.

It happened this way. One Mustafa Pasha, a Bosnian, had purchased the governorship of Habesh but preferred to stay in the Hijaz while sending a deputy to administer the province. Treating the assignment as a money-making opportunity, the deputy hired an inexperienced young man to assist him in assessing exorbitant customs duties on Habeshi merchants importing goods through the Red Sea port of Suakin (today in northeastern Sudan). Outraged, the merchants appealed to the Ottoman soldiers garrisoning the province, who rose up and imprisoned the deputy and his assistant. When Mustafa Pasha, the absentee governor, sent a delegation to negotiate, the soldiers killed them all, along with the deputy governor's assistant. Mustafa next sent a ship to attack the rebels, but they easily repulsed it.

Without ever setting foot in Habesh himself, Mustafa Pasha then appealed to the governor of Egypt, Hasseki Mehmed Pasha, for an expeditionary force to crush the rebellion. Hasseki Mehmed dutifully called up Egypt's regiments, but it was a difficult time for the soldiers, who had recently seen action on the Iranian and Habsburg fronts, in addition to the "ordinary" round of punitive expeditions to shore up the *sharif* of Mecca against his rivals and to quash rebellious Bedouin in the Egyptian countryside. They therefore replied, according to Naima:

> We are always assigned to quash the Bedouin bandits and send the tribute [to Istanbul] and serve the pilgrimage commander; we never lack for service. This time, let the eunuchs' slaves and followers go to perform this service. They have so much money and property from the sultan's state that they should do something.[80]

The Cairo eunuchs unquestionably had a sense of themselves as a community, for Naima reports that they took offense at the soldiers' remarks and staged a public protest, which probably centered on the neighborhood in which they lived. We would have to imagine a few dozen East African eunuchs, most of them middle-aged or elderly, marching around Birkat al-Fil, or through the neighboring streets. Their "slaves and followers," meanwhile, confronted the soldiers directly, even coming to blows.

In the end, the soldiers, under Ahmed Bey Bushnaq ("the Bosnian"), did go to Habesh to put down the rebellion. They won a pyrrhic victory of sorts when Hasseki Mehmed Pasha elected to imprison several of the most prominent exiled eunuchs in the remote fortress of Ibrim, on the border separating Egypt from Sudan. One of those imprisoned was the infamous Lala Süleyman Agha, whom we encountered in Chapter 6 as the alleged murderer of Mehmed IV's grandmother, Kösem Sultan, in 1651. Yet he returned to Cairo, along with the other imprisoned eunuchs, several years later and lived there until the 1670s. In 1676, though, perhaps feeling a bit overconfident, he joined a delegation of

---

[80] Naima, *Tarih-i Naima*, IV: 1555–56, 1638–40, quotation at 1640.

soldiers traveling to Sultan Mehmed IV's court in Edirne to announce the deposition of the latest governor of Egypt; there, he was arrested for "interfering with the soldiers," although at least one source claims that he was recognized as the murderer of Kösem Sultan. He was exiled to Lemnos, where he was eventually executed.[81]

Meanwhile, former Chief Eunuch Taş Yatur Ali Agha and former sultan's companion Mes'ud Agha managed to flee to Damascus, then make their way back to Edirne, where they were reinstated as sultan's companions. From this secure position, they vented their indignation at Hasseki Mehmed Pasha, whose career was consequently ruined.[82]

What the Abyssinia Incident shows is that the soldiers in Egypt's regiments, and perhaps the population of Cairo at large, regarded the exiled harem eunuchs as a cohesive body, with a common status and interests. They were also painfully aware of the wealth and manpower that the eunuchs commanded; in fact, their suggestion that the eunuchs' followers put down the rebellion in Habesh implies that these followers were armed – perhaps even that the eunuchs had small private armies, as Moralı Beshir Agha would in Istanbul a century later.[83] Regardless of whether they did or not, the eunuch community was clearly capable of taking collective action.

Conclusion

Egypt was an integral part of a harem eunuch's life and career. Most African eunuchs were castrated in Upper Egypt and first sold into slavery in Cairo's enormous slave market. Their first posting was often the household of Egypt's governor or one of the province's grandees. And of course, exile in Cairo awaited most harem eunuchs, chief and otherwise, at the end of their careers, and often at intervals before deposition. A number of Chief Eunuchs are buried in Cairo.

Exiled eunuchs gave something back to Egypt, though. As we have seen, they contributed in significant, even vital, ways to the province's commercial and agricultural economy through their endowment of *wakala*s for flax and coffee beans, as well as what amounted to factories and shopping complexes for the finished products produced from these commodities. The effects of these enterprises on Egypt's infrastructure were profound. Osman, Davud, and el-Hajj Mustafa Aghas collectively resuscitated the area between Birkat al-Fil

---

[81] Abdurrahman Abdi, *Vekayiname*, 397; Silahdar, *Silahdar Tarihi*, I: 650; al-Hallaq, *Tarih-i Mısr-ı Kahire*, fols. 211b–212b.
[82] Naima, *Tarih-i Naima*, IV: 1556, 1640.
[83] Al-Hallaq, *Tarih-i Mısr-ı Kahire*, fol. 174b: an apparent eunuch military troop.

and the Khan al-Khalili, establishing a new neighborhood in the process, while Abbas Agha appears to have given the Nile Delta town of Minyat Zifta a new lease on life.

None of these projects would have been possible, of course, without the eunuchs' *vekil*s, who scouted out locations for these undertakings, purchased the properties and lands that would be endowed to finance them, dealt with the farmers and artisans who made them run, and probably even went to the *shari'a* courts to register the endowment deeds. While the Vekil-i Darüssaade handled transactions related to the Evkafü'l-Haremeyn, a eunuch's personal *vekil* – who might be the same person – made sure that his wants were supplied in retirement and that the investments he had made in preparation for his Egyptian exile produced income once he arrived in Cairo.

The practice of exiling harem eunuchs to Cairo, then, gave rise to physical reminders of their presence, in the form of caravanserais, linen factories, coffeehouses, and, of course, lavish residential compounds. These were more than simply reminders, though, since they resulted in commercial and residential architecture that, in some cases, permanently altered Cairo's urban topography and that of other Egyptian cities and towns. The eunuchs themselves, though, were the most visceral reminder. Concentrated in one strategically located neighborhood near Cairo's citadel, they had a definite sense of themselves as a distinct element in Cairene society, even as they hobnobbed with and lived among the military and administrative elite. When necessary, they could even act as a pressure group, demanding the privileges, such as not having their followers called up for military service, that went with this distinctive form of retirement in exile.

When exiled Chief Harem Eunuchs established endowments, though, their goal was not simply to invest in commerce and reap revenues. They also established a large number of religious and educational institutions. Osman Agha's small mosque and el-Hajj Beshir Agha's *sebil-mekteb*, mentioned above, are only a tiny sample of the institutions of this kind that acting and exiled Chief Harem Eunuchs founded. These foundations are the subject of Chapter 9.

9   The Chief Harem Eunuch and Ottoman Religious and Intellectual Life

Thus far, we have seen ample evidence of the Chief Harem Eunuch's political and economic influence, both at the imperial center and in the Ottoman provinces. But intertwined with these elements of his influence was his influence on the Ottoman Empire's intellectual and religious life. To a large degree, he exercised this influence through pious endowments of religious, educational, and charitable institutions, above all Qur'an schools, madrasas, libraries, and Sufi lodges. But these endowments also serve as indicators of the Chief Harem Eunuch's own religious and intellectual proclivities. In brief, these consisted mainly of promotion of Sunni Islam, adherence to mainstream Sufi orders, opposition to Shi'ism, particularly Twelver Shi'ism as it developed in Safavid (and to a lesser extent Qajar) Iran, and devotion to the Prophet Muhammad. Complementary to the emphasis on Sunnism was promotion of the Hanafi legal rite, the official Ottoman rite, although rather surprisingly, this element did not become pronounced until the early eighteenth century.

Though not all Chief Eunuchs shared the same religious and intellectual preferences, there was a general consistency to their leanings, with one significant exception: when the puritanical tendency known as the Kadızadeli movement was at its height in the late seventeenth century, some high-placed harem eunuchs espoused it, while others, including at least one Chief Harem Eunuch, persisted in promoting the very forms of Sufism that the Kadızadelis regarded as an intolerable innovation to the practices of the Prophet Muhammad. This seeming divergence of opinion did not result in open discord among the harem eunuchs. Still, it probably helps to explain at least a few depositions and exiles. It also comes as no surprise that this kind of ideological rift occurred during the seventeenth century, a period of society-wide crisis when social and ideological categories of all kinds were being contested.

This chapter explores the Chief Harem Eunuchs' religious and intellectual tendencies, above all as they were manifested in the religio-educational institutions – not so much mosques as schools of various kinds – founded by key Chief Harem Eunuchs. These were located chiefly in Istanbul, Cairo, and Medina but occasionally in other locales. We then move on to a consideration of the ways in which the Chief Eunuch contributed to Ottoman intellectual life by endowing books and founding libraries. Finally, a discussion of Sufi institutions endowed by Chief Eunuchs leads to an attempt to untangle the Chief Eunuchs' responses to the largely anti-Sufi Kadızadeli movement within the broader context of Ottoman confessionalization

Qur'an Schools/*Sebil-Mekteb*s

By far the most frequent Chief Eunuch–endowed educational institution was the Qur'an school (*mekteb* in Turkish, *kuttab* in Arabic), a modest foundation that offered basic religious education, and in the process rudimentary literacy, to young, usually pre-teenage, boys – all at no charge. In the case of schools endowed by Chief Eunuchs, these boys were often orphans. Typically, the goal of such schools was to enable boys to memorize the Qur'an through repeated recitation; sophisticated exegesis was not part of the agenda. By endowing a Qur'an school, a Chief Eunuch was performing a pious duty by teaching the sacred scripture to other Muslims; for this he would be rewarded in heaven.

Although Chief Eunuch–endowed Qur'an schools survive as part of large religious complexes, today known as *külliye*s, elsewhere in the Ottoman Empire, by far the largest number of extant free-standing schools is in Cairo. This has a great deal to do with a distinctive type of Qur'an school that developed in Cairo during the late Mamluk period and carried over into the Ottoman era: the *sebil-mekteb* or *sabil-kuttab*, a Qur'an school (*mekteb* or *kuttab*) built on top of a public water fountain (*sebil* or *sabil*). The *sebil*, an enclosed chamber in which one to three employees dip up cups of water from an underground cistern and hand it out through a metal grill, thus serves as the lower story of the structure, the *mekteb*, an open or enclosed loggia, as the upper story; an enclosed staircase usually occupies one side of the structure.[1] The original rationale for such a combination is unknown, but providing water to Muslims, like teaching them the Qur'an, is a pious act that earns the provider a heavenly reward. Since the *mekteb* is sometimes open to the elements, Cairo's mild climate may well have determined the popularity of the architectural form there.

Habeshi Mehmed Agha. Interestingly enough, the very first Chief Harem Eunuch, Habeshi Mehmed Agha, seems to have experimented with transplanting this architectural form to the Ottoman imperial capital, perhaps inspired by his prior residence in Egypt. Around 1580, he commissioned two *sebil-mekteb*s along the processional route known as Divan Yolu in the center of old Istanbul.

---

[1] *EI*[2], s.v. "Sabil, 2. As an Architectural Term," by Doris Behrens-Abouseif; Behrens-Abouseif, *Islamic Architecture in Cairo*, 147; Doris Behrens-Abouseif, *Cairo of the Mamluks: A History of the Architecture and Its Culture* (London, 2007), 84, 86, 221, 320.

One stood near Constantine's Column, a.k.a. the Burnt Column or Çemberli-taş, the other near Ayasofya. (Neither structure exists today.)[2] This experiment was never repeated; all other Chief Eunuch–endowed *sebil-mekteb*s were erected in Cairo.

El-Hajj Mustafa Agha. In Cairo, the *sebil-mekteb* was a common part of the Mamluk sultans' mosque–madrasa complexes by the late fourteenth century, building on the earlier practice of situating a *sebil* (with no *mekteb*) at the corner of a religious building. Sultan Qaytbay (r. 1468–96) commissioned the first known free-standing *sebil-mekteb*, which still stands in the Saliba neighborhood, below Cairo's citadel. Completed in 1479, it is a linear stone building decorated with elaborate polychrome stone inlay over the *sebil* grill.

As it happens, this structure became the first *sebil-mekteb* to be endowed in Cairo by an Ottoman Chief Harem Eunuch, for in 1620, the powerful el-Hajj Mustafa Agha restored it. The lengthy Arabic endowment deed that describes the properties he endowed in Egypt notes that the school was to educate ten orphan boys, to be hand-picked by Mustafa Agha himself or, in his absence, by the local endowment supervisor (*mütevelli*). The boys were to be taught by a "virtuous" (*'afif*) man of religion who had memorized the Qur'an, along with a student assistant (*'arif*). Students and teachers alike received a daily bread ration and a new set of clothes during the holy month of Ramadan. Overall, we can regard this restoration as part of Mustafa Agha's urban development project in Cairo, discussed in Chapter 8, for most of his commercial structures were likewise located in the Saliba neighborhood, as was his residence, which stood just across the street from the *sebil*.[3] All these sites were near Birkat al-Fil, future site of the eunuch enclave, as well.

Abbas Agha. Mustafa Agha's restoration of Qaytbay's *sebil-mekteb* seems to have set something of a precedent, although admittedly with a substantial delay. Nearly half a century later, Abbas Agha, before his exile to Cairo, founded a *sebil-mekteb* whose fountain Evliya Çelebi describes as "so ornamented and decorated that it resembles a pagan temple with Chinese drawings";[4] otherwise, not much is known about this structure, which no longer exists. But it was part of a veritable *sebil-mekteb* explosion in Cairo during the 1660s and 1670s: "In seven years," Evliya marvels, "seventy new *sebil*s were built,"[5] by both exiled harem eunuchs (chief and otherwise) and by local military officers.

---

[2] Ayvansarayi, *Garden of the Mosques*, 110–11; Necipoğlu, *Age of Sinan*, 498.
[3] Cairo, Wizarat al-Awqaf, No. 302/51, pp. 13, 24–26, 38–39.
[4] Evliya Çelebi, *Seyahatname*, X: 152.
[5] Ibid.; Hamza Abd al-Aziz Badr and Daniel Crecelius, "The *Waqf*s of Shahin Ahmad Agha," *Annales islamologiques* 26 (1992): 79–114.

Yusuf Agha. One of these military officers was Mehmed, the lieutenant commander (*kethüda*) of Cairo's Janissary regiment, who built a *sebil-mekteb*, along with a *wakala*, or urban caravanserai, on Darb al-Ahmar, a major artery connecting Bab Zuwayla to the citadel in the southeast. The site is not far to the east of Mustafa Agha's *sebil*. In 1677, Yusuf Agha, then acting Chief Harem Eunuch, ordered his agent, the grandee Mustafa Agha (later Bey) Kızlar, to purchase these structures and reendow the *sebil-mekteb*.

The resulting endowment deed has been studied by André Raymond, who points out that Yusuf's *mekteb*, much like el-Hajj Mustafa's, was to teach the Qur'an to ten orphan boys, who would also receive a monthly stipend and new clothes at Ramadan. Unlike Mustafa's *sebil-mekteb*, which is, after all, a restored Mamluk Sultanate structure, Yusuf's is decorated with blue and white Iznik tiles, a few of which can still be glimpsed inside the *sebil* even though the structure is, to quote Raymond, "in an advanced state of decay."[6] And unlike Mustafa's *sebil-mekteb*, Yusuf's was not located in close proximity to the founder's residence but instead was situated several kilometers east of Yusuf's house at Birkat al-Fil. Revenue for the *mekteb* came from the adjoining *wakala*, from a sort of urban tenement known as a *rab'* above the *wakala*, and from a coffeehouse, complete with roasting and grinding facilities, across the way.[7] These neighboring structures seem to duplicate on a smaller scale the kind of infrastructural development that el-Hajj Mustafa, Osman, and Davud Aghas had undertaken farther west and north, as described in Chapter 8.

The endowment deed contains a couple of somewhat unusual, or at least noteworthy, provisions. It stipulates that Yusuf's agent Mustafa Agha Kızlar (the future bey) is to be superintendent (*nazir*) of the foundation during his lifetime; he presumably looked after it until his death in 1730. At the same time, the deed allocates thirty Egyptian silver coins (singular, *para*) per month for a foundation administrator (Arabic, *shadd*) "from among the founder's manumitted slaves." More surprisingly, the endowment funds a Friday preacher (*khatib*) and a daily prayer leader (*imam*) at the Mosque of the Prophet in Medina. When he endowed the structure in 1677, Yusuf Agha presumably had no idea that he would one day command the corps of eunuchs who guarded the Prophet's mosque and tomb; at the time, no former Chief Harem Eunuch had ever held that position. Yet the acting Chief Harem Eunuch was constantly aware of the tomb eunuchs, many of whom were, after all, former harem eunuchs, and more broadly of the "other harem" – that is, the

---

[6] Raymond, "*Sabil* of Yusuf Agha," 223–28, 230–32; Evliya Çelebi, *Seyahatname*, X: 152; Williams, *Islamic Monuments in Cairo*, 98.

[7] Raymond, "*Sabil* of Yusuf Agha," 228–29; Williams, *Islamic Monuments in Cairo*, 98; André Raymond, "The *Rab'*: A Type of Collective Housing in Cairo during the Ottoman Period," in *Architecture as Symbol and Self-Identity*, ed. Jonathan G. Katz (Philadelphia, PA, 1980), 55–61.

haram, or sacred precinct, surrounding the Prophet's mosque and tomb. This helps to explain why Yusuf's predecessor Abbas Agha had a volume of the late fifteenth-century historian al-Samhudi's panegyric history of Medina in his collection of books in Cairo, even though he probably never set foot in Medina.[8]

El-Hajj Beshir Agha. El-Hajj Beshir Agha was not part of the wave of *sebil-mekteb* construction remarked by Evliya Çelebi, yet he arguably revived it by building his own *sebil* – or, rather, having it built for him by one of his trusty *vekil*s, just as he was leaving Cairo to return to Topkapı. It was located along the shore of Birkat al-Fil, to the north of the *sebil*s of Mustafa and Yusuf Aghas, southwest of Bab Zuwayla and southeast of the nineteenth-century 'Abdin Palace.[9] Like Mustafa Agha (but unlike Yusuf), el-Hajj Beshir had his residence near his *sebil-mekteb* – in his case, right next-door to it.

The endowment deed of Beshir Agha's *sebil-mekteb* has been published by Daniel Crecelius and Hamza Abd al-Aziz Badr. It stipulates that the *mekteb* is to educate twenty orphan boys (twice the number of either el-Hajj Mustafa's or Yusuf's *mekteb*) but that, intriguingly, they are to be taught by a "Hanafi *faqih*." Ordinarily, *faqih* would refer to an expert in Islamic jurisprudence (*fiqh*), but here, as in el-Hajj Mustafa's endowment deed, it probably means simply a Qur'an instructor. The insistence on hiring a Hanafi is significant, though. While the Hanafi legal rite (*mezhep* or *madhhab*) was the official rite of the Ottoman Empire, so that the chief judge and the head of the descendants of the Prophet in Egypt always belonged to that rite, the province counted a large number of adherents of the other Sunni rites, above all the Shafi'i and the Maliki. Still, the deeds for el-Hajj Mustafa's and Yusuf's *sebil-mekteb*s make no mention of the instructors' legal rite, so we might conclude that by the time el-Hajj Beshir built his structure, the other rites were perceived as more of a threat to Hanafi dominance.

This makes sense, for in fact the Shafi'is and Malikis were more prominent among Egypt's ulema in the early eighteenth century. Cairo's famed al-Azhar madrasa was now the preeminent institution of higher Islamic learning in the city, and it was headed by a new official: the Shaykh al-Azhar, an office that seems to have emerged in the late seventeenth century. The first several Shaykhs were Maliki, but in 1724, a Shafi'i won the office, setting a lasting precedent: until 1870, no member of any other rite held the office. When we add to this the growth of al-Azhar's Shafi'i and Maliki student population during these years, with many Maliki students arriving from Upper Egypt, West Africa, and Morocco, and Shafi'i students from Indonesia and Malaysia,

---

[8] Hathaway, "Wealth and Influence," 295, 297, 309.
[9] Williams, *Islamic Monuments in Cairo*, 157; personal observation; Süleymaniye Library, MS Hacı Beşir Ağa 682, fols. 38b–39a, 42b–43a, 44a–b.

we can see why Hanafis in Cairo might have felt a bit beleaguered.[10] In general, too, Shafi'is and Malikis simply outnumbered Hanafis on the ground in Egypt, and had for centuries, despite the later Mamluk sultans' patronage of Hanafism. Given all these circumstances, it was logical for el-Hajj Beshir to attempt to bolster his *mezhep* by training up orphans – who had no preexisting ties to any legal rite – as Hanafis.

Moralı Beshir Agha. El-Hajj Beshir Agha established something of a Hanafi "beachhead" at Birkat al-Fil before he returned to Istanbul. His successor as Chief Harem Eunuch, Moralı Beshir Agha, went farther. In 1750, two years before his execution, he oversaw, from Istanbul, the construction of the first madrasa that an Ottoman sultan had ever commissioned in Cairo, to the immediate north of el-Hajj Beshir's *sebil-mekteb*. The Mahmudiyye Madrasa – named, naturally, for Sultan Mahmud I – was part of a religious complex that included a lodge for Halveti Sufis and, at the southernmost corner, another *sebil-mekteb* (see Figure 9.1). While the madrasa housed forty students, the new *sebil-mekteb* accommodated twenty, the same number as el-Hajj Beshir's structure. This new *mekteb* faces that of el-Hajj Beshir across a narrow lane, today known as Sikkatat al-Habbaniyya. The two structures could hardly be more different: el-Hajj Beshir's spare and linear, Moralı Beshir's a curvaceous Baroque edifice, stylistically up to date and, in its way, reminiscent of Baroque confections in the imperial capital, notably the fountain of Ahmed III in front of Topkapı's outer gate. Moralı Beshir himself, a skilled calligrapher, may have designed the calligraphic panels that adorn the *sebil*.[11] Inside, Moralı Beshir's *sebil* is lined with blue and white Iznik tiles. Clearly, no expense was spared for the Mahmudiyye complex, which also featured white marble paving stones imported from Istanbul.[12]

---

[10] Daniel Crecelius, "The Emergence of the Shaykh al-Azhar as the Pre-Eminent Religious Leader in Egypt," in *Colloque international sur l'histoire du Caire, 27 mars–5 avril 1969*, eds. Andrée Assabgui et al. (Cairo, 1972), 109–23; Afaf Lutfi al-Sayyid Marsot, "The Ulama of Cairo in the Eighteenth and Nineteenth Centuries," in *Scholars, Saints, and Sufis: Muslim Religious Institutions after 1500*, ed. Nikki R. Keddie (Berkeley, CA, 1972), 149–65; Michael Winter, *Egyptian Society under Ottoman Rule, 1517–1798* (London, 1992), 118–23; Jane Hathaway, "The Role of the 'Ulama' in Social Protest in Late Eighteenth-Century Egypt," unpublished M.A. thesis, University of Texas at Austin, 1986, 17–19, 34–37.

[11] Doris Behrens-Abouseif, "The Complex of Sultan Mahmud I in Cairo," *Muqarnas* 28 (2011): 195–220; Flachat, *Observations*, II: 129.

[12] Personal observation; Behrens-Abouseif, "Complex of Sultan Mahmud I," 197, 198–99; Williams, *Islamic Monuments of Cairo*, 157; BOA, C.MF.648 (end of Şevval 1166/end of August 1753) and BOA Tahvil Defteri 11/93 (13 Receb 1164/7 June 1751), published in *Misr fi al-watha'iq al-'uthmaniyya/Osmanlı Belgelerinde Mısır/Egypt in the [sic] Ottoman Documents* (Istanbul, 2007), 12–13; BOA, Mühimme-i Mısır, vol. 7, nos. 98 (1 Zilkade 1166/29 August 1753) and 99 (1 Şevval 1166/31 July 1753); Hamadeh, *City's Pleasures*, 90, 96, 103–4, 114, 137, 175–76, 196–97.

Figure 9.1 El-Hajj Beshir Agha's (right) and Moralı Beshir Agha's *sebil-mekteb*s in Cairo. Author's photos.

In fact, the Mahmudiyye religious complex marked this entire neighborhood next to Birkat al-Fil – where virtually all exiled harem eunuchs had their residences – as a site of Hanafi learning. But in addition to serving as an implicit riposte to the strength in Egypt of the Shafiʻi and Maliki legal rites, the complex, along with el-Hajj Beshir's *sebil-mekteb*, offered institutional competition to the growing number of madrasas and *mekteb*s being founded by Egypt's grandees, above all the ascendant Kazdağlı household. The Kazdağlıs, like virtually all of Egypt's grandees, were Hanafis themselves, but the religious institutions they founded were neither sanctioned nor supported by the imperial government; instead, they functioned wholly autonomously. In 1744, Abdurrahman Kethüda al-Kazdağlı, one of the greatest architectural patrons in Ottoman Cairo, founded a free-standing *sebil-mekteb* in the heart of the original Fatimid city that today is arguably the best-known example of the genre in the world.[13] Mahmud's new religious complex showed that the imperial center was still, so to speak, in the game where Hanafi education in Cairo was concerned.

---

[13] Doris Behrens-Abouseif, "The ʻAbd al-Rahman Katkhuda Style in Eighteenth-Century Cairo," *Annales islamologiques* 26 (1992): 117–26; André Raymond, *Le Caire des Janissaires: l'apogée de la ville ottomane sous ʻAbd al-Rahman Katkhuda* (Paris, 1995), 98–114.

The sultanic interest in the Birkat al-Fil district may be one reason why Osman Kethüda al-Kazdağlı, the powerful Janissary officer who headed the household during the 1720s, established his residence and a religious complex in the northwestern district of Azbakiyya, which had only just begun to challenge Birkat al-Fil as an elite residential neighborhood.[14] A later Chief Eunuch–founded *sebil-mekteb*, that of Ebu'l-Vukuf Ahmed Agha (term 1755–57) stayed well to the south of Azbakiyya, at Qanatir al-Siba', a district located just south and west of Birkat al-Fil that at the time was not much of an elite residential hub, even though Ebu'l-Vukuf's former residence was located there.[15]

Collectively, these *sebil-mekteb*s reflect the Chief Harem Eunuch's desire to teach the Qur'an and impart literacy to orphan boys. In this connection, we can hardly overlook the fact that three of the structures mentioned here were located in close proximity to the sponsoring Chief Eunuchs' local residences. To some degree, this echoes the arrangement that prevailed in Mecca, where the subordinate members of the eunuch corps who guarded the Ka'ba lived in the home of the eunuch in charge while they completed their training. The orphans who attended the *mekteb*s in Cairo may not have belonged to the Chief Harem Eunuch's household, but they were nonetheless, in a sense, his clients. We might even say they were his surrogate children, rather like the young eunuchs in Mecca, for by means of the *sebil-mekteb*, he raised a new generation of literate Sunni Muslims – and, in el-Hajj and Moralı Beshir Aghas' cases, at least, Hanafis, as well.

Madrasas

Founding a Qur'an school was one thing. It was quite another for a Chief Harem Eunuch to found a madrasa, the Muslim equivalent of a theological seminary, although with a heavy emphasis on jurisprudence (*fiqh*) as well as on Qur'anic exegesis (*tefsir*) and study of *hadith*, or sayings attributed to the Prophet Muhammad. In general, a madrasa required more of everything: space, food, fuel, personnel, cash. Students – whose numbers could range from ten or twenty to multiple hundreds, in the case of al-Azhar – generally lived on

---

[14] Behrens-Abouseif, *Azbakiyya and Its Environs*, 55ff.; Raymond, "Essai de géographie," 66, 73–75, 78, 80–81, 97–103; Hathaway, *Politics of Households*, 78, 127.

[15] BOA, Mühimme-i Mısır, vol. 7, nos. 411 (1 Rebiülevvel 1171/12 November 1757), 431 (mid-Receb 1171/late March 1758), 442 (1 Şa'ban 1171/9 April 1758), 450 (same date), 451 (same date), 454 (mid-Şa'ban 1171/late April 1758), 455 (same date), 503 (1 Rebiülevvel 1172/1 November 1758), 504 (30 Receb 1172/28 March 1759), 563 (1 Şa'ban 1172/29 March 1759), 566 (mid-Şa'ban 1172/mid-April 1759), 607 (1 Cemaziyelevvel 1173/20 December 1759), 678 (mid-Zilhicce 1173/28 July 1760), 680 (same date); Raymond, "Essai de géographie," 80–81, 98, 100–102.

the grounds of the madrasa, often relocating from great distances. In addition
to lodgings, they required a mosque for daily worship, a library to house the
books they studied, a kitchen, a bath, and toilets. For all these reasons, a
madrasa required a much larger physical space than a Qur'an school. And
instead of a single teacher, multiple instructors were necessary, as well as
librarians, mosque preachers, and various maintenance people to light the
lamps, sweep the floors, and so on (although the endowment deeds for
many madrasas stipulate that the students themselves will perform these
duties). All employees received cash salaries and often food and clothing
allotments, as well. To found a madrasa, then, was a huge undertaking requiring vast resources.

Not surprisingly, there are relatively few madrasas founded by Chief Harem
Eunuchs. And whereas Chief Eunuchs were particularly active in founding
*mekteb*s in Cairo, none of them founded a madrasa in that city, albeit Moralı
Beshir Agha supervised construction of the Mahmudiyye Madrasa from afar.[16]
Instead, Chief Eunuch–founded madrasas exist in the holy cities, in the
imperial capital, and in the Ottoman Balkans.

Habeshi Mehmed Agha. Once again, the first Chief Eunuch, Habeshi
Mehmed Agha, set a precedent by founding a madrasa, with accommodations
for ten students, in 1582–83. The great Sinan designed this no-longer-extant
structure, which seems to have been a kind of supplement to Habeshi Mehmed's *sebil-mekteb* near Çemberlitaş. At a madrasa in the imperial capital, the
students would presumably have belonged to the Hanafi rite.[17]

El-Hajj Mustafa Agha. And once again, el-Hajj Mustafa Agha continued
the tradition by founding a madrasa in Mecca during his pilgrimage to that city
in 1602 – that is, three years before he became Chief Harem Eunuch. His
madrasa was unusual in providing for instruction in *both* the Hanafi and Shafi'i
legal rites. This was almost unheard-of among Ottoman imperial foundations
of any kind since Hanafism was the empire's official legal rite. Yet Shafi'ism
was well represented among the resident population of Mecca, as well as
among pilgrims to the city, and in the Red Sea region generally: Lower Egypt
and coastal Yemen were majority Shafi'i. El-Hajj Mustafa may have wished to
accommodate this not insignificant element of Mecca's population, perhaps
seeking at the same time to counteract the ideological appeal of the Zaydi
imams of Yemen, who in the early seventeenth century were in the process of
ousting the Ottomans from that province.[18]

---

[16] Badr and Crecelius, "*Awqaf* of al-Hajj Bashir Agha in Cairo," 301.
[17] Necipoğlu, *Age of Sinan*, 498.
[18] BOA, MD 112, no. 1000 (1 Safer 1114/26 June 1702), shows Solak Nezir Agha providing for
both Hanafi and Shafi'i *teravih* (*tarawih*), or supplementary, prayers for the Prophet's birthday.

In Cairo, as well, el-Hajj Mustafa accommodated both the Hanafi and Shafi'i rites when he endowed thirty Qur'an readers to recite verses before and after the dawn and evening prayers; his endowment deed stipulates that a shaykh from each rite will preside over his own circle (*majlis*) of readers. The same provision is made for nine people whom he endowed to pray at al-Azhar.[19] As if to underline his respect for the Shafi'i rite, he also provided for three people to recite the Fatiha (the opening verse of the Qur'an) at the tomb of al-Shafi'i himself, located in Cairo's enormous Qarafa cemetery.[20] Abbas Agha, who died in Cairo during the 1690s, is buried near al-Shafi'i's tomb, a choice of location that seems more than coincidental; an order for repairs to the tomb nearly eighty years later reveals that the superintendent of the endowment for al-Shafi'i's tomb was the once and future Chief Eunuch Cevher Mehmed Agha (terms 1772–74, 1779–83).[21]

One possible explanation for this devotion to al-Shafi'i comes from the eunuchs' Ethiopian homeland. Most Ethiopian Muslims have historically adhered to the Shafi'i rite.[22] If Mustafa, Abbas, and perhaps other harem eunuchs (including Habeshi Mehmed, if we believe the tale of his capture) were, in fact, Muslims by birth – as African eunuchs very occasionally were[23] – then their families may have belonged to the Shafi'i rite, in which case they may have retained a certain loyalty to the rite and its eponymous founder.

El-Hajj Beshir Agha. No Chief Harem Eunuch founded more educational institutions than the long-serving el-Hajj Beshir Agha. In Medina alone, he founded a madrasa and a *dar al-hadith*, or school for the study of sayings attributed to the Prophet Muhammad. Both institutions are described in the massive endowment deed preserved in Istanbul's Süleymaniye Library. Founded in 1738, the modest, eight-room madrasa was a restoration of an earlier structure, with an attached library (*kitabhane*) and a *mu'allimhane* to train Qur'an-school teachers. This complex offered "hands-on learning" at its finest: madrasa students staffed the library, led daily prayers, and kept the grounds and the washroom clean. Meanwhile, students from the madrasa and the *mu'allimhane* teamed up to teach the Qur'an to children. In effect, then, this institution functioned as three schools in one. The endowment deed mentions no restrictions on the provenances of students who could enroll in the madrasa or *mu'allimhane*, so presumably, it was open to anyone capable of mastering the curriculum.

---

[19] Wizarat al-Awqaf, No. 302/51, pp. 39–41. The Hanafi *'asr* (afternoon) prayer is roughly an hour later than that of the other three rites.

[20] Topkapı Palace Archive, D 7911 (undated).

[21] Topkapı Palace Archive, E 4787 (1194/1780).

[22] Hussein Ahmed, *Islam in Nineteenth-Century Wallo, Ethiopia: Revival, Reform, and Reaction* (Leiden, 2001), 65–66.

[23] See Chapter 10 on the late Ottoman eunuch Nadir Agha.

Beshir's *dar al-hadith*, apparently purpose-built and funded by revenues from lands around Damascus, had a somewhat different agenda. It was for "the useful knowledge of people originally from Rum" (*fi-ül-asıl diyar-i Rum ahalisinin 'ulum-u nafi'e*) – that is, the Ottoman central lands, more particularly Anatolia and the eastern Balkans. Specifically, the resident students must comprise twenty Rumi bachelors. To hammer this point home, the document adds, "the twenty rooms will not be for married people, North Africans (*Magribi*), Indians (*Hindi*), Persians (*A'cam*), peasants (*fellah*), Shi'ites (*revafiz*, implying heretics), or people of other races (*ecnas*)."[24] These provisions guaranteed that the students would be uniformly Hanafi, since virtually all Rumis belonged to this rite. Their teacher (*müderris*) would likewise be a native of Rum, selected by the Chief Tomb Eunuch, who was the superintendent of the endowment, and the chief judge of Medina. If no Rumi sufficiently knowledgeable in Qur'anic exegesis, Prophetic traditions, and Islamic jurisprudence (*fiqh*) could be found in Medina, these two officials could petition to have one dispatched from Istanbul.

These stipulations imply that there was no shortage of Rumi students in Medina, although they clearly coexisted with would-be students from a wide variety of locales and backgrounds, so that it would have been very easy for them to absorb the doctrinal interpretations and practices of those places. Arguably, then, the core aim of the foundation was to ensure that such students received a uniform legal and religious education according to the Hanafi legal rite. In other words, the *dar al-hadith* prevented the localization of Rumi students in the Hijaz while, at the same time, reinforcing the status in the region of the Hanafi rite, which was, after all, the official Ottoman rite.

Like the madrasa students, those enrolled in the *dar al-hadith* had to cook, clean, fetch, and carry for themselves. The endowment deed includes a list of books in the *dar al-hadith*'s library; these constitute the canon of Hanafi jurisprudence and exegesis. Taken together, the *dar al-hadith* and the madrasa had the effect of shoring up Hanafism in Medina, a city whose population had historically been majority Zaydi and Ismaili Shi'ite. In addition to training new students in this rite, the institutions supplied manuscripts of classic Hanafi works to existing Hanafi ulema in the city and to Hanafi pilgrims visiting the city.

At the opposite end of the empire from Medina, in the Danube River port of Sistova (today Svishtov, Bulgaria), el-Hajj Beshir Agha founded another madrasa, apparently in 1745. This might seem an odd site for a Chief Eunuch–endowed madrasa; after all, the population of the region was overwhelmingly Orthodox Christian, and what Muslims there were all belonged to the Hanafi

---

[24] Süleymaniye Library, MS Hacı Beşir 682, fols. 23b–34a, especially 24a.

rite. Yet, as we saw in Chapter 7, Beshir was intensely interested in the Danube valley because of its strategic location vis-à-vis the Habsburgs and Russia, and the key role it played in supplying Istanbul with grain.

The Svishtov madrasa was part of a much larger constellation of infrastructural projects in this key Danubian port. Today, no trace of the madrasa remains, nor any record of what must have been its sizable library, which must have consisted mainly of critical Hanafi works, much like the library of the Medina *dar al-hadith*. Even Beshir's mammoth endowment deed mentions only the neighboring sheep-trotter shop.[25] Nonetheless, we can easily see that in a majority Christian city so far removed from the imperial capital, and even from the provincial capital, Sofia, manuscripts of the classics of Hanafi exegesis and jurisprudence would have been much harder to obtain than they were in Medina. Beshir's madrasa would have kept Hanafi education viable in this town, supplying, for example, imams and Qur'an school teachers for Svishtov and the surrounding region.

Less than a year before his paralyzing stroke, el-Hajj Beshir Agha commissioned a madrasa as part of his religious complex (today know as a *külliye*) just south of Topkapı Palace in Istanbul. This complex, much of which still stands in good repair, included, besides the madrasa, a mosque, a Qur'an school, a lodge for Naqshbandi Sufis (discussed below), a public fountain in the corner of the perimeter wall, and a library. Conditions for this madrasa were nearly as stringent as those for Beshir's *dar al-hadith* in Medina: students must not be married and must not leave their places at the madrasa to pursue other activities besides the study of Islamic law and theology. If they violated the rules, their places would be given to others. All the same, there was no ethnoregional limitation, as there was for the Medina *dar al-hadith*. Since the madrasa was in Istanbul, most of the students would presumably have been Rumi, anyway; still, the absence of dire warnings against interlopers is in striking contrast to the conditions for the *dar al-hadith*.[26]

As in other madrasas, the students took on various routine jobs – gatekeeper (*bevvab*), sweeper (*ferraş*), lamp-lighter (*siraçı*), library aide (*mustahfız*) – all of which were assigned according to the chamber in which the student lived and all of which paid a token salary. As was apparently customary, the complex also included a *mekteb*, so that it offered the possibility of a continuous Muslim education that could equip a boy – even an orphan – for some sort of ulema career – not, of course, the top positions in the imperial ulema hierarchy, which drew from the great sultanic madrasas of Istanbul, Edirne, and Bursa, but more modest instructorships and mosque preacher positions.

[25] Ibid., fol. 104b; fol. 81a (madrasa in Eyüp).
[26] Ibid., fols. 105b–113a; Ayvansarayi, *Garden of the Mosques*, 55–56.

Yet this was not a run-of-the-mill educational complex. It was clearly a showcase institution, designed to attract elite ulema and high-ranking palace officials, up to and including the sultan. The mosque was clearly not the standard madrasa mosque, used by the students for their daily prayers. It employed a small army of salaried preachers, sermonizers, Qur'an-reciters, and muezzins, several of them specifically assigned to the Friday public noontime prayers. It also featured a gallery (*mahfil*) for the sultan, complete with its own muezzin. This suggests that Mahmud I and his successors occasionally visited the mosque, which was, after all, very close to the palace. By the same token, the *mekteb* was more sophisticated than usual, equipped with a calligraphy teacher and even a "higher *mekteb*" (*mekteb-i mu'alla*) where students studied "useful sciences" (*'ulum-u nafi'e*), probably meaning basic exegesis, two days a week. The *mekteb* may not even have been for orphan boys, as Chief Eunuch–endowed *mekteb*s usually were. The endowment deed says nothing about orphans, and the clothing that the students received at Ramadan consisted of accessories (cloak, fez, sash, socks) rather than the basics.[27]

As for the library, it housed what had to be one of the largest and most important book collections in Istanbul, if not in the entire empire. (This collection forms the core of the Süleymaniye Library's Hacı Beşir classification today.) Comprising 690 different works in 1,007 volumes, the book collection encompassed the usual classics of Qur'anic exegesis, *hadith* commentaries, and Hanafi jurisprudence but, in addition, histories and geographies, biographical compilations, works on grammar and morphology, medical works, mystical writings, poetry and *belles lettres* in Ottoman Turkish, Arabic, and Persian.[28] This was, in other words, not simply a collection of standard texts for madrasa students to consult. Small wonder that the library employed four "professional" librarians, each with the title *hafiz-i kütüb*, or "guardian of the books," as well as a book-binder (*mücellid*) and someone to sweep the library floor. The books, the endowment deed insists, must not be removed from the library; this prohibition applied even to books that were frequently studied or copied. We sense Beshir Agha's anxiety about damage to his collection, which must have taken him many years to amass and which undoubtedly included rare manuscripts presented to him as gifts by Ottoman and foreign dignitaries. When not in use, tellingly, the books were stored in a depot inside the complex's mosque, to the right of the *mihrab* (see Figure 9.2). Such a strategy conveyed the message that the books were a sacred treasure that potential readers should regard as somewhat taboo.

---

[27] Suleymaniye Library, MS Hacı Beşir 682, fols. 106a–109a, 112b–113a.
[28] Anonymous, *Defter-i kütübhane-i Beşir Ağa* (Istanbul, 1303/1885); Hathaway, *Beshir Agha*, 88–94.

Figure 9.2 El-Hajj Beshir's complex near Topkapı Palace and the book depot inside the mosque. Author's photos.

Founding a major Hanafi madrasa right next to the palace made a statement: while it was all well and good to train palace pages – and Beshir Agha had reaped the benefits of this education – the training of the ulema, including ulema who might help staff the imperial bureaucracy, was of at least equal importance. We can imagine, too, that Beshir's madrasa and library gave *imam*s, *khatib*s, *qadi*s, and muftis employed in the palace – perhaps including the Chief Mufti, with whom el-Hajj Beshir cultivated ties – a place to consult key books and scope out ulema-in-training.

Libraries and Book Endowments

A library did not have to be part of a madrasa or *dar al-hadith*, although it was ordinarily attached to a larger religious or educational complex. Nonetheless, the eighteenth century is known as an age of free-standing libraries. The first of note was actually established before the turn of the century: the Köprülü library, founded in 1678 by the future grand vizier Köprülü Fazıl Mustafa Pasha on the central Istanbul artery known as Divan Yolu, just east of the religious complex founded by his father Köprülü Mehmed Pasha.[29]

But library-building really took off during the reign of Ahmed III. The sultan's mother, Gülnuş Emetullah, included a library housing sixty-six book manuscripts in her mosque complex in Üsküdar, completed, as we saw in

---

[29] Istanbul, Köprülü Library, MS no. 4, fols. 20a–53a (25 Safer 1089/17 April 1678).

Chapter 7, in 1711.[30] Her son, not to be outdone, commissioned a free-standing library in the Third Court of Topkapı Palace in 1719. The building now houses various curatorial offices associated with the palace museum. The manuscripts that the library housed would form the core of the current Topkapı Palace Museum Library's collection, a major resource for scholars of Ottoman and Islamic history.[31] Ahmed's successor, Mahmud I, founded a small library inside Ayasofya in 1739, and another adjoining the Mosque of Mehmed the Conqueror in 1742.[32] A couple of decades later, the grand vizier and prolific intellectual Raghib Mehmed Pasha founded a 1,000-volume library in Istanbul's Laleli district.[33]

El-Hajj Beshir Agha is widely believed to have played a pivotal role in the palace library's construction, and even to have suggested it to the sultan. Notwithstanding, neither of the two major court chroniclers of this period, Mehmed Raşid Efendi and Silahdar Mehmed Agha, mentions any hand the Chief Eunuch may have had in it.[34] If he were, at least in part, responsible for the library's construction, then this was a foretaste of his impressive book-endowment activities later in his career. He ultimately endowed at least half a dozen major book collections, the most prominent of which were those connected to his complex near Topkapı, his *dar al-hadith* in Medina, a similar foundation at Eyüp, and possibly his madrasa in Svishtov. These endowments seem to go a step beyond the book-collecting of previous Chief Eunuchs. While, for example, Abbas Agha, who died in Cairo during the 1690s, left behind an impressive collection of illuminated Qur'ans and books on Hanafi law and a variety of other subjects,[35] neither he nor any other of el-Hajj Beshir's predecessors seems to have taken such pains to ensure the books' circulation and use.

Beshir also endowed more modest collections of books to existing institutions, notably al-Azhar in Cairo and the tomb of Abu Hanifa in Baghdad. At al-Azhar, he endowed a number of books to the residential college of the Turks (Riwaq al-Atrak), one of the ancient madrasa's twenty-five residential colleges, or *riwaq*s, each of which accommodated students from a particular region. The Riwaq al-Atrak was one of the few exclusively Hanafi colleges, and its students would have welcomed this infusion of seminal works of

---

[30] İpşirli Argıt, *Rabia Gülnuş Emetullah*, 184–85.
[31] *TDVİA*, s.v. "Ahmed III Kütüphanesi," by Semavi Eyice; Esin Atıl, *Levni and the* Surname: *The Story of an Eighteenth-Century Ottoman Festival* (Istanbul, 1999), 24, 26.
[32] http://ayasofyamuzesi.gov.tr/tr/içmi-mahmud-kütüphanesi; *TDVİA*, s.v. "Fatih Kütüphanesi," by İsmail Erünsal.
[33] Sadullah Enveri Efendi, *Sadullah Enveri Tarihi* (Bulaq, 1243/1827), II: 163, 178–79.
[34] Raşid, *Tarih-i Raşid*, V: 128–29; Silahdar, *Nusretname*, II: 384–85.
[35] Hathaway, "Wealth and Influence," 295, 297–301, 308–15; Hathaway, *Politics of Households*, 142 n. 15.

Hanafi jurisprudence and Qur'anic exegesis. This endowment was folded into the endowment of el-Hajj Beshir's *sebil-mekteb* in Cairo.[36] The endowment deed does not specify the conditions under which the books were to circulate.

Beshir's endowment to the mosque and tomb of Abu Hanifa is a different matter. A four-page endowment deed, housed in the Süleymaniye Library, lists the thirteen endowed books – all canonical works of Hanafi jurisprudence and exegesis – and stipulates that they may be borrowed but not taken out of the "neighborhood" (*mahalle*).[37] This last condition implies that the neighborhood around the mosque and tomb was inhabited by a solidly Hanafi population, including ulema and students in a position to use the books; in fact, the deed insists that the books are to be used by students. This was undoubtedly the case, for Abu Hanifa (d. 767 CE), the namesake of the Hanafi legal rite to which the Ottomans belonged, is regarded by Hanafis as "the greatest imam" (*al-imam al-a'dham*), and the tomb neighborhood is today known as Adhamiyya. The tombs of such luminaries attract pilgrims and the devout who simply wish to live nearby. So it probably seemed safe to allow limited circulation of the books so that, for example, elderly, shut-in scholars and scholars who taught students in their homes could have access to them.

There is no question that the Chief Harem Eunuch, and el-Hajj Beshir Agha above all, used *vakıf* to promote the circulation and use of books, above all books of Hanafi scholarship. But did the Chief Eunuch himself read the books that he endowed? In the case of a number of Chief Eunuchs and other high-ranking harem eunuchs, the answer is an unequivocal "Yes." These books were more than simply luxury gifts or canny investments. The Hanafi texts in Abbas Agha's and el-Hajj Beshir Agha's collections were, to a large extent, the works that harem eunuchs would have studied during their education in Topkapı Palace. At the very least, then, high-ranking harem eunuchs would have read these works as students. For many of them, though, reading went far beyond these student requirements. The scholarly Hoca Reyhan Agha, a companion of Turhan Sultan whom we encountered in Chapter 6 and will encounter again later, was as learned in the Islamic sciences as any member of the ulema. And Moralı Beshir Agha, according to the French merchant Jean-Claude Flachat, spent several hours a day reading in his impressive book collection.[38] In general, the Chief Eunuchs were known as bibliophiles, and to be a bibliophile certainly meant being a reader.[39]

[36] Badr and Crecelius, "*Awqaf* of al-Hajj Bashir Agha in Cairo," 301.
[37] Istanbul, Süleymaniye Library, MS Yazma Bağışlar 2524 (1146/1734).
[38] Flachat, *Observations*, II: 128.
[39] Pierre A. MacKay, "The Manuscripts of the *Seyahatname* of Evliya Çelebi – Part I: The Archetype," *Der Islam* 52, 2 (1975): 278.

El-Hajj Beshir Agha and Evliya Çelebi's *Seyahatname*. Only a committed reader could have reproduced and disseminated the great travel book, or *Seyahatname*, of the seventeenth-century courtier known as Evliya Çelebi (ca. 1611–82). El-Hajj Beshir Agha carried out this task in the last years of his life, and it may be his most important contribution to Ottoman intellectual culture.

Beshir acquired the *Seyahatname* from Cairo toward the end of his career. The author, Evliya Çelebi, had himself spent the last decade or so of his life in Cairo as the guest of the Qasimi grandee and pilgrimage commander Özbek Bey ibn Abu al-Shawarib Rıdvan Bey, whom he had met on the *hajj* in 1671–72. He completed his opus in Cairo, and there it remained when he died around 1682. Özbek Bey seems to have taken custody of it; on his death in 1719, it passed to his son Ibrahim Çelebi. In 1742, someone – perhaps one of Ibrahim Çelebi's sons – sent the original manuscript, ostensibly in Evliya's own hand, to Istanbul as a gift for el-Hajj Beshir Agha. We may speculate that the eunuch was already aware of the work, having perhaps learned of its existence during one of his brief sojourns in Cairo before he became Chief Harem Eunuch. El-Hajj Beshir dispatched the manuscript, in numerous portions, to Galatasaray, one of the sites outside Topkapı where palace pages were trained. Here, it was copied by some of these very pages.

The checkered history of the *Seyahatname* manuscripts has been exhaustively explored by the late Pierre MacKay.[40] Suffice it to say that el-Hajj Beshir endowed a complete copy to his library, but after his death, the volumes were dispersed and reassembled only decades later. Today, only different manuscripts of scattered volumes of the work remain in the Süleymaniye Library's Hacı Beşir Ağa collection, along with the other books from the eunuch's religious complex.

Beshir Agha almost certainly never met Evliya Çelebi, but he knew very well how important the *Seyahatname* was. In ten volumes, it covers most of the territory of the Ottoman Empire (with the notable exception of North Africa), offering descriptions and appraisals of the entire spectrum of Ottoman society: elites and commoners, urban and rural populations, religious and social institutions, samples of the languages of different populations, descriptions of key battles and important government officials, legends and tall tales. Nothing quite like it had ever been produced in Ottoman territory (or anywhere else), nor would ever be again. Introducing this unique work to the readership

---

[40] MacKay, "Manuscripts of the *Seyahatname*," 278–79, 293–94; Hathaway, *A Tale of Two Factions*, 152, 163–64; Jane Hathaway, "The Exalted Lineage of Rıdvan Bey Revisited: A Reinterpretation of the Spurious Genealogy of a Grandee in Ottoman Egypt," *International Journal of Turkish Studies* 13, 1–2 (2007): 99, 110.

of the Ottoman central lands was one of the greatest contributions to Ottoman literature that any individual ever made.

Yet even this landmark accomplishment was part of a broader tradition of Chief Eunuch contributions to Ottoman intellectual life. As we will see in Chapter 11, a number of Chief Eunuchs commissioned manuscripts, illuminated and otherwise, of histories of the Ottoman dynasty, festival books, and the like. These activities, combined with the Chief Eunuchs' habitual use of *vakıf* to endow books, helped to make books available, in a pre-print era, to the fraction of Ottoman society that was literate, meaning predominantly members of the court, the government bureaucracy, and the ulema. The books in turn helped to inculcate the forms of Sunni orthodoxy and Ottoman identity that the Chief Eunuchs endorsed.

Sufi Lodges (*Zaviyes*)

Quite a number of Chief Harem Eunuchs had Sufi tendencies, although few of them seem to have been attached to a single order (*tariqa*). The books that Abbas Agha left behind in Cairo at the time of his death include several classic works of medieval Muslim mysticism, before Sufi orders had taken shape to any significant degree: the medieval Persian mystic Farid al-Din 'Attar's (d. ca. 1221) *Conference of the Birds* (*Mantiq al-tayr*), an allegory of the soul's quest for spiritual fulfillment, the same author's compendium of the lives of mystical saints (*Tabaqat al-awliya'*), and *Kimiya-i sa'ada* (*The Alchemy of Happiness*), a late work by the great theologian al-Ghazali (d. 1111 CE) that helps to reconcile Sunni orthopraxy with mystical/spiritual fulfillment. (These, incidentally, were in the original Arabic and Persian, which Abbas and other Chief Harem Eunuchs read.) Another work in his collection was called *Qira'at al-awrad*, which can refer to parts of the Qur'an, known as *awrad*, to be read during private devotions supplemental to the five daily prayers, but also to the vocalized part of a Sufi mystical exercise, or *dhikr*.

Owning and reading mystical works paled in comparison to founding a lodge (*zaviye*) where members of specific Sufi orders could live and pursue mystical fulfillment. Such a lodge required many of the same things that a madrasa required: lodging, a mosque for daily prayers, kitchens, baths, toilets, maintenance workers. (This helps to explain why such lodges were often built as part of larger religious complexes.) Above all else, though, a lodge required a communal space, usually a round hall, where the order's distinctive mystical exercise, or *dhikr*, could be performed. And since each Sufi order's *dhikr* was distinctive, lodges were often, though not always, custom-built for specific orders.

The Ottoman court was famously close to the Mevlevi order, founded by the son of Mevlana ("our master") Jelal al-Din Rumi (1207–73) and particularly

active in the Ottoman central lands.[41] Yet no Chief Harem Eunuch ever
founded a Mevlevi lodge. On the other hand, several Chief Eunuchs
patronized two other mainstream orders, the Halvetis (Khalwatis) and the
Naqshbandis. Overall, though, the eunuchs seem to have been fairly eclectic
in the orders whose lodges they chose to patronize, so that we may speak of a
general support for "*tariqa* Sufism" – that is, Sufism that involved adherence to
an order – rather than, for example, the non-*tariqa erfan* mysticism popular in
Safavid and Qajar Iran (and in present-day Iran, for that matter).

Habeshi Mehmed Agha. We recall that Habeshi Mehmed Agha's landmark
religious complex in Istanbul's Çarşamba district included a Sufi lodge. This
lodge was affiliated with the Halveti order, which had taken shape in Azerbaijan in the fifteenth century and spread into Ottoman territory in the following
century as the order's shaykhs fled the expanding Safavids.[42] As Hafız
Hüseyin Ayvansarayi, the eighteenth-century author of a compendium of
descriptions of Istanbul's mosques, points out, the first shaykh of the lodge
was Yayabaşızade Hızır Efendi, who also offered instruction in Qur'anic
exegesis at Habeshi Mehmed's *dar al-hadith*; Habeshi Mehmed Agha apparently became his personal disciple. Habeshi Mehmed's adherence to the
Halveti order conformed to the spiritual proclivities of the Ottoman court
during the reign of his patron, Murad III. Murad's own obsessive devotion
to the Halveti shaykh known as Şeyh Şuca (d. 1582), who became his spiritual
confidant, has received quite a bit of scholarly attention.[43] Murad's mother,
Nurbanu Sultan, and the grand vizier Shemsi Ahmed Pasha (d. 1580), a
member of her circle, likewise endowed Halveti convents.[44]

El-Hajj Mustafa and Abbas Aghas. Two of the seventeenth-century Chief
Eunuchs whose endowments we have examined above, el-Hajj Mustafa Agha
and Abbas Agha, endowed Sufi lodges in Cairo whose *tariqa*s are unspecified.
El-Hajj Mustafa's was a restored *zaviye* adjoining a *wakala* on the Nile, en

---

[41] Halil Inalcik, *The Ottoman Empire: The Classical Age, 1300–1600*, trans. Norman Itzkowitz
   and Colin Imber (London, 1973), 190–91, 200–202.
[42] Ayvansarayi, *Garden of the Mosques*, 219; Necipoğlu, *Age of Sinan*, 500; John J. Curry, *The
   Transformation of Muslim Mystical Thought in the Ottoman Empire: The Rise of the Halveti
   Order, 1350–1650* (Edinburgh, 2010), 21–86; Nathalie Clayer, *Mystiques, état et société: les
   Halvetis dans l'aire balkanique de la fin du XVe siècle à nos jours* (Leiden, 1994). 6–35; B.G.
   Martin, "A Short History of the Khalwati Order of Dervishes," in *Scholars, Saints, and Sufis*,
   ed. Nikki R. Keddie (Berkeley, CA, 1972), 275–85, 290–97.
[43] Fleischer, *Bureaucrat and Intellectual in the Ottoman Empire*, 72, 74–75; Curry, *Transform-
   ation of Muslim Mystical Thought*, 76–77, 171, 175, 189, 215, 279.
[44] Zeynep Yürekli, "A Building between the Public and Private Realms of the Ottoman Elite: The
   Sufi Convent of Sokollu Mehmed Pasha in Istanbul," *Muqarnas* 20 (2003): 159–85; Aslı
   Niyazioğlu, "Dreams, Ottoman Biography Writing, and the Halveti Sünbüli Şeyhs of 16th-
   Century Istanbul," in *Many Ways of Speaking about the Self: Middle Eastern Ego-Documents
   in Arabic, Persian, and Turkish (14th–20th Century)*, eds. Ralf Elger and Yavuz Köse (Wiesbaden, 2010), 173.

route to Bulaq.[45] A document from the Topkapı archive dealing with Abbas Agha's endowments in Istanbul mentions a *zaviye* that he founded in Istanbul's Beşiktaş neighborhood, part of a small religious complex that also included a mosque (still standing); a *dershane*, seemingly a place for lectures; and a *mu'allimhane*, a training facility for Qur'an school teachers. He also founded a *zaviye*, along with a mosque, in Üsküdar on the Asian side of the Bosphorus. Remarkably, Abbas's agent (*vekil*), Cafer Bey (previously Agha) ibn Mehmed, is described as the former *baba*, or shaykh, of the Beşiktaş *zaviye*.[46] His Egyptian estate inventory likewise mentions a *zaviye* in Cairo.[47]

Unfortunately, neither document provides any details at all; in the case of the Cairo *zaviye*, this silence extends to where the structure is located. It is listed right after two properties outside Bab al-Futuh, the northern gate of the original Fatimid city of al-Qahira. Since a branch of the Halveti order was popular in this neighborhood,[48] we might speculate that Abbas's *zaviye* was likewise Halveti, but it is impossible to be sure. Perhaps these structures were used by more than one Sufi order, as occasionally happened.

El-Hajj Beshir Agha. As for el-Hajj Beshir Agha, he was quite eclectic in his Sufi endowments, to judge from the huge endowment deed that details many of his projects outside Egypt. He endowed stipends for food for several existing Istanbul lodges, including a lodge for archers near the Okmeydanı, the archery field north of the Golden Horn, and the lodge attached to the tomb of Lalizade Seyyid Abdülbaki Efendi (d. 1738) in Eyüp.[49] Neither lodge's affiliation is mentioned in the deed, and in the case of the archers, we simply do not know. But Lalizade, who served as chief judge (*qadi*) of Jerusalem, Cairo, Mecca, and finally Istanbul, was a "Bayrami-Melami," referring to the mystical tradition founded by the fourteenth-century Anatolian mystic Hajji Bayram-ı Veli, who was active in and around Ankara, and to the Melami "supra-order," as Victoria Holbrook has called it, a loose collectivity of Sufi shaykhs who had trained in other orders.[50] Lalizade himself wrote an authoritative description and history of the Melamis and the Bayramis.

[45] Wizarat al-Awqaf, No. 302/51, pp. 8–11.
[46] Topkapi Palace Archive, E 3941/2 (1082–83/1672–73), E 7833/2–7, cited in Chapter 6, n. 14.
[47] Topkapı Palace Archive D 7657 (undated); Hathaway, "Wealth and Influence," 296, 302, 305.
[48] Behrens-Abouseif, *Cairo of the Mamluks*, 283–84; Doris Behrens-Abouseif, "An Unlisted Monument of the Fifteenth Century: The Dome of Zawiyat al-Damirdaš," *Annales islamologiques* 18 (1982): 105–21; Doris Behrens-Abouseif, "Four Domes of the Late Mamluk Period," *Annales islamologiques* 17 (1981): 191–201; Doris Behrens-Abouseif and Leonor Fernandes, "Sufi Architecture in Early Ottoman Cairo," *Annales islamologiques* 20 (1984): 103–14.
[49] Süleymaniye Library, MS Hacı Beşir Ağa 682, fols. 115a, 116a.
[50] Süreyya, *Sicill-i Osmani*, III: 298–99; Victoria Rowe Holbrook, "Ibn 'Arabi and Ottoman Dervish Traditions: The Melami Supra-Order," Parts 1–2, *Journal of the Muhyiddin Ibn Arabi Society* 9 (1991): 18–35; 12 (1992): 15–33.

The rather mysterious and controversial Melamis combined devotion to the legendary medieval mystic Ibn Arabi's (1165–1240) concept of "unity of being" (*wahdat al-wujud*), according to which God is present in all of creation, with extreme humility and abhorrence of any sort of public profile. Melamis were sporadically persecuted during the sixteenth and seventeenth centuries, and went completely underground during the eighteenth, yet the order attracted influential Ottoman intellectuals and powerful government officials[51] – possibly including el-Hajj Beshir Agha.

On the other hand, Beshir Agha also restored the tomb of one of the greatest Halveti shaykhs buried in Istanbul, Sünbül Sinan Efendi (d. 1529),[52] which abuts the mosque of the grand vizier Koca Mustafa Pasha (d. 1512). Koca Mustafa's son-in-law, a devotee of Sünbül Efendi, constructed a lodge on the site for the Halveti suborder, known as the Sünbüliyye, that the shaykh founded, complete with forty cells for the distinctive Halveti seclusion rituals.[53] The shaykh is interred near the lodge, alongside several other Sünbüliyye leaders.[54]

As we saw in Chapter 7, el-Hajj Beshir endowed a number of infrastructural improvements in the neighborhood to which Koca Mustafa Pasha gave his name, north of the Sea of Marmara. His attraction to this quarter may have had more than a little to do with the presence there of Sünbül Efendi's lodge and tomb. By 1738, when Beshir restored the tomb, patronage of the Halveti order would have seemed even more natural than it had during Habeshi Mehmed Agha's day, for the Halvetis were now one of the most widespread Sufi orders in the Ottoman Empire, with branches in Anatolia, the Balkans, and the Arab lands.[55] (As noted above, the Sufi lodge attached to Cairo's Mahmudiyye madrasa, whose construction was overseen by el-Hajj Beshir's successor, was a Halveti lodge.) In addition to the tomb, he restored a small public fountain originally built in the early sixteenth century by one Hüsrev Bey.[56] Toward the end of his life, he provided for Qur'an recitation, prayers, and candle-lighting at the tomb.[57]

Even with all this, though, el-Hajj Beshir's most pronounced Sufi preference was for the Naqshbandi order. This order, which originated in Central Asia in the fourteenth century, spread to newly conquered Istanbul in the late fifteenth century and was present, though not entrenched, throughout much of the

---

[51] Holbrook, "Ibn 'Arabi and Ottoman Dervish Traditions," Part 1, 25–27.
[52] Süleymaniye Library, MS Hacı Beşir Ağa 682, fols. 114b–115a.
[53] *TDVİA*, s.v. "Sünbül Sinan," by Hür Mahmut Yücer; http://sumbulefendicami.com.
[54] Curry, *Transformation of Muslim Mystical Thought*, 70–73.
[55] Ibid., 89–291; Clayer, *Mystiques, état et société*, 143–79; Martin, "Short History of the Khalwati Order of Dervishes," 285–90, 297–305.
[56] Süleymaniye Library, MS Hacı Beşir Ağa 682, fols. 44b–45b.   [57] Ibid., fol. 115a.

empire by the late seventeenth century.[58] The Naqshbandi *tariqa* is known for its insistence on Sunni orthopraxy, which made it especially loathsome to the Safavids in Iran; a number of shaykhs fled before the Safavid advance. During el-Hajj Beshir Agha's tenure as Chief Harem Eunuch, the Mujaddidi variant of the Naqshbandi order, an uncompromisingly *shari'a*-minded interpretation of the Naqshbandi way pioneered by the reformist Indian mystic Ahmad Sirhindi (1564–1624), was sweeping through the Ottoman Arab lands and beginning to encroach on the imperial center. More pervasive than earlier incarnations of the order, it inspired exactly the kinds of endowments that el-Hajj Beshir made.

El-Hajj Beshir endowed a stipend for a Naqshbandi shaykh to teach al-Ghazali's magnum opus, *Ihya 'ulum al-din* (*Revivification of the Religious Sciences*) at the Shaykh ibn Wafa' Mosque near Abu Ayyub's tomb in Istanbul, where there had been a Naqshbandi presence since at least the mid-sixteenth century.[59] Meanwhile, the Sufi lodge at his religious complex near Topkapı Palace was a Naqhsbandi institution. This lodge was a residential compound run in much the same way as the nearby madrasa. The shaykh and his disciples lived in nine chambers surrounding the lodge proper, and most routine duties – sweeping, cooking, gate-keeping, the call to prayer – were divided among the residents. Like the complex's madrasa, the Sufi lodge was strictly for bachelors. "Apart from the shakyh," the endowment deed warns, "the residents are not to be married. If one of the residents marries, moves to another place, or dies, his place will be given to a sound student of the [religious] sciences."[60]

The Sufis and the madrasa students apparently ate together; the endowment deed is remarkably specific about their food, which on ordinary days consisted of bread, rice soup, rice pilaf, and mutton. On Friday nights, on 'Id al-Fitr and 'Id al-Adha, and during the entire month of Ramadan, the Sufis and disciples received additional rice and meat, and on completing a full Qur'an recitation, they received dates. Dates were also the reward for completing the *khatm al-Khwajagan*, a partially silent, partially vocalized recitation that the endowment deed describes as taking place on Mondays and Fridays "according to the

---

[58] Dina Le Gall, *A Culture of Sufism: Naqshbandis in the Ottoman World, 1450–1700* (Albany, NY, 2005), 17–94; Jürgen Paul, *Doctrine and Organization: The Khwajagan/Naqshbandiya in the First Generation after Baha'uddin* (Berlin, 1998); Arthur F. Buehler, *Sufi Heirs of the Prophet: The Indian Naqshbandiyya and the Rise of the Meditating Sufi Shaykh* (Columbia, SC, 1998); Halil İbrahim Şimşek, *Osmanlı'da Müceddidilik, XII./XVIII. Yüzyıl* (Ankara, 2004).

[59] Süleymaniye Library, MS Hacı Beşir Ağa 682, fols. 41b–42a; Le Gall, *A Culture of Sufism*, 18, 22, 43, 54.

[60] Süleymaniye Library, MS Hacı Beşir Ağa 682, fols. 109a–110b.

requirements of the Naqshbandi *tariqa*."[61] The deed also calls for occasional infusions of *zerde*, a festive "special occasion" pilaf made with saffron.

At his religious complex, then, el-Hajj Beshir Agha was not simply subsidizing an existing Sufi institution but founding a new one in order to train young, unmarried men in the rituals of the Naqshbandi order. The elaborate conditions for this Naqshbandi lodge spelled out in his endowment deed suggest the founder's genuine attachment to the order. These provisions also allowed for regular contact between the Naqshbandis-in-training and the madrasa students. Perhaps some madrasa students later joined the lodge. So while Beshir's ministrations to the lodge of Lalizade and the tomb of Sünbül suggest a healthy respect for the Bayrami-Melamis and the Halvetis, the lodge in his complex reflects a desire to spread, or at least to reinforce, the Naqshbandi order in the imperial capital.

The Kadızadeli Movement

In view of this consistent support, over a long period, for *tariqa* Sufism on the part of Chief Harem Eunuchs, it may come as a surprise that some influential harem eunuchs supported the greatest threat to organized Sufism ever to emerge in Ottoman territory. This was the Kadızadeli movement, a puritanical, militantly anti-innovationist strain of Hanafi Sunnism that first came to light in the early decades of the seventeenth century. As Madeline Zilfi has pointed out, the Kadızadelis' base consisted of provincial mosque preachers, mainly in Anatolia, who resented the Halvetis' near-monopoly of high-profile mosque preacher positions in Istanbul, Edirne, and Bursa toward the middle of the seventeenth century. In fact, the movement took its name from Kadızade Mehmed Efendi, a mosque preacher from Balıkesir in western Anatolia who won appointment to Istanbul's great Ayasofya mosque in 1631. The high point of Kadızade Mehmed's career came two years later, when, on the occasion of the Prophet's birthday, he successfully debated the Halveti shaykh Sivasi Efendi at the Sultan Ahmed Mosque in the presence of Sultan Murad IV. Yet the sultan was not particularly close to Kadızade Mehmed, and his movement's influence inside the palace remained limited.[62]

This situation changed with the next generation of Kadızadelis, led by Üstüvani Mehmed Efendi, a native of Damascus. In an attempt to garner influence inside the palace, Üstüvani appealed to those members of the court who could read and write, including the harem eunuchs. Among his chief targets was the influential harem eunuch Hoca ("Teacher") Reyhan Agha, the

---

[61] Ibid., fols. 110b–111a, 112a.
[62] Katib Çelebi, *The Balance of Truth*, trans. Geoffrey L. Lewis (London, 1957), 132–34; Zilfi, *Politics of Piety*, 131–38.

companion of Mehmed IV's mother, Turhan Sultan. Reyhan had been one of the harem eunuchs implicated in the murder of Turhan's hated mother-in-law, Kösem Sultan, in 1651; a few years later, he had helped to save the young Sultan Mehmed IV from assassination by the *hass oda* pages. Well known for his knowledge of Islamic theology and law, Reyhan tutored Mehmed IV in these and related subjects.

By the 1650s, Hoca Reyhan's influence was such that he, like the Chief Eunuch Behram Agha, could get virtually anyone he liked appointed to any court position.[63] According to Naima, Reyhan invited Üstüvani into the Third Court of Topkapı Palace so that he could counsel the young sultan; as a result, Üstüvani came to be known as the "sultan's shaykh" (*padişah şeyhi*).[64] The other side of this coin, of course, was that Reyhan Agha could arrange the deposition, ruination, or even death of anyone who ran afoul of him. The Kadızadelis benefited from this negative influence, too. When, in 1653, Üstüvani Mehmed Efendi and his fellow Kadızadelis took offense at a book by the popular mosque preacher Kürd ("Kurdish") Molla Mehmed, Hoca Reyhan intervened, along with the Chief Mufti, to have him exiled.[65] Even after Chief Eunuch Behram Agha was killed in the March 1656 Plane Tree Incident, the palace soldiery supported Üstüvani in their dealings with Behram's replacement, Dilaver Agha, who was Chief Eunuch from 1656 to 1658.[66]

Üstüvani's influence came to an abrupt end just a few months later, with Köprülü Mehmed Pasha's appointment as grand vizier, just as the Kadızadelis were preparing to launch an all-out assault on Istanbul's Sufi lodges. Alarmed at the public disorder that the movement appeared to be fomenting, Köprülü Mehmed exiled three Kadızadeli leaders, including Üstüvani, to Cyprus.[67] Generally speaking, Köprülü Mehmed's insistence on total administrative control meant that he could not tolerate the Kadızadelis as an alternative locus of power. Conversely, the extent of the Kadızadelis' influence at court by 1656 was one reason that he wanted unfettered authority.

For the Kadızadelis, this was unquestionably a setback, but the height of their influence was still to come – ironically, with the help of Köprülü Mehmed's son and successor as grand vizier, Köprülü Fazıl Ahmed Pasha. While governor of the northeastern Anatolian province of Erzurum, Fazıl Ahmed befriended the third great Kadızadeli leader, Vani Mehmed Efendi, then a mosque preacher in Erzurum. Recalled to Istanbul in 1661 to assume the grand vizierate, Fazıl Ahmed brought Vani Mehmed back with him.

---

[63] E.g., Naima, *Tarih-i Naima*, III: 1515.

[64] Ibid., III: 1290; IV: 1576–77, 1708; Zilfi, *Politics of Piety*, 141–43, 146.

[65] Naima, *Tarih-i Naima*, III: 1435.

[66] Topkapı Palace Archive, E 3606 (undated), implying that Reyhan may have outlived Dilaver.

[67] Abdurrahman Abdi, *Vekayiname*, 83–84; Silahdar, *Silahdar Tarihi*, I: 57–59; Zilfi, *Politics of Piety*, 146–47.

The Kadızadeli leader in short order became twenty-year-old Mehmed IV's personal spiritual counselor.

Yet there is no indication that the Chief Eunuchs of the later part of Mehmed IV's reign shared the Kadızadeli sympathies of the sultan or his grand vizier. As we saw above, Abbas Agha, who died in Cairo in the 1690s, left behind several mystical works and a Sufi lodge.[68] It is, of course, possible that Abbas's exile to Cairo in 1671 had something to do with his Sufi tendencies being unpalatable to Vani Mehmed and other Kadızadelis. If that were the case, though, we would expect to see pronounced Kadızadeli tendencies in his successors. But we do not. His immediate successor, the long-serving Yusuf Agha, showed no particular affinity for Vani Mehmed or for the Kadızadeli agenda in general. Yusuf, as we saw in Chapter 6, was instrumental in the execution of the grand vizier Kara Mustafa Pasha after the failed 1683 Ottoman siege of Vienna, which Vani had encouraged; this could hardly have been the action of someone close to Vani, who was rusticated as a result of the debacle.

The upshot seems to be that while the Kadızadelis definitely had sympathizers among the highest-ranking harem eunuchs, and counted perhaps the most scholarly harem eunuch in Ottoman history – who was, moreover, the sultan's mother's boon companion – as an adherent, the harem eunuchs' spiritual preferences and doctrinal sympathies at any given time were mixed. Sympathy for *tariqa* Sufism seems to have been deeply enough ingrained among the harem eunuchs as a whole that it never disappeared, even when the Kadızadelis were at the peak of their influence. The status of Kadızadeli influence among the eunuchs may reflect its status in Ottoman society at large: the Kadızadeli movement was not an all-encompassing ideology but a collection of puritanical attitudes that varied in intensity from place to place and from one sector of society to another, and that changed over time, much like the movement's membership.

Confessionalization and the Struggle for Orthodoxy

Perhaps above all else, the Kadızadeli movement reflects a struggle over the nature of Hanafi orthodoxy in the Ottoman realm, more specifically over the question of whether official Ottoman orthodoxy should accommodate a range of popular traditions, such as various Sufi rituals and visitation of the tombs of holy men. This struggle was an integral part of the seventeenth-century crisis, tied as it was to class tensions, tensions between the imperial capital and the provinces, and urban-rural tensions. Like these other sources of dissension within Ottoman society, the struggle between the Kadızadelis and the Sufi

---

[68] Hathaway, "Wealth and Influence," 295, 296, 299–300, 312–14.

orders played itself out over the course of the seventeenth century but was largely resolved, in favor of the Sufis, by the eighteenth.

At the same time, though, the Kadızadeli movement taps into the broader question of what historians of early modern Europe call confessionalization, that is, the adoption by a state of an official religious orthodoxy. In Europe, the "age of confessionalization" spanned the fifteenth through the seventeenth centuries, the period when each of the major western European kingdoms and empires officially adopted a particular branch of Christianity. The subjects of these polities constructed and publicly performed these various Christian orthodoxies by, for example, participating in state-sanctioned rituals and adopting state-sanctioned symbols.[69]

In recent years, the notion of "confessionalization" has caught on in the Ottoman field, as well, as a means of framing the Ottomans' increasing official emphasis, during roughly the same period, on their adherence to the majority Sunni sect of Islam and to the Hanafi legal rite of Sunnism.[70] In the Ottoman case, recognition of the sultan as caliph of the world's Sunni Muslims and public disparagement of the enemy Shi'ite Safavids were manifestations of confessionalization, as were the increasing numbers of conversions from Christianity to Sunni Islam. Public affirmation of Hanafi identity, through the use of running water for ablution before prayer and through observance of the later afternoon prayer, could also count as part of Ottoman confessionalization. So could ostentatious participation in or, on the other hand, vehement rejection of Sufi rituals.

The Kadızadeli movement represented something of a watershed in Ottoman confessionalization since it forced Ottoman society to take a public stand on whether *tariqa* Sufism could be part of Sunni Hanafi orthodoxy. An indicator of the Kadızadeli movement's divisiveness is the fact that it split the ranks of the harem eunuchs during the seventeenth century, with at least a few championing it while others held fast to Sufi practices. While stringently *shari'a*-minded and even puritanical, Kadızadeli-ism was by no means

---

[69] E.g., Heinz Schilling, "Confessional Europe," in *Handbook of European History, 1400–1600*, eds. Thomas A. Brady et al. (Leiden, 1995), II: 641–70; Wolfgang Reinhard, "Reformation, Counter-Reformation, and the Early Modern State: A Reassessment," *Catholic Historical Review* 75, 3 (1989): 385–403.

[70] Derin Terzioğlu, "Where *'Ilm-i hal* Meets Catechism: Islamic Manuals of Religious Instruction in the Ottoman Empire in the Age of Confessionalization," *Past and Present* 220 (2013): 79–114; Derin Terzioğlu, "How to Conceptualize Ottoman Sunnitization: A Historiographical Discussion," *Turcica* 44 (2012–13): 301–38; Guy Burak, "Faith, Law, and Empire in the Ottoman 'Age of Confessionalization' (15th–17th Century): The Case of 'Renewal of Faith,'" *Mediterranean Historical Review* 28, 1 (2013): 1–23; Guy Burak, *The Second Formation of Islamic Law: The Hanafi School in the Early Modern Ottoman Empire* (New York, NY, 2015); Tijana Krstić, *Contested Conversions to Islam: Narratives of Religious Change and Communal Politics in the Early Modern Ottoman Empire* (Stanford, CA, 2011).

anti-intellectual or anti-rationalist; some of its most famous proponents advocated the sort of rational inquiry that, as Khaled El-Rouayheb has shown, was permeating Ottoman intellectual life in the seventeenth century. This helps to explain its appeal to intellectuals such as Hoca Reyhan Agha.[71] But by the early eighteenth century, Sufism had won out and cemented its status as an integral part of Ottoman orthodoxy, even though pockets of anti-Sufi sentiment remained long after the Vienna debacle.

In opposing many Sufi practices as "unorthodox," though, the Kadızadelis enabled Ottoman society to espouse a related element of Sunni orthodoxy, namely, devotion to the Prophet Muhammad. Part of the Kadızadeli agenda was channeling the zeal of believers toward the Prophet and away from Sufi "saints" and other figures of popular piety. One of their chief intellectual inspirations for this stance was the sixteenth-century scholar (and mystic) Birgevi (a.k.a. Birgili) Mehmed Efendi, whose treatise *Al-Tariqat al-muhammadiyya* (*The Path of Muhammad*) describes a spiritual path that is not unlike that of certain Sufi orders (above all the Naqshbandis)[72] but that focuses exclusively on the Prophet and is devoid of mystical adepts who can serve as intermediaries. The Chief Harem Eunuch's professional identification with the Prophet Muhammad, through his supervision of the Evkafü'l-Haremeyn and his links to the Prophet's tomb in Medina, can only have impressed the Kadızadelis, perhaps even overriding Sufi sympathies among several occupants of the office.

Clearly, Chief Eunuch–endowed institutions conveyed the various elements of Ottoman orthodoxy – Sunnism, Hanafism, devotion to the Prophet, and, apart from the Kadızadeli interlude, *tariqa* Sufism – in different ways and to different degrees. El-Hajj Beshir Agha's *dar al-hadith* in Medina, for example, embodied devotion to the Prophet, but the works of Hanafi exegesis and jurisprudence that dominated its library simultaneously projected the Ottomans' official Hanafi identity. All Chief Eunuch foundations in Mecca and Medina, rather like the corps of eunuchs at the Prophet's tomb and the Ka'ba, likewise underlined the Sunni Ottomans' control of these holy sites in contradistinction to the Safavid Shi'ites and, later, Nadir Shah.

Overall, the Chief Eunuchs' overtly Hanafi endowments conveyed the broadest range of spiritual messages, for their connotations varied depending on where and when the institutions that they funded were established. El-Hajj Beshir Agha's book endowment at Abu Hanifa's tomb in Baghdad carried an implicitly anti-Shi'ite subtext, for Iraq was the historical zone of contention

---

[71] Khaled El-Rouayheb, *Islamic Intellectual History in the Seventeenth Century: Scholarly Currents in the Ottoman Empire and the Maghreb* (New York, NY, 2015), 14–18, 24–26, 175, 190–93, 294; Le Gall, *A Culture of Sufism*, 150–56.

[72] Le Gall, *A Culture of Sufism*, 112, 153; Michael A. Cook, *Commanding Right and Forbidding Wrong in Islamic Thought* (Cambridge, 2000), 323–30.

between the Ottomans and the Safavids, and Abu Hanifa's tomb was a prime symbol of the two empires' struggle. Whenever the Safavids conquered Baghdad, they promptly razed the tomb, only to have the Ottomans restore it when they won the city back.[73] The same eunuch's madrasa in Svishtov, on the other hand, served as an island of Hanafi Sunnism in an Orthodox Christian sea. In Cairo, meanwhile, el-Hajj Beshir's and Moralı Beshir's Hanafi Qur'an schools took up the implicit challenge of similar structures erected by powerful local notables.

Generally speaking, the Hanafi emphasis is noticeably heavier in the eighteenth-century endowments, for reasons that are not immediately clear. The Kadızadeli movement, despite its ultimate defeat, may have galvanized Hanafi identity among Ottoman ulema. In Egypt, the growing prominence of Shafi'i and Maliki ulema, above all at al-Azhar, was also surely a factor. In Iraq, and perhaps in the holy cities as well, the challenge of Nadir Shah's proposed Ja'fari *madhhab* could have something to do with the Hanafi reaction since it potentially gave Twelver Shi'ism a new Sunni framework within which to win sympathizers. By the early eighteenth century, the days when the Chief Eunuch could endow a foundation catering to a non-Hanafi rite, as el-Hajj Mustafa Agha had done a century earlier, were clearly over.

Confessionalization was a social process that manifested itself in public spaces. As such, it was performative inasmuch as the community of believers publicly enacted their orthodoxy, for example by publicly washing with running water before the Friday noontime prayer. Not surprisingly, the Chief Harem Eunuch's endowments provided for public performance of Ottoman orthodoxy. The Qur'an schools, madrasas, and religious complexes that various Chief Eunuchs founded were all publicly visible as architectural spaces, and the students, dervishes, mendicants, and religious functionaries who took part in the activities of these institutions were publicly visible in and around them. Calls to prayer, Friday sermons, recitation of Hanafi texts, and even some Sufi rituals were publicly audible. Repeated public performance of orthodox identity, of the sort that these eunuch-sponsored institutions made possible, contributed to Ottoman confessionalization.

Though they were not, technically, contributions to Ottoman religious or intellectual life, the Chief Eunuchs' graves or tombs were part of their public visibility and could express devotion to the Prophet, to the sultan, or to some other highly charged figure through their placement, inscriptions, and decoration. Pictorial representations of the Chief Eunuch could serve a similar purpose, even though they were seen by far fewer people. Chapter 11 explores these monuments as a means of memorializing the Chief Harem Eunuch.

---

[73] Alvise Contarini, in *Relazioni di ambasciatori veneti al Senato*, XIII: 389.

10   Reformed Out of Existence
The Dénouement of the Chief Harem Eunuch

All the noteworthy examples that Chapter 9 provided of Chief Harem Eunuch sponsorship of Ottoman religious and intellectual life came from before the end of the eighteenth century. This is no coincidence, for the Chief Harem Eunuch's influence was unquestionably waning by then (see Table 10.1). Ottoman court chronicles of the late eighteenth and early nineteenth centuries give us some idea of the Chief Eunuch's changing status in the wake of the lengthy and distinguished career of el-Hajj Beshir Agha and the (relatively) short and (very) tumultuous careers of Moralı Beshir and Ebu'l-Vukuf Ahmed. Whereas the Chief Eunuch is a frequent character in the political narratives of the seventeenth and early eighteenth centuries, he is very seldom mentioned in the major chronicles of the later period, such as those of Sadullah Enveri (1735–94), Ahmed Vasif (ca. 1730–1806), Ayntabi Ahmed Asım (a.k.a. Mütercim Seyyid Ahmed Asım, 1755–1820), and Şanizade Mehmed Ataullah (1771–1826). In an unmistakable sign of the times, the most space that Sadullah devotes to any Chief Eunuch in his chronicle occurs in his account of the death of Ebu'l-Vukuf Ahmed Agha's successor, Musahib Beshir Agha (term 1757–68), who was accidentally poisoned by a medical quack.[1]

The Chief Eunuch's scribe (Darüssaade Ağası *katibi* or *yazıcı*), who registered pious donations to the holy cities, was almost more likely to receive mention, not least because this office occasionally appears along the career trajectory leading to the grand vizierate. The post had been a path to influential office since at least the later seventeenth century; as we saw in Chapter 6, Hamza Pasha, the governor of Egypt just before Yusuf Agha's deposition, owed his position to his earlier service as Yusuf's scribe. A century later, İzzet Mehmed Pasha, briefly grand vizier on two separate occasions (1774–75 and 1781–82), was named Darüssaade Ağası *katibi* early in his career, largely because of his links to the Teberdar corps, that is, the Old Palace halberdier

---

[1] Sadullah Enveri, *Sadullah Enveri Tarihi*, II: 251. On Ahmed Vasif, see Ethan L. Menchinger, *The First of the Modern Ottomans: The Intellectual History of Ahmed Vasif* (New York, NY, 2017).

Table 10.1 *Major officers of the harem and Third Court from the late eighteenth to the early twentieth centuries*[a]

	Harem	Third Court (or equivalent in later palaces)	
		Sword-Bearer (Silahdar) (until 1830)	
Sultan's Mother	Chief Harem Eunuch	**Gate of Felicity**	**Privy Chamber**
	Cevher Mehmed (twice)	**(Babüssaade)**	**(Hass Oda)**
	Sarıkçı Beshir		
	Idris	Palace Treasurer	Valet (Çuhadar)
	Büyük Bilal	(Hazinedar Başı)	*Abdulfettah*
	Halid	*Ebe Selim (deputy)*	
	Küçük Bilal		Stirrup-Holder
	Mercan		(Rikabdar)
	Kasım		
	Anber		Privy Chamber Head
	Hafız Isa		(Hass Oda Başı)
	Harem Treasurer (Hazinedar-i Şehriyari)		
	Bekir		
	Büyük Bilal		
	Halid		
	Küçük Bilal		
	Anber		
	Treasury Agent (Hazine Vekili)		
	Büyük Bilal		
	Küçük Bilal		
	Nezir		
	Mehmed Lazoğlu (in Egypt)		
	Companions (Musahibs)		
	Büyük Bilal		
	Küçük Bilal		
	Cevher		
	Nadir		

[a] Italics indicate individuals named in the chapter.

regiment that was close to the Chief Eunuch.[2] But this post was no longer the exclusive preserve of high-ranking military administrators. In the 1760s,

[2] Ahmed Vasif Efendi, *Mehasinü'l-asar ve haka'ikü'l-ahbar*, ed. Mücteba İlgürel (Ankara, 1994), 125; Ahmed Asım Efendi, *Asım Tarihi* (Istanbul, 1284/1867), II: 53; d'Ohsson, *Tableau général*, VII: 32; II: 363, 368; Subhi, *Subhi Efendi Tarihi*, I: 41.

Sadullah Enveri has at least two bureaucrats holding the office, while in 1789, according to Ahmed Asım, the Second Coffee-Maker assumed the position.[3]

In contrast, the grand vizier is virtually omnipresent in these chronicles. Over the course of the eighteenth century, in fact, the Ottoman Empire's grand viziers steadily increased their influence at the expense not only of the Chief Eunuch and the other officers of the harem but also of the *hass oda* officials, notably the *silahdar*, or sultan's sword-bearer, who, as we saw in Chapters 6 and 7, now headed the Third Court pages. This kind of displacement became possible only when the grand vizier ceased to come from among the officers of the *hass oda* himself. By the mid-eighteenth century, grand viziers were routinely coming from the Ottoman chancery, notably from the office of *reisü'l-küttab*, or chief scribe, whose importance was increasing as he began to take the lead in foreign diplomacy. Rami Mehmed Pasha was the first *reisü'l-küttab* to become grand vizier, although he served in the latter post for only seven months in 1703 before being deposed in the wake of the Edirne Incident. He was succeeded by a string of more traditional military types. By the mid-eighteenth century, though, the pattern was well established and culminated in the grand vizierate of the much-revered Koca Raghib Mehmed Pasha from 1757 to 1763.

Raghib Pasha, as we have seen, went to some lengths early in his grand vizierate to rein in the Chief Harem Eunuch Ebu'l-Vukuf Ahmed Agha. His efforts were part of a trend dating to the attempts of Silahdar Damad Ali Pasha (term 1713–16) to halt the importation of eunuchs from East Africa, which went hand-in-hand with his efforts, and those of his predecessor Çorlulu Ali Pasha (term 1701–10), to make the *silahdar*, as opposed to the Chief Threshold Eunuch, the leading figure in the Third Court. These grand vizierial initiatives seem to reflect an awareness that the harem and threshold eunuchs could still wield significant influence over palace politics. And yet the growing number of grand viziers from the chancery and their increasing authority as the eighteenth century wore on meant that the chancery was able effectively to transcend the competition between the harem and the Third Court. By the late eighteenth century, the locus of political authority in the imperial capital had, to a large degree, shifted from inside the palace to the grand vizier's residence at Bab-i Ali. Inside the palace, meanwhile, the sultan's household was still headed by the familiar duo of the *silahdar*, or alternatively the Baş Çuhadar (chief valet), representing the Third Court, and the Chief Harem Eunuch, representing the harem. Now, though, they functioned more as a team than as rivals.

---

[3] Sadullah Enveri, *Sadullah Enveri Tarihi*, 175, 215, 235; Ahmed Asım, *Asım Tarihi*, II: 53.

The Late Eighteenth-Century Reform Trajectory

In these altered circumstances, the Ottoman state confronted the need for military and administrative reform in the wake of a string of disastrous military losses to the Russian and Habsburg empires. Following the humiliating 1774 treaty of Küçük Kaynarca, which brought the first Russo-Ottoman war to a close, the Ottomans were obliged to cede masses of territory to Russia and the Habsburg Empire and to declare the Crimea independent, while allowing Russia the right to intervene on behalf of Orthodox Christians in Ottoman territory.[4]

Sultan Abdülhamid I (r. 1774–89), who had the grim duty of presiding over the empire during this debacle, recognized the necessity of bringing new European military practices and strategies to the Ottoman armed forces, just as Russia had done under Peter the Great several decades earlier. Earlier sultans had already hired what today would be called European military advisors, most notably Comte de Bonneval, the French renegade artillery expert who came to be known as Humbaracı Ahmed Pasha (1675–1747), and the Franco-Hungarian officer Baron de Tott (1733–93).[5] De Tott organized the empire's first formal course in naval science, which he offered at the fledgling naval engineering school opened in 1773 near the imperial shipyards in Istanbul's Kasımpaşa neighborhood. The school's instructors were initially European experts like de Tott. Abdülhamid's government expanded the school, renaming it the Imperial Naval Engineering School, and provided for the translation into Ottoman Turkish of European technical manuals.[6]

Selim III, a nephew of Abdülhamid who succeeded his uncle in April 1789, not only retained Abdülhamid's innovations but embarked upon the most sweeping military and administrative reforms that the Ottoman Empire had seen up to that point. He brought in more European military instructors and technical advisors, added a military science school to the naval engineering school, and, most controversially, created an entirely new army on the European model, complete with European-style form-fitting uniforms – the first ever seen in Ottoman lands – and a brand-new barracks (still standing) on the Sea of Marmara. Here, the soldiers could drill and maintain preparedness, very much unlike the Janissaries, who by 1789 were a fighting force only on paper. (Those who still called themselves Janissaries and, most importantly,

---

[4] Gabriel Noradounghian, *Recueil d'actes internationaux de l'Empire ottoman*, vol. 1: *1300–1789* (Paris, 1897), 319–34; Aksan, *An Ottoman Statesman in War and Peace*, 166–67.

[5] Virginia H. Aksan, "Enlightening the Ottomans: Tott and Mustafa III," in *International Congress on Learning and Education in the Ottoman World: Istanbul, 12–15 April 1999*, ed. Ali Çaksu (Istanbul, 2001), 163–74.

[6] Stanford J. Shaw, *Between Old and New: The Ottoman Empire under Selim III, 1789–1807* (Cambridge, MA, 1971), 153–54.

still collected the Janissary salary, were for the most part merchants of various kinds.)[7] The army and the new administrative apparatus that went with it were known collectively as the Nizam-i Cedid, or New Order. To pay for the new army, Selim created a special treasury, the İrad-i Cedid, whose agents reviewed the military payrolls and removed those who were receiving salaries or grants of revenue-collection rights without performing service.[8]

Although most of Selim's reforms were military and fiscal, he did introduce a far-reaching diplomatic innovation. For the first time in history, the Ottoman Empire opened permanent embassies in the capitals of Europe, beginning with London in 1792 and proceeding through Berlin and Vienna in 1795 to post-revolution Paris in 1796.[9] The new ambassadors came from the ulema and the chancery, and in many respects, they can be seen as the logical outcome of the increasing importance of diplomacy in Ottoman geopolitical strategy ever since the 1699 Treaty of Karlowitz, and the corresponding growth in influence of the *reisü'l-küttab*.[10] The *reisü'l-küttab*'s newly authoritative position, in turn, reflects the steadily escalating influence of the grand vizier and his chancery in the course of the eighteenth century, at the expense of palace officials, very much including the Chief Eunuch.

New Harem Eunuch Career Trajectories

The Chief Harem Eunuchs were not at the forefront of these reforms. No Chief Eunuch joined the inner circle around Selim that proposed, debated, and attempted to implement the reforms, even though the sultan's mother was a member. In general, harem eunuchs, and the Chief Eunuch above all, took the role of conservatives, preserving the traditions of the empire that had made their careers possible. El-Hajj Beshir Agha's stand against Nadir Shah's Ja'fari legal rite proposal was thus in many respects typical of the Chief Eunuch's conservative attitude, although Beshir Agha's successors did not interfere in foreign policy to the extent that he did. (The only exception to this rule was the attempts of Cevher Mehmed Agha, Chief Harem Eunuch under Mustafa III and Abdülhamid I, to promote British mediation to end the Russo-Ottoman war of 1768–74.)[11]

---

[7] Virginia H. Aksan, "Whatever Happened to the Janissaries? Mobilization for the 1768–1774 Russo-Ottoman War," *War in History* 5, 1 (1998): 23–36.

[8] Shaw, *Between Old and New*, 112–79.

[9] Ibid., 186–91; Stéphane Yerasimos, ed. and trans., *Deux ottomans à Paris sous le Directoire et l'Empire: relations d'ambassade* (Paris, 1998).

[10] Rifaat A. Abou-El-Haj, "Ottoman Diplomacy at Karlowitz," *Journal of the American Oriental Society* 87, 4 (1967): 498–512.

[11] M.S. Anderson, "Britain and the Russo-Turkish War of 1768–74," *English Historical Review* 69, 270 (1954): 51–52.

This did not mean, however, that all Chief Harem Eunuchs were implacably opposed to the reforms. A famous miniature painting shows one of Selim III's early Chief Eunuchs standing just behind the grand vizier Koca Yusuf Pasha (term 1791–92), who in turn stands just behind Selim, as they review the new Nizam-i Cedid troops from a ceremonial tent.[12] Since the scene took place in 1792, the pictured Eunuch must be Halid Agha, who served from 1791 to 1798.

At the same time, the career path that led to the office of Chief Eunuch during Selim's reign reflected the reform agenda. Offices attached to the harem treasury loomed larger than ever. We recall that during the late seventeenth century, under the Köprülü grand viziers, the office of harem treasurer (*hazinedar-i şehriyari*) became a veritable prerequisite for those who would be Chief Eunuch. A century later, a new post entered the promotional track: *hazine vekili*, literally "agent of the treasury," which now became a stepping-stone to harem treasurer. This office apparently originated in the Old Palace, home to the concubines and female family members of deceased or deposed sultans; the Armenian dragoman Mouradgea d'Ohsson, writing at the end of the eighteenth century, describes the *hazine vekili* as a prime candidate to succeed the chief of the Old Palace eunuchs.[13] Harem treasurer, though, remained the immediate precursor to the office of Chief Eunuch. If this new office worked in the same manner as that of harem treasurer, then part of its purpose was to check the power of the Chief Eunuch by filling the ranks below him with eunuchs who were not his protégés.

Significantly, this new office first emerged as a critical step in the Chief Harem Eunuch career trajectory at the time of Selim's accession, when one of his *musahib*s, Bilal Agha (later known as Büyük Bilal, or Bilal the Elder), assumed it. Bilal must certainly have been part of Selim's household in the *kafes*, the "cage" at the rear of the harem where Selim spent the dozen or so years between reaching puberty and taking the throne. In the space of a few months, Bilal rose to harem treasurer, then, on the deposition of Idris Agha in 1790, to Chief Eunuch. In an unusual twist to the typical harem eunuch career trajectory, Bekir Agha, the harem eunuch who served as treasurer for a number of years while Idris was Chief Eunuch, was not allowed to slip easily into the highest office.[14] This suggests that Selim and his advisors were eager to install a Chief Eunuch who was unequivocally a member of the new sultan's household. Büyük Bilal might conceivably have assisted in the reforms but for health problems that confined him to his quarters for long periods and

---

[12] This painting has been reproduced repeatedly, yet attribution is hard to come by.
[13] D'Ohsson, *Tableau général*, VII: 55; Tayyarzade Ahmed Ata, *Osmanlı Saray Tarihi: Tarih-i Enderun*, ed. Mehmet Arslan (Istanbul, 2010), I: 362, 364.
[14] Vasif, *Mehasinü'l-asar*, 112, 240.

caused him to delay in handling harem matters. He died in office in 1792 and was, predictably, succeeded by the harem treasurer, Halid Agha.

While Halid had not been *hazine vekili* before becoming harem treasurer, his successor, Küçük Bilal, or Bilal "the Younger," did follow this trajectory. The historian Ahmed Asım Efendi provides a necrology for the younger Bilal that reveals that he was raised in the household of Ivaz Mehmed Pashazade Halil Pasha, who was briefly (December 1769–December 1770) grand vizier under Mustafa III, and entered the palace when Halil Pasha presented him to the sultan.[15] His palace career recapitulates that of Büyük Bilal and suggests that he, too, belonged to Selim's princely household. Like the elder Bilal, he became a *musahib* when Selim was enthroned, then quickly moved through the ranks of *hazine vekili* and *hazinedar* while Halid Agha was Chief Eunuch. He certainly impressed Ahmed Asım: "He was like a second Koca Beshir Agha," the historian enthuses, referring to the legendary el-Hajj Beshir.[16] When he died in March 1807, Küçük Bilal was succeeded by Mercan Agha, who, in the opinion of both Ahmed Asım and the late nineteenth-century historian Ahmed Cevdet Pasha, paved the way for Selim III's downfall and was abetted by the *hazine vekili* Nezir Agha.[17]

Reform and the Evkafü'l-Haremeyn

The Hijaz was a bigger problem for Selim than it had been for his predecessors. The region had been administered by the *sharif*s of Mecca, descendants of the Prophet Muhammad and originally Zaydi Shi'ites, since the early thirteenth century.[18] At the time of Selim's enthronement, the legendary Sharif Sarur ibn Mas'ad (r. 1772–88) had just died, a paragon of bravery and justice who expelled the rival sharifian families from the Hijaz and ushered in a period of unity and commercial prosperity. On his death, however, his ambitious younger brother Ghalib usurped the sharifate, which Sarur had hoped would pass to one of his two sons.

The eunuchs of the *sharif*'s court became entangled in the struggle, too. The historian Abdüşşekür Efendi, as quoted by Ahmed Cevdet, relates how Ghalib, well familiar with the influence of court eunuchs, imprisoned Sarur's personal chief eunuch, Yahya Saltuh Agha, "who secretly planned to cause upheaval and rebellion," according to Abdüşşekür. Yet the eunuch managed to escape and flee to Sarur's two sons, Muhammad and Abdallah, who hid him. Muhammad then challenged Ghalib militarily, bombarding his house so

[15] Ahmed Asım, *Asım Tarihi*, I: 246; Süreyya, *Sicill-i Osmani*, II: 24.
[16] Ahmed Asım, *Asım Tarihi*, I: 246.
[17] Ibid., II: 163, 183, 197; Ahmed Cevdet, *Tarih-i Cevdet* (Istanbul, 1854–85), VIII: 418.
[18] Peters, *Mecca*, 232, 351–52, 370–71.

heavily that "in the *harem-i şerif* [the Great Mosque of Mecca] prayers could not be performed, not even the Friday prayer."[19] In the end, though, Muhammad was defeated and captured, along with Abdallah, who was still only a young boy.

At this point, Yahya Saltuh fled to Istanbul, where he petitioned Selim III to transfer the late Sarur's charitable soup kitchen (*imaret*) to Abdallah's nominal supervision rather than allowing Sharif Ghalib to administer it. But the new sultan did not act on the petition, and Yahya Saltuh departed for Cairo, where he presumably lived out his life. "Look at this crook," Abdüşşekür rants, "who transfers an *imaret* to an underage boy in order to take the reins of power into his own hands, and causes a huge insurrection in Mecca, the dwelling-place of God!"[20] This, Abdüşşekkür – and by extension Cevdet – clearly believed, was what happened when eunuchs interfered in politics. Abdüşşekür's diatribes may not be as vitriolic as those of Mustafa Ali (Chapter 8) and Derviş Abdullah Efendi (Chapter 7), but they amply demonstrate that bias against African eunuchs was still alive and well among the Ottoman intelligentsia.

This incident would have been worrisome to the Chief Eunuch, at the time Idris Agha, not because a court eunuch was mistreated – or fomented rebellion, depending on one's viewpoint – but because charitable foundations such as Sarur's *imaret* were attached to the Evkafü'l-Haremeyn. Selim himself was concerned that such *imaret*s were in poor repair empire-wide. For this reason, a key measure of his reform program was to overhaul the administration of the Evkaf.

Collection of revenues for the foundations had long been farmed out to provincial grandees, as we saw in Chapter 8. Notables such as Hasan Agha Bilifya, whom we met in that chapter, had held the tax farms of particular Evkaf villages for decades, well before Sultan Mustafa III (r. 1757–74) officially extended the life-tenure tax farm known as *malikane* to the Evkafü'l-Haremeyn, in effect giving official sanction to a practice that was already entrenched. Mustafa III's formidable grand vizier Raghib Mehmed Pasha, as part of his overall campaign to curb the Chief Harem Eunuch's influence, ordered the imperial chief financial officer, or *defterdar*, to inspect the Evkaf registers, but after Raghib's death in 1763, this duty reverted to the Chief Eunuch, who, at least by d'Ohsson's account, became even more influential than ever in assigning vacant supervisory positions to his clients.[21] But now, the reform treasury, or İrad-i Cedid, took over the tax farms and reassigned them to the *mütevelli*s of the foundations, that is, the local supervisors under the ultimate jurisdiction of the Chief Eunuch. The *mütevelli*s would have been provincial notables themselves, of course, but there were only a handful of

---

[19] Cited in Ahmed Cevdet, *Tarih-i Cevdet*, IV: 379.   [20] Ibid., IV: 380.
[21] D'Ohsson, *Tableau général*, II: 534–36.

them, as opposed to tens of tax-farmers of the old kind, and so they were presumably far easier to control.[22]

When Selim deposed Idris Agha in 1790, replacing him with his client Büyük Bilal, he sent Idris not to Cairo but to Medina, where he became head of the eunuchs guarding the Prophet Muhammad's tomb. So far from representing a departure from the norm, however, this was part of an ongoing trend. The trend seems to have begun with Sarıkçı ("Turban-Bearer") Beshir Agha, Abdülhamid I's first Chief Eunuch, who was sent to Medina on his deposition in 1779. He was joined there four years later by his successor, Cevher Mehmed Agha, who was serving his second term as Chief Eunuch: from July 1772 to February 1774, he had been Mustafa III's last Chief Eunuch but had been recalled to the palace from Cairo shortly before Sarıkçı Beshir was deposed. From that point until the office of Chief Eunuch was discontinued in the wake of the Young Turk Revolution, virtually all Chief Eunuchs who did not die in the palace headed for Medina when they left office.

Sending deposed Chief Eunuchs directly to Medina may have begun when Sarur was *sharif* of Mecca in order to keep watch over him since, after all, there were no rival sharifian families to keep him in check. Once he was dead, however, a permanent palace representative in the Hijaz became imperative to keep tabs on the wily Sharif Ghalib. Ghalib profited immensely from the customs duties at Jidda, where Indian ships bearing coffee from Yemen called en route to Suez, and from provisioning the pilgrims who came to Mecca every year.[23]

When the French occupied Egypt in 1798, Napoleon magnanimously allowed the pilgrimage caravan to continue going to Mecca every year and appointed the deputy (*kethüda*) of the Ottoman governor of Egypt as the pilgrimage commander for 1799. Sharif Ghalib happily accepted the French, who occupied Suez in December of that year, as protectors of the Red Sea coffee trade, in which he had an enormous stake.[24] In other words, the Prophetic descendant who governed Mecca on behalf of the Ottoman sultan was, for all practical purposes, in league with the occupier of the Ottomans' most lucrative province. With the French in residence, Cairo was off-limits as a destination for deposed Chief Eunuchs, and with the subsequent rise of Mehmed Ali Pasha, the practice of exiling Ottoman harem eunuchs to Cairo came to an end.

The Wahhabis. Scarcely had the French departed Egypt in 1801, under an agreement negotiated with the Ottomans and the British,[25] when the Wahhabis erupted into the Hijaz from their native territory of the Najd, deep in the interior of the Arabian Peninsula. Followers of a stringently puritanical

---

[22] Ibid., II: 536–39; Ahmed Cevdet, *Tarih-i Cevdet*, VI: 151–52, 219–20.
[23] Peters, *Mecca*, 226–28.   [24] Ibid., 232–36.   [25] Al-Jabarti, *'Aja'ib al-athar*, III: 213–28.

interpretation of Sunni Islam promulgated by the Najdi scholar Muhammad ibn 'Abd al-Wahhab, they regarded the rule of the Ottoman sultan as illegitimate; hence the territories in the Arabian Peninsula that their tribal armies, commanded by the chieftain Muhammad ibn Saud, conquered were effectively removed from the Ottoman domains. Their swift camel cavalry occupied Medina in 1803 and Mecca in 1805, leaving Sharif Ghalib, to say nothing of Sultan Selim, in a state of shock.

By the terms of Wahhabi doctrine of that era, the corps of eunuchs who guarded the Prophet's tomb in Medina and the smaller corps who guarded the Ka'ba were an unacceptable innovation to the *sunna*, or custom, of the Prophet Muhammad. After all, the eunuch corps dated only to the Ayyubid, or perhaps the Zengid, era, some 550 years after the Prophet's death. When they occupied the holy cities, then, the Wahhabis removed the eunuchs from their positions, even though they did not punish them or threaten them with violence. Many eunuchs fled to Egypt, including the Chief Tomb Eunuch at the time, Anber Agha, who arrived in Cairo with the Ottoman chief judge of Medina.[26]

Mehmed Ali Pasha, the enterprising governor of Egypt from 1805 to 1848, finally removed the Wahhabis from the Hijaz with the sultan's blessing in 1811. This did not mean, however, that Ottoman control of the Hijaz resumed as if nothing had happened. For one thing, the Wahhabis and their Saudi allies remained in control of the Najd, despite periodic expeditions into that region by Mehmed Ali's sons and their armies. This meant that the Wahhabis posed a constant threat right up until they reconquered the Hijaz in the early twentieth century. Meanwhile, Mehmed Ali did not simply hand the Hijaz back to Mahmud II once he had ousted the Wahhabis. Instead, he administered it himself through the redoubtable Sharif Ghalib, who died in 1813, and his successors. Full Ottoman authority was restored to the holy cities only in 1841, after Mehmed Ali's armies had withdrawn from Syria, which they occupied from 1830 to 1840, under a British-brokered agreement.

Even during this period of Egyptian control, however, deposed Chief Harem Eunuchs continued to arrive in Medina to lead the corps of tomb eunuchs. No doubt in part because of the Wahhabi threat, moreover, the number of eunuchs guarding the Prophet's tomb and the Ka'ba increased dramatically over the course of the nineteenth century. While visitors at the end of the eighteenth century and the beginning of the nineteenth century counted forty to fifty eunuchs at the Prophet's tomb and twenty to forty at the Ka'ba, Sir Richard Francis Burton, who made the pilgrimage in disguise in the 1850s, reports 120 eunuchs at the tomb and eighty at the Ka'ba.[27] Larger numbers of pilgrims, taking advantage of nineteenth-century improvements in long-distance

---

[26] Ahmed Asım, *Asım Tarihi*, 305, 310.
[27] Burckhardt, *Travels in Arabia*, 158; Burton, *Personal Narrative*, II: 319.

transportation and communication, also help to explain the bigger eunuch guard. In view of the Wahhabi presence so close to the Hijaz, the Ottoman central government probably felt that a well-connected Şeyhü'l-Harem and formidable retinues of eunuchs at the Prophet's tomb – which the Wahhabis had wanted to destroy to prevent visitors from "worshipping" it – and the Ka'ba would underline the Ottomans' authority in the holy cities.

Selim III's Deposition and Execution

Selim III's reforms had their vocal critics and their implacable enemies. Chief among these were the Janissaries and the mercenaries who served as their auxiliaries, all of whom saw their interests threatened by the Nizam-i Cedid army. They were joined by the entrenched palace interest groups, who were similarly threatened by the new treasury's review of their grants of revenue and the reformists' dependence on European advisors. In view of this opposition, perhaps the wonder is that the reformist regime survived for nearly twenty years. But finally, in 1807, a division of mercenaries (singular, *yamak*) rose in rebellion and descended on Istanbul; they were soon joined by the main body of Janissaries. Numerous court chronicles recount how the soldiers massed near Topkapı Palace, demanding that Selim abolish the Nizam-i Cedid and remove the most unpopular of his advisors; when he acquiesced, they pressed for him to abdicate. After a few days of pressure, he agreed, whereupon the rebels proclaimed Selim's cousin Mustafa as sultan.[28]

Along the Danube River in what is now Bulgaria, however, the governor of the district of Rusçuk (modern-day Ruse), not far east of Svishtov, now took matters into his own hands. Alemdar Mustafa Pasha was a provincial notable with a large private army, a category of functionary who in earlier years had posed an *obstacle* to the implementation of reforms in the provinces. As Stanford Shaw points out, Alemdar had never been favorably disposed toward the Nizam-i Cedid, yet once the Janissaries and their allies had taken over Istanbul, he found that they opposed the growing freedom of action of provincial notables like him.[29] He therefore took up arms against them and marched on Istanbul in July 1808, determined to restore Selim to the throne.[30]

By the time Alemdar's army reached the imperial capital, those palace officials close to the new sultan, Mustafa IV, had begun to consider doing away with Selim, now relegated to the harem, in order to foil Alemdar's plans. These officials comprised the chief officers of the harem and the *hass oda*;

---

[28] Ahmed Asım, *Asım Tarihi*, II: 26, 33–34, 38, 178–82; Ahmed Cevdet, *Tarih-i Cevdet*, VIII: 206–29; Shaw, *Between Old and New*, chapter 21.

[29] Shaw, *Between Old and New*, 397–404.

[30] Ahmed Asım, *Asım Tarihi*, II: 191; Shaw, *Between Old and New*, 386, 397.

these two components of the palace's private spaces were not in competition, as they had been in the seventeenth century, but acting in concert. Thus, the conspirators included the Baş Çuhadar Abdulfettah Agha, a Georgian mamluk of a former grand vizier, and the deputy palace treasurer (not to be confused with the harem treasurer) Ebe Selim Agha, on the one hand, and the Chief Eunuch Mercan Agha, the last Chief Eunuch appointed by Selim, and the *hazine vekili* Nezir Agha, on the other.[31]

The chroniclers' blow-by-blow description of Selim's murder, which reads like the screenplay of an action movie, makes it clear why Ahmed Cevdet, even at a remove of several decades, describes these two eunuchs in truly poisonous terms. Cevdet, who deploys color prejudice freely in his lengthy chronicle, condemns Nezir as a "pig named Nezir whose face will be black in this world and the next."[32] His attitude toward Mercan Agha, while unequivocally negative, is a bit more complicated. "For someone as black of face and soul as Mercan Agha to become Chief Eunuch provides a clue to Sultan Selim's black fate," declares the chronicler (whereas Şanizade simply calls Mercan "a son of a whore who stoked the fire of rebellion and sedition").[33] Yet to some degree, Mercan seems an accessory rather than a perpetrator, doing little more than delivering messages, as the Chief Eunuch was expected to do. At the beginning of the rebellion, he delivered the news to Selim that the rebels wanted to enthrone Mustafa, at which point Selim abdicated. Once Alemdar Pasha had secured the grand vizier's seal, Mercan informed Mustafa, at Alemdar's behest, that the ulema and high officials wanted Selim to return. When Mustafa and those close to him hatched the plot to kill Selim, though, Mercan went along with it. "Either he agreed with these death-deserving [reprobates], or he was afraid and anxious about what they were going to do," concludes Cevdet. But at the same time, he ran the harem; no one entered without his permission. Yet he did nothing to stop the murderers from entering and seizing their prey.[34]

As Alemdar Mustafa approached the Babüssaade, the gate separating Topkapı's Second Court from the sultan's audience chamber at the head of the Third Court, the conspirators entered the harem and hurried to Selim's chambers, where they stabbed him to death. They then headed for the chambers of his cousin, twenty-four-year-old Prince Mahmud. Alemdar's forces were now pounding on the Babüssaade, attempting to break it down, while the conspirators advanced along the harem's twisting passageways. Suddenly,

[31] Ahmed Asım, *Asım Tarihi*, II: 53, 163, 183, 197, 201; Süreyya, *Sicill-i Osmani*, III: 343.
[32] Ahmed Cevdet, *Tarih-i Cevdet*, VIII: 391.
[33] Ibid., VIII: 171; Şanizade Mehmed Ataullah Efendi, *Şanizade Tarihi*, ed. Ziya Yılmazer (Istanbul, 2008), I: 30.
[34] Ahmed Cevdet, *Tarih-i Cevdet*, VIII: 229, 390, 392, 417–18; Ahmed Asım, *Asım Tarihi*, II: 189, 191.

Selim's Georgian concubine sprang into the assassins' path and hurled hot ashes from the harem bath into their eyes. This delayed their progress long enough to allow two harem eunuchs in Mahmud's entourage, his tutor (*lala*) Anber Agha and Anber's assistant Hafız Isa Agha, to rush the prince to the roof of the harem, where, in Cevdet's words, he appeared "like the rising Bayram moon,"[35] though bleeding from a stab wound to his left shoulder and a cut over his eyebrow where the harem door had hit him. Down below, Alemdar finally broke through the Babüssaade, only to find Selim's lifeless body stretched out in front of the audience chamber. Alemdar's forces now swarmed over the palace, capturing most of the conspirators, including Mercan and Nezir Aghas. Alemdar and his men swore allegiance to Mahmud, who was formally invested as sultan that very night.[36]

The struggle between the reformers and the conservatives, and by extension between the supporters of Selim III and the supporters of Mustafa IV, split not the harem and the *hass oda* but the entourages of rival candidates for the throne and, in this context, the harem eunuchs above all. Mercan, despite having attained his post under Selim, and Nezir favored Mustafa, while Anber and Isa favored the reformers as represented by Mahmud II.

Once Mahmud was firmly on the throne, revenge could be taken. Mustafa IV returned to the harem, where he was killed the following November on Mahmud's orders. The other conspirators suffered similar fates. Şanizade recounts where each of them was captured and how and where each of them was executed. Nezir, the *hazine vekili*, was apprehended in Üsküdar, on the Asian side of the Bosphorus, and hanged in front of the Alay Köşkü in the palace walls, across from the Sublime Porte. Baş Cuhadar Abdulfettah Agha had fled across the Sea of Marmara to Kabataş but was caught and hanged in front of the Bab-i Hümayun, the outer gate to the Topkapı complex. The deputy treasurer Ebe Selim was not captured until a year later, but when he was finally taken, he was beheaded outside the Alay Köşkü. As for Chief Eunuch Mercan, he did not flee but was deposed and sent to the Balıkhane Kasrı ("Fishhouse Castle") just outside the palace, a standard place of execution for disgraced court officials. There, he was beheaded and his body hung outside the Orta Kapı, the turreted gate giving onto Topkapı's Second Court, as punishment for allowing the murderers into the harem. Two other harem eunuchs, Cevher and Anber (not to be confused with Mahmud's tutor), were beheaded in front of the Bab-i Hümayun. The harem treasurer Kasım Agha became Chief Harem Eunuch, following the familiar pattern, while the faithful

---

[35] Ahmed Cevdet, *Tarih-i Cevdet*, VIII: 394, referring to the new moon signaling the end of Ramadan.
[36] Ahmed Asım, *Asım Tarihi*, II: 206, 254, 260; Ahmed Cevdet, *Tarih-i Cevdet*, VIII: 393–99, IX: 35; Shaw, *Between Old and New*, 404–5.

tutor Anber Agha became treasurer, virtually ensuring his eventual promotion to Chief Eunuch.[37]

The dénouement of Alemdar's rebellion and Mahmud's enthronement has been narrated in numerous other studies. Briefly, Alemdar's victory emboldened him to press the new young sultan for concessions for provincial notables (*ayan*); the result was the *Sened-i İttifak*, or "Memorandum of Agreement," signed between Mahmud and the notables of several Balkan and Anatolian provinces in September 1808. Yet Alemdar's overbearing ways as grand vizier stirred opposition within the palace and the implacable Janissary corps, leading Mahmud to depose him only four months after Alemdar had helped him to the throne. Cornered, Alemdar, with his flair for the operatic, committed suicide by blowing up an ammunition depot rather than let himself be taken alive.[38]

Mehmed Ali and the Holy Cities

Mahmud was now sultan in his own right – or was he? He still did not control the Hijaz, even though the Wahhabis were gone, and he was in a highly ambivalent position vis-à-vis Egypt, where Mehmed Ali Pasha had consolidated his power. Mehmed Ali, as is well known, had come to Egypt in 1801 with the Ottoman army dispatched to oversee the French withdrawal; with the title *ser çeşme*, designating a commander of irregular forces, he led a mostly Albanian division. Over the next four years, he weathered the competition among a series of Ottoman governors and the clients of the Georgian grandees Ibrahim and Murad Beys, until finally, in 1805, he was himself appointed governor.[39]

Mehmed Ali was now officially the Ottoman governor of Egypt; in that capacity, he, in contrast to the Wahhabis, had an obligation to uphold the established Ottoman infrastructure in the Hijaz. This included the annual pilgrimage caravan from Cairo, which he now oversaw, and which transported grain for the holy cities; the ritual covering (*kiswa*) for the Ka'ba; and the *mahmal* (known in Egypt as *mahfil*), the wooden litter, carried on camel-back, that symbolized the Prophet's presence.[40] It also included the Evkafü'l-Haremeyn, which endowed specific grain-producing villages in Upper Egypt to Mecca and Medina, as well as providing for the establishment and maintenance of wells, soup kitchens, hospitals, and schools in the holy cities. And it

---

[37] Şanizade, *Şanizade Tarihi*, I: 30–32, 48–49; Ahmed Cevdet, *Tarih-i Cevdet*, VIII: 363, 400, 417–18, 425, 463; Ahmed Asım, *Asım Tarihi*, II: 163.

[38] Ahmed Cevdet, *Tarih-i Cevdet*, VIII: 420, IX: 2–8, 14–33, 46, 50–52, 332–39.

[39] Al-Jabarti, *'Aja'ib al-athar*, III: 349–434, passim; IV: 1–12.

[40] D'Ohsson, *Tableau général*, III: 263–65; Burton, *Personal Narrative*, I: 261, 415; Edward W. Lane, *An Account of the Manners and Customs of the Modern Egyptians: The Definitive 1860 Edition*, introduction by Jason Thompson (Cairo, 2003), 437, 438–40.

included the eunuchs who guarded the Ka'ba and the Prophet's tomb in Medina, who by the nineteenth century came mainly from Istanbul.[41]

Mehmed Ali had his own East African eunuchs at his court in Cairo; he even occasionally sent eunuchs to serve at the Ka'ba.[42] At the same time, there was still quite a degree of fluidity between Mehmed Ali's court eunuchs and the imperial harem eunuchs in Istanbul. The same Hafız Isa Agha who assisted Anber Agha in rescuing Prince Mahmud from the murderers of Selim III, for example, had earlier served at Mehmed Ali's court.[43] Mehmed Ali also had ties to one Cezayırlı ("Algerian") Ali Agha, who later headed the eunuch guard at Istanbul's Old Palace, home to the mothers and unmarried sisters and daughters of past sultans.[44]

Although deposed Chief Eunuchs and other harem eunuchs were rarely exiled to Cairo during the nineteenth century, the Evkafü'l-Haremeyn continued to draw much of their revenue, to say nothing of grain, from Egypt, and so, not surprisingly, the imperial palace sought to retain the Chief Eunuch's permanent agent (vekil) in Cairo. Mehmed Ali wasted little time in trying to wrest control of the entire Evkaf bureaucracy from the imperial government. First, he arranged to have members of his own administration, notably his deputy, the famous Mehmed Lazoğlu, appointed vekil.[45] Several years later, he wrote to the hazine vekili and acting Chief Eunuch, the same Hafız Isa Agha, proposing to transform the administration and funding of the holy cities to a system that he himself would, naturally, dominate.[46] Tension between the Ottoman central authority and Mehmed Ali's dynasty in Egypt over the administration of the holy cities would continue until the collapse of the Ottoman Empire, by which time the Wahhabis were encroaching on the Hijaz again. Thus, it is hardly surprising that the new pattern of sending deposed Chief Eunuchs directly to Medina continued during Mehmed Ali's reign.

The Tanzimat

When Sultan Mahmud II resurrected the reforms of his uncle, Selim III, he launched the Ottoman Empire on a trajectory of westernizing change that lasted until 1876. In the early years of his reign, Mahmud faced a constant

---

[41] Peters, Mecca, 264.   [42] Burckhardt, Travels in Arabia, 158.

[43] Patrick Scharfe, "Muslim Scholars and the Public Sphere in Mehmed Ali Pasha's Egypt, 1801–1841," unpublished Ph.D. dissertation, Ohio State University, 2015, 146–47; Burton, Personal Narrative, II: 319.

[44] Scharfe, "Muslim Scholars and the Public Sphere," 150 n. 415; Süreyya, Sicill-i Osmani, III: 556.

[45] Al-Jabarti, 'Aja'ib al-athar, IV: 170; Scharfe, "Muslim Scholars and the Public Sphere," 152 n. 417.

[46] Scharfe, "Muslim Scholars and the Public Sphere," 206; Şanizade, Şanizade Tarihi, II: 403.

threat of Janissary rebellion, but he ultimately solved this problem by eliminating the Janissary corps entirely in 1826. He declared a general ban of the regiment, along with the affiliated Bektashi Sufi order; the sultan's men hunted down stray Janissaries throughout the Ottoman central lands.[47] This left the revived Nizam-i Cedid troops as the core of a professional, European-style Ottoman army.

While Selim and Mahmud initiated the reforming trend, their successors, Abdülmecid I (r. 1839–61) and Abdülaziz (r. 1861–76), oversaw the sweeping mid-century reforms known collectively as the Tanzimat, or "reordering," which were implemented by their reforming grand viziers and other government ministers. This new reform trajectory affected the palace eunuchs no less than any other member of the Ottoman court, and in many respects more. By the end of Mahmud's reign, the white eunuchs who had patrolled the Third Court of Topkapı Palace had all but ceased to exist. To quote the British army colonel Charles White, who resided in Istanbul for three years during the mid-1840s, "The office of kapoo aghaassy [sic] no longer exists, and, with the exception of some old and worn-out white eunuchs, and some three or four youths sent as presents, the whole white department has been done away with." "The present chief," he later adds, "is an old man, and the greater part of his subordinates are equally aged. The office will be allowed to cease at his death."[48] Mahmud's changes rang the death knell for the *hass oda* establishment, as well; the office of *silahdar*, which replaced the Kapı Ağası as de facto chief of the privy chamber, had already been abolished in 1830 (see Chapter 6).[49]

For the Chief Harem Eunuch, the era of reform was nearly as perilous. By the time the first major reform decree of the Tanzimat, the 1839 Gülhane Rescript, was promulgated by Abdülmecid I, the office of Chief Harem Eunuch was, by White's account, "in abeyance." "The office of Kislar Aghassy [sic]," he goes on to explain, "although not absolutely abolished, has remained unoccupied since the demise of the last tenant ... soon after the inauguration of the present Sultan. His functions are performed by the Khaznadar Agha (treasury or privy purse), who is next in the black hierarchy."[50] White's observation cannot be entirely accurate: the *Defter-i Ağayan-i Darüsssaade*, published in 1898, records Chief Harem Eunuchs up through that year, and indeed we will encounter the graves of some of them in the next chapter. But it is quite telling that he received the impression that the office had been suspended. His confusion may have stemmed from the fact that

---

[47] Ahmed Rasim, *Resimli ve Haritalı Osmanlı Tarihi* (Istanbul, 1328–30/1910–12), IV: 1826–33.

[48] Charles White, *Three Years in Constantinople, or, Domestic Manners of the Turks in 1844*, 2nd ed. (London, 1846), I: 246; II: 352, 360.

[49] Ibid., II: 361.   [50] Ibid., I: 206; II: 352–53.

bureaucrats and chroniclers increasingly used the title Kızlar Ağası ("Agha of the Girls") as an alternative to Darüssaade Ağası during the Tanzimat years. (They may have preferred this term because the Darüssaade, or "Abode of Felicity," evoked the harem of Topkapı, as opposed to the European-style palaces that the Tanzimat-era sultans favored, or because the title Darüssaade Ağası was associated with supervision of the Evkafü'l-Haremeyn.)[51] Clearly, in any case, the Chief Eunuch's importance and visibility had plummeted relative to that of other, formerly subordinate, members of the harem eunuch hierarchy.

These changes represented, first of all, the final triumph of the career trajectory that the Köprülü grand viziers had put in place nearly two centuries earlier. We can easily see why the reforming grand viziers of the Tanzimat era would, like the Köprülüs, have preferred to have a financial officer dominate the harem hierarchy – and not an official who was merely a client of the current Chief Harem Eunuch. Meanwhile, not surprisingly, the authority of the *hazine vekili*, added in the late eighteenth century to augment central control over harem expenditures, increased; he took the *silahdar*'s old place as overall head of the palace household.[52] And in general, the flexible post of companion (*musahib*) to the sultan became more important than it had ever been. During the eighteenth century, a hierarchy of *musahib*s had occupied the rungs of the harem eunuch ladder below the Chief Eunuch and the harem treasurer.[53] By the final years of the empire, the sultan's Head Companion (*Baş Musahib*) was in actual fact the most powerful eunuch in the palace.

Well before the promulgation of the Gülhane Rescript, Mahmud II had stripped the Chief Eunuch of supervisory power over the holy cities pious foundations. "Although he was permitted to retain the nominal inspectorship of the holy cities and domains," White remarks, "he was shorn of all real influence, and limited to the mere superintendence of the harem."[54] To replace him, Mahmud in 1826 founded an imperial Pious Foundations Supervision Bureau (*Evkaf-ı Hümayun Nezareti*), connected to the imperial treasury. In 1845, his successor, Abdülmecid, converted the bureau into a European-style Ministry of Pious Endowments (*Vizaretü'l-Evkaf*), run by a reformist pasha.[55]

Even the harem eunuchs' appearance changed with the Tanzimat, as did that of the sultan, his army, and all government officials. Gone were the floor-length robes and massive, awe-inspiring headgear of the pre-reform

---

[51] E.g., Ahmed Cevdet, *Tarih-i Cevdet*, VIII: 390, 392.
[52] White, *Three Years in Constantinople*, II: 358–60.   [53] Ata, *Osmanlı Saray Tarihi*, I: 363.
[54] White, *Three Years in Constantinople*, II: 357.
[55] Barnes, *Introduction to Religious Foundations in the Ottoman Empire*, 109–13; Mustafa N. Alkan, "Tanzimattan Sonra Vakıflar İdaresinde Yeniden Yapılanmaya Dair bir Örnek: Adana Evkaf Müdürlüğü," *Ankara Üniversitesi Osmanlı Tarihi Araştırma ve Uygulama Merkezi Dergisi* 19 (2006): 13–15.

era. Now everyone wore the comparatively humble fez, combined with a variation on European dress uniform – accessorized, in many cases, with European-style medals and orders.[56] This meant that the Chief Harem Eunuch had to give up the distinctive high sugar-loaf headdress that he had worn in official public ceremonies and become just one fez-wearing official among many. But since the office of Chief Harem Eunuch was much reduced in its influence and visibility after 1839, perhaps this sartorial transformation was not quite the rude shock that we might expect.

The British and Mehmed Ali

While Mahmud II and his successor were implementing these internal changes to the status of the Chief Harem Eunuch and other palace eunuchs, external forces were forcing farther-reaching changes. The British government, beginning in the 1830s, began to press for the abolition of the slave trade worldwide. Eunuchs, not surprisingly, came in for special attention on the part of abolitionists. Responding to British pressure, Mahmud prohibited castration and the employment of eunuchs by Ottoman subjects outside the imperial household. As a result, even though quite a number of wealthy households violated the prohibition, White estimated that no more than 400 eunuchs remained in Istanbul by 1843.[57]

Perhaps even more than the British abolition campaign, Mehmed Ali Pasha's assumption of near-autocratic authority in Egypt, which was complete by 1805, had a profound impact on the trade in East African eunuchs into Ottoman territory. More than previous governors of Egypt, he imported eunuchs and other African slaves to Cairo for the use of his own court so that he was, to some degree, competing with the imperial court for the (dwindling) supply of African eunuchs. He established a court in Cairo that was a virtual duplicate of the Ottoman court, with his own harem eunuch hierarchy – although, tellingly, there were no white privy chamber eunuchs; these were largely a thing of the past by the time Mehmed Ali was first appointed governor.[58] This new situation created a degree of overlap in duties and perquisites between the Ottoman harem eunuchs and those attached to Mehmed Ali's court and, as noted above, the possibility of service to both regimes in the course of a eunuch's career.

---

[56] Selim Deringil, *The Well-Protected Domains: Ideology and the Legitimation of Power in the Ottoman Empire, 1876–1909* (London, 1998), 26–28, 35–37.

[57] White, *Three Years in Constantinople*, II: 353; Ehud R. Toledano, *The Ottoman Slave Trade and Its Suppression, 1840–1890* (Princeton, NJ, 1982), especially chapters 3–4, 6–8.

[58] Afaf Lutfi al-Sayyid Marsot, *Egypt in the Reign of Muhammad Ali* (Cambridge, 1984), chapter 5; Khaled Fahmy, *Mehmed Ali: From Ottoman Governor to Ruler of Egypt* (Oxford, 2009), 57–58.

But it was Mehmed Ali's territorial expansion that triggered the most profound changes in the supply of African eunuchs to the Ottoman court. His intervention in the Hijaz in 1811 to crush the Wahhabi rebellion gave him a permanent presence in Mecca and Medina and in the Red Sea area in general. This meant that he had direct access to what at the time was the most popular route for the transport of newly enslaved boys from the Horn of Africa. In 1821, his son Ibrahim Pasha led the invasion and conquest of Sudan, putting an end to the venerable Funj Sultanate and founding the city of Khartoum in the process.[59] From then until 1956, Egypt controlled Sudan and, with it, the caravan routes that ran into Egypt from Darfur and from the old Funj capital of Sennar. Slaves, occasionally including future eunuchs, transported along these routes were now subject to the authority of Mehmed Ali and his descendants.

Mehmed Ali's control over Egypt – and his foundation of a dynasty that ruled Egypt until 1952 – explains why no Ottoman Chief Harem Eunuch was exiled to Cairo after 1800, although as we saw in Chapter 8, the Hijaz had become the main destination for deposed Chief Eunuchs well before Mehmed Ali came to power. During the nineteenth century, most deposed harem eunuchs were exiled to Medina, where they joined the corps of eunuchs guarding the Prophet's tomb, and where a good many of them ended their days. Some of Mehmed Ali Pasha's harem eunuchs also joined the tomb contingent after deposition, with some even serving as Şeyhü'l-Harem. In Cairo, meanwhile, the extensive urban renewal projects undertaken by Mehmed Ali and his descendants put an end to what little might have remained of the eunuch enclave at Birkat al-Fil (and to Birkat al-Fil itself, which was filled in the mid-nineteenth century).[60]

Decreasing Visibility

Apart from Mehmed Ali, the most dramatic changes in what we might call Ottoman harem eunuch culture resulted from the growing professionalization of the Ottoman imperial administration under the Tanzimat reforms. The grand vizier, who had already successfully challenged the Chief Eunuch's authority during the latter half of the eighteenth century, became more and more a prime minister equivalent while other members of the imperial governing council, or *divan*, came to resemble cabinet ministers. These circumstances curtailed the Chief Eunuch's ability to intervene informally in political matters. By the time

---

[59] Marsot, *Egypt in the Reign of Muhammad Ali*, 205–6; Holt and Daly, *A History of the Sudan*, chapter 3; Khaled Fahmy, *All the Pasha's Men: Mehmed Ali, His Army, and the Making of Modern Egypt* (Cambridge, 1997), 86–89, 92–93.

[60] Al-Jabarti, *'Aja'ib al-athar*, III: 377–78; Nadia Fouad Younes, "The Evolution of Birkat al-Fil from the Fatimids to the Twentieth Century," unpublished M.A. thesis, American University in Cairo, 2010, chapter 4 (unpaginated).

Mahmud II took the throne, an exercise of Chief Harem Eunuch leverage similar to el-Hajj Beshir Agha's subversion of negotiations with Nadir Shah was unthinkable.

At the same time, the Chief Eunuch's public visibility decreased dramatically. We no longer see Chief Eunuch–founded mosques, madrasas, or even *sebil-mektebs*; imposing Chief Eunuch tombs; or illuminated manuscripts featuring the Chief Eunuch. Photography came to the Ottoman Empire in the mid-nineteenth century, but by then, the office of Chief Eunuch was, at least according to White, "in abeyance," so that only lower-ranking harem eunuchs appear in late Ottoman photographs. Correspondingly, while harem eunuchs still joined the sultan in official public processions, they were far more likely to be rank-and-file eunuchs.

In addition, the physical space occupied by harem eunuchs changed dramatically in the course of the nineteenth century as the sultans abandoned Topkapı Palace for new European-style palaces on the western shore of the Bosphorus. Abdülmecid relocated to the enormous, glittering Dolmabahçe, right on the water; his son Abdülhamid II preferred Yıldız, up the hill in the Beşiktaş district. In both these palaces, the harem occupied a completely separate section of the complex from the public spaces where the sultan met with the grand vizier and other officials and received foreign emissaries and other visitors.[61] It was not accessible from the same public spaces as the sultan's audience chamber; in this feature, the nineteenth-century palaces differed fundamentally from Topkapı. This change severely limited the harem eunuchs' contact with anyone beyond the harem residents and the sultan himself, who still spent much of his private time in the harem.

By 1908, when the Young Turk Revolution effectively ended Abdülhamid II's authority, the harem eunuchs had very little meaningful political influence left. Abdülhamid did have a full complement of harem eunuchs, including his Head Companion (*Baş Musahib*), Cevher Agha, and his Second Companion (*İkinci Musahib*), the youthful Nadir Agha. Tellingly, though, he did not have anyone who held the title Darüssaade Ağası. Cevher was regarded as his chief eunuch, and sometimes called Kızlar Ağası. The Young Turks viewed Cevher with intense suspicion and accused him of complicity in the April 1909 mutiny that sought to restore Abdülhamid's political authority. He was hanged from the recently opened Galata Bridge after the counter-coup failed.[62] Nadir Agha and other harem eunuchs fared better after the botched counter-coup

---

[61] Personal observation; Chris Hellier, *Splendors of Istanbul: Houses and Palaces along the Bosphorus* (New York, NY, 1993), 151–73, 200–220.

[62] Francis McCullagh, *The Fall of Abd-ul-Hamid* (London, 1910), 275; Ayşe Osmanoğlu, in Douglas Scott Brookes, ed. and trans., *The Concubine, the Princess, and the Teacher: Voices from the Ottoman Harem* (Austin, TX, 2010), 172–73.

Figure 10.1 Photographs of Nadir Agha in the palace and as an older man.
Hayat, 29 November 1957, and *Yedigün* 83, 10 Birinciteşrin (October) 1934.
Courtesy of Ata Potok.

effectively put an end to the harem eunuch institution, ultimately carving out
lives for themselves in the nascent Turkish Republic.

Nadir Agha

Nadir Agha's experience provides unique insight into the much-changed
circumstances of imperial harem eunuchs in the waning years of the Ottoman
Empire. During the 1950s, Nadir, by then an elderly man, gave an extensive
interview to *Hayat* (*Life*) magazine (see Figure 10.1). This was supplemented
by a summation, published in the journal *Toplumsal Tarih*, of extensive
conversations between him and a woman, Nihal Ertuğ, who lived near him
toward the end of his life.[63] The accounts that Nadir gave to these two sources
do not always tally; details of his native village, his family members, the age at
which he was captured, and the years in which certain events occurred vary
from one telling to another.

---

[63] Hasan Ferit Ertuğ, "Musahib-i Sani-i Hazret-i Şehr-yari Nadir Ağa'nın Hatiratı," Parts 1–2,
Toplumsal Tarih 49 (January 1998): 7–15; 50 (February 1998): 6–14.

Like so many Ottoman harem eunuchs down the centuries, Nadir came from Ethiopia, more specifically from one of that kingdom's geographically marginal territories in the south. "I am Galla," he told his neighbor, referring to what today is known as the Oromo population, but "I was a Muslim." By the time he was enslaved, a majority of Ethiopia's Oromos were indeed Muslim, whereas a century or so earlier, they would have been largely animist. And he was apparently far from unique as an Oromo in Ottoman employ in the late nineteenth century: the long-suffering British traveler Charles Doughty describes large numbers of "Galla" slaves in the shaykhdoms of the Arabian Peninsula, among the Ottoman troops in the region, and even accompanying a "Persian aga" on the pilgrimage.[64]

As a small child, perhaps around 1880, Nadir was captured during a savage raid on his home village; the attackers, he claimed, killed his father in front of him and slaughtered many of his fellow villagers. His captors apparently castrated him and left him to bleed to death, yet he revived and managed to make his way through the forest to his family home, where his sister, aghast, exclaimed, "You are not a human being any more!"[65] Thus his enslavement and castration were far more random and haphazard than those of earlier harem eunuchs, who were taken to Upper Egypt and "surgically" castrated in a Coptic monastery with a lengthy tradition of carrying out the procedure. This difference may stem from changes to the trade in African eunuchs resulting from Mahmud II's and Mehmed Ali Pasha's reforms in response to British abolition efforts, which made large-scale, systematic provision of African eunuchs virtually impossible. Equally striking is the extreme insecurity of southern Ethiopia in the late nineteenth century, with slave raiders apparently able to strike anywhere at any time. The lack of security resulted in part from the Ethiopian government's preoccupation with staving off invasion by Italy and by the Sudanese Mahdi. This points up the fact that the Ottoman eunuch trade was vulnerable to political upheavals throughout the Horn of Africa, as well.

A year or two later, Nadir was captured a second time and sent across the Red Sea to Mecca, where he was put up for sale with 200 other African boys.[66] By his account, he was so thin and weak that his captors despaired of selling him. Finally, Seyyare Hanım, the wife of Emir Abdullah, brother of the *sharif* of Mecca, purchased him and took him into her household. It was she who named him Nadir, after a eunuch whom the couple had owned previously. Nadir lived in Mecca and Taif for three years, during which time his

---

[64] Charles M. Doughty, *Arabia Deserta*, ed. H.L. MacRitchie (London, 1989), 43, 102, 142, 145, 160, 163, 187.

[65] Ertuğ, "Nadir Ağa'nın Hatiratı," part 1, 7. It is possible that his sister's remark referred to the dehumanizing experience of captivity and that Nadir was castrated later in Mecca.

[66] Ibid., 9–11.

benefactress dressed him in the Turkish style and hired a tutor to teach him Arabic.[67] This part of his career, then, fit the harem eunuch "norm": the local notable's household as finishing school. This household's location in Mecca points up Egypt's displacement by the holy cities during the nineteenth century as the standard site of a eunuch's pre-palace life and exile. (There is, of course, a certain irony in the enhanced connection between harem eunuchs and the holy cities during this period, given that the Chief Eunuch no longer supervised the pious foundations for Mecca and Medina.)

Three years later, though, the *sharif* of Mecca presented Nadir to the palace, along with eleven other young eunuchs; here again, Nadir's career followed the established pattern, despite the fact that he was never part of the *sharif*'s household. He arrived at Yıldız Palace at an opportune time, for Sultan Abdülhamid was replacing his Sudanese eunuchs, whom he mistrusted, with Ethiopian ones and snapped Nadir up, along with twenty-two other young Ethiopian eunuchs.[68] Nadir was still quite young, seventeen or under, when he entered Abdülhamid's service, yet within four years, he had become the sultan's favorite eunuch companion. He was able to give the American journalist Francis McCullagh details about the famously paranoid sultan's hobbies, fears, and obsessions that few other people, even Abdülhamid's concubines, would have known, notably his promotion of an elaborate network of spies within the palace, who delivered "intelligence" by means of written reports known by the French name *djournal*. This intelligence, much of it inaccurate, only added to his paranoia and his distrust of those around him.[69]

Nadir played a critical role in the 1909 mutiny against the Young Turk government. McCullagh establishes that he, along with Cevher Agha, co-founded the Muhammadan League that laid the groundwork for the revolt, and helped to distribute the bribes that persuaded the lower-ranking soldiers to rise up. Yet, following Abdülhamid's deposition, Nadir escaped execution by providing the Young Turks with useful information on the ex-sultan, above all the locations where he had hidden valuables.[70] He seems genuinely to have turned against his former master, telling McCullagh, "Abdülhamid had a stone in the place where his heart ought to be, and innocent blood flowing in floods had no effect on him whatever."[71]

---

[67] Ibid., 12.

[68] Ibid., 10, 12–13. An 1893 inventory of palace eunuchs gives the date as 1889 and estimates Nadir's birth date as 1874.

[69] McCullagh, *Fall of Abd-ul-Hamid*, 18–21.

[70] Ibid., 53–56, 251; M. Süleyman (Çapanoğlu), "Abdülhamidin En Yakın Adamı Nadir Ağa Eski Efendisi İçin Ne Söylüyör?" *Yedigün* 83 (10 Birinciteşrin [October] 1934), 19–21, reproduced in Ertuğ, "Nadir Ağa'nın Hatiratı," part 2, 12.

[71] McCullagh, *Fall of Abd-ul-Hamid*, 132.

Following the failure of the 1909 counter-coup, Nadir Agha, like all the remaining harem eunuchs and the concubines, was obliged to leave the palace. McCullagh described the pathetic scene when the concubines, almost all of them Circassian, were assembled in Topkapı Palace to be reunited with such of their relatives as might have come to claim them after receiving telegrams from the Young Turk government.[72] No such reunions took place for the harem eunuchs. The East African slave trade had always been dislocating and anonymous, so that retaining contact with families of origin was virtually impossible, in marked contrast to the manner in which some *devshirme* recruits and mamluks from the Caucasus stayed in touch with their families and even brought family members to the Ottoman court. Turmoil in Ethiopia only added to the difficulty of tracking down relatives.

Coincidentally, Nadir Agha is the only harem eunuch who we know attempted to locate his remaining family members. Sultan Abdülhamid himself asked the special representative of the emperor of Ethiopia, Menelik II (r. 1889–1913), to assist in finding Nadir's two younger sisters. Eventually, by Nadir's account, he learned that his sisters had fled to Kenya, then under British rule, from the upheaval in Ethiopia. But Menelik's envoy had been unable to obtain further information. After a lengthy wait, a letter arrived from him reading, as Nadir recalled:

His Majesty Emperor Menelik took a personal interest in your case. We sent a delegation from Addis Ababa to Limmu [Nadir's village] to investigate. Unfortunately, it was unable to find anyone from your family. As a result of our investigation, we learned that your entire family emigrated from southern Ethiopia to Kenya. We are very sorry that despite our wishes, we were unable to give you happy news.

With this letter, we are sending you two elephant tusks and a gold coin. In addition, you are receiving two Orders of the Lion [of Ethiopia] of the first rank that His Majesty the Emperor has bestowed on you. The elephant tusks belong to elephants hunted down near Limmu. We send you our deepest respects.

On receiving this news, Nadir abandoned any hope of ever finding his sisters; years later, he told *Hayat*, he learned that they had both died.[73]

With no remaining connection to Ethiopia, Nadir, like many former harem eunuchs, remained in Istanbul following the collapse of the Ottoman Empire after World War I, although, like most of them, he relocated to the Asian side of the Bosphorus. The historical taboo against having the eunuchs' "pollution" at large within the city walls may have played some role in this decision, along with the eunuchs' understandable desire to distance themselves from the former imperial capital's busy commercial centers, where they would be conspicuous. At the time, in contrast, Asiatic Istanbul consisted mostly of

---

[72] Ibid., 276–78.   [73] Ertuğ, "Nadir Ağa'nın Hatıratı," part 2, 10.

small villages and undeveloped agricultural land. Nadir moved to the Göztepe district on the shore of the Sea of Marmara and purchased a house and land there. He eventually bought a herd of Crimean dairy cows and opened a dairy. By his own account, he became the first person in Istanbul to deliver milk in bottles.[74] He died in 1957, apparently of natural causes. By this time, he would have been in his late eighties.[75]

A number of other former harem eunuchs pooled their money to buy a house in Üsküdar, on the Asian side of the Bosphorus, where they lived as in a dormitory or hostel. We can only imagine the difficulties they faced in post-Ottoman Turkish society. They were instantly recognizable as ex-harem eunuchs, and employment opportunities must have been few and far between, not simply because employers in the new Turkish Republic were reluctant to hire them but because their palace service had left them with few practical skills – although photographs of late Ottoman harem eunuchs do show at least one of them peeling apples and carrying out other mundane household chores.[76] A few of them remained in the entourages of members of the imperial family in exile, but anti-slavery laws meant that they now had to be salaried employees. Not all imperial family members could afford to keep such servants, and in any case, not all former harem eunuchs wanted to remain in service to the imperial family. In a rather ironic twist, Mustafa Kemal Atatürk employed an African eunuch, one Nesip Efendi, to look after his adopted daughters, though whether this was a former palace eunuch is not clear.[77]

At least fifty former harem eunuchs living in Istanbul formed a Eunuchs' Mutual Assistance Society, which met periodically for a couple of decades after the abolition of the empire. Nadir Agha was among the participants. The organization's purpose was, not surprisingly, to provide a sense of community and material aid to this unique population.[78]

Medina, meanwhile, had fallen (again) to the Saudis and their Wahhabi allies in 1925. Abdulaziz ibn Saud declared the Kingdom of Saudi Arabia in 1932, and ever since, the Saudi monarchy has taken great pride in its status as servitor of the holy cities. Given the Wahhabis' rejection of any innovation to the practice of the Prophet Muhammad, we would naturally expect the Saudi government to have abolished the institution of tomb eunuchs and to have

---

[74] Ibid., 8.
[75] *Hayat* reported his death on 29 November 1957, in connection with the publication of his interview, which he had given only a few days before.
[76] Ok, *Harem Dünyası*, 52, 54, 56.
[77] Haldun Derin, *Çankaya Özel Kalemini Anımsarken (1933–1951)* (Istanbul, 1995), 38.
[78] US Department of State, Papers Relating to Internal Affairs of Turkey, 1910–29, 867.9111/226: Review of the Turkish Press for 28 June–11 July 1928, p. 17. I am grateful to the late Professor John Burnham for providing me with a copy of this document. Cf. Ertuğ, "Nadir Ağa'nın Hatıratı," part 2, 9.

pensioned off or exiled those eunuchs who remained in Medina at the time of the Saudi takeover. This, after all, was what they had begun to do in the early nineteenth century, as we saw above. But this time, they did not do so. Instead, the Saudis continued to import and castrate enslaved boys from eastern Africa and India until slavery was officially abolished in the kingdom in 1962. A handful of these eunuchs still guard the Prophet's tomb, although they are steadily dying out.[79] Although these men were never harem eunuchs, they are arguably the last remaining vestiges of the eunuch culture that this book has examined.

Conclusion

We get the sense that the dramas through which Nadir Agha and the ill-fated Cevher Agha lived were the rather pathetic last gasps of a harem eunuch institution whose glory days were long behind it. Nonetheless, we should not jump to the conclusion that westernizing reform was somehow inimical to the office of Chief Harem Eunuch and its extraordinary influence. Had that been the case, the Tanzimat might have abolished the office of Agha of the Abode of Felicity outright. But there was no cataclysm of the sort that followed the abolition of the Janissaries in 1826. Instead, there is some degree of confusion as to whether the office of Chief Eunuch even existed after the 1830s and, assuming it did, what duties the occupants of the office performed at this point.

What brought the office to this state was the transformation of the Evkafü'l-Haremeyn. Mahmud II's creation of a Directorate of Pious Foundations effectively robbed the Chief Eunuch of the responsibility that had defined his office since its inception under Murad III. Official court chronicles give us next to no idea of the effects this move had on the nineteenth-century Chief Eunuchs, but it is not hard to guess. There would no longer have been a need for a permanent Vekil-i Darüssaade in Cairo, no need for the carefully constructed networks of clients in Egypt, in Damascus, and in other key provinces. Correspondingly, there would have been little opportunity for the elaborate religious and educational facilities that the Chief Eunuch had historically founded in the provinces. When the office of Chief Harem Eunuch lost control of the Evkafü'l-Haremeyn, it effectively lost its main channel of influence and, from a certain standpoint, its reason for being. This has to be the reason for the confusion over the status of Chief Eunuch during the later nineteenth century, and why the sultan's chief companion (Baş Musahib) had displaced him by at least the reign of Abdülhamid II.

---

[79] Adel Quraishi, photo exhibition "The Guardians," Leighton House, London, October–November 2015.

Supervision of the Evkaf bookended the Chief Harem Eunuch's existence: it enabled him to outstrip the Chief Threshold Eunuch in influence and to begin to exercise the political and economic influence that would make him one of the most powerful figures in the entire empire (and occasionally, during the seventeenth and early eighteenth centuries, the most powerful). But when supervision of the Evkaf was removed from the office, the office quickly became little more than an accessory to the sultanate.

The harem eunuchs at large, of course, survived this transformation. From one standpoint, the permanent weakening of the office of Chief Harem Eunuch gave other members of the harem eunuch hierarchy room to maneuver. In few other circumstances would it have been possible for Nadir Agha, the Second Companion, to become so close to Abdülhamid or, once the old sultan had been ousted, to occupy such a visible role – though, of course, his ability to take advantage of circumstances should not be underestimated.

In short, the Tanzimat reforms robbed the harem eunuchs of their extra-harem significance. In these new circumstances, rather ironically, personal ties to the sultan and other members of the imperial family again assumed paramount importance, bringing the harem eunuchs back to the status they had held before Murad III transferred supervision of the Evkafü'l-Haremeyn to Habeshi Mehmed Agha. Correspondingly, the Chief Harem Eunuch lost his capacity to leave a mark on the Ottoman Empire outside the palace.

All this helps to explain why there are comparatively few "mementos" of late Ottoman harem eunuchs. There are a few photos of Cevher, Nadir, and other late Ottoman harem eunuchs, but many of these were taken after the empire collapsed. Very few architectural monuments exist, and the graves of these eunuchs tend to be clustered around those of sultans or female members of the royal family or concentrated near Yıldız Palace. Chapter 11 will take up these sorts of eunuch memorials.

11   Memorializing the Chief Harem Eunuch

There are numerous ways to memorialize a person. Flowery eulogies at funerals and laudatory tombstone inscriptions are two tried and true ways, and they were certainly employed in the case of a good number of deceased Chief Harem Eunuchs. In life, though, a Chief Harem Eunuch could be memorialized in other ways, notably through the architectural monuments that he endowed and through the miniature paintings that he commissioned. We have already reviewed a number of mosques, schools, and Sufi lodges commissioned by Chief Harem Eunuchs. While these stand as testaments to the eunuchs' wealth, influence, and piety, they do not represent the eunuchs personally, except perhaps in their inscriptions, which literally inscribe the Chief Eunuch founder as a pious Muslim, staunch Hanafi, devoted Halveti or Naqshbandi, and, above all, committed Ottoman. These attributes are somewhat impersonal, however.

Miniatures, tombs, and graves are a bit different. They directly represent the Chief Eunuch as an individual, not simply as one of a population of good Muslims or sincere Sufis. Of course, they do appear in certain contexts, so that we must read or view them in the context of narrative texts and other paintings, in the case of miniatures, or in the context of a mosque complex or a group of other graves, in the case of burials.

This chapter, then, explores miniature paintings featuring the Chief Harem Eunuch, as well as Chief Eunuch tombs and graves, with the aim of determining how the Chief Eunuch is represented in these matrixes. Since the Chief Eunuch usually commissioned the miniatures in which he was represented and, in a surprisingly large number of cases, determined the site of his own burial, this exercise also allows us to gauge how the Chief Eunuch wished to be represented and remembered. For this reason, miniatures and graves allow us to come as close as we will probably ever be able to come to a sense of the Chief Harem Eunuch's self-fashioning.

Chief Harem Eunuchs in Miniature Paintings

The Palace Atelier and Its Work. Ottoman miniature paintings, single-page paintings intended to illustrate books, are justifiably famous for their vivid

248

colors and intricate detail. They were produced by the palace atelier, which was established under Süleyman I and staffed by the most talented painters, draftsmen, calligraphers, and book-binders in the Islamic world. The artists' workshop was probably located just outside the palace grounds; for special projects, an additional temporary studio was apparently installed in Topkapı's First Court.[1] Here, this artistic "dream team" laboriously copied out, illustrated, and bound manuscripts of a variety of works, both literary and historical.[2]

While the court atelier of the enemy Shi'ite Safavid empire in Iran was renowned for its illuminated manuscripts of the classics of medieval Persian literature, the Ottoman atelier tended to produce illustrated historical chronicles and religious histories. Murad III's reign saw the production of numerous chronicles of contemporary and near-contemporary Ottoman history, a number of which were the work of the court chronicler (*şehnameci*) Seyyid Lokman, who appears to have overseen the production of illuminated manuscripts at the court during these years.[3] The chief illustrator of many of these works was the legendary Nakkaş Osman ("Osman the Illustrator"), who directed the atelier during much of Murad's reign.[4] He was likewise the chief contributor of miniatures to the *Süleymanname*, the official history of Süleyman I's reign, produced under Murad III, and to an illuminated Ottoman Turkish translation of a magnificent *Shahname* that had been presented to Sultan Selim II (r. 1566–74) at his coronation by the Safavid shah Tahmasp.

Palace eunuchs appear, sometimes in quantity, in the *Süleymanname*, but they are all white threshold eunuchs associated with Topkapı's Third Court. (Whether any of them is meant to represent a specific personage is difficult to determine.)[5] Given the influence of the threshold eunuchs before and during Süleyman's reign, this is hardly surprising. In contrast, not a single African harem eunuch is depicted in this work.

Habeshi Mehmed Agha. Harem eunuchs are better represented in imperial histories dealing with the reign of Murad himself, not least because Murad III's Chief Harem Eunuch, Habeshi Mehmed Agha, was active in commissioning illuminated manuscripts of such contemporary histories. He was thus in a

---

[1] Fetvacı, *Picturing History*, 74, 150; Alan W. Fisher and Carol G. Fisher, "A Note on the Location of the Royal Ottoman Painting Ateliers," *Muqarnas* 3 (1985): 118–20; Filiz Çağman, "Saray Nakkaşhanesinin Yeri Üzerine Düşünceler," in *Sanat Tarihinde Doğudan Batıya: Ünsal Yücel Anısına Sempozyum Bildirileri* (Istanbul, 1989), 35–46; Zeren Tanındı, "Manuscript Production in the Ottoman Palace Workshop," *Manuscripts of the Middle East* 5 (1990–91): 67–98; Zeren Tanındı, "Topkapı Sarayı'nın Ağaları ve Kitaplar," *Uludağ Üniversitesi Fen-Edebiyat Fakültesi Sosyal Bilimler Dergisi* 3, 3 (2002): 42–46; Topçular Katibi, *Topçular Katibi Tarihi*, I: 654, 664; Artan, "Making of the Sublime Porte,"162.

[2] Fetvacı, *Picturing History*, 71–72.   [3] Ibid., 71.   [4] Ibid., 71, 78–79, 83, 91–92.

[5] E.g., Esin Atıl, *Süleymanname: The Illustrated History of Süleyman the Magnificent* (Washington, DC, 1986), 93, 97, 99, 199, 227.

unique position to influence the image (literal and figurative) of the Ottoman dynasty and those who served it.

Emine Fetvacı has argued convincingly that each of Habeshi Mehmed's major pictorial commissions carries a specific agenda for the projection of sultanic authority or imperial identity while also contributing to a definition of the Chief Harem Eunuch's role. Thus, the 1583 *Zübdetü't-tevarih* (*Quintessence of Histories*), a universal history by Seyyid Lokman, with miniatures by Nakkaş Osman, draws a connection between the Ottoman sultans and the Abrahamic prophets, and in so doing presents the Ottoman dynasty as foreordained.[6] The *Surname*, or *Book of Festivals*, composed in 1588 by the poet known as Intizami to commemorate the 1582 circumcision of Murad III's son and heir, Mehmed III, portrays the hierarchy of the Ottoman court, in which the Chief Harem Eunuch occupied a higher rank than ever before, while emphasizing the continuity of the Ottoman dynasty and its adherence to the Prophet Muhammad's tradition. At the same time, the repetitive representations of craft guilds parading through Istanbul's hippodrome and receiving the sultan's largesse highlight the sultan's wealth and generosity.[7] And the *Kitab-i Gencine-i Feth-i Gence* (*Treasury on the Conquest of Ganja*) celebrates the conquest of Ganja in Azerbaijan by Habeshi Mehmed's protégé Ferhad Pasha, thereby cementing Habeshi Mehmed's reputation as a vizier-maker while allowing us a glimpse of the competing factions at Murad III's court.[8]

One of Habeshi Mehmed's earliest commissions, Lokman's 1581 *Şahanşahname* (*Book of the King of Kings*), deserves special mention for its extraordinary depiction of the eunuch. It is a history of Murad III's reign in which, Fetvacı argues, Habeshi Mehmed Agha symbolizes the triumph of justice and the resilience of Ottoman dynastic authority in the face of political crisis and uncertainty. Habeshi Mehmed is the central figure in a series of miniatures from this work dealing with the 1579 assassination of the extraordinarily powerful grand vizier Sokollu Mehmed Pasha, whom we met in Chapter 4. As noted there, the eunuch was not Sokollu's client but belonged to the rival patronage network of Murad III's mother.

So it seems a bit odd that in the *Şahanşahname*, Habeshi Mehmed, his skin painted a brownish gray, is depicted as the hero who literally rides in to rescue the situation after Sokollu is stabbed (see Figure 11.1). He is shown riding (on horseback) to visit the stricken Sokollu, examining Sokollu on his deathbed, informing Murad III of the vizier's demise, and ordering the arrest of his assassin.[9] Here, he is physically at the center of almost every folio; the only figure to whom he yields pride of place is the sultan himself. He is clearly the embodiment of sultanic authority and continuity who brings closure to this

---

[6] Fetvacı, *Picturing History*, 158, 164–75.   [7] Ibid., 175–81, 183–85.
[8] Ibid., 81, 83, 85, 86, 185–87, 210–12.   [9] Ibid., 86, 153–57.

Figure 11.1 Habeshi Mehmed Agha. From Lokman, *Şahanşahname*, vol. 1 (1581). Istanbul University Library, MS F. 1404, fol. 131b. By permission of Istanbul University Library.

horrific episode without necessarily being a partisan of Sokollu himself. After all, this is a book about the Ottoman sultan ("king of kings"), not about his grand vizier. A double-folio illustration positioned earlier in the same work, it is worth noting, depicts no fewer than seventeen lower-ranking African harem eunuchs in a scene in which the future Mehmed III meets with a vizier, as if to suggest that the harem's influence will continue during his reign, Sokollu or no Sokollu.[10]

Although Habeshi Mehmed Agha is depicted in other chronicles – both those he commissioned and those he did not – he appears in far fewer folios and then usually as a decidedly subordinate figure. In the extravagant *Surname*, to take one of the best-known manuscripts of Murad III's reign, Habeshi Mehmed is not depicted in any of the many folios in which Murad views Istanbul's craft guilds marching through the hippodrome from the balcony of the palace of Süleyman's grand vizier Ibrahim Pasha (tenure 1523–36). Instead, the eunuch appears only in the manuscript's final folio, where he and the influential eunuch dwarf Zeyrek Agha, seated side-by-side at the center of the composition, receive the *Surname*'s author, Intizami. Yet the not-so-subtle subtext of this image is that the two eunuchs are responsible for the work since they interceded with Murad to win the commission for the little-known poet.[11] As if to underline this point, Habeshi Mehmed, who is the largest figure in the picture, holds an intricately bound volume – presumably the *Surname* itself – as does Intizami.[12]

Habeshi Mehmed Agha's strategy of commissioning illuminated manuscripts that conveyed specific messages about Ottoman sovereignty, as well as about his own function, paralleled the agenda of his architectural commissions, examined in Chapter 4. Collectively, the artistic and architectural commissions projected the image of a powerful Sunni Muslim empire that was triumphantly expansionist yet just and well administered. It was ruled by a pious dynasty that, although not descended from the Abrahamic prophets, fulfilled their spiritual mission. The Chief Harem Eunuch, meanwhile, supported the dynasty, even stepping in to fill power vacuums such as the one created by Sokollu's assassination, and enabled it to carry out that task.

In the Seventeenth Century. After this wave of lavish commissions by Habeshi Mehmed Agha, the production of illuminated court chronicles dropped off sharply, although it did not come to a complete halt. Murad III's immediate successors commissioned illustrated histories on a more modest scale, as well as a newly diverse range of albums and treatises. The generalized crisis of the seventeenth century doubtless played a role in this reduced

---

[10] Ibid., 160.
[11] Ibid., 176–77; Tanındı, "Topkapı Sarayı'nın Ağaları ve Kitaplar," 44–45; Zeren Tanındı, "Bibliophile Aghas (Eunuchs) at Topkapı Sarayı," *Muqarnas* 21 (2004): 337–38.
[12] Fetvacı, *Picturing History*, 177–78.

production, siphoning resources away from the court and toward the Ottoman Empire's multilateral military efforts, which included staving off the Jelali rebels. At a time when the Ottoman dynasty faced an existential threat from the Jelalis, on one hand, and a lack of mature princes, on the other, lavish festival books must have seemed the height of waste and frivolity.

Under the circumstances, it seems remarkable that Murad's successors commissioned as many works as they did, let alone that the Chief Harem Eunuch was pictured in them. Yet the powerful el-Hajj Mustafa Agha was interested in illuminated manuscripts and patronized several court painters, including one who assembled a pastiche album for Ahmed I in which Mustafa Agha appears alongside the sultan.[13]

The eunuch appears in far more striking fashion in a Turkish translation of the *Shahname* (*Book of Kings*), the Iranian national epic, that he commissioned from the poet Mehdi during the reign of Ahmed's son and successor, the ill-fated Osman II. In a double-folio frontispiece, el-Hajj Mustafa presents the book to the enthroned sultan (see Figure 11.2). The layout of the painting is extraordinary: Osman II's throne divides the pictorial space vertically in two, with the white Third Court eunuchs, along with the principal officers of the *hass oda*, populating the left side and the African harem eunuchs the right. The scene graphically illustrates the spatial division between the harem and the Third Court while picturing the sultan as caught between the two, though his throne sits firmly on the "harem" side of the picture. Particularly striking is the painter's individualized rendering of the harem eunuchs. While el-Hajj Mustafa is a delicate-featured figure with pale gray skin, his assistant, who holds prayer beads, is much larger and darker. The rank-and-file harem eunuchs, meanwhile, have a mix of pale brown, pale gray, and charcoal-gray skin, their facial features are varied, and several of them are rendered in profile. In contrast, the Third Court eunuchs, apart from the Chief Threshold Eunuch, form a largely undifferentiated, front-facing mass. Less viscerally striking but equally telling is Mustafa Agha's positioning in the painting: just below the sultan, on a level with the *hass oda* officers, and definitely above the Chief Threshold Eunuch.

Mustafa Agha's protégé and successor, Süleyman Agha, figures prominently in an account of Osman II's expedition to Hotin by the court poet Nadiri. Tall, with charcoal-gray skin, the eunuch stands or rides on the sultan's left throughout the ill-fated campaign; he is also present, standing behind the Chief Mufti and other religious officials, when the imperial governing council takes

---

[13] Tülün Değirmenci, *İktidar Oyunları ve Resimli Kitaplar: II. Osman Devrinde Değişen Güç Simgeleri* (Istanbul, 2012), 76–77, 181. I am grateful to Emine Fetvacı for bringing this book to my attention.

Figure 11.2 Osman II with harem and Third Court eunuchs. From Mehdi, *Şehname-i Türki*, Uppsala University Library, MS O. Celsig 1, fols. 1b–2a. By permission of Uppsala University Library.

the decision to launch the expedition.[14] His positioning echoes the chronicler Ibrahim Peçevi's description of his closeness to the sultan. At the same time, his centrality to this series of paintings recalls the heroic depiction of Habeshi Mehmed Agha in the *Şahanşahname*.

By the end of the seventeenth century, the *şehnameci*, a court poet such as Nadiri who produced a laudatory but abbreviated account of a sultan's reign, had given way to the *vak'anüvis*, an official court historian who was expected to add to an annalistic chronicle of the Ottoman dynasty's history.[15] Historical chronicles, official and otherwise, proliferated during the later seventeenth and early eighteenth centuries, often featuring minutely detailed accounts of particular events, as well as long lists of turnovers in administrative offices. These text-oriented chronicles were less amenable to serial illustration than the

---

[14] Ibid., 171–74, 210–17, 231, 264–69.

[15] Lewis V. Thomas, *A Study of Naima*, ed. Norman Itzkowitz (New York, NY, 1972), 149–55; *TDVİA*, s.v. "Vak'anüvis," by Bekir Kütükoğlu.

work of *şehnameci*s (it's hard to imagine a vibrantly colored double-folio miniature of, for example, one *qadi* succeeding another). At the same time, single-sheet drawings were becoming popular, both at court and among the growing class of tax-paying merchants and other subjects with disposable incomes. Outside the 1720 *Surname*, discussed below, and two portrait books of the Ottoman sultans, the oeuvre of the court painter known as Levni consists mostly of such drawings,[16] whereas Nakkaş Osman and his atelier produced multiple illuminated chronicles at the courts of Murad III and Mehmed III.

But this did not mean that gigantic imperial celebrations did not occur between the 1580s and the 1720s, or that the Chief Harem Eunuch did not participate in them. Chapter 5 mentions a 1612 procession, described by the chronicler Topçular Katibi, celebrating the betrothal of the grand vizier Nasuh Pasha to the daughter of Ahmed I, as well as a second procession, two years later, that escorted the groom to the Topkapı harem; a similar procession occurred in Edirne in 1614.[17] Such processions must have been routine when the sultan's daughter or sister married.

As we saw in Chapter 6, Yusuf Agha presided over Mehmed IV's lavish two-week commemoration (*şenlik*) of the circumcision of his two sons, followed by an eighteen-day celebration of his daughter's marriage. Abdi Efendi, a court poet who had previously served as Yusuf Agha's scribe (*yazıcı*), composed his own *surname* of the circumcision celebrations.[18] Yet no miniatures appear to be associated with Abdi's *surname* (at least none that survive), and in fact no image of Yusuf Agha survives at all, to the best of my knowledge. As in the case of the 1588 *Surname*, the author appears to have been chosen by the Chief Eunuch himself, and even to be his protégé.

The 1720 *Surname*. In the autumn of 1720, Sultan Ahmed III had his four sons, aged between two and ten, circumcised, occasioning a two-week festival in the imperial capital. As in 1675, the circumcision festival was associated with weddings: in this case, two daughters of the late Sultan Mustafa II were married *before* the circumcisions.[19] As in 1582, these festivities resulted in a lavishly illustrated *Surname* (Book of Festivals), which was self-consciously

---

[16] Atıl, *Levni and the* Surname, 33–35.

[17] Topçular Katibi, *Topçular Katibi Tarihi*, I: 596–98, 601 n., 617, 622–23.

[18] Abdi, *Surname*, in *Osmanlı Saray Düğünleri ve Şenlikleri*, ed. Arslan, V: 485–537; Efdal Sevinçli, "Festivals and Their Documentation: *Surname*s Covering the Festivities of 1675 and 1724," in *Celebration, Entertainment, and Theatre in the Ottoman World*, eds. Suraiya Faroqhi and Arzu Öztürkmen (London, 2014), 186–207; Efdal Sevinçli, "Şenliklerimiz ve Surnameler-imiz: 1675 ve 1724 Şenliklerine İlişkin İki Surname," *Journal of Yaşar University* 1, 4 (2011): 377–416.

[19] Raşid, *Tarih-i Raşid*, V: 215; Vehbi, *Surname: Sultan Ahmed'in Düğün Kitabı*, transcribed and translated into modern Turkish by Mertol Tulum, ed. Ahmet Ertuğ (Bern, 2000), fols. 5b, 9a (pp. 56, 60 of the modern text); Uluçay, *Padişahların Kadınları ve Kızları*, 76, 78. Atıl, *Levni and the* Surname, 41–42, seems to have misread this passage.

modeled on its predecessor. Its miniatures were prepared by the court painter Levni, while the text, dominated by description of the circumcision festivities, was composed by Seyyid Vehbi Efendi, a poet and member of the ulema who later served as judge in several important provincial cities. Vehbi's text overflows with praise of grand vizier Damad Ibrahim Pasha,[20] and in fact he seems to have owed his commission to the grand vizier and the sultan, rather than to the Chief Harem Eunuch of the time, el-Hajj Beshir Agha.

In comparison to its 1588 precursor, this *Surname* employs a somewhat more muted color palette and includes elements of perspective, particularly in the rendering of processions. As Esin Atıl has pointed out, the sultan is not as segregated from the action as he is in the 1588 work – no Ibrahim Pasha Palace balcony – although he is depicted in a rather static "observer" mode in various locations. Furthermore, the sultan is almost never isolated but instead shares the "observer's" space with other officials, notably Damad Ibrahim Pasha and his deputy, the *kethüda bey* Mehmed Pasha.[21] Even the intimate space immediately adjacent to the sultan, which in the 1588 *Surname* is inhabited only by two *silahdars* and Prince Mehmed in most cases,[22] is frequently crowded with the three participating princes and the subordinate harem eunuchs who attend them.

El-Hajj Beshir was probably closer to the court painter, Levni, than to the chronicler, Vehbi. He may even, like Habeshi Mehmed Agha, have directed the palace atelier, in which case he would have known Levni rather well. Probably not coincidentally, Beshir is far better represented in Levni's illustrations than he is in Vehbi's text, where he is mentioned only four times, and only once by name.[23] In contrast, he appears in nine of Levni's miniatures (while other harem eunuchs appear in twenty-four); compare this with Habeshi Mehmed Agha, who appears in only one miniature at the very end of the 1588 *Surname*, although he is prominently mentioned in the text at the beginning of the work.[24]

El-Hajj Beshir is particularly well represented in Levni's illustrations of the rituals connected with the actual circumcisions, which occurred a week after the official festivities had ended. In the "circumcision parade" that brought the princes back to Topkapı for the operations, Beshir appears alongside the Chief Threshold Eunuch, both on horseback, bringing up the rear of a small army of palace officials (see Figure 11.3); once back at the palace, he looks on as the grand vizier bows to the sultan, requesting permission to proceed with the surgery. His placement in most of these miniatures is either at the center or at

---

[20] E.g., Vehbi, *Surname*, fols. 61b, 103a, 136a, 147a (Tulum's text, 132, 144, 177, 195).
[21] Atıl, *Levni and the* Surname, 85.   [22] Fetvacı, *Picturing History*, 179–80.
[23] Vehbi, *Surname*, fols. 12a, 144b, 145b, 155a (Tulum's text, 65, 191, 193, 208).
[24] Fetvacı, *Picturing History*, 177–78.

Figure 11.3 El-Hajj Beshir Agha in procession with the Chief Threshold
Eunuch. From Vehbi, *Surname-i Vehbi* (1720). Topkapı Palace Museum
Library, MS A. 3593, fol. 170b. By permission of the Topkapı Palace
Museum Library.

the front of the picture plane, implying that he is the most important figure in any given illustration. This is entirely appropriate since, after all, he would have directed the princes' education and supervised the subordinate harem eunuchs who attended them on a daily basis and who are also well represented in the *Surname*.

There are even telling discrepancies between Vehbi's descriptions of Beshir Agha's participation and the manner in which he appears in Levni's miniatures. In an early folio, Beshir presents Damad Ibrahim Pasha's gifts to the sultan, who is seated in a tent with three of his four sons, and their attendant African harem eunuchs, deployed around him (the two-year-old prince, because of his tender age, did not participate in the festivities). Here, Beshir Agha is positioned at the painting's exact center (Figure 11.4). Vehbi's text notes the presentation of the grand vizier's gifts but makes no mention of Beshir Agha presenting them.[25]

And in the last folio but one, reproduced on the cover of this book, Beshir Agha leads the three princes past the new library in the palace's Third Court to the circumcision room in the Fourth Court. Here, he is right at the front of the picture frame, in front of Damad Ibrahim Pasha (in white), who, along with another vizier, is guiding ten-year-old Prince Süleyman by the arms. But what Vehbi's text says is that Damad Ibrahim took Prince Süleyman's right arm while the Chief Eunuch took his left and four other viziers guided the other two princes.[26] In short, Levni has quite literally taken Beshir Agha from the margins of Vehbi's narrative description of the circumcision festivities and relocated him front and center.

Eunuchs' Physical Rendering. If we compare the physical depiction of el-Hajj Beshir Agha and his harem eunuch underlings in Levni's *Surname* with that of Habeshi Mehmed Agha and the other harem eunuchs with whom he is occasionally pictured in the late sixteenth-century manuscripts covered here, we see that conventions of rendering an East African eunuch's facial features and skin tone had changed between the reign of Murad III and that of Ahmed III. In the earlier works, the harem eunuchs' facial features are generic, differing little, if at all, from those of other palace personnel. What marks Habeshi Mehmed and other harem eunuchs out as African is a simple wash of paint, usually pale blue. Only in the *Şahanşahname* are different colors used to render the Chief Eunuch's skin (pale gray-brown) and that of the rank-and-file harem eunuchs (blackish-brown).[27] This is perhaps in keeping with the idiosyncratic nature of the *Şahanşahname*, which celebrates Habeshi Mehmed as a breed apart from ordinary harem eunuchs.

---

[25] Vehbi, *Surname*, fols. 25a–26a (Tulum's text, 72–73).
[26] Ibid., fol. 155a (Tulum's text, 208).   [27] Fol. 146a.

Figure 11.4 El-Hajj Beshir Agha presents the grand vizier's gifts to Sultan Ahmed III. From Vehbi, *Surname-i Vehbi* (1720). Topkapı Palace Museum Library, MS A. 3593, fol. 26b. By permission of the Topkapı Palace Museum Library.

Greater variety, if not realism, creeps in during the early decades of the seventeenth century. While el-Hajj Mustafa Agha, as portrayed in Ahmed I's pastiche album, is not terribly different from the eunuchs in Nakkaş Osman's illustrations from the 1580s, he and his assistant are both given distinctive physical attributes and skin tones in Mehdi's *Shahname* for Osman II. The rank-and-file eunuchs in the latter work, meanwhile, display a variety of skin tones, even if their facial features are not highly differentiated.

In Levni's 1720 *Surname*, meanwhile, the harem eunuchs' skin is a dark brown, similar to coffee beans, or occasionally gray-brown. Moreover, Levni or his assistants seem to have tried to approximate the distinctive features of castrated East Africans, giving the harem eunuchs relatively broad noses and broad cheeks of the type caused by testosterone deficiency. These are, naturally, subjective impressions of the eunuchs' rendering, and it is, of course, very hazardous to attribute motive to such impressionistic effects. Nonetheless, the harem eunuchs' features are noticeably different from those of non-African, and above all non-eunuch, figures in Levni's paintings. To put this innovation in context, the facial features of virtually all the human (and even many of the animal) figures in Levni's *Surname* are more individualized than those in the late sixteenth-century and even the early seventeenth-century works. This could perhaps reflect the influence of European painting, and also of the portrait-like rendering of faces in Mughal court painting.[28]

Generally speaking, these differences in painterly rendering suggest a gradual shift toward depicting the variety of physical types represented among the African harem eunuchs – and among palace personnel more broadly. Beyond that, though, they may point to the court artists' increasing familiarity with African harem eunuchs as the years passed. Under Murad III, after all, African eunuchs were just coming into their own at Topkapı Palace, though their numbers were greater than they would ever be again. At the beginning of Murad's reign, as well, the Kapı Ağası still headed the sultan's household, so African harem eunuchs, despite their numbers, were presumably less visible around the palace than they would be by the early eighteenth century. Add to this the fact, noted in Chapter 7, that by the early eighteenth century the imperial family was increasingly celebrating momentous occasions in semi-public spaces removed from Topkapı, so that Istanbul's growing middle classes would have glimpsed the large numbers of African eunuchs who surrounded the sultan, princes, and imperial women, and become familiar with their overall appearance.

As for the shift in colors of pigment used to render the skin tones of East African eunuchs, this could well represent no more than increasing or

---

[28] Stuart Cary Welch, *Imperial Mughal Painting* (New York, NY, 1978); Hamadeh, *City's Pleasures*, 199–200, 204, 236, stressing decorative elements, not portraiture.

decreasing availability of certain pigment sources. It could also be part of the overall shift in color palette between the 1580s and the 1720s, or part of a shift in painterly conventions. But if our hypothesis about the court painters' increasing familiarity with African eunuchs is at all valid, then the change could represent an attempt to render the eunuchs' skin tones more accurately. This would accord with the trend toward more individualized facial features, too. We notice that in the case of non-African personages, Levni usually uses more or less the same generic off-white that Nakkaş Osman and his contemporaries do; at times, however, he employs peaches, yellows, tans, and grays to render slight variations in non-African skin color, something the sixteenth-century miniatures very rarely do. Again, the overall effect is a greater realism in the later paintings.

Eunuch Pairings and Positioning. Outside these lavish manuscripts executed by the palace atelier, surviving paintings of harem eunuchs produced by Ottoman artists are few and far between. In fact, only one comes to mind: an illustration from an Arabic-language book of animal fables (*Fables Recounted by Learned Men*, a.k.a. *Luqman's Fables*) produced in seventeenth-century Egypt or Syria, showing two young eunuchs hunting a stag with a bow and arrow.[29] One of the eunuchs is black, the other white. Both wear short tunics: an orange one for the black eunuch, a purple one for the white eunuch. Both wear small gold headdresses, resembling European-style crowns, a very curious addition. The accompanying text gives no clue as to who these eunuchs are or why they are depicted as a color-coordinated pair; instead, it recounts the well-known fable of the stag who scorns his thin legs and prides himself on his magnificent antlers, only to have his antlers entangle him in the brush as he tries to flee from the hunters. The two eunuchs function as the hunters in the fable: the white eunuch aims the bow while the black one grabs the stag's thin legs.

Nonetheless, the pictorial motif of a black and a white eunuch together apparently had fairly wide currency among both Ottoman painters and European painters observing Ottoman court life. A book of Ottoman costumes prepared by the late sixteenth-century Flemish painter Lambert DeVos includes a colored drawing of a matched black and white eunuch pair – labeled the Kapı Ağası and the Hazinedar Başı, or head treasurer (i.e., the Hazinedar-i Şehriyari) – on horseback (Figure 11.5).[30] We saw in Chapter 5 that Topçular Katibi's description of the above-mentioned 1612 betrothal procession has the great el-Hajj Mustafa Agha riding on horseback alongside the Chief Threshold

---

[29] Stefano Carboni, "The Arabic Manuscripts," in *Pages of Perfection: Islamic Paintings and Calligraphy from the Russian Academy of Sciences, St. Petersburg*, eds. Yuri A. Petrosyan et al. (Lugano, 1995), 86, 284.

[30] I am grateful to Professor Bernard Lewis for providing me with a photographic reproduction of this drawing in 1995.

Figure 11.5 Two palace eunuchs. From Lambert DeVos, *Turkish Costumes* (1574). American School of Classical Studies at Athens, Gennadius Library, MS A986q, plate 42. By permission of the Gennadius Library.

Eunuch. Levni, over a century later, includes a scene of el-Hajj Beshir Agha and the Chief Threshold Eunuch bringing up the rear of the "circumcision parade" that accompanied the princes from the Okmeydanı to Topkapı Palace for the actual operation. As in the Egyptian (or Syrian) painting, the two eunuchs are color-coordinated: el-Hajj Beshir in a dark red surcoat, the Chief Threshold Eunuch in a dark green one, both lined with black fur, both worn over white caftans. If this motif began, as we suggested in Chapter 5, as a pictorial representation of the harem–Third Court division, whereby black eunuchs were automatically associated with the harem and white eunuchs with the Third Court, then it endured long after the harem had outstripped the Third Court in influence and the rivalry had metamorphosed into a partnership.

Finally, a word on the Chief Eunuch's placement in these paintings. In numerous examples, both Habeshi Mehmed and el-Hajj Beshir Agha occupy the front or center of the paintings in which they appear. Nowhere is this effect more striking than in the *Şahanşahname*, which portrays Habeshi Mehmed Agha as the hero who rescues the empire after Sokollu Mehmed's assassination. Likewise, Habeshi Mehmed takes pride of place in the final folio of the *Surname*, receiving the author along with Zeyrek Agha. And of course, el-Hajj Beshir Agha stands right on the picture frame as he leads three princes and six viziers through Topkapı's Third Court. But this positioning almost never occurs when the sultan is also present in the painting. In that case, the Chief Eunuch is almost always a subordinate figure. Still, he is not *just* a subordinate figure but, even in a painting, plays his familiar role of demarcating a boundary between the sultan's personal space and the space populated by a larger body of palace officials. In the 1584 *Hünername* (*Book of Skills*), for example, Habeshi Mehmed appears alone with Murad III outside the harem in one corner of a double-folio scheme of Topkapı Palace.[31] The eunuch's back is to the harem, so that he is, in effect, separating Murad from this space ordinarily restricted to palace women (even though Murad more or less lived there).

As for el-Hajj Beshir Agha, even when he is at the center of a *Surname* miniature, presenting the grand vizier's gifts to Ahmed III, he stands at the edge of the sultan's tent, below the sultan and separating him from the procession of gift-bearing Baltacıs. In the penultimate folio of the 1720 *Surname*, he separates the sultan and the grand vizier, who is asking permission to proceed with the circumcision, from the subordinate viziers and the redoubtable Baltacıs. Even in the remarkable painting in which he leads the three princes toward the circumcision chamber, he stands at the picture frame, separating the Third Court from the space of the hypothetical observer. As for the lower-ranking harem eunuchs, who are depicted in numerous miniatures

---

[31] Topkapı Palace Library, MS Hazine 1523, fol. 232a: http://commons.wikimedia.org/wiki/File: Hunername_231b-232_detail.jpg.

from the 1720 work, they always stand slightly behind the sultan or the princes, creating a figurative barrier between them and the rest of the court, on the one hand, or between them and an unseen public space, on the other.

At the same time, the positioning of both Habeshi Mehmed Agha and el-Hajj Beshir Agha at the ends of so many illustrated manuscripts seems like more than a coincidence. In this position, the Chief Harem Eunuch serves as a sort of a "seal" to end the official proceedings and, by extension, the works that commemorate them. In some respects, then, he – or at least his pictorial self – acts as a boundary between the "world" of the narrated and painted events and the real world in which they are produced.

Tombs and Graves

Celebrated though they might be in miniatures and texts during their lifetimes, Chief Harem Eunuchs, like all mortals, ultimately died – even though many Chief Eunuchs lived well into their eighties or, in the case of el-Hajj Beshir Agha and Yusuf Agha, even their nineties. They were memorialized in death no less than they were in life – often more so – but now in inscriptions on gravestones and tomb lintels rather than in miniatures. This section examines how Chief Eunuchs died, to the extent we can know, and what happened after they died, above all the appearance and location of their graves or tombs, and what these monuments can tell us about how the eunuchs wished to be remembered.

Eunuch Deaths. Rare was the Chief Eunuch who, like Osman Agha in 1603, perished during a rebellion. And although several – Moralı Beshir Agha, Lala and Uzun Süleyman Aghas – were quietly executed by sultanic decree, this fate, too, was uncommon. Most Chief Eunuchs died in old age, of diseases associated with age or the lingering aftereffects of castration and hormonal deficiencies. Generally speaking, Ottoman chroniclers who note the death of an acting or former Chief Eunuch do not specify a cause, as if age itself were sufficient explanation. Thus, the Cairene chronicler Ahmed Çelebi, speaking of Yusuf Agha, says only, "On the night of 12 Rabi' al-Awwal [1129/23 February 1717], Yusuf Agha Kızlar died; he was ninety-six years old."[32]

In the case of el-Hajj Beshir Agha, as we saw in Chapter 7, Russian diplomatic sources fill in the silences of the Ottoman chronicles, giving us a visceral sense of the aged eunuch's slow, painful expiration following a debilitating stroke. This sort of lingering death cannot have been uncommon among Chief Harem Eunuchs, many of whom lived to ripe old ages. What was

---

[32] Ahmed Çelebi, *Awdah al-isharat*, 290.

uncommon was dying while in office; most Chief Eunuchs spent the last several years or even decades of their lives in exile, far from Istanbul.

Little information is available concerning the funerals of Chief Eunuchs, regardless of where they died. We gather that men did not ordinarily partici-pate in the funeral prayers; thus the chronicler Selaniki reports that prayers for Habeshi Mehmed Agha were recited in the harem portion of Mehmed the Conqueror's Mosque in Istanbul's Fatih district before the body was trans-ported to Habeshi Mehmed's mosque complex in Çarşamba, not far to the west.[33] This may have been, above all else, a way for female members of the imperial household to participate in the funeral of the Ottoman high official to whom they were closest. Interment was an outdoor, far more public activity, probably dominated by men. As for the eleven Chief Eunuchs who were buried in Istanbul's Eyüp cemetery, we can surmise that prayers were performed in the on-site Mosque of Abu Ayyub al-Ansari, which certainly contained a harem; the chronicles, however, are silent on this point. As for deposed Chief Eunuchs who died in Cairo or Medina, neither provincial chronicles nor court chronicles say anything about their funerals, preferring to focus on seizure of their assets and the like.[34]

Burial Places: Tombs. Only three Chief Eunuchs are buried in free-standing tombs: Habeshi Mehmed Agha, el-Hajj Mustafa Agha, and el-Hajj Beshir Agha. As we saw in Chapter 4, the tomb of Habeshi Mehmed, the first Chief Harem Eunuch, who died in 1591, is located just outside his mosque in Çarşamba, built by Sinan's apprentice and eventual successor Davud Agha. He is the only occupant of the tomb; obviously, he had no wives or children who might have been interred in adjacent coffins. While the tomb, at least in its present state, bears no inscription, the inscription over the entrance to the mosque reads "May God illuminate Mehmed's grave!" a chronogram that gives the date 999, or 1590–91 CE.[35]

Although other Chief Harem Eunuchs commissioned their own mosques and even full-fledged religious complexes, Habeshi Mehmed is one of only two actually buried in their own complexes: the other is Süleyman Agha (term 1620–22), who was killed in the rebellion that brought down Sultan Osman II and was buried on the grounds of his small mosque in the Kumkapı district. This may have had a great deal to do with Habeshi Mehmed's position as the first head of the harem eunuchs to outstrip the Kapı Ağası – in his case the powerful Gazanfer Agha – in status. The free-standing tomb in the mosque complex underlined the message that Habeshi Mehmed was now the most powerful palace eunuch. Gazanfer, possibly in response, included a tomb in his own religious complex in Saraçhane.

---

[33] See Chapter 4, n. 54.   [34] E.g., Ahmed Çelebi, *Awdah al-isharat*, 181, 182, 184.
[35] Ayvansarayi, *Garden of the Mosques*, 218 and n. 1706.

Figure 11.6 El-Hajj Mustafa's (right) and el-Hajj Beshir's tombs on either side of the tomb of Abu Ayyub al-Ansari. Photo by Doğa Öztürk.

El-Hajj Mustafa Agha and el-Hajj Beshir Agha, in contrast, are buried in tombs on either side of the tomb of Abu Ayyub al-Ansari in Istanbul's famed Eyüp cemetery (Figure 11.6). El-Hajj Mustafa's tomb is accessible only through the entryway of Abu Ayyub's tomb. Today, the tomb contains a large, rather spartan brown casket and a wall-hanging depicting the Ka'ba, in testament to the deceased Chief Eunuch's position as supervisor of the Evkafü'l-Haremeyn. El-Hajj Beshir's tomb is altogether more elaborate, featuring a separate entry and two gold-painted inscriptions at right angles to each other on the exterior walls. One inscription, positioned above a grilled window to the left of the entrance to Abu Ayyub's tomb, is the *Fatiha*, the opening chapter of the Qur'an commonly read at funerals and inscribed on tombstones. The other, atop the wall abutting the public square and directly over the entrance to Beshir's tomb, reads as follows:

> The former support of the Abode of Felicity [Darüssaade, i.e., the harem],
> Beshir Agha, possessor of virtue, commander of nobility,
> Lies here. For many years, with his acts of generosity, which were the
>   most brilliant adornment of the seat of power,

He behaved as a slave to the summons to prayer.
When he left the world, His Excellency found another position.
For when he realized that the happiness of the world was not everlasting,
See the sincerity with which he set out on his final journey.
A halting place was made for him in the vicinity of Khalid [i.e.,
    Abu Ayyub al-Ansari].
May God forgive his sins.
May his place be in the paradise of his boon-companions, the men of
    learning.[36]

Inside is a casket topped with the Chief Harem Eunuch's headdress.

The placement of these two tombs is telling: the two deceased eunuchs are, in effect, guarding the entrance to Abu Ayyub al-Ansari's tomb. This is, I believe, a deliberate allusion to the eunuchs who guarded the Prophet Muhammad's mosque and tomb in Medina. The analogy is, furthermore, continually reinforced through the person of Abu Ayyub al-Ansari himself. He was one of the Medinese "helpers" (*ansar* in Arabic) who welcomed the Prophet to Medina after his flight from Mecca in 622 CE. When Muhammad arrived in Medina, according to the *hadith* and the Prophetic biographical literature, Abu Ayyub offered him a floor of his house as a temporary residence. Later, he served as Muhammad's standard-bearer in the battles that the early Muslim community fought with the polytheists of Mecca. As an old man, he joined the armies of the early Umayyad caliphate when they besieged Constantinople in 672. Falling mortally ill, he asked to be buried beneath the Byzantine land walls.[37] When the Ottoman sultan Mehmed II conquered Constantinople 781 years later, his men miraculously discovered Abu Ayyub's grave, and the Conqueror built a mosque and tomb on the spot.

Abu Ayyub, in sum, was a convert to Islam who served the Prophet in Medina, then died in Constantinople while in the service of the nascent Islamic state and was buried there. El-Hajj Beshir Agha could say much the same thing: he, too, was a convert who served the (deceased) Prophet in Medina, then relocated to Istanbul to spend the rest of his days serving a Muslim dynasty. El-Hajj Mustafa's experience was the same, minus the sojourn in Medina.

---

[36] Hathaway, *Beshir Agha*, 105; Recep Akakuş, *Eyyüp Sultan ve Mukaddes Emanetler* (Istanbul, 1973), 190; Yıldız Demiriz, *Eyüp'te Türbeler* (Ankara, 1982), 38–39; Ayvansarayi, *Garden of the Mosques*, 56, 270. I am grateful to Mr. Erman Güven, former head of Istanbul's Tomb Directorate, for permitting me to enter el-Hajj Beshir's and el-Hajj Mustafa's tombs and sharing his photographs of gravestones in Eyüp cemetery.

[37] Ibn Ishaq, *The Life of Muhammad: A Translation of Ishaq's* Sirat Rasul Allah, ed. 'Abd al-Malik Ibn Hisham, trans. Alfred Guillaume (London, 1955), 228–30; al-Tabari, *History of al-Tabari*, vol. 39: *Biographies of the Prophet's Companions and Their Successors*, trans. Ella Landau-Tasseron (Albany, NY, 1998), 40.

Burial Places: Graves. The vast majority of Chief Eunuchs and other harem eunuchs were buried in "ordinary" graves, consisting of a headstone and a footstone on either end of the burial plot. As in the case of all Ottoman officials and religious figures, the top of the headstone is carved in the shape of the Chief Eunuch's official headgear. This means that Chief Eunuch headstones from before the mid-nineteenth century are easy to recognize since they are topped with the Eunuch's distinctive high sugarloaf hat. Post-Tanzimat headstones, in contrast, bear only a fez, making them visually indistinguishable from the tombstones of other Ottoman bureaucrats. Inscriptions on these tombstones are perfunctory, never providing more than the Chief Eunuch's name, often preceded by a few flowery encomia, and "the *Fatiha* was read for his soul," followed by the year of death. A fairly typical, if somewhat verbose, example is the tombstone of Küçük Bilal Agha, Chief Eunuch from 1798 to 1807, under Selim III, in Eyüp cemetery:

> He [God] is the eternal creator.
> The late, the forgiven, the one in need of the mercy of his Lord the
>   all-forgiving,
> The agha of the noble Abode of Felicity,
> Bilal Agha, [former slave of] Halil Pasha;[38]
> For his noble soul, may God, be he exalted, be pleased with him,
> The *Fatiha*.
> In M[uharrem] of the year 1222 [March 1807].

Apart from the specially designed tombs, the locations of Chief Eunuch graves, to say nothing of those of lower-ranking harem eunuchs, appear not to follow any particular pattern, except for the fact that all are buried in the cities where they died since, by Muslim law, burial should occur within twenty-four hours of death. In addition to el-Hajj Mustafa and el-Hajj Beshir Aghas, nine Chief Eunuchs are buried in various locations in Eyüp cemetery; the earliest of these is Küçük Abdurrahman Agha, who was Chief Eunuch from 1703 to 1704 and died in 1727. Certain of these graves are grouped together, although, since tombstones in ancient Muslim cemeteries are moved around with a fair degree of frequency, these groupings may reflect much later interventions. The graves of Halid Agha, who served from 1791 to 1798, and the above-mentioned Küçük Bilal are both located in an enclosure outside the tomb of Mihrişah Sultan, the mother of Selim III, the sultan whom they served. (Mihrişah herself died in 1805, after Halid but before Küçük Bilal, which suggests that Halid's tombstone may have been moved to its present location.) Meanwhile, the grave of Paşaçırağı ("Pasha's Protégé") Abdullah Agha (1839–40) is next to that of his successor, Tahir Agha (1840–44).

---

[38] Ivaz Mehmed Pashazade Halil Pasha, grand vizier 1769–70, in whose household Bilal was raised.

Outside Eyüp, the locations of eunuch graves seem to be rather random, at least before the mid-eighteenth century. Thus, Server, or Sünbül, Agha (term 1591–92) is buried somewhere on Divan Yolu, the thoroughfare running from Topkapı Palace to the Byzantine land walls; the first Mercan Agha, who served for a few months in 1717, somewhere in Çarşıkapı, the neighborhood just south of Istanbul's covered bazaar. But in the latter half of the mid-eighteenth century, we start to see graves of Chief Eunuchs who died in Istanbul located near structures associated with the rulers whom they served. The most striking example is the Ayazma Mosque, founded by Mustafa III (r. 1757–74) in the southern part of Üsküdar, on the Asian side of the Bosphorus. Behind the mosque is a small graveyard containing the graves of the second Mercan Agha (term 1768–72), and the main officers of the sultan's privy chamber, or *hass oda*: the *silahdar* (sword-bearer), the *çuhadar* (valet), and the *hass oda başı*, or nominal supervisor of the privy chamber, who was a white eunuch. Also included are the graves of several mosque functionaries and two female harem functionaries. Death dates range from 1173/1759 to 1202/1787–88, well after Sultan Mustafa had died.[39] Mercan Agha's tombstone is one of the largest on the premises, standing a good two feet taller than that of the *hass oda başı*.

Of particular note is that Mustafa III himself is buried not at Ayazma but on the grounds of the other great mosque complex he founded, the Laleli complex, in the middle of the old city of Istanbul; the tombs of his son Selim III and three daughters are also located there. It is almost as if a topographical distinction had been made between imperial family members, who had the privilege of burial in the center of the imperial capital, and functionaries of the imperial household, who were relegated to Üsküdar. Regardless, though, these guardians of the imperial family's private space are reassembled in death behind the more remote of their sultan's two mosques; their placing can be read symbolically either as a calculated distancing from the imperial family or, on the other hand, as a breed of posthumous honor: they are the proxies in Üsküdar for the sultan, who, even in death, cannot be in two places at once.

Mustafa III's successor, his nephew Abdülhamid I (r. 1774–89), turned this architectural strategy on its head by founding a mosque in the Beylerbeyi district, on the Asian side of the Bosphorus, but placing its associated structures – *imaret*, or public soup kitchen, madrasa, library, public fountain, and his own tomb – in Istanbul's central Sirkeci neighborhood. Of the support structures, only the tomb remains. Alongside Abdülhamid's sepulcher lies that of his son Mustafa IV, who reigned briefly after the deposition of Selim III, and the tiny caskets of a large number of sons and daughters who died in infancy or early childhood. The tomb also houses the purported footprint of the Prophet Muhammad, which was

---

[39] Personal observation. I thank Davidson McLaren for pointing out the cemetery to me.

transported from a village near Damascus at Abdülhamid's request. Outside the tomb is a small graveyard containing the graves of a number of harem and privy chamber officials, in a striking parallel to the arrangement at Ayazma, except that here, the officials are separated from the royal family by only a few meters. The graves include those of the treasurer (*hazinedar başı*) of the privy chamber and the Chief Eunuch Ebu Bekir Agha, who died in 1825 after roughly two years in office. His grave is quite elaborate, elevated above most others and consisting of a carved stone sarcophagus, in addition to the head and footstones. To the right of his tomb, and distinctly lower to the ground, is the grave of a subordinate harem eunuch named Mehmed Reşid, who died in 1812.[40]

Most of the people interred in this graveyard served at the court of the reforming sultan Mahmud II and died during his reign. The conclusion we would logically draw is that since Mahmud II's own tomb had not yet been built when they died, they were buried near the tomb of his immediate predecessor, Mustafa IV, which also happened to be the tomb of Abdülhamid I.

Like his cousin Mustafa IV, Mahmud II founded no mosques during his reign. When he died in 1839, he was buried in a lavish free-standing tomb prominently located on Divan Yolu in the heart of Istanbul, not far from the Blue Mosque and the hippodrome. His tomb eventually came to accommodate the caskets of Sultans Abdülaziz (r. 1861–76) and Abdülhamid II (r. 1876–1909), as well as various concubines and children. In the tomb's garden are quite a number of other graves, including that of Talha Agha, who was Chief Harem Eunuch for virtually all of Abdülaziz's reign. His tombstone is a tapered cylinder with no carved headgear of any kind. Although his grave is across the garden from the sultans' tomb, separated from it by numerous other graves, he could be said to be symbolically guarding the resting place of the sultan he served.[41]

By the mid-nineteenth century, the Ottoman court had relocated from Topkapı to "modern" palaces on the European side of the Bosphorus: first Dolmabahçe, built between 1843 and 1856, later Yıldız, originally constructed during the late eighteenth century, the preferred dwelling of the authoritarian Abdülhamid II. This meant that harem eunuchs, not to speak of other palace personnel, were now dying considerably to the north of the core area of old Istanbul where most sultanic tombs were located. Although several nineteenth-century Chief Eunuchs are buried at Eyüp, at least two, along with numerous lower-ranking harem eunuchs, are interred outside the tomb of Yahya Efendi (d. 1571), the sixteenth-century religious scholar, Sufi shaykh, and milk-brother of Süleyman the Magnificent, located in Beşiktaş, near the

---

[40] Personal observation; Ayvansarayi, *Garden of the Mosques*, 480–86.
[41] Personal observation. The *Defter-i Ağayan-ı Darü's-sa'ade* claims that Talha's successor Cevher Agha, who was Chief Eunuch for only two months in 1875 but died in 1887, is also buried in the garden of this tomb. However, I was unable to find his grave.

southeastern entrance of the Yıldız complex. The two Chief Eunuch graves are those of Mehmed Rasim, who served for five months in 1856 and died in November 1874, and Mehmed Yaver (term 1888–98), who died in office. But in addition, there are quite a number of lower-ranking harem eunuch graves scattered about, both those of the imperial harem and those attached to the households of various officials. The tombstones are fairly uniform, all carved with post-Tanzimat fezzes, although some display higher-quality carving and are attached to stone sarcophagi, as at Abdülhamid I's tomb. Death dates range from the 1850s to the 1890s, with most falling in the latter part of that range. The graves could be construed as "guarding" the tomb of the revered Yahya Efendi, whose intercession some visitors seek even today, although the manner in which they are scattered, mainly uphill from the tomb, almost suggests that Yahya Efendi's tomb is protecting them. Regardless, this graveyard seems to be something of a harem eunuch cemetery, serving mainly nearby Yıldız Palace. The remarkable thing is that we cannot name such a repository for earlier periods of Ottoman history.

Or can we? Once again, Üsküdar looms as a possible "go-to" site for eunuch graves from an earlier era, as well as for the graves of eunuchs who were somehow persona non grata – these in addition to the graveyard behind the Ayazma Mosque. The massive Karaca Ahmet cemetery at Üsküdar's southeastern edge once contained a designated burial ground for harem eunuchs. A plan of this graveyard, dating from 1881, is housed in the Topkapı Archive,[42] but the graveyard itself seems to have vanished into the mists of time.

In addition to this "mass" eunuch graveyard, several individual Chief Eunuchs who came to bad ends are buried in Üsküdar. The earliest of these is Behram Agha, who, as noted in Chapter 5, was executed in the course of the 1656 Plane Tree Incident.[43] Moralı Beshir Agha, executed in 1752 as a result of his own excesses, was buried near the tomb of the Halveti Sufi shaykh Nasuhi Mehmed Efendi in the Üsküdar neighborhood known as Doğancılar, although his tombstone is no longer present in the very well-tended graveyard abutting the mosque. Also reportedly buried in Doğancılar is Mehmed Arif Agha (term 1850–55), Chief Eunuch late in the reign of Abdülmecid I (r. 1839–61), who died at the end of 1863. Here once again, Üsküdar serves as a zone outside the core areas of Istanbul that was therefore a "safe" location for the graves of eunuchs, particularly those who had died in disgrace. (It is worth noting in this connection that the so-called Traitors' Graveyard [Hainler Mezarlığı] designated by the mayor of Istanbul for deceased perpetrators of the abortive July 2016 military coup in Turkey is located in Pendik, on what is today Istanbul's eastern edge.)

---

[42] Topkapı Palace Archive, E 9467 (14 Şa'ban 1298/11 July 1881).
[43] *Defter-i Ağayan-ı Darü's-sa'ade*, appendix to *Hamiletü'l-kübera*, 168; Ayvansarayi, *Garden of the Mosques*, 245, 262.

Graves outside Istanbul

A majority of Chief Harem Eunuchs are buried outside Istanbul. Most of these died either in Cairo, where they had been exiled, or in Medina while serving as Chief Tomb Eunuch. At least sixteen are buried in Cairo, although rather astonishingly, only one of their graves can be located with any degree of certainty: that of Abbas Agha (term 1667–71), who was buried near the mausoleum of the great jurist Muhammad ibn Idris al-Shafiʻi (767–820 CE), eponym of the Shafiʻi legal rite of Sunni Islam, in the enormous "City of the Dead" necropolis southeast of Cairo's citadel. Al-Shafiʻi's ornate domed tomb was built in the early thirteenth century by the Ayyubid sultans, who followed the Shafiʻi rite, by that time the most widespread rite in Lower Egypt.[44] Despite its Fatimid architectural touches, the tomb represents the Sunni reclamation of Cairo after two hundred years of Ismaili Shiʻite rule. Saladin founded a madrasa, the theological seminary that he used to great effect to combat Fatimid Ismaili ideology, near al-Shafiʻi's original grave, and the Ayyubid sultan who commissioned the mausoleum is buried inside it, along with his mother. Under the Ottomans, a newly appointed governor of Egypt often made a ritual stop at al-Shafiʻi's mausoleum on his way up to the citadel.[45]

In this context, it seems only natural that a former Chief Harem Eunuch would wish to be buried near al-Shafiʻi, regardless of the lingering rivalry between the Shafiʻi legal rite and the Hanafi rite, official rite of the Ottoman Empire. After all, the Chief Eunuch had a huge stake in projecting the Ottomans' identity as the Sunni world's chief defender against heretical Shiʻism. (There is also the issue, discussed in Chapter 9, of Ethiopian Muslims' adherence to the Shafiʻi rite, although we do not know if Abbas were born a Muslim.) Al-Shafiʻi's mausoleum serves as the same sort of "halting place" for Abbas that Abu Ayyub al-Ansari's tomb is for el-Hajj Beshir Agha. By the same token, Abbas could be said to be "guarding" al-Shafiʻi's tomb – defending a pillar of Sunni Islam – just as el-Hajj Beshir and el-Hajj Mustafa guard Abu Ayyub's tomb, or as Talha Agha guards Abdülaziz's tomb.

By the late eighteenth century, as we saw in Chapter 7, a deposed Chief Harem Eunuch routinely served a stint as chief of the eunuchs who guarded the Prophet Muhammad's tomb in Medina. Once Mehmed Ali Pasha and his descendants had taken over Egypt, Medina replaced Cairo as the standard place of exile for deposed Chief Eunuchs. This, of course, meant that more and more Chief Eunuchs died and were buried in Medina: at least eleven total.

Eunuchs who died in Medina were buried in the town's cemetery, known as Jannat al-Baqiʻ or simply al-Baqiʻ. It was located just outside Bab al-Jumaʻa,

---

[44] Williams, *Islamic Monuments in Cairo*, 134–35.
[45] E.g., al-Damurdashi, *Al-Durra al-musana*, 58, 90.

the city gate nearest the Prophet's mosque and tomb, which was adjacent to the eunuchs' quarter just east of the tomb. This was a true celebrity graveyard, since some of the most important members of the original Muslim community were buried there, including all of the Prophet's wives except his first wife, Khadija, who died in Mecca; all of his daughters, with the possible exception of Fatima; his uncle al-'Abbas, ancestor of the Abbasid caliphs; 'Uthman ibn 'Affan, the third caliph recognized by Sunnis; and Hasan ibn 'Ali ibn Abi Talib. The last Ottoman caliph, Abdülmecid II, was buried there in 1924, only two years before the cemetery was demolished by the Saudis. This was heady company for the deceased eunuchs, and their proximity to the Prophet's tomb meant that they continued guarding his tomb in spirit after they had left the earthly corps of tomb eunuchs. This, in effect, completed the "*hijra* to God and his Prophet" that they had undertaken when they were first assigned to Medina.

A handful of Chief Harem Eunuchs died in still other locales. Those who were executed shortly after being exiled to Aegean islands, such as Lala Süleyman Agha, who was packed off to Lemnos in 1676, and Uzun Süleyman Agha, who was exiled to Cyprus with el-Hajj Beshir in 1713, were buried on site, and their graves have apparently not survived. Three who died in Edirne, where the Ottoman court resided for much of the reigns of Mehmed IV and his three immediate successors, were buried there, presumably in one of the numerous historic graveyards in that city.

Conclusion

In death, then, many Chief Harem Eunuchs symbolically pursued their customary roles of guarding access to an exalted Muslim personage, whether the Ottoman sultan, one of the imperial women, the Prophet Muhammad, his standard-bearer, a Sufi shaykh, or one of the early masters of Islamic law. Naturally, this function was hardly the only concern that came to bear on the choice of a Chief Eunuch's burial site. A corollary was the benefit to the deceased eunuch of burial near such an eminent figure; a religious luminary in particular could impart his or her sacred aura and possibly play an intercessory role. Beyond that, though, convenience and proximity would have had to be overriding concerns in view of the Muslim strictures on burying the dead within twenty-four hours. Disgraced eunuchs, furthermore, would not have been honored with burial near an eminent Muslim. For them, as for many other eunuchs, particularly the harem rank and file, burial in Üsküdar, across the Bosphorus from the Ottoman palace and major sultanic mosques, and thus symbolically cut off from the sultanic space, seemed more suitable.

The idea that buried eunuchs symbolically guarded the tombs of such eminent personages might seem a bit far-fetched until we consider the resonances of such strategic grave positioning. A eunuch grave near the tomb of Abu Ayyub unquestionably evokes the eunuch guard at the Prophet Muhammad's tomb in Medina. Similarly, eunuch burials near the tombs of Ottoman sultans and imperial women evoke the eunuchs of the Mamluk Sultanate guarding the tombs of the sultans and even their counterparts in Ming dynasty China guarding the tombs of the Ming emperors. But beyond that, these "tomb guardian burials" echo the manufactured tomb guardians used so extensively by various Chinese dynasties: the famous terracotta warriors guarding the tomb of China's first emperor, the autocratic Qin Shi Huang (r. 221–210 BCE) outside Xi'an, and the much smaller clay figurines, sculpted nude but dressed in real clothing, similarly employed by the later Han emperors. To these we may add the tomb guardian statues found outside numerous tomb mounds in China and Korea.[46]

When we consider how sacred and dangerous the space of a royal tomb was considered historically – hence, for example, curses carved into Egypt's pyramids to prevent disturbance of the Pharaohs' tombs – the eunuchs' tomb guardian function makes sense. For the eunuchs, moreover, burial near an exalted personage provided an appropriate "halting place," to use the language of el-Hajj Beshir Agha's epitaph, en route to the paradise that they believed they attained as a reward for performing just this sort of service.

If tombs memorialized the Chief Harem Eunuch in death, miniature paintings fulfilled the same purpose while he lived, displaying his influence and visibility at the time of the production of the illuminated manuscript in question. In these paintings, moreover, the Chief Eunuch often performed the same function that he did in his grave or tomb: that of a guardian figure, symbolically patrolling the boundary that separated – and protected – the sultan from the mass of palace functionaries, from the public at large, even from the viewers of the painting or the visitors to his tomb. Yet on certain rather rare occasions, he occupied a prominent, even central place in a painting, just as certain rare eunuchs, above all el-Hajj Mustafa and el-Hajj Beshir Agha, were laid to rest in centrally located tombs of extraordinary visibility, in their cases on either side of Abu Ayyub al-Ansari. But in all these cases, the Chief Eunuch's impact resulted from his relation to the sultan, to other imperial family members, or, in the case of graves and tombs at Eyüp, to the Prophet Muhammad and his companions. In this sense, the Chief Eunuch's memorialization in paintings and tombs was always contingent on his position vis-à-vis the more exalted personage whom he served. In death as in life, painted or unpainted, he remained the quintessential guardian figure.

---

[46] Personal observations, Qin Shi Huang mausoleum, Lintong district, Xi'an; Shaanxi Provincial Museum, Xi'an; Hanyingling mausoleum, Zhangjiawan, Shaanxi Province, China; tomb of King Wonseong of Silla (d. 798 CE), Gyeongju, South Korea.

12   Conclusion

The Imperial Trajectory

This book has tried to convey the trajectory of the Chief Harem Eunuch's career, both in terms of the individual career and with respect to the aggregate of the Chief Eunuchs over some three centuries. We have seen that the office of Chief Harem Eunuch to a remarkable extent follows the overall trajectory of the Ottoman Empire. The office was created at a time when the Ottoman sultan was growing increasingly secluded from public view and spending much of his private time in the harem of Topkapı Palace. Although the first Chief Eunuch, Habeshi Mehmed Agha, probably received the duties and perquisites that he did because of his personal influence, they became entrenched and institutionalized after his death. Among these duties, supervision of the Holy Cities Pious Foundations stands out, for once Habeshi Mehmed assumed it, it remained in the Chief Harem Eunuch's hands until Mahmud II's creation of the Imperial Pious Foundations Directorate in 1826 – and this despite the emergence of powerful Chief Threshold Eunuchs, above all Gazanfer Agha, in the sixteenth and seventeenth centuries who might have reclaimed the supervision.

The Chief Harem Eunuch's influence arguably peaked during the crisis of the seventeenth century, when a string of underaged and/or mentally unstable sultans made the sultan's mother, and the Chief Eunuch in partnership with her, a locus of authority within the palace. This tumultuous era saw rival factions within the harem competing for primacy in access to the sultan, court appointments, selection of the grand vizier, and general imperial policy. The 1651 murder of the formidable Kösem Sultan, in which the Chief Eunuch Lala Süleyman Agha allegedly played a leading role, is no doubt the key proof of how deep-rooted and dangerous this rivalry was. The rivalry subsided when the Köprülü grand viziers took office in the second half of the seventeenth century; the first two Köprülüs in particular used their households to circumvent the competing pools of potential courtiers, even appointing Chief Eunuchs from among their personal clients.

During the first half of the eighteenth century, a time of economic recovery and cultural efflorescence for the Ottoman Empire, the Chief Harem Eunuch took a leading role in fostering international commerce, above all with western Europe, and what has been termed a new culture of public sociability. French and Italian luxury imports and lavish garden-based entertainments were hallmarks of the so-called Tulip Era (*Lale Devri*), a term referring to a moment of peaceful cultural flowering that el-Hajj Beshir Agha, along with the grand vizier Nevşehirli Damad Ibrahim Pasha, helped to pioneer. El-Hajj Beshir and his successor, Moralı Beshir, took the lead in planning the outdoor festivities known as Çırağan Entertainments, which celebrated the blooming of the tulips each spring, and the *helva sohbetleri*, wintertime indoor gatherings at which the sweet helva was prepared and consumed.

In other words, the Chief Harem Eunuch was at the forefront of all the Ottoman Empire's major "eras" over the roughly 200 years between the office's creation and the beginnings of westernizing reform under Selim III: the era of seclusion, the era of crisis, the Tulip Era. But this trend came to an end with the westernizing reforms of the nineteenth century, culminating in the Tanzimat. While various Chief Eunuchs supported or opposed these reforms, none of them took the lead in proposing or implementing them. Instead, the grand vizier and the reformist officials whom he and the sultan appointed to the governing *divan* guided the reforms. By the time the Tanzimat reforms took effect, in any case, the office of Chief Harem Eunuch had apparently become something of a dead letter. The era of Chief Harem Eunuch influence was effectively over.

Reproduction and Continuity

What allowed the Chief Harem Eunuch to exert such a degree of influence over the 252 years between 1574 and 1826? The critical factor was the essential role that he played in dynastic reproduction in an era when Ottoman princes were borne by concubines and raised in the harem. Generally speaking, in absolutist empires such as the Ottoman, Mughal, Ming, and Qing, the harem or inner sanctum was the site of dynastic reproduction, where the emperor's wives and/or concubines bore and reared the successors to the throne. The Chief Eunuch was an integral part of this process because of his status as the quintessential guardian, remarked at the end of Chapter 11. His was a "life in between," literally marginal, policing the boundary that separated the harem from male-gendered spaces even as he policed the sexuality of its inhabitants.

It was this liminality that enabled him to perform this function. His inability to procreate, combined with what we might call his permanent state of pre-pubescence and the "otherness" of his color and geographical orgins, removed any threat he might have posed to the space occupied by imperial women and children. At the same time, his outwardly male gender enabled him to function in the space inhabited by the sultan and his pages, on the one hand, and the grand vizier and his bureaucrats, on the other. His could thus mediate among all these spaces while never belonging to any of them.

Thus empowered, the Chief Eunuch helped to reproduce the Ottoman dynasty literally by guiding concubines, often selected by the sultan's mother, to the sultan's bedchamber. Perhaps more importantly, though, he aided dynastic reproduction figuratively by overseeing the princes' education, on the one hand, and by aiding the sultan's mother, grandmother, or favorite concubine in her political struggles, on the other – whether with other harem residents, with the sultan and his pages, or with the grand vizier.

But this concern for reproduction and generational continuity extended far beyond the palace harem. Through the various educational institutions that he founded throughout the empire by means of pious endowments – Qur'an schools, madrasas, schools for the study of *hadith* – the Chief Eunuch achieved intellectual and religious reproduction by shaping a new generation of Sunni Muslims. In eunuch-founded Qur'an schools, these newly educated young Muslims were usually orphans, meaning that the Chief Eunuch really did help to give definitive confessional shape to a mass of unformed human raw material. These institutions by at least the early eighteenth century came to stress indoctrination into the Hanafi legal rite, which had become a key marker of Ottoman confessionalization. This was in line with a hardening of attitudes toward the Twelver Shi'ite Safavid dynasty and its self-proclaimed savior, Nadir Shah, in Iran and with a desire to emphasize the Hanafism of the imperial court against that of provincial notables. Through these endowments, then, the Chief Eunuch's doctrinal and intellectual goals meshed with his provincial and foreign policy aims.

The Chief Eunuch's concern with ensuring generational continuity applied not simply to the Ottoman dynasty, nor even to the Sunni Muslim community at large, but to the community of harem eunuchs, as well. An astute Chief Harem Eunuch cultivated protégés among the younger "generation" of eunuchs. He was in a position to promote their careers and, through canny use of *vakıf* and networks of clients in places such as Cairo, to pass along houses, books, and even commercial enterprises. In this way, the Chief Harem Eunuch helped to reproduce the harem eunuch establishment, too.

Vakıf, Infrastructure, and Influence

For most of its history, the office of Chief Harem Eunuch was linked to supervision of the Evkafü'l-Haremeyn. These foundations enabled the Chief Eunuch to make major contributions to the Ottoman Empire's urban infrastructure, some of which are still apparent today. These infrastructural projects in turn served as vehicles for the Chief Harem Eunuch's religious, educational, and economic influence.

Physical infrastructure in numerous Ottoman cities and along the pilgrimage route was transformed by the Chief Harem Eunuch's endowments. We can probably say that the early seventeenth-century Chief Eunuchs Osman Agha and el-Hajj Mustafa Agha, with the substantial help of the agent (*vekil*) Davud Agha, transformed Cairo, making it more of a hub for regional and international commerce than it had ever been before. The very first Chief Eunuch, Habeshi Mehmed Agha, created the city of Ismail Geçidi (today Izmail) in the Danube Delta in what is now Ukraine; his infrastructural projects were reinforced in the early eighteenth century by el-Hajj Beshir Agha. And el-Hajj Beshir himself established commercial infrastructure throughout the Ottoman Empire's territories, from Cairo to Svishtov in Bulgaria, from Chios to Aleppo.

Commercial infrastructure was inseparable from religious and educational infrastructure, in no small part because of the way that the Muslim pious endowment (*vakıf*) expressed itself physically: a mosque or madrasa, for example, would usually adjoin the shops, bazaar, or bath that provided its revenue, so that founding a major *vakıf* often resulted in a whole new urban neighborhood or, in the case of a rural area, a whole new village. In every province of the empire, Chief Harem Eunuchs founded dozens of mosques, madrasas, Qur'an schools (including *sebil-mekteb*s), Sufi lodges, public fountains, libraries, and religious complexes combining all these elements. Their effect on the empire's urban infrastructure is thus incalculable, but so, too, is their effect on religious education and practice. As we have seen, the stipulations of el-Hajj Beshir Agha's many foundations in particular provided education in the Hanafi legal rite of Sunni Islam to orphans and other young boys in Cairo, Medina, and Svishtov; manuscripts of seminal works of Hanafi exegesis and law to students and ulema in Cairo, Baghdad, Medina, and Istanbul; and accommodation for Sufi orders in Istanbul and Cairo. Collectively, these Chief Eunuch religious foundations promoted Sunni Islam, the Hanafi legal rite, *tariqa* Sufism, and devotion to the Prophet Muhammad among the Ottoman population at large.

Where the Muslim holy cities were concerned, the Chief Eunuch's foundations facilitated the pilgrimage to Mecca and visitation of the Prophet's mosque and tomb in Medina by providing roads, wells, and lodging along the pilgrimage routes and religio-educational institutions in the holy cities themselves. These foundations reinforced the Ottoman sultan's status as "servitor of the two holy sanctuaries" (*khadim al-Haramayn* in Arabic). Both terms of this expression have connotations referring to eunuchs: *khadim*, literally "servant," as early as the ninth century CE was a euphemism for a eunuch, as it still is in modern Turkish, while *haram* refers to a sacred or taboo site, whether the mosque at Mecca or Medina or the sultan's harem. Under the circumstances, we can assert that the Chief Harem Eunuch was himself a *khadim al-Haramayn* in all senses of the phrase: a servant and a eunuch who served both the holy cities and the palace harem. In his case, *Haramayn* (*Haremeyn*), or "two holy sanctuaries," can refer specifically to the Prophet's mosque and tomb at Medina, on the one hand, and the imperial harem, on the other.

This religious patronage looms especially large in relation to the question of Ottoman "confessionalization" during the sixteenth and seventeenth centuries: that is, the adoption and public performance of an official religious identity. The official religious identity that took shape in the Ottoman Empire during this period was Sunni, Hanafi, Sufi – meaning membership in one of three or four "mainstream" orders – and devotee of the Prophet. Through his endowments above all but, in the case of devotion to the Prophet, through service as chief of the tomb eunuchs and in his choice of burial site, the Chief Eunuch modeled official Ottoman orthodoxy and helped to reinforce and spread it, too.

These multiple roles that the Chief Eunuch played were facilitated by the lack of well-defined professional duties among the members of the Ottoman court in the pre-Tanzimat era. Increasing professionalization and standardization of official roles, beginning in the eighteenth century, curtailed the Chief Eunuch's influence, as well as that of other "informal officials," such as the sultan's mother and the *silahdar*, or sword-bearer. The grand vizier, now more or less a prime minister equivalent, and the *reisü'l-küttab*, now a foreign minister equivalent, grew correspondingly more influential. In other words, offices whose power had been enhanced by steadily increasing institutionalization and independence from the sultan's household benefited, from the eighteenth century onward, at the expense of offices, very much including that of Chief Harem Eunuch, whose duties were still largely defined by personal relationships with the sultan and other members of the imperial family, as well as membership in their households. Once supervision of the Evkafü'l-Haremeyn was removed from the office of Chief Harem Eunuch, in fact, that office became even more closely attached to the sultan's household, and arguably suffered the consequences.

The Global Picture

Much the same could be said of head eunuchs, and court eunuchs in general, in other empires, including the Mughal in India, the Qajar in Iran, the Qing in China, and the Chosun in Korea. With westernizing reform came professionalization of administrative offices, and as a result the influence of palace eunuchs waned, generally speaking. There were exceptions, of course: in late Qing China, for a well-known example, the tender age of the Guangxu emperor (r. 1875–1908) and the untimely death of his mother allowed his aunt, the ferocious dowager empress Cixi (1835–1908), effectively to run the empire from 1881 until her death, assisted by the eunuchs who guarded the Forbidden City.[1]

In all these polities, nonetheless, as well as earlier polities such as the Roman and Byzantine empires, Ming China, and virtually all medieval Islamic empires, court eunuchs played key roles in enabling the ruler's household, and the state apparatus that existed within it during the premodern era, to function. At the same time, they ensured dynastic succession and continuity. Apart from this essential role, their attributes and functions varied from one empire to another. Ottoman eunuchs are comparable only to Byzantine eunuchs in their effect on religious education and performance, even though, unlike their Byzantine counterparts, they could not join the religious hierarchy. Chinese eunuchs, in contrast, were often illiterate, although they might donate to Buddhist and Confucian shrines of various types. In Mughal India and Safavid Iran, meanwhile, the continuous transfer of the emperor's court from one city to another seems to have prevented court eunuchs from participating so extensively in urban infrastructural development.

While court eunuchs strike modern-day students as bizarre, even freakish, they were in use throughout much of the world, excluding Russia and Latin America, until roughly 200 years ago – and far more recently in the case of the Ottoman Empire and Saudi Arabia. Even in western Europe, where direct analogs to the Ottoman harem eunuchs cannot be found, the singers known as castrati were a fixture in the Vatican, where they arguably originated as a holdover from eunuch court singers in the Byzantine Empire. They achieved rock-star-like popularity in western Europe's capitals during the eighteenth century.

In general, court eunuchs were the aides, advisors, and personal secretaries of the premodern world. Their inability to reproduce and, in most cases, their lack of ties to the subject populations of the kingdoms and empires they served functioned as the equivalent of a security clearance to keep them loyal to the dynasties that they served. Because of the fluidity in the functions of early modern courtiers, they could fill a variety of roles: guardian, confidant, message-bearer, funeral attendant, advisor, mentor, entertainment director, educator. They came to identify strongly with the dynasties they served, even if, as in many cases, they had originated in distant lands, been forcibly enslaved, and arrived at the imperial court through no choice of their own. Few people were as loyal to an imperial dynasty as the eunuchs who served it.

---

[1] Jung Chang, *Empress Dowager Cixi: The Concubine Who Launched Modern China* (London, 2013); Pamela K. Crossley, "In the Hornet's Nest," *London Review of Books* 36, 8 (17 April 2014), 9–10.

The story of Sun Yaoting, the last surviving eunuch of the last emperor of China, is instructive in this regard. A highly recognizable figure in Beijing during the first half of the twentieth century, he died toward the end of 1996, aged ninety-four. His obituary in the *New York Times* recounts how his own family arranged his castration, hoping that he would lift them out of poverty through service to the ruling Qing dynasty. Yet, in a cruel irony, the Qing were overthrown in 1911, only a few months after his castration, marking the end of nearly 2,000 years of imperial rule in China. Although Sun Yaoting served the wife of the deposed last emperor Pu Yi, he "never stopped lamenting the fall of the imperial system he had aspired to serve," according to his official biographer, who added, "That was the regret of his whole life."[2] A eunuch without an imperial system, and more specifically an imperial household, to serve, had no purpose. At the same time, an imperial household without eunuchs (or close equivalents, as in Christian Ethiopia) lacked the means to ensure dynastic reproduction in all senses of the word. In short, the imperial household could not function without eunuchs, and vice versa. The one was inconceivable without the other.

Self and Personhood

Eunuchs' identification with the dynasties they served raises a final question, however: Is the Chief Harem Eunuch's selfhood really accessible to us? That is, do the Chief Eunuch's policies, choice of clients, endowment of particular structures, patronage of particular artists or Sufi orders, and so on really reflect his personal preferences, or are they simply a projection of the sultan's priorities or those of the imperial family? This is a legitimate question since, after all, the boundary between the sultan's agenda (or that of his mother) and that of his Chief Eunuch could be rather blurry. The sultan, too, wished to promote Sunni Islam; he, too, patronized mainstream Sufi orders. Safiye Sultan's usurpation of Osman Agha's mosque endowment in Cairo, noted in Chapter 8, suggests that even the Chief Eunuch's endowments were not wholly his own but metamorphosed into dynastic endowments on his death.

Yet I maintain that the Chief Eunuch's own desires, and even his own personality, are indeed accessible, even if they do not always occupy the foreground of the available sources. These elements come through in the interstices of the narrative of Ottoman history, as articulated in chronicles and archival documents. In the literally marginal tale of Habeshi Mehmed Agha's enslavement, in el-Hajj Beshir Agha's denunciation of Nadir Shah's

---

[2] Jia Yinghua, quoted in Seth Faison, "The Death of the Last Emperor's Last Eunuch," *New York Times*, 20 December 1996; Jia Yinghua, *The Last Eunuch of China: The Life of Sun Yaoting*, trans. Sun Haichen (Beijing, 2009).

Ja'fari rite – occupying a single line in Şemdanizade's text – in the same eunuch's plea, captured in a few words in a 119-page endowment deed, that his books not be removed from his religious complex, we glimpse the priorities and self-fashioning of the Chief Eunuch himself, quite separate from the priorities of the Ottoman dynasty or the Ottoman state. These glimpses are even more vivid in atextual sources, above all miniature paintings and tombs. Habeshi Mehmed's depiction as savior of the state in the *Şahanşahname*, el-Hajj Beshir's foregrounding in the *Surname* (subverting Vehbi's text), and perhaps above all, el-Hajj Beshir's and el-Hajj Mustafa's interment on either side of the Prophet's standard-bearer – these point to the personal priorities of the Darüssaade Ağası, which admittedly cannot be entirely separated from devotion to the Ottoman dynasty, to Sunni Islam, and to the Prophet Muhammad. At the same time, these priorities must be read within the context of the sultan's, the dynasty's, and the state's master narrative, which frames them and gives them meaning, in the same way that the main body of a text gives meaning to marginalia, or to accompanying miniatures (and vice versa). This is what I have tried to do here.

In light of the above considerations, it seems fitting to end with the atextual source with which we started: the image on this book's cover, which shows el-Hajj Beshir Agha leading Ahmed III's three sons to the circumcision room in the Fourth Court of Topkapı Palace. We now know that Levni, the illustrator of the festival book in which this miniature appears, gave Beshir Agha a much more prominent place than he occupies in the poet Vehbi's text. Levni moved him to the very front of the picture frame, as if to emphasize the critical role that Beshir Agha played in this life-cycle ceremony and, more generally, in patrolling the boundary separating the imperial family from the subjects they ruled. But perhaps Levni was right all along, for as we have seen, Beshir Agha – and the Chief Harem Eunuch in general – was indeed indispensable to royal circumcisions and all other such rituals that contributed to the reproduction and continuation of the House of Osman. Without him, there would be no picture.

Appendix: Ottoman Chief Harem Eunuchs

Name	Sultan	Term (Hijri)	Term (Gregorian)	Death
Habeshi Mehmed	Murad III	981–99	1574–91	1591, Istanbul
Server or Sünbül	Murad III	999–1001	1591–93	Cairo
Beyazi Mustafa	Murad III	1001–4	1593–96	1596, Varcar Vakuf, Bosnia[a]
Osman	Murad III, Mehmed III	1004–11	1596–1603	1603, Istanbul*
Abdurrezzak	Ahmed I	1011–12	1603	1604, Istanbul*
Cevher	Ahmed I	1012–13	1604–5	Cairo
El-Hajj Mustafa	Ahmed I, Osman II	1014–29, 1032–33	1605–20, 1623–24	1624, Istanbul
Süleyman	Osman II	1029–31	1620–22	1622, Istanbul*
Malatyalı Ismail	Mustafa I	1031–32	1622–23	1635, Malatya
Idris	Murad IV	1032–49	1624–40	1640
Ibrahim (Çaçu?)	Murad IV	1049–50	1639–40	1656, Istanbul*[b]
Sünbül	Ibrahim	1050–54	1640–44	1644, near Karpathos in the Aegean
Taş Yatur Ali	Ibrahim	1054–55	1644–45	1655, Edirne
Celali Ibrahim	Ibrahim, Mehmed IV	1055–57, 1058–59	1645–47, 1648–49	1651, Cairo*
Ishak	Ibrahim	Rebiülahir-Receb 1057, Şa'ban-Ramazan 1057	May–August 1647, September 1647	Cairo
Musahib Mehmed	Ibrahim	Receb-Şa'ban 1057	August–September 1647	1647, Istanbul

(cont.)

Name	Sultan	Term (Hijri)	Term (Gregorian)	Death
Mes'ud	Ibrahim	1057–58	1647–48	1650, Istanbul
Mehmed	Mehmed IV	1059–61	1649–51	Cairo
Lala/Uzun Süleyman	Mehmed IV	1061–62	1651–52	1676, Lemnos*
Behram	Mehmed IV	1062–66	1652–56	1656, Istanbul*
Dilaver	Mehmed IV	1066–68	1656–58	Cairo
Solak Mehmed	Mehmed IV	1068–73	1658–62	Cairo
Musli	Mehmed IV	1073–78	1663–68	1668, Edirne
Abbas	Mehmed IV	1078–82	1668–71	ca. 1697, Cairo
Yusuf	Mehmed IV	1082–98	1671–87	1717, Cairo
Hazinedar Ali	Süleyman II	1098–99	1687–88	ca. 1713, Cairo
Mustafa	Süleyman II	1099–1101	1688–89	Cairo
Karagöz Gedai Ahmed	Süleyman II, Ahmed II	1101–2	1690–91	1691, Edirne
Uzun Ismail	Ahmed II	1102–3	1691–92	Cairo
Kaba/Uzun Nezir	Ahmed II	1103–5	1692–94	Cairo
Uzun Ishak	Ahmed II	1105–6	1694–95	Cairo
Yapraksız Ali	Mustafa II	1106–12	1695–1700	Cairo
Solak Nezir	Mustafa II	1112–15	1700–1703	1703, Lemnos*
Küçük Abdurrahman	Ahmed III	1115–16	1703–4	1727, Istanbul
Uzun Süleyman	Ahmed III	1116–25	1704–13	1715, Cyprus*
Anber Mehmed	Ahmed III	1125–29	1713–17	Cairo
Mercan	Ahmed III	1129	1717	1721, Istanbul
El-Hajj Beshir	Ahmed III, Mahmud I	1129–59	1717–46	1746, Istanbul
Moralı Beshir	Mahmud I	1159–65	1746–52	1752, Istanbul*
Hazinedar Beshir	Mahmud I, Osman III	1165–68	1752–55	1759, Cairo
Ebu'l-Vukuf Ahmed	Osman III	1168–71	1755–57	1757, Çanakkale*
Musahib Beshir	Mustafa III	1171–82	1757–68	1768, Istanbul
Mercan	Mustafa III	1182–86	1768–72	1772, Istanbul
Cevher Mehmed	Mustafa III, Abdülhamid I	1186–87, 1193–97	1772–74, 1779–83	Medina

(cont.)

Name	Sultan	Term (Hijri)	Term (Gregorian)	Death
Sarıkçı Beshir	Abdülhamid I	1187–93	1774–79	Medina
Idris	Abdülhamid I, Selim III	1197–1204	1783–89	1796, Medina
Büyük Bilal	Selim III	1204–6	1789–91	1791, Istanbul
Halid	Selim III	1206–13	1791–98	1798, Istanbul
Küçük Bilal	Selim III	1213–22	1798–1807	1807, Istanbul
Mercan	Selim III, Mustafa IV	1222–23	1807–8	1808, Istanbul*
Kasım	Mahmud II	1223–27	1808–12	1822, Medina
Anber Mehmed	Mahmud II	1228–30	1813–15	1826, Medina
Hafız Isa	Mahmud II	1230–39	1815–23	1845, Medina
Ebu Bekir	Mahmud II	1239–41	1823–25	1825, Istanbul
Leylek/Uzun Abdullah	Mahmud II	1241–55	1825–39	1840, Istanbul
Paşaçırağı Abdullah	Abdülmecid I	1255–56	1839–40	1841, Istanbul
Tahir	Abdülmecid I	1256–60	1840–44	1844, Istanbul
Tayfur	Abdülmecid I	1260–66	1844–50	1850, Medina
Mehmed Arif	Abdülmecid I	1266–71	1850–55	1863, Istanbul
Mehmed Besim	Abdülmecid I	1271	1855	1871, Medina
Hüseyin	Abdülmecid I	1271–72	1855–56	1857, Istanbul
Mehmed Rasim	Abdülmecid I	1272	1856	1874, Istanbul
Tahsin	Abdülmecid I	1273–75	1856–59	1859, Medina
Hayreddin	Abdülmecid I	1275–77	1859–60	1873, Medina
Visaleddin	Abdülmecid I	1277	1860–61	1888, Medina
Talha	Abdülaziz	1277–92	1861–75	1875, Istanbul
Cevher	Abdülaziz	1292	1875	1887, Istanbul
Lala Süleyman	Murad V	1293	1876	1880, Istanbul
Nureddin	Abdülhamid II	1293–97	1876–80	1880, Istanbul
Hafız Behram	Abdülhamid II	1297–1304	1880–87	1887, Istanbul
Şerefeddin	Abdülhamid II	1304–6	1887–88	1889, Medina
Mehmed Yaver	Abdülhamid II	1306–15	1888–98	1898, Istanbul
Abdülgani	Abdülhamid II	1315–18	1898–1901	

(cont.)

Name	Sultan	Term (Hijri)	Term (Gregorian)	Death
Thakib Tayfur	Abdülhamid II	1318–25	1901–8	
Cevher (Baş Musahib)	Abdülhamid II	1325–26	1908–9	1909, Istanbul*
Fahreddin	Mehmed V Reşad	1326	1909	1976, Cairo

*Indicates execution.

*a*Thanks to Sanja Kadrić for this information.

*b*It is unclear whether he is identical to Çaçu Ibrahim Agha, who was killed in the 1656 Plane Tree Incident.

Works Cited

Archival Documents

Ankara, Türk Tarih Kurumu (Turkish History Foundation) Archives. *Defter-i Ağayân-i Darüssaade* (1898). MS Y 86. Published as an appendix to Ahmed Resmi Efendi, *Hamiletü'l-kübera*, ed. Ahmet Nezihi Turan, 163–75. Istanbul, 2000.

Cairo, Wizarat al-Awqaf (Ministry of Pious Endowments). MS No. 302/51 (1032/1623).

Istanbul, Başbakanlık Osmanlı Arşivi (Ottoman Prime Ministry Archives). Cevdet Maarif (C.MF) 648 (1166/1753). Published in *Misr fi al-watha'iq al-'uthmaniyya/ Osmanlı Belgelerinde Mısır/Egypt in the [sic] Ottoman Documents*, 13. Istanbul, 2007.

Maliyeden Müdevver (MAD.d). 169 (1013/1604–5), 7816 (1066–70/1655–59).

Mühimme Defteri (A.DVNS.MHM.d). Volumes 6, 29, 62, 90, 91, 99, 102, 104, 108, 110, 112, 114, 115, 160 (973/1565–1172/1758).

Mühimme-i Mısır (A.DVNS.MSR.MHM.d). Volumes 3, 4, 5, 6, 7 (1131/1718–1174/ 1761).

Tahvil Defteri (A.DVNS.NŞT.d) 11/93 (1164/1751). Published in *Misr fi al-watha'iq al-'uthmaniyya/Osmanlı Belgelerinde Mısır/Egypt in the [sic] Ottoman Documents*, 12. Istanbul, 2007.

Istanbul, Köprülü Library. MS No. 4 (1089/1678).

Istanbul, Süleymaniye Library. MS Hacı Beşir Ağa 682 (1151/1738–1158/1745).

MS Yazma Bağışlar 2524 (1146/1734).

Istanbul, Topkapı Sarayı Müzesi Arşivi (Topkapı Palace Museum Archive). D 34, 2025, 4124, 5599, 7244/2, 7657, 7911, 8786/2 (1012/1604–1167/1754).

E 33, 79, 153, 2429, 3606, 3941, 4787, 5211, 5215, 7737, 7833, 7844, 7884, 7900, 7920, 7926, 8211, 9467, 11691 (1013/1604–1298/1881).

Moscow, Archive of the Foreign Policy of the Russian Empire. Fund 89: Relations of Russia with Turkey. Files 2, 5, 6 (1745–46).

Washington, DC, National Archives. United States Department of State. Papers Relating to Internal Affairs of Turkey, 1910–29, 867.9111/226 (1928).

Chronicles and Other Primary Narrative Sources

Abdi Efendi. *Abdi Tarihi: 1730 Patrona İhtilali Hakkında bir Eser*, ed. Faik Reşit Unat. Ankara, 1943.

Abdi Efendi. *Surname*. In *Osmanlı Saray Düğünleri ve Şenlikleri*, ed. Mehmet Arslan. Volume 5, 485–537. Istanbul, 2008.

Abdullah Efendi, Derviş. *Risale-i Teberdariye fi ahval-ı ağa-yı Darü's-sa'ade.* Istanbul, Köprülü Library, MS II/233.

Abdurrahman Abdi Pasha. "Abdurrahman Abdi Paşa Vekayi'name'si: Tahlil ve Metin Tenkidi, 1058–1053/1648–1682," ed. Fahri Çetin Derin. Unpublished Ph.D. dissertation, Istanbul University, 1993.

Al-Abshihi, Shihab al-Din ibn Ahmad. *Kitab al-mustatraf fi kulli fannin mustazraf.* 2 vols. Cairo, 1902.

Ahmed Çelebi ibn 'Abd al-Ghani. *Awdah al-isharat fi man tawalla Misr al-Qahira min al-wuzara' wa-l-bashat,* ed. A. A. 'Abd al-Rahim. Cairo, 1978.

Alberti, Tommaso. *Viaggio a Costantinopoli di Tommaso Alberti (1620–1621), pubblicato da Alberto Bacchi della Lega.* Bologna, 1889.

Ali, Mustafa. *Halatü'l-Kahire mine'l-'adati'z-zahire.* Istanbul, Süleymaniye Library, MS Fatih 5427/14. MS Esad Efendi 2407.

Mustafa Ali's Counsel for Sultans of 1581: Edition, Translation, Notes, ed. and trans. Andreas Tietze. 2 vols. Vienna, 1979–82.

Mustafa Ali's Description of Cairo of 1599, ed. and trans. Andreas Tietze. Vienna, 1975.

Anonymous. *Akhbar al-nuwwab min dawlat Al 'Uthman min hin istawala 'alayha al-sultan Salim Khan.* Istanbul, Topkapı Palace Museum Library, MS Hazine 1623.

Anonymous. *Coppie d'une lettre escrite de Constantinople à un Gentil-homme François, contenant la trahison du Bascha Nassouf, sa mort estrange, & des grandes richesses qui luy ont esté trouees.* Paris, 1615.

Anonymous. *Defter-i kütübhane-i Beşir Ağa-yı İstanbul'da Bab-i A'li civarında vaki'dir.* Istanbul, 1303/1885.

Arrowsmith-Brown, J. H., ed. and trans. *Prutky's Travels in Ethiopia and Other Countries.* London, 1991.

Asım Efendi, Ahmed. *Asım Tarihi.* 2 vols. Istanbul, 1284/1867.

Asım Efendi, Ismail (Küçük Çelebizade). *Tarih-i İsmail Asım Efendi.* Istanbul, 1282/1865.

Ata, Tayyarzade Ahmed. *Osmanlı Saray Tarihi: Tarih-i Enderun,* ed. Mehmet Arslan. 5 vols. Istanbul, 2010.

Ayvansarayi, Hafız Hüseyin. *The Garden of the Mosques: Hafız Hüseyin Ayvansarayî's Guide to the Muslim Monuments of Ottoman Istanbul,* trans. Howard Crane. Leiden, 2000.

Barkan, Ömer Lütfi, ed. "Kanunname-i Mısır." In *XV ve XVıncı Asırlarda Osmanlı İmparatorluğunda Ziraî Ekonominin Hukuki ve Mali Esasları,* ed. Ömer Lütfi Barkan. Volume 1: *Kanunlar.* Istanbul, 1943.

Brookes, Douglas Scott, ed. and trans. *The Concubine, the Princess, and the Teacher: Voices from the Ottoman Harem.* Austin, TX, 2008.

Bruce, James. *Travels to Discover the Source of the Nile in the Years 1768, 1769, 1770, 1771, 1772, and 1773.* 6 vols. Dublin, 1790–91.

Al-Budayri, Ahmad, al-Hallaq. *Hawadith Dimashq al-yawmiyya, 1154–1175 h./ 1741–1762,* ed. Ahmad Izzat Abd al-Karim. Condensed by Muhammad Sa'id al-Qasimi. Cairo, 1959.

Burckhardt, John Lewis (Johann Ludwig). *Notes on the Bedouins and the Wahabys, Collected during His Travels in the East.* 2 vols. London, 1831.

Travels in Arabia. Beirut, 1972.

Travels in Nubia. New York, NY, 1978.

Burstein, Stanley, ed. *Ancient African Civilizations: Kush and Axum*. Princeton, NJ, 1998.

Burton, Richard Francis. *First Footsteps in East Africa, or, An Exploration of Harar*, ed. Isabel Burton. 2 vols. London, 1894.

Personal Narrative of a Pilgrimage to al-Madinah and Meccah. Memorial ed. 2 vols. London, 1893. Reprint, New York, NY, 1964.

Çapanoğlu, M. Süleyman. "Abdülhamidin En Yakın Adamı Nadir Ağa Eski Efendisi İçin Ne Söylüyör?" *Yedigün* 83 (10 Birinciteşrin [October] 1934): 19–21.

Carlier de Pinon, Jean. *Relation du voyage en Orient de Carlier de Pinon (1579)*, ed. Edgar Blochet. *Revue de l'Orient latin* 12 (1909–11): 112–203, 327–421.

Cevdet, Ahmed. *Tarih-i Cevdet*. 10 vols. Istanbul, 1854–85.

Al-Damurdashi, Ahmad Katkhuda 'Azeban. *Al-Durra al-musana fi akhbar al-Kinana*. British Library, MS OR 1073–74.

Dankoff, Robert, trans. and commentary. *The Intimate Life of an Ottoman Statesman: Melek Ahmed Pasha (1599–1662) as Portrayed in Evliya Çelebi's Book of Travels*. Albany, NY, 1991.

Dawood, N. J., trans. *Tales from the Thousand and One Nights*. Hammondsworth, Middlesex, 1954. Reprint, 1985.

De la Croix, Sieur. *Le Sérail des empereurs turcs: relation manuscrite du sieur de la Croix à la fin du règne du sultan Mehmed IV*, ed. Corinne Thépaut-Cabasset. Paris, 2007.

Defterdar Sarı Mehmed Pasha. *Zübde-i Vekayiât*, ed. Abdülkadir Özcan. Ankara, 1995.

Delbare, François-Thomas. *Histoire des ministres-favoris, anciens et modernes*. Paris, 1820.

Destari Salih Efendi. *Destari Salih Tarihi: Patrona Halil Ayaklanması Hakkında bir Kaynak*, ed. Bekir Sıtkı Baykal. Ankara, 1962.

DeVos, Lambert. *Turkish Costumes* (ca. 1574). American School of Classical Studies at Athens, Gennadius Library, MS No. A986q.

D'Ohsson, Ignatius Mouradgea. *Tableau général de l'Empire othoman*. 7 vols. Paris, 1787–1820.

Doughty, Charles M. *Arabia Deserta*, ed. H. L. MacRitchie. London, 1989.

Duran, Tülay, ed. *Tarihimizde Vakıf Kuran Kadınlar: Hanım Sultan Vakfiyyeleri*. Istanbul, 1990.

Ertuğ, Hasan Ferit. "Musahib-i Sani-i Hazret-i Şehr-yari Nadir Ağa'nın Hatiratı." Parts 1 and 2. *Toplumsal Tarih* 49 (January 1998): 7–15; 50 (February 1998): 6–14.

Evliya Çelebi. *Seyahatname*, eds. Orhan Şaik Gökyay, Seyit Ali Kahraman, Yücel Dağlı, Robert Dankoff, et al. 10 vols. Istanbul, 1996–2007.

Firpo, Luigi, ed. *Relazioni di ambasciatori veneti al Senato*. Volume 13: *Costantinopoli (1590–1793)*. Turin, 1984.

Flachat, Jean-Claude. *Observations sur le commerce et sur les arts d'une partie de l'Europe, de l'Asie, de l'Afrique et même des Indes orientales*. 2 vols. Lyon, 1766.

Foster, Sir William, ed. *The Red Sea and Adjacent Countries at the Close of the Seventeenth Century, as Described by Joseph Pitts, William Daniel, and Charles Jacques Poncet*. London, 1949.

Frank, Louis. "Memoir on the Traffic in Negroes to Cairo and on the Illnesses to Which They Are Subject upon Arrival There," trans. Michel Le Gall. In *Slavery in the Islamic Middle East*, ed. Shaun Marmon, 69–88. Princeton, NJ, 1999.

Girard, P. S. *Mémoire sur l'agriculture, l'industrie et le commerce de l'Égypte*. Volume 17 of *Description de l'Égypte*, 2nd ed. Paris, 1824.

Gold, Milton, trans. *Tarikh-e Sistan*. Rome, 1976.

El-Habeşi, Ali b. Abdurrauf. *Rafa'ilü'l-gubuş fi feza'ilü'l-Hubuş*. Istanbul, Süleymaniye Library, MS Fatih 4360.

Al-Hallaq, Mehmed b. Yusuf. *Tarih-i Mısr-ı Kahire*. Istanbul University Library, MS T.Y. 628.

Hasanbeyzade Ahmed Pasha. *Hasan Bey-zade Tarihi*, ed. Şevki Nezihi Aykut. 2 vols. Ankara, 2004.

Holt, P. M., ed. and trans. *The Sudan of the Three Niles: The Funj Chronicles, 910–1288/1504–1871*. Leiden, 1999.

Ibn Battuta, Muhammad b. 'Abdallah. *Rihla Ibn Battuta*. Beirut, 1964.

Ibn Ishaq, Muhammad. *The Life of Muhammad: A Translation of Ishaq's* Sirat Rasul Allah, ed. 'Abd al-Malik Ibn Hisham. Translated by Alfred Guillaume. London, 1955.

Al-Ishaqi, Muhammad 'Abd al-Mu'ti. *Akhbar al-uwal fi man tasarrafa fi Misr al-Qahira min arbab al-duwal*. Bulaq, 1304/1886–87.

Al-Jabarti, 'Abd al-Rahman. *'Aja'ib al-athar fi-l-tarajim wa-l-akhbar*, ed. Shmuel Moreh. 4 vols. Jerusalem, 2013.

   Al-Jabarti's History of Egypt: 'Aja'ib al-athar fi-l-tarajim wa-l-akhbar, eds. Thomas Philipp and Moshe Perlmann. Stuttgart, 1994.

Al-Jahiz, 'Amr b. Bahr. *Risalat mufakharat al-sudan 'ala al-bidan*. In *Rasa'il al-Jahiz*, ed. 'Abd al-Salam Muhammad Harun, I: 173–226. Cairo, 1385/1965.

Johnson, Samuel. *A Voyage to Abyssinia*, ed. Joel L. Gold. Translated from the French. New Haven, CT, 1985.

Katib Çelebi. *The Balance of Truth*, trans. Geoffrey L. Lewis. London, 1957.

   Fezleke. 2 vols. Istanbul, 1286–87/1869–71.

Koçi Bey. *Koçi Bey Risaleleri*, ed. Zuhuri Danışman. Prepared by Seda Çakmakoğlu. Istanbul, 2008.

Lane, Edward W. *An Account of the Manners and Customs of the Modern Egyptians: The Definitive 1860 Edition*. Cairo, 2003.

Lello, Henry. *The Report of Lello, Third English Ambassador to the Sublime Porte*, ed. Orhan Burian. Ankara, 1952.

Lewis, Bernard, trans. *Islam from the Prophet Muhammad to the Capture of Constantinople*. Volume 1: *Politics and War*. Volume 2: *Religion and Society*. Oxford, 1974. Reprint, 1987.

Luther, Kenneth Allin, trans. *The History of the Seljuq Turks from the* Jami' al-Tawarikh, *an Ilkhanid Adaption [sic] of the* Saljuq-nama *of Zahir al-Din Nishapuri*, ed. C. Edmund Bosworth. Richmond, Surrey, UK, 2001.

McCullagh, Francis. *The Fall of Abd-ul-Hamid*. London, 1910.

Mehmed bin Mehmed. "Mehmed bin Mehmed Er-Rumi (Edirneli)'nin *Nuhbetü't-tevarih ve'l-ahbar*'ı ile *Tarih-i Al-i Osman*'ının Metni ve Tahlilleri," ed. Abdurrahman Sağırlı. Unpublished Ph.D. dissertation, Istanbul University, 2000.

Naima, Mustafa. *Tarih-i Naima: Ravzatü'l-Hüseyn fi hulasat-i ahbari'l-hafikayn*, ed. Mehmed İpşirli. 4 vols. Ankara, 2007.

Peçevi, Ibrahim. *Tarih-i Peçevi*, ed. Bekir Sıtkı Baykal. 2 vols. Ankara, 1981.

Raşid, Mehmed, Efendi. *Tarih-i Raşid*. 5 vols. Istanbul, 1282/1865.

Rasim, Ahmed. *Resimli ve Haritalı Osmanlı Tarihi*. 4 vols. Istanbul, 1328–30/1910–12.

Resmi, Ahmed. *Hamiletü'l-kübera*, ed. Ahmet Nezihi Turan. Istanbul, 2000.

Richards, Donald S., ed. and trans. *The Annals of the Saljuq Turks: Selections from al-Kamil fi'l-Ta'rikh of 'Izz al-Din Ibn al-Athir*. London, 2002.

Rycaut, Paul. *A History of the Turkish Empire from the Year 1623 to the Year 1677*. London, 1680.

Al-Sabi, Hilal. *Rusum dar al-khilafa: The Rules and Regulations of the 'Abbasid Court*, trans. Elie A. Salem. Beirut, 1977.

Sadullah Enveri Efendi. *Sadullah Enveri Tarihi*. 2 vols. Bulaq, 1243/1827.

Safi, Mustafa. *Mustafa Safi'nin* Zübdetü't-Tevarih'*i*, ed. İbrahim Hakkı Çuhadar. 2 vols. Ankara, 2003.

Salt, Henry. *A Voyage to Abyssinia, and Travels into the Interior of That Country*. Philadelphia, 1816.

Şanizade Mehmed Ataullah Efendi. *Şanizade Tarihi*, ed. Ziya Yılmazer. 4 vols. Istanbul, 2008.

Selaniki Mustafa Efendi. *Selaniki Tarihi*, ed. Mehmet İpşirli. 2 vols. Istanbul, 1989.

Şemdanizade Fındıklılı Süleyman Efendi. *Şem'dani-zade Fındıklılı Süleyman Efendi Tarihi: Mür'i't-tevarih*, ed. M. Münir Aktepe. 2 parts in 3 vols. Istanbul, 1976.

Silahdar Fındıklılı Mehmed Agha. *Nusretname*, ed. İsmet Parmaksızoğlu. 2 vols. Istanbul, 1962.

Silahdar Tarihi. 2 vols. Istanbul, 1928.

Subhi Efendi. *Subhi Efendi Tarihi*. In *Tarih-i Sami ve Şakir ve Subhi*. Istanbul, 1198/1783.

Süreyya, Mehmed. *Sicill-i Osmani*. 4 vols. Istanbul, 1308–15/1890–97. Reprint, Westmead, Farnborough, UK, 1971.

Al-Tabari, Muhammad b. Jarir. *The History of al-Tabari*. Volume 31: *The War between Brothers: The Caliphate of Muhammad al-Amin, A.D. 809–813/A.H. 193–198*, trans. Michael Fishbein. Albany, NY, 1992.

History of al-Tabari. Volume 39: *Biographies of the Prophet's Companions and Their Successors*, trans. Ella Landau-Tasseron. Albany, NY, 1998.

Topçular Katibi. *Topçular Kâtibi 'Abdülkadir (Kadrı) Efendi Tarihi: Metin ve Tahlil*, ed. Ziya Yılmazer. 2 vols. Ankara, 2003.

Vasif, Ahmed, Efendi. *Mehasinü'l-asar ve haka'ikü'l-ahbar*, ed. Mücteba İlgürel. Ankara, 1994.

Vehbi Efendi, Seyyid. *Surname: Sultan Ahmed'in Düğün Kitabı*, dir. Ahmet Ertuğ. Transcribed into Latin letters and with a modern Turkish translation by Mertol Tulum. Bern, 2000.

White, Charles. *Three Years in Constantinople, or, Domestic Manners of the Turks in 1844*. 2nd ed. 2 vols. London, 1846.

Yerasimos, Stéphane, ed. and trans. *Deux ottomans à Paris sous le Directoire et l'Empire: relations d'ambassade*. Paris, 1998.

Secondary Sources

Ottoman and Islamic History

Abou-El-Haj, Rifaat A. *The 1703 Rebellion and the Structure of Ottoman Politics*. Leiden, 1984.

"Ottoman Diplomacy at Karlowitz." *Journal of the American Oriental Society* 87, 4 (1967): 498–512.

"The Ottoman Vezir and Paşa Households, 1683–1703: A Preliminary Report." *Journal of the American Oriental Society* 94 (1974): 438–47.

Akakuş, Recep. *Eyyüp Sultan ve Mukaddes Emanetler.* Istanbul, 1973.

Akdağ, Mustafa. *Celali İsyanları (1550–1603).* Ankara, 1963.

Aksan, Virginia H. "Enlightening the Ottomans: Tott and Mustafa III." In *International Congress on Learning and Education in the Ottoman World: Istanbul, 12–15 April 1999*, ed. Ali Çaksu, 163–74. Istanbul, 2001.

An Ottoman Statesman in War and Peace: Ahmed Resmi Efendi, 1700–1783. Leiden, 1995.

"Whatever Happened to the Janissaries? Mobilization for the 1768–1774 Russo-Ottoman War." *War in History* 5, 1 (1998): 23–36.

Aktepe, M. Münir. *Patrona İsyanı, 1730.* Istanbul, 1958.

Ali, Omar H. *Malik Ambar: Power and Slavery across the Indian Ocean.* Oxford, 2016.

Alkan, Mustafa N. "Tanzimattan Sonra Vakıflar İdaresinde Yeniden Yapılanmaya Dair bir Örnek: Adana Evkaf Müdürlüğü." *Ankara Üniversitesi Osmanlı Tarihi Araştırma ve Uygulama Merkezi Dergisi* 19 (2006): 13–31.

Anderson, Matthew S. "Great Britain and the Russo-Turkish War of 1768–74." *English Historical Review* 69, 270 (1954): 39–58.

Arbel, Benjamin. "Nur Banu (c. 1530–1583): A Venetian Sultana?" *Turcica* 24 (1992): 241–59.

Artan, Tülay. "The Making of the Sublime Porte Near the Alay Köşkü and a Tour of a Grand Vizierial Palace at Süleymaniye." *Turcica* 43 (2011): 145–206.

Ashtor, Eliyahu. *The Jews of Moslem Spain.* 3 vols. in 2. Philadelphia, 1973. Reissued 1992.

Atıl, Esin. *Levni and the* Surname*: The Story of an Eighteenth-Century Ottoman Festival.* Istanbul, 1999.

Süleymanname: The Illustrated History of Süleyman the Magnificent. Washington, DC, 1986.

Ayalon, David. *L'esclavage du mamelouk.* Jerusalem, 1951.

Eunuchs, Caliphs, and Sultans: A Study in Power Relationships. Jerusalem, 1999.

"The Muslim City and the Mamluk Military Aristocracy." *Proceedings of the Israel Academy of Sciences and Humanities* 2 (1968): 311–29.

"On the Eunuchs in Islam." *Jerusalem Studies in Arabic and Islam* 1 (1979): 67–124.

Badr, Hamza Abd al-Aziz, and Daniel Crecelius. "The *Awqaf* of al-Hajj Bashir Agha in Cairo." *Annales islamologiques* 27 (1993): 291–311.

"The *Waqf*s of Shahin Ahmad Agha." *Annales islamologiques* 26 (1992): 79–114.

Baer, Marc David. "The Great Fire of 1660 and the Islamization of Christian and Jewish Space in Istanbul." *International Journal of Middle East Studies* 36 (2004): 159–81.

Barbir, Karl K. *Ottoman Rule in Damascus, 1700–1758.* Princeton, NJ, 1980.

Barkan, Ömer Lutfi. "The Price Revolution of the Sixteenth Century: A Turning Point in the Economic History of the Near East," trans. Justin McCarthy. *International Journal of Middle East Studies* 6 (1975): 3–28.

Barnes, John Robert. *An Introduction to Religious Foundations in the Ottoman Empire.* Leiden, 1987.

Behrens-Abouseif, Doris. "The 'Abd al-Rahman Katkhuda Style in Eighteenth-Century Cairo." *Annales islamologiques* 26 (1992): 117–26.

Azbakiyya and Its Environs from Azbak to Ismail, 1476–1879. Cairo, 1985.
Cairo of the Mamluks: A History of the Architecture and Its Culture. London, 2007.
"The Complex of Sultan Mahmud I in Cairo." *Muqarnas* 28 (2011): 195–220.
Egypt's Adjustment to Ottoman Rule: Institutions, Waqf, *and Architecture (16th and 17th Centuries).* Leiden, 1994.
"Four Domes of the Late Mamluk Period." *Annales islamologiques* 17 (1981): 191–201.
Islamic Architecture in Cairo: An Introduction. Leiden, 1989. New ed. Cairo, 1993.
"Sultan Qaytbay's Foundation in Medina: The *Madrasah*, the *Ribat*, and the *Dashisha*." *Mamluk Studies Review* 2 (1998): 61–72.
"An Unlisted Monument of the Fifteenth Century: The Dome of Zawiyat al-Damirdaš." *Annales islamologiques* 18 (1982): 105–21.
Behrens-Abouseif, Doris, and Leonor Fernandes. "Sufi Architecture in Early Ottoman Cairo." *Annales islamologiques* 20 (1984): 103–14.
Beyhan, Mehmet Ali. "Amusements in the Ottoman Palace of the Early Nineteenth Century: Revelations from a Newly Analysed *Ruzname*." In *Celebration, Entertainment, and Theatre in the Ottoman World*, eds. Suraiya Faroqhi and Arzu Öztürkmen, 225–36. London, 2014.
Börekçi, Günhan. "Factions and Favorites at the Courts of Ahmed I (r. 1603–1617) and His Immediate Predecessors." Unpublished Ph.D. dissertation, Ohio State University, 2010.
Bosworth, C. Edmund. "The Army of the Ghaznavids." In *Warfare and Weaponry in South Asia, 1000–1800*, eds. Jos J. L. Gommans and Dirk H. A. Kolff, 153–84. New Delhi, 2001.
Brookes, Douglas S. "Of Swords and Tombs: Symbolism in the Ottoman Accession Ritual." *Turkish Studies Association Bulletin* 17, 2 (1993): 1–22.
Buehler, Arthur F. *Sufi Heirs of the Prophet: The Indian Naqshbandiyya and the Rise of the Meditating Sufi Shaykh.* Columbia, SC, 1998.
Burak, Guy. "Faith, Law, and Empire in the Ottoman 'Age of Confessionalization' (15th-17th Century): The Case of 'Renewal of Faith.'" *Mediterranean Historical Review* 28, 1 (2013): 1–23.
The Second Formation of Islamic Law: The Hanafi School in the Early Modern Ottoman Empire. New York, NY, 2015.
Çağman, Filiz. "Saray Nakkaşhanesinin Yeri Üzerine Düsünceler." In *Sanat Tarihinde Doğudan Batıya: Ünsal Yücel Anısına Sempozyum Bildirileri*, 35–46. Istanbul, 1989.
Carboni, Stefano. "The Arabic Manuscripts." In *Pages of Perfection: Islamic Paintings and Calligraphy from the Russian Academy of Sciences, St. Petersburg*, eds. Yuri A. Petrosyan et al., 77–91. Lugano, Switzerland, 1995.
Casale, Giancarlo. *The Ottoman Age of Exploration.* Oxford, 2010.
Clayer, Nathalie. *Mystiques, état et société: les Halvetis dans l'aire balkanique de la fin du XVe siècle à nos jours.* Leiden, 1994.
Cook, Michael A. *Commanding Right and Forbidding Wrong in Islamic Thought.* Cambridge, 2000.
Population Pressure in Rural Anatolia, 1450–1600. London, 1972.
Cortese, Delia, and Simonetta Calderini. *Women and the Fatimids in the World of Islam.* Edinburgh, 2006.

Crecelius, Daniel. "The Emergence of the Shaykh al-Azhar as the Pre-Eminent Religious Leader in Egypt." In *Colloque international sur l'histoire du Caire, 27 mars-5 avril 1969*, eds. Andrée Assabgui et al., 109–23. Cairo, 1972.

"The *Waqf* of Muhammad Bey Abu al-Dhahab in Cairo." *International Journal of Middle East Studies* 23, 1 (1991): 57–81.

Curry, John J. *The Transformation of Muslim Mystical Thought in the Ottoman Empire: The Rise of the Halveti Order, 1350–1650*. Edinburgh, 2010.

Değirmenci, Tülün. *İktidar Oyunları ve Resimli Kitaplar: II. Osman Devrinde Değişen Güç Simgeleri*. Istanbul, 2012.

Demiriz, Yıldız. *Eyüp'te Türbeler*. Ankara, 1982.

Derin, Haldun. *Çankaya Özel Kalemini Anımsarken (1933–1951)*. Istanbul, 1995.

Deringil, Selim. *The Well-Protected Domains: Ideology and the Legitimation of Power in the Ottoman Empire, 1876–1909*. London, 1998.

El-Rouayheb, Khaled. *Islamic Intellectual History in the Seventeenth Century: Scholarly Currents in the Ottoman Empire and the Maghreb*. New York, NY, 2015.

Encyclopaedia Iranica. London, 1985– .

Encyclopaedia of Islam, 2nd ed. Leiden, 1960–2002.

Encyclopaedia of Islam Three. Leiden, 2007– .

Erder, Leila, and Suraiya Faroqhi. "Population Rise and Fall in Anatolia, 1550–1620." *Middle Eastern Studies* 15 (1979): 322–45.

Erimtan, Can. *Ottomans Facing West? The Origins of the Tulip Age and Its Development in Modern Turkey*. London, 2008.

Fahmy, Khaled. *All the Pasha's Men: Mehmed Ali, His Army, and the Making of Modern Egypt*. Cambridge, 1997.

Mehmed Ali: From Ottoman Governor to Ruler of Egypt. Oxford, 2009.

Faroqhi, Suraiya. *Pilgrims and Sultans: The Hajj under the Ottomans*. London, 1994.

Fetvacı, Emine. *Picturing History at the Ottoman Court*. Bloomington, IN, 2013.

Finkel, Caroline. *Osman's Dream: History of the Ottoman Empire*. London, 2005.

Fisher, Alan W., and Carol G. Fisher. "A Note on the Location of the Royal Ottoman Painting Ateliers." *Muqarnas* 3 (1985): 118–20.

Fleischer, Cornell H. *Bureaucrat and Intellectual in the Ottoman Empire: The Historian Mustafa Ali (1541–1600)*. Princeton, NJ, 1986.

Gemil, Tahsin. "Vakifuri otomane fondate pe teritoriul României (sec. XV-XIII)." In *Fațetele istoriei: existențe, identități, dinamici – Omagiu academicianului Ștefan Ștefănescu*, eds. Tudor Teoteoi et al., 193–97. Bucharest, 2000.

Gibb, H. A. R., and Harold Bowen. *Islamic Society and the West: A Study of the Impact of Western Civilization on Moslem Culture in the Near East*. Volume 1, Part 1. London, 1950.

Goitein, S. D. *A Mediterranean Society*. Volume 1: *Economic Foundations*. Volume 2: *The Community*. Berkeley, CA, 1967, 1971.

Gordon, Matthew S. *The Breaking of a Thousand Swords: A History of the Turkish Military of Samarra, A.H. 200–275/815–889 C.E.* Albany, NY, 2001.

Grehan, James. "Smoking and 'Early Modern' Sociability: The Great Tobacco Debate in the Ottoman Middle East (Seventeenth to Eighteenth Centuries)." *American Historical Review* 111, 5 (2006): 1352–77.

Griswold, William J. *The Great Anatolian Rebellion, 1000–1020/1591–1611*. Berlin, 1983.

Güler, Mustafa. *Osmanlı Devlet'inde Haremeyn Vakıfları (XVI.–XVII. Yüzyıllar)*. Istanbul, 2002.

Hamadeh, Shirine. *The City's Pleasures: Istanbul in the Eighteenth Century*. Seattle, WA, 2008.

Hambly, Gavin. "A Note on the Trade in Eunuchs in Mughal Bengal." *Journal of the American Oriental Society* 94, 1 (1974): 125–30.

Hanna, Nelly. *Artisan Entrepreneurs in Cairo and Early-Modern Capitalism (1600–1800)*. Syracuse, NY, 2014.

Har-El, Shai. *The Struggle for Domination in the Middle East: The Ottoman-Mamluk War, 1485–91*. Leiden, 1995.

Hathaway, Jane. *The Arab Lands under Ottoman Rule, 1516–1800*. With contributions by Karl K. Barbir. Harlow, Essex, UK, 2008.

Beshir Agha, Chief Eunuch of the Ottoman Imperial Harem. Oxford, 2006.

"The *Evlâd-i 'Arab* ('Sons of the Arabs') in Ottoman Egypt: A Rereading." In *Frontiers of Ottoman Studies: State, Province, and the West*. Volume 1, eds. Colin Imber and Keiko Kiyotaki, 203–16. London, 2005.

"The Exalted Lineage of Rıdvan Bey Revisited: A Reinterpretation of the Spurious Genealogy of a Grandee in Ottoman Egypt." *International Journal of Turkish Studies* 13, 1–2 (2007): 97–111.

"Exiled Harem Eunuchs as Proponents of the Hanafi *Madhhab* in Egypt." *Annales islamologiques* 37 (2003): 191–99.

"Habeşi Mehmed Agha: The First Chief Harem Eunuch (Darüssaade Ağası) of the Ottoman Empire." In *The Islamic Scholarly Tradition: Studies in History, Law, and Thought in Honor of Professor Michael Allan Cook*, eds. Asad Q. Ahmed, Behnam Sadeghi, and Michael Bonner, 179–95. Leiden, 2011.

"The 'Mamluk Breaker' Who Was Really a *Kul* Breaker: A Fresh Look at Kul Kıran Mehmed Pasha, Governor of Egypt 1607–1611." In *The Arab Lands in the Ottoman Era: Essays in Honor of Professor Caesar Farah*, ed. Jane Hathaway, 93–109. Minneapolis, MN, 2009.

"The Ottomans and the Yemeni Coffee Trade." In *The Ottomans and Trade*, eds. Ebru Boyar and Kate Fleet. Special issue of *Oriente Moderno* 25, 1 (2006): 161–71.

"Out of Africa, into the Palace: The Ottoman Chief Harem Eunuch." In *Living in the Ottoman Realm*, eds. Christine Isom-Verhaaren and Kent F. Schull, 225–38. Bloomington, IN, 2015.

The Politics of Households in Ottoman Egypt: The Rise of the Qazdağlıs. Cambridge, 1997.

"The Role of the Kızlar Ağası in 17th–18th Century Ottoman Egypt." *Studia Islamica* 75 (1992): 141–58.

"The Role of the 'Ulama' in Social Protest in Late Eighteenth-Century Egypt." Unpublished MA thesis, University of Texas at Austin, 1986.

A Tale of Two Factions: Myth, Memory, and Identity in Ottoman Egypt and Yemen. Albany, NY, 2003.

"A Twelfth-Century Partnership in Silk-Trading in the Egyptian Delta: A Geniza Study." *Journal of the Middle East Studies Society at Columbia University* 2, 1 (1988): 23–37.

"The Wealth and Influence of an Exiled Ottoman Eunuch in Egypt: The *Waqf* Inventory of Abbas Agha." *Journal of the Economic and Social History of the Orient* 37 (1994): 293–317.

Hellier, Chris. *Splendors of Istanbul: Houses and Palaces along the Bosphorus.* New York, NY, 1993.

Hinchy, Jessica. "Eunuchs and the East India Company in North India." In *Celibate and Childless Men in Power: Ruling Eunuchs and Bishops in the Pre-Modern World*, eds. Almut Höfert, Matthew M. Mesley, and Serena Tolino, 149–74. London, 2018.

Holbrook, Victoria Rowe. "Ibn 'Arabi and Ottoman Dervish Traditions: The Melami Supra-Order." Parts 1 and 2. *Journal of the Muhyiddin Ibn Arabi Society* 9 (1991): 18–35; 12 (1992): 15–33.

Holt, P. M. *Egypt and the Fertile Crescent: A Political History, 1516–1922.* Ithaca, NY, 1966.

Hourani, Albert. "Ottoman Reform and the Politics of Notables." In *Beginnings of Modernization in the Middle East in the Nineteenth Century*, eds. William R. Polk and Richard L. Chambers, 41–68. Chicago, IL, 1968.

Imber, Colin. *The Ottoman Empire, 1300–1650: The Structure of Power.* 2nd ed. New York, NY, 2009 [2002].

Inalcik, Halil. "The Conquest of Edirne, 1361." *Archivum Ottomanicum* 3 (1971): 185–210.

The Ottoman Empire: The Classical Age, 1300–1600, trans. Norman Itzkowitz and Colin Imber. London, 1973.

"The Question of the Closing of the Black Sea under the Ottomans." In Halil Inalcik, *Essays in Ottoman History*, 415–45. Istanbul, 1998.

İpşirli Argıt, Betül. *Rabia Gülnuş Emetullah Sultan, 1640–1715.* Istanbul, 2014.

Irwin, Robert. *The Middle East in the Middle Ages: The Early Mamluk Sultanate, 1250–1382.* London, 1986.

İtez, Özüm. "Osmanlı Arkeolojisinin Daha Sağlam Temeller Üzerinde Gelişmesine Öncüllük Etmek İstiyoruz." *Arkitera*, 24 March 2016. www.arktitera.com/soylesi/831/osmanli-arkeolojisinin-daha-saglam-temeller-uzerinde-gelismesine-onculluk-etmek-istiyoruz.

Itzkowitz, Norman. "Eighteenth-Century Ottoman Realities." *Studia Islamica* 16 (1962): 73–94.

"Mehmed Raghip Paşa: The Making of an Ottoman Grand Vizier." Unpublished Ph.D. dissertation, Princeton University, 1958.

Ottoman Empire and Islamic Tradition. Chicago, IL, 1972.

Junne, George H. *The Black Eunuchs of the Ottoman Empire: Networks of Power in the Court of the Sultan.* London, 2016.

Kafesçioğlu, Çiğdem. *Constantinopolis/Istanbul: Cultural Encounter, Imperial Vision, and the Construction of the Ottoman Capital.* University Park, PA, 2009.

Kayaoğlu, İsmet. "Beşir Ağa Vakfı." *Belgeler* 15, 2 (1981–86): 77–87.

Krstić, Tijana. *Contested Conversions to Islam: Narratives of Religious Change and Communal Politics in the Early Modern Ottoman Empire.* Stanford, CA, 2011.

Kunt, Metin. "Ethno-Regional (*Cins*) Solidarity in the Seventeenth-Century Ottoman Establishment." *International Journal of Middle East Studies* 5 (1974): 233–39.

The Sultan's Servants: The Transformation of Ottoman Provincial Government, 1550–1650. New York, NY, 1983.

Le Gall, Dina. *A Culture of Sufism: Naqshbandis in the Ottoman World, 1450–1700.* Albany, NY, 2005.

Lev, Yaacov. "Army, Regime, and Society in Fatimid Egypt, 358–487/968–1094." *International Journal of Middle East Studies* 19 (1987): 337–65.

Lewis, Bernard. *Race and Slavery in the Middle East: An Historical Enquiry.* New York, NY, 1990.

Lowry, Heath W. *The Nature of the Early Ottoman State.* Albany, NY, 2003.

MacKay, Pierre A. "The Manuscripts of the *Seyahatname* of Evliya Çelebi – Part I: The Archetype." *Der Islam* 52, 2 (1975): 278–98.

Marmon, Shaun. *Eunuchs and Sacred Boundaries in Islamic Society.* New York, NY, 1995.

Marsot, Afaf Lutfi al-Sayyid. *Egypt in the Reign of Muhammad Ali.* Cambridge, 1984.
     "The Ulama of Cairo in the Eighteenth and Nineteenth Centuries." In *Scholars, Saints, and Sufis: Muslim Religious Institutions since 1500*, ed. Nikki R. Keddie, 149–65. Berkeley, CA, 1972.

Martin, B. G. "A Short History of the Khalwati Order of Dervishes." In *Scholars, Saints, and Sufis: Muslim Religious Institutions since 1500*, ed. Nikki R. Keddie, 275–305. Berkeley, CA, 1972.

Ménage, V. L. "Sidelights on the Devshirme from Idris and Sa'duddin." *Bulletin of the School of Oriental and African Studies* 18 (1956): 181–83.

Menchinger, Ethan L. *The First of the Modern Ottomans: The Intellectual History of Ahmed Vasif.* New York, NY, 2017.

Menemencioğlu, Nermin, ed., with Fahir İz. *The Penguin Book of Turkish Verse.* Hammondsworth, 1978.

Murphey, Rhoads. "Mustafa Safi's Version of the Kingly Virtues as Presented in His *Zübdetü't-tevarih*, or Annals of Sultan Ahmed, 1012–1023 A.H./1603–1614 A.D." In *Frontiers of Ottoman Studies: State, Province, and the West.* Volume 1, eds. Colin Imber and Keiko Kiyotaki, 5–24. London, 2005.
     "Twists and Turns in the Diplomatic Dialogue: The Politics of Peace-Making in the Early Eighteenth Century." In *The Peace of Passarowitz, 1718*, eds. Charles Ingrao, Nikola Samardžić, and Jovan Pešalj, 73–91. West Lafayette, IN, 2011.

Nayir, Zeynep. *Osmanlı Mimarlığında Sultan Ahmet Külliyesi ve Sonrası.* Istanbul, 1975.

Necipoğlu, Gülru. *The Age of Sinan: Architectural Culture in the Ottoman Empire.* London, 2005.
     Architecture, Ceremonial, and Power: The Topkapı Palace in the Fifteenth and Sixteenth Centuries. New York, NY, 1991.

Niyazioğlu, Aslı. "Dreams, Ottoman Biography Writing, and the Halveti Sünbüli Şeyhs of Sixteenth-Century Istanbul." In *Many Ways of Speaking about the Self: Middle Eastern Ego-Documents in Arabic, Persian, and Turkish (14th–20th Century)*, eds. Ralf Elger and Yavuz Köse, 171–84. Wiesbaden, 2010.

Nizri, Michael. *Ottoman High Politics and the Ulema Household.* New York, NY, 2014.

Noradounghian, Gabriel. *Recueil d'actes internationaux de l'Empire ottoman.* Volume 1: *1300–1789.* Paris, 1897.

Nutku, Özdemir. *IV. Mehmet'in Edirne Şenliği (1675).* Ankara, 1972. 2nd printing, 1987.

Ok, Sema. *Harem Dünyası: Harem Ağaları*. Istanbul, 1997.

Orhonlu, Cengiz. *Osmanlı İmparatorluğu'nun Güney Siyaseti: Habeş Eyaleti*. Ankara, 1974. 2nd printing, 1996.

Osman, Tosyavizade Rifat. *Edirne Rehnüması*. Istanbul, 1994.

"Ottoman Palace Suffers from Flooding, Neglect." *Hürriyet Daily News*, 31 January 2012.

Özer, Mustafa. "Edirne Sarayı Kazıları'nda Son Bulgular." İstanbul Araştırmalar Enstitüsü, 26 November 2015. www.iae.org.tr/Aktivite-Detay/Edirne-Sarayi-Kazilarinda-Son-Bulgular-Mustafa-Ozer/53.

Palmer, J. A. B. "The Origin of the Janissaries." *Bulletin of the John Rylands Library* 35 (1952–53): 448–81.

Pamuk, Şevket. *A Monetary History of the Ottoman Empire*. Cambridge, 2000.

Parlayan, Ayşegül. "Osmanlı'nın Kayıp Sarayı: Edirne Sarayı'nda Arkeoloji, Koruma, ve Restorasyon." *Atlas Tarih* 45 (2017): 80–91.

Paul, Jürgen. *Doctrine and Organization: The Khwajagan/Naqshbandiya in the First Generation after Baha'uddin*. Berlin, 1998.

Pedani, Maria Pia. "Safiye's Household and Venetian Diplomacy." *Turcica* 32 (2000): 9–32.

Peirce, Leslie. *The Imperial Harem: Women and Sovereignty in the Ottoman Empire*. New York, NY, 1993.

Penzer, N. M. *The Harem: An Account of the Institution as It Existed in the Palace of the Turkish Sultans, with a History of the Grand Seraglio from Its Foundation to Modern Times*. Philadelphia, PA, 1936. 2nd ed., London, 1965. Reprint, New York, 1993.

Peters, F. E. *Mecca: A Literary History of the Muslim Holy Land*. Princeton, NJ, 1994.

Piterberg, Gabriel. "The Alleged Rebellion of Abaza Mehmed Pasha: Historiography and the State in the Seventeenth Century." In *Mutiny and Rebellion in the Ottoman Empire*, ed. Jane Hathaway, 13–24. Madison, WI, 2002.

An Ottoman Tragedy: History and Historiography at Play. Berkeley, CA, 2003.

Quraishi, Adel. "The Guardians" photo exhibition. Leighton House, London, October–November 2015.

Raymond, André. *Artisans et commerçants au Caire au XVIIIe siècle*. 2 vols. Damascus, 1973–74. Reprint Cairo, 1999.

"Les Bains publics au Caire à la fin du XVIIIe siècle." *Annales islamologiques* 8 (1969): 129–50.

Le Caire des Janissaires: l'apogée de la ville ottomane sous 'Abd al-Rahman Katkhuda. Paris, 1995.

"Le Déplacement des tanneries à Alep, au Caire et à Tunis à l'époque ottomane: un 'indicateur' de croissance urbaine." *Revue du monde musulman et de la Méditerranée* 55–56 (1990): 34–43.

"Essai de géographie des quartiers de résidence aristocratique au Caire au XVIIIe siècle. *Journal of the Economic and Social History of the Orient* 3 (1963): 58–103.

"The Rab': A Type of Collective Housing in Cairo during the Ottoman Period." In *Architecture as Symbol and Self-Identity*, ed. Jonathan G. Katz, 55–61. Philadelphia, PA, 1980.

"The Residential Districts of Cairo's Elite in the Mamluk and Ottoman Periods (Fourteenth to Eighteenth Centuries)." In *The Mamluks in Egyptian Politics and Society*, eds. Thomas Philipp and Ulrich Haarmann, 207–23. Cambridge, 1998.

"Une 'révolution' au Caire sous les mamelouks: la crise de 1123/1711." *Annales islamologiques* 6 (1966): 95–120.

"The *Sabil* of Yusuf Agha Dar al-Saʿada (1088/1677) According to Its *Waqf* Document." In *The Cairo Heritage: Essays in Honor of Laila Ali Ibrahim*, ed. Doris Behrens-Abouseif, 223–33. Cairo, 2003.

Refik, Ahmet (Altınay). *Lale Devri, 1130–1143*. Istanbul, 1331/1915.

Sajdi, Dana. *The Barber of Damascus: Nouveau Literacy in the Eighteenth-Century Ottoman Levant*. Stanford, CA, 2013.

Salzmann, Ariel. "An Ancien Régime Revisited: 'Privatization' and Political Economy in the Eighteenth-Century Ottoman Empire." *Politics and Society* 21, 4 (1993): 393–423.

Scharfe, Patrick. "Muslim Scholars and the Public Sphere in Mehmed Ali Pasha's Egypt, 1801–1841." Unpublished Ph.D. dissertation, Ohio State University, 2015.

Sevinçli, Efdal. "Festivals and Their Documentation: *Surname*s Covering the Festivities of 1675 and 1724." In *Celebration, Entertainment, and Theatre in the Ottoman World*, eds. Suraiya Faroqhi and Arzu Öztürkmen, 186–207. London, 2014.

"Şenliklerimiz ve Surnamelerimiz: 1675 ve 1724 Şenliklerine İlişkin İki Surname." *Journal of Yaşar University* 1, 4 (2011): 377–416.

Shaw, Stanford J. *Between Old and New: The Ottoman Empire under Selim III, 1789–1807*. Cambridge, MA, 1971.

The Financial and Administrative Organization and Development of Ottoman Egypt, 1517–1798. Princeton, NJ, 1962.

Shaw, Stanford J., and Ezel Kural Shaw. *History of the Ottoman Empire and Modern Turkey*. 2 vols. Cambridge, 1976–77.

Sievert, Henning. "Der schwarze Obereunuch Moralı Beşir Ağa in den Augen von Ahmed Resmi Efendi." In *Islamwissenschaft als Kuturwissenschaft*. Volume 1: *Historische Anthropologie: Ansätze und Möglichkeiten*, eds. Stephan Conermann and Syrinx von Hees, 345–78. Hamburg, 2007.

Zwischen arabischer Provinz und Hoher Pforte: Beziehungen, Bildung und Politik des osmanischen Bürokraten Ragib Mehmed Paşa (st. 1763). Würzburg, 2008.

Şimşek, Halil İbrahim. *Osmanlı'da Müceddidilik, XII./XVIII. Yüzyıl*. Ankara, 2004.

Sumner-Boyd, Hillary, and John Freely. *Strolling through Istanbul: The Classic Guide to the City*. Revised ed. London, 2010 [1972].

Tanındı, Zeren. "Bibliophile Aghas (Eunuchs) at Topkapı Saray." *Muqarnas* 21 (2004): 333–43.

"Manucript Production in the Ottoman Palace Workshop." *Manuscripts of the Middle East* 5 (1990–91): 67–98.

"Topkapı Sarayı'nın Ağaları ve Kitaplar." *Uludağ Üniversitesi Fen-Edebiyat Fakültesi Sosyal Bilimler Dergisi* 3, 3 (2002): 41–56.

Terzioğlu, Derin. "How to Conceptualize Ottoman Sunnitization: A Historiographical Discussion." *Turcica* 44 (2012–13): 301–38.

"Where *'Ilm-i hal* Meets Catechism: Islamic Manuals of Religious Instruction in the Ottoman Empire in the Age of Confessionalization." *Past and Present* 220 (2013): 79–114.

Tezcan, Baki. "The 1622 Military Rebellion in Istanbul." In *Mutiny and Rebellion in the Ottoman Empire*, ed. Jane Hathaway, 25–43. Madison, WI, 2002.

"*Dispelling the Darkness*: The Politics of 'Race' in the Early Seventeenth-Century Ottoman Empire in the Light of the Life and Work of Mullah Ali." *International Journal of Turkish Studies* 13, 1–2 (2007): 85–91.

"Searching for Osman." Unpublished Ph.D. dissertation, Princeton University, 2001.

The Second Ottoman Empire: Political and Social Transformation in the Early Modern World. New York, NY, 2010.

Thomas, Lewis V. *A Study of Naima*, ed. Norman Itzkowitz. New York, NY, 1972.

Toledano, Ehud R. *The Ottoman Slave Trade and Its Suppression, 1840–1890.* Princeton, NJ, 1982.

Tuchscherer, Michel. "Le Pèlerinage de l'émir Sulaymân Ğâwiš al-Qazduġlî, sirdâr de la caravane de la Mekke en 1739." *Annales islamologiques* 24 (1988): 155–206.

Tucker, Ernest S. *Nadir Shah's Quest for Legitimacy in Post-Safavid Iran.* Gainesville, FL, 2006.

Turan, Ebru. "The Sultan's Favorite: Ibrahim Paşa and the Making of the Ottoman Universal Sovereignty." Unpublished Ph.D. dissertation, University of Chicago, 2007.

Türkiye Diyanet Vakfı İslam Ansiklopedisi. Istanbul, 1988–2013.

Uluçay, M. Çağatay. *Harem II.* Ankara, 1971.

Padişahların Kadınları ve Kızları. Ankara, 1980. Reprinted 1985, 1992.

Uzunçarşılı, İsmail Hakkı. "*Gazi* Orhan Bey Vakfiyesi." *Belleten* 5 (1941): 277–88.

Osmanlı Devletinin Saray Teşkilatı. Ankara, 1945. Reprinted 1984, 1988.

Osmanlı Tarihi. 8 vols. Ankara, 1947–62.

Vryonis, Speros Jr. "Seljuk Gulams and Ottoman Devshirmes." *Der Islam* 41 (1965): 224–52.

Welch, Stuart Cary. *Imperial Mughal Painting.* New York, NY, 1978.

White, Sam. *The Climate of Rebellion in the Early Modern Ottoman Empire.* Cambridge, 2011.

Williams, Caroline. *Islamic Monuments in Cairo: The Practical Guide.* New revised ed. Cairo, 2008.

Winter, Michael. *Egyptian Society under Ottoman Rule, 1517–1798.* London, 1992.

Winter, Stefan. *The Shi'ites of Lebanon under Ottoman Rule, 1516–1788.* Cambridge, 2010.

Wishnitzer, Avner. "Into the Dark: Power, Light, and Nocturnal Life in Eighteenth-Century Istanbul." *International Journal of Middle East Studies* 46, 3 (2014): 513–31.

Wittek, Paul. "Devshirme and Shari'a." *Bulletin of the School of Oriental and African Studies* 17 (1955): 271–78.

Yenişehirlioğlu, Filiz. "Architectural Patronage of *Ayan* Families in Anatolia." In *Provincial Elites in the Ottoman Empire*, ed. Antonis Anastasopoulos, 321–29. Rethmyno, 2005.

Yılmaz, Hüseyin. *Caliphate Redefined: The Mystical Turn in Ottoman Political Thought.* Princeton, NJ, 2018.

Younes, Nadia Fouad. "The Evolution of Birkat al-Fil from the Fatimids to the Twentieth Century." Unpublished M.A. thesis, American University in Cairo, 2010.

Yüksel Muslu, Cihan. *The Ottomans and the Mamluks: Imperial Diplomacy and Warfare in the Islamic World.* London, 2014.

Yürekli, Zeynep. "A Building between the Public and Private Realms of the Ottoman Elite: The Sufi Convent of Sokollu Mehmed Pasha in Istanbul." *Muqarnas* 20 (2003): 159–85.

Zarinebaf, Fariba. *Crime and Punishment in Istanbul, 1700–1800*. Berkeley, CA, 2010.

Zilfi, Madeline C. *The Politics of Piety: The Ottoman Ulema in the Post-Classical Age, 1600–1800*. Minneapolis, MN, 1988.

Eunuchs in Africa and Related Topics

Ahmed, Hussein. *Islam in Nineteenth-Century Wallo, Ethiopia: Revival, Reform, and Reaction*. Leiden, 2001.

Beachey, R. W. *The Slave Trade of Eastern Africa*. New York, NY, 1976.

Boston, J. S. *The Igala Kingdom*. Ibadan, 1968.

Cameron, John. "The Anatomy of the Mummies." In *The Tomb of Two Brothers*, ed. Margaret Alice Murray, 33–47. Manchester, 1910.

Eades, J. S. *The Yoruba Today*. Cambridge, 1980.

Fisher, Humphrey. *Slavery in the History of Muslim Black Africa*. New York, NY, 2001.

Goldenberg, David M. *The Curse of Ham: Race and Slavery in Early Judaism, Christianity, and Islam*. Princeton, NJ, 2003.

Holt, P. M., and M. W. Daly. *A History of the Sudan from the Coming of Islam to the Present Day*. 5th ed. Harlow, Essex, UK, 2000.

Jonckheere, Franz. "L'Eunuque dans l'Égypte pharaonique." *Revue d'histoire des sciences* 7, 2 (1954): 139–55.

Kadish, Gerald E. "Eunuchs in Ancient Egypt?" In *Studies in Honor of John A. Wilson*. Studies in Ancient Oriental Civilization No. 35, the Oriental Institute of the University of Chicago, 55–62. Chicago, 1969.

Kirwan, Laurence. *Studies on the History of Late Antique and Christian Nubia*, eds. Tomas Hägg, László Török, and Derek A. Welsby. Aldershot, Hampshire, UK, 2002.

Marcus, Harold G. *A History of Ethiopia*. Berkeley, CA, 1994.

Moore-Harell, Alice. "Economic and Political Aspects of the Slave Trade in Ethiopia and the Sudan in the Second Half of the Nineteenth Century." *International Journal of African Historical Studies* 32, 2 (1999): 407–21.

Muhammad, Akbar. "The Image of Africans in Arabic Literature: Some Unpublished Manuscripts." In *Slaves and Slavery in Muslim Africa*, ed. John R. Willis. Volume 1: *Islam and the Ideology of Enslavement*, 47–65. London, 1985.

Tamrat, Taddesse. *Church and State in Ethiopia, 1270–1527*. Oxford, 1972.

Török, László. *The Kingdom of Kush: Handbook of the Napatan-Meroitic Civilization*. Leiden, 1997.

Trimingham, J. Spencer. *Islam in Ethiopia*. London, 1965.

Eunuchs in Other Societies

Anderson, Mary M. *Hidden Power: The Palace Eunuchs of Imperial China*. Buffalo, NY, 1990.

Berry, Helen. *The Castrato and His Wife*. Oxford, 2011.

Boulhol, Pascal, and Isabelle Cochelin. "La Réhabilitation de l'eunuque dans l'hagiographie antique (IVe–VIe siècles)." *Studi di antichita cristiana* 48 (1992): 48, 49–76.

Chang, Jung. *Empress Dowager Cixi: The Concubine Who Launched Modern China.* London, 2013.

Crossley, Pamela K. "In the Hornet's Nest." Review of Jung Chang, *Empress Dowager Cixi: The Concubine Who Launched Modern China. London Review of Books* 36, 8 (17 April 2014): 9–10.

Encyclopaedia Iranica, s.v. "Eunuchs, I. The Achaemenid Period," by Muhammad Dandamayev, and s.v. "Eunuchs, II. The Sasanian Period," by Aly Kolesnikov. London, 1985.

Faison, Seth. "The Death of the Last Emperor's Last Eunuch." *New York Times*, 20 December 1996.

Gaul, Niels. "Eunuchs in the Late Byzantine Empire, c. 1250–1400." In *Eunuchs in Antiquity and Beyond*, ed. Shaun Tougher, 199–219. Swansea, 2002.

Grayson, Albert Kirk. "Eunuchs in Power: Their Role in the Assyrian Bureaucracy." *Festschrift für Wolfram Freiherrn von Soden – Alter Orient und Altes Testament* 240 (1995): 85–98.

Kuefler, Mathew. *The Manly Eunuch: Masculinity, Gender Ambiguity, and Christian Ideology in Late Antiquity.* Chicago, IL, 2001.

Llewellyn-Jones, Lloyd. "Eunuchs in the Royal Harem in Achaemenid Persia (559–331 B.C.)." In *Eunuchs in Antiquity and Beyond*, ed. Shaun Tougher, 19–49. Swansea, 2002.

Mitamura, Taisuke. *Chinese Eunuchs: The Structure of Intimate Politics*, trans. Charles A. Pomeroy. Rutland, VT, 1970.

Moran, Neil. "The Choir of the Hagia Sophia." *Oriens Christianus* 89 (2005): 1–7.

Phillips, William D. Jr. *Slavery from Roman Times to the Early Transatlantic Trade.* Minneapolis, MN, 1985.

Ringrose, Kathryn M. *The Perfect Servant: Eunuchs and the Social Construction of Gender in Byzantium.* Chicago, IL, 2003.

Sidéris, Georges. "'Eunuchs of Light': Power, Imperial Ceremonial and Positive Representations of Eunuchs in Byzantium (4th–12th Centuries A.D.)." In *Eunuchs in Antiquity and Beyond*, ed. Shaun Tougher, 161–75. Swansea, 2002.

    "Une Société de ville capitale: les eunuques dans la Constantinople byzantine (IVe–XIIe siècle)." In *Les Villes capitales au Moyen Âge – XXXVIe Congrès de la SHMES (Istanbul, 1er–6 juin 2005)*, 243–73. Paris, 2006.

Tougher, Shaun. *The Eunuch in Byzantine History and Society.* London, 2008.

    "In or Out? Origins of Court Eunuchs." In *Eunuchs in Antiquity and Beyond*, ed. Shaun Tougher, 143–59. Swansea, 2002.

Tsai, Shih-shan Henry. "Eunuch Power in Imperial China." In *Eunuchs in Antiquity and Beyond*, ed. Shaun Tougher, 221–33. Swansea, 2002.

    The Eunuchs in the Ming Dynasty. Albany, NY, 1996.

Yinghua, Jia. *The Last Eunuch of China: The Life of Sun Yaoting*, trans. Sun Haichen. Beijing, 2009.

Other Topics

Norwich, John Julius. *A Short History of Byzantium*. New York, NY, 1997.

Patterson, Orlando. *Slavery and Social Death: A Comparative Study*. Cambridge, MA, 1982.

Reinhard, Wolfgang. "Reformation, Counter-Reformation, and the Early Modern State: A Reassessment." *Catholic Historical Review* 75, 3 (1989): 385–403.

Schilling, Heinz. "Confessional Europe." In *Handbook of European History, 1400–1600*. Volume 2, eds. Thomas A. Brady, Heiko A. Oberman, and James D. Tracy, 641–70. Leiden, 1995.

Schulz, Juergen. *The New Palaces of Medieval Venice*. University Park, PA, 2004.

Websites

Archnet. https://archnet.org/resources. Subheadings "Atik Valide Külliyesi," "Iskele Camii," "Masjid al-Malika Safiyya," "Semsi Pasa," and "Sultan Ahmet."

Ayasofya Museum, Istanbul. http://ayasofyamuzesi.gov.tr/tr/içmi-mahmud-kütüphanesi

Ottoman Inscriptions. www.ottomaninscriptions.com/verse.aspx?ref=list&bid=2974&hid=4616

Sünbül Efendi Mosque. http://sumbulefendicamii.com

Üsküdar Municipality. www.uskudar.bel.tr/tr/main/erehber/tarihi-mekanlar/39

Index